Dan Taylor (1738–1816), Baptist Leader and Pioneering Evangelical

Monographs in Baptist History

VOLUME 9

Ours is a day in which not only the gaze of western culture but also increasingly that of Evangelicals is riveted to the present. The past seems to be nowhere in view and hence it is disparagingly dismissed as being of little value for our rapidly changing world. Such historical amnesia is fatal for any culture, but particularly so for Christian communities whose identity is profoundly bound up with their history. The goal of this new series of monographs, Studies in Baptist History, seeks to provide one of these Christian communities, that of evangelical Baptists, with reasons and resources for remembering the past. The editors are deeply convinced that Baptist history contains rich resources of theological reflection, praxis and spirituality that can help Baptists, as well as other Christians, live more Christianly in the present. The monographs in this series will therefore aim at illuminating various aspects of the Baptist tradition and in the process provide Baptists with a usable past.

Dan Taylor (1738–1816), Baptist Leader and Pioneering Evangelical

Richard T. Pollard

FOREWORD BY
Peter J. Morden

☞PICKWICK *Publications* · Eugene, Oregon

DAN TAYLOR (1738–1816), BAPTIST LEADER AND
PIONEERING EVANGELICAL

Monographs in Baptist History 9

Pickwick Publications
An Imprint of Wipf and Stock Publishers
199 W. 8th Ave., Suite 3
Eugene, OR 97401

www.wipfandstock.com

PAPERBACK ISBN: 978-1-5326-3619-6
HARDCOVER ISBN: 978-1-5326-3621-9
EBOOK ISBN: 978-1-5326-3620-2

Cataloguing-in-Publication data:

Names: Pollard, Richard T., author | Morden, Peter J., foreword.

Title: Dan Taylor (1738–1816), Baptist leader and pioneering evangelical / Richard T. Pollard.

Description: Eugene, OR: Pickwick Publications, 2018 | Series: Monographs in Baptist History 9 | Includes bibliographical references.

Identifiers: ISBN 978-1-5326-3619-6 (paperback) | ISBN 978-1-5326-3621-9 (hardcover) | ISBN 978-1-5326-3620-2 (ebook)

Subjects: LCSH: Taylor, Dan (1738–1816) | Evangelicalism—History | Evangelical Revival—Biography—History and criticism | Wesley, John (1703–1791)

Classification: BR758.P67 2018 (print) | BR758.P67 (ebook)

Manufactured in the U.S.A.   07/30/18

To my wife Nikki, and our sons Joel and Cameron

Contents

Foreword

IN FEBRUARY 1786 THE well-known Baptist minister and theologian Andrew Fuller (1754–1815) made the following entry in his diary: "received *another* treatise written against me." His underlining of "another" suggests his weariness and—perhaps—frustration at the frequent and often ill-tempered attacks on his published work. However, once Fuller had read this particular treatise the tone of his diary entries changed. "The author discovers an amiable spirit and there is a good deal of plausibility in some things which he maintains," Fuller wrote. A few days later he added, "My mind has been much employed all the week in thinking on the above piece" which, he said, was "ingeniously wrought together."[1] He soon responded to his opponent with a pamphlet of his own, and the two men continued to debate in print for several years. Both sought to challenge the other, and their engagement was incisive and robust. They disagreed on several points (for example, Fuller was a Calvinist, his adversary was not). Yet they still held each other in high regard and their very public disagreement was always conducted in the "amiable" tone Fuller had first noted in his diary.

Fuller's adversary was another Baptist Minister, Dan Taylor (1738–1816), founder of the New Connexion of General Baptists. At the time of their debate they were both respected and influential figures in the evangelical world, prolific writers with a passion for mission and ministry. Both men continued to be remembered and indeed revered after their deaths, but more recently there has been a marked divergence in the ways the two men have been treated. Fuller has been the subject of many scholarly studies examining different dimensions of his life and—especially—his theology. The flow

---

1. Andrew Fuller, Diary and Spiritual Thoughts [1784–1801], Bristol Baptist College (G 95 b), 5–12 Feb 1786.

of articles and books shows no sign of abating. He is increasingly recognized as an important historical figure and as a theologian of considerable merit. Consequently, there are many who are appropriating insights from Fuller in order to enrich Christian thinking and praxis today. By contrast, Taylor's life and thought have been almost completely neglected. Hardly any scholarly work has been done, and the little that has been written is decidedly uneven in quality. This lack of attention would surely have surprised Taylor's contemporaries, not least Fuller himself. It has left a significant gap in our understanding of eighteenth- and nineteenth-century English Baptist life.

This fine study by Richard Pollard fills the scholarly lacuna. It sets Taylor in historical and cultural context and draws the contours of his wide-ranging and influential ministry on the map of Baptist life, showing how he was especially shaped by the eighteenth-century Evangelical Revival. Taylor emerges as a creative thinker who was determined to put his principles into practice. Dr Pollard describes him as the "Baptist Wesley" and makes a convincing case for this bold claim. He has mined a rich seam of primary material and the scholarship on display here is impeccable. Both the details and the broad sweep of Taylor's ministry are brought into focus as never before and this study makes a real contribution to our understanding of Baptist heritage, as well as illuminating wider trends. In my view, it is the best study of an English General Baptist figure ever written.

This very readable book also has real contemporary significance. Taylor was a pioneer, an entrepreneur and a strategic thinker who shaped the life of a denomination around key evangelical priorities whilst holding firm to core Baptist principles. Above all, in his thinking and practice he prioritized gospel mission. Unlike Fuller, Taylor was not primarily a theologian, but, like him, his life and work have many insights to offer the church today. Pollard wisely refrains from drawing out lessons for the twenty-first century, instead focusing on writing good history. Yet for those with eyes to see there is much here that is relevant to contemporary contexts. This study is, therefore, a resource not only for scholars but for all who seek to engage in ministry and mission today.

Peter J. Morden is Senior Pastor and Team Leader, South Parade Baptist Church, Leeds, Distinguished Visiting Scholar, Spurgeon's College, London, and an Associate Tutor, St Hild College, Barnabas Centre, Sheffield.

Preface

THIS BOOK IS A lightly revised version of my PhD thesis. The desire to pursue doctoral research on Dan Taylor's evangelicalism was initially stimulated by Ian Randall who, along with Peter Morden, assumed a supervisory role. Some of the material which now takes its place in this book has already appeared in various articles and papers. The substance of chapter 4 which examines Taylor's theological engagement with Andrew Fuller was delivered at a Spurgeon's College post-graduate seminar. The essential content of chapter 7 was published in the *Baptist Quarterly* as "Dan Taylor: A Baptist Entrepreneur." I presented the key distinctives of Taylor's evangelicalism in my delivery of the 2017 Whitley Lecture in the UK at Spurgeon's College, Bristol Baptist College, Regent's Park College, Northern Baptist College and South Wales Baptist College. This was subsequently published as "The Pioneering Evangelicalism of Dan Taylor (1738–1816)." The nature of Taylor's ministry and central tenets of his evangelicalism also formed the subject of a lecture I gave at a conference on Dan Taylor and the New Connexion which was facilitated by the Centre for Baptist History and Heritage with the Baptist Historical Society at Regent's Park College in 2017. On all the occasions when I have presented material I have received stimulating feedback which has proved formative in the writing of this book.

Richard T. Pollard

Bristol, England
July 2018

Preface

Acknowledgments

I WOULD LIKE TO acknowledge the support and guidance of Peter Morden and Ian Randall. My initial interest in Dan Taylor was inspired as a consequence of attending one of Ian's lectures during my training as a ministerial student at Spurgeon's College, London. Peter and Ian both served as my supervisors through my doctoral research and their contribution at so many levels has been invaluable and I am immensely grateful. I am privileged to count them as friends. I express my gratitude to the Angus Library, Regent's Park College, Oxford, particularly for granting me unhindered access to Dan Taylor's works and letters. I am also thankful for the assistance I have received from The John Rylands Library, Manchester, and the West Yorkshire Archives Office, Wakefield. I am indebted to my PhD examiners, Geordan Hammond and Keith Jones, and to the chair of my viva voce, Stephen Wright, for their helpful comments. Particular thanks must be given to Ernie Whalley—the former Baptist Regional Minister (Team Leader) for Yorkshire. During my time as Associate Minister at South Parade Baptist Church in Leeds I received much encouragement from Ernie, and within our conversations we regularly spoke about Dan Taylor. I also extend thanks to Brian Nicholls my senior colleague at South Parade for his friendship, interest in my research and time that he and the church gave me to pursue my studies. Since my appointment as Senior Minister at Fishponds Baptist Church, Bristol, I have also appreciated the support given to me by the leadership team and congregation. In addition, I am thankful for the grants I have received from the Baptist Union of Great Britain's Further Studies Fund and from the Whitley Committee. Most of all, I have to thank my wife Nikki, and our sons Joel and Cameron for their endless encouragement and inspiration. It is to them that this book is dedicated.

Abbreviations

ANF   *Ante-Nicene Fathers.* Vol. 1, *The Apostolic Fathers, Justin Martyr, Ireneaus.* Edited by Alexander Roberts and James Donaldson. 1885. Peabody, MA: Hendrickson, 2004.

BE   John Wesley, *The Bicentennial Edition of the Works of John Wesley*, edited by Frank Baker and Richard P. Heitzenrater (Oxford: Clarendon, 1975–83)

BQ   *The Baptist Quarterly*

PWHS   *Proceedings of the Wesley Historical Society*

Introduction

ON 11 JUNE 1800 Dan Taylor (1738–1816) represented the General Body of Protestant Dissenting Ministers in a direct address to King George III.[1] Given Taylor's background, this was something that he would not have envisaged.[2] His selection for this role was a reflection of the respect he commanded as a leading evangelical figure. Within Baptist life his stature as a minister was widely recognized. John Morris, in his memoirs of the influential Particular Baptist minister Andrew Fuller (1754–1815), noted that Fuller considered Taylor "an invincible opponent."[3] Among Taylor's General Baptist contemporaries, his status was unrivaled. Within the General Baptists he was held as the pre-eminent defender of evangelical truth and a key innovator in the cause of mission.[4]

This book provides a detailed examination of Taylor's evangelicalism. The introductory chapter begins by considering the distinguishing marks and origins of evangelicalism as a movement, followed by an outline of the historic and current state of the study of Taylor. An attempt to provide a working understanding of the Enlightenment is then undertaken.

1. Adam Taylor, *Memoirs*, 220. The wider context of Taylor's representation of the Protestant Dissenting Ministers before King George III will be considered in chapter 7. As with this reference, it should be noted that in my use of all primary sources, I have endeavored to follow the capitalization, grammar, spelling, and formatting of the original titles.

2. For a description of the material constraints that were apparent in Taylor's upbringing, see ibid., 2–3.

3. Morris, *Memoirs*, 205. This publication is a copy of the second edition of Morris's *Memoirs* that was published in London in 1826. The first edition was published in 1816.

4. It should be noted that both here and throughout this book I use the word "innovator" as a convenient term to describe Taylor's pioneering evangelicalism. It was not a term that was used by Taylor or by his contemporaries to describe him.

Attention is also given to the primary evidence that forms the raw material of the book. In addition, an overview of Taylor's life is included, which contains biographical and narrative details that are pertinent to an understanding of the nature of his character, life, and ministry, but which fall outside of the more evaluative aspects of the book. The introduction finishes with reference to the core subject matter of each chapter, a summary of my overarching argument and the general direction it will take. Each of the seven main chapters will examine a different aspect of Taylor's evangelicalism as I aim to offer new understanding of its central facets and reflect on how these accorded with that which was new and distinct within eighteenth-century evangelicalism.

The Study of Evangelicalism

As Derek Tidball observes, defining evangelicalism can be like "attempts to pick up a slippery bar of soap with wet hands."[5] While the word "evangelical" derives from the Greek noun *euangelion* meaning "glad tidings" or "joyful news," this is inadequate in establishing effective conceptual limits to the term.[6] An unhelpful broadness also surrounds definitions that simply focus on evangelicals as being committed to the Bible. This is apparent in the way that the fourteenth-century theologian and reformer John Wyclif was known as "doctor evangelicus" due to his emphasis on the centrality and sufficiency of Scripture as, for example, evident in his unfinished *Opus Evangelicum*.[7] On the other hand, narrow conceptions of evangelicalism have emerged when the parameters of definition have been too limited. Kenneth Myer's focus on evangelicalism as a subculture of certain behavioral patterns, is one such example.[8] Neither should an understanding of the movement be restricted to a definition provided by any one group of believers. For example Martin Luther, the sixteenth-century Protestant Reformer, described the commitment of his followers to justification by grace through faith and the supreme authority of Scripture, as constituting the evangelical church.[9] However, the professions and practices of evangelicalism have always extended beyond the confines of a particular ecclesiastical tradition.[10]

5. Tidball, *Who are the Evangelicals?* 12.

6. For an examination of the meaning of "evangelical," see Pierard, "Evangelicalism," 379–82.

7. See Lahey, *Wyclif*, 135; Wyclif, *Opus Evangelicum*.

8. Myers, "Better Way," 39–57.

9. For consideration of this, see Gerstner, "Theological Boundaries," 23–24.

10. See, e.g., Marsden's emphasis on evangelicalism as a "transdenominational

Mindful of the pitfalls of delineations of the essential nature of evangelicalism that are too broad or limited, I have utilized David Bebbington's influential definition from the 1989 publication of his landmark *Evangelicalism in Modern Britain*.[11] The "special marks" that Bebbington attributes to evangelicalism consist of "conversionism"—the belief that human beings need to be converted; "activism"—that the gospel needs to be expressed in effort; "biblicism"—a special regard for the Bible as the source of spiritual truth; and "crucicentrism"—a particular focus on the atoning work of Christ on the cross.[12] While Bebbington does not present the movement as entirely uniform but as comprising numerous strands, he is clear that this "quadrilateral of priorities" forms "the basis of Evangelicalism" and provides it with a "self-conscious unity."[13] The "Bebbington quadrilateral," as it is known, has generally been well received. Criticism has largely been restricted to concerns about the equality between its four elements. It has, for example, been suggested that he should have emphasized the greater importance of conversionism than activism.[14] Surprise has also been expressed at the importance Bebbington places on evangelicals possessing a confident assurance of faith when he does not designate this as one of the four special marks of the movement.[15] In addition, it is legitimate to ask whether the church is more crucial to evangelicalism than is apparent in Bebbington's definition. However, his knowledge of the subject, thorough approach and balanced reasoning have provided a framework that helps to identify the core facets of evangelicalism.

A valuable aspect of Bebbington's framework is his emphasis on the need for evangelicalism to be understood culturally as well as theologically. Pertinent to the study of eighteenth-century evangelicalism within this book is his identification of the ways in which its central values and practices were shaped by the Enlightenment.[16] The way Bebbington roots his examination of evangelicalism within a close consideration of the surrounding context of the English Enlightenment provides a further reason for the attention I have placed on his understanding of evangelicalism. While Reginald Ward, for

---

community" in "Evangelical Denomination," ix.

11. Bebbington, *Evangelicalism*.

12. Ibid., 2–17.

13. Ibid., 3, 27.

14. See, e.g., McGowan, "Evangelicalism," 64.

15. See, e.g., Williams, "Enlightenment Epistemology," 348.

16. Bebbington, *Evangelicalism*, 50–69. Bebbington was not the first to note the influence of the Enlightenment on evangelicalism. Examples of earlier works where this point was made, albeit in more limited scope, include McLoughlin, *Isaac Backus*; and Anstey, *Atlantic Slave Trade*.

example, provides insights into the origins and nature of evangelicalism, the thrust of his focus is the influence of Continental Pietism.[17] However, there is no evidence of direct continental influences on Taylor or on his formation of the New Connexion of General Baptists which was a thoroughly English movement.[18] Bebbington highlights significant elements of congruence between evangelicalism and the Enlightenment and this has led to previous dominant understandings of evangelicalism, which were almost exclusively anti-Enlightenment, being displaced.[19] A further core dimension of Bebbington's approach is that he does not assume an unbroken tradition of gospel based evangelical Christianity reaching back through the Evangelical Revival, the Puritans, the Reformers, the Lollards, and other Dissenters to New Testament Christianity. Instead, he views evangelicalism as inseparable from the beginnings of the Evangelical Revival in the 1730s.[20] Its key figures included Church of England clergy—John Wesley (1703–91) and George Whitefield (1714–70) who were both influential on the founding of Methodism; and in New England—the American philosopher, eminent theologian and Congregational church pastor and preacher Jonathan Edwards (1703–58). It is this aspect of Bebbington's understanding of evangelicalism that has proved most contentious.

New impetus was given to the study of the origins and essential nature of evangelicalism in the 2008 publication *The Emergence of Evangelicalism*, edited by Michael Haykin and Kenneth Stewart. In the main, its contributors, several of whom I engage with in this book, contest what is referred to as the "Bebbington thesis"—namely that which Bebbington stipulates regarding the eighteenth-century inception of evangelicalism.[21] They instead seek to demonstrate that eighteenth-century evangelicalism was no more than a continuum of theological thinking and practices, particularly those associated with the Reformation and Puritanism.[22] The same publication includes a response from Bebbington.[23] He acknowledges that he had underappreciated certain evangelical emphases that pre-dated the eighteenth century, and ceases to refer to evangelicalism as "created" by the Enlightenment

17. See, e.g., Ward, *Protestant Evangelical Awakening*, and *Early Evangelicalism*.

18. It should be noted that my spelling of "Connexion" is the same as that of Dan Taylor. Some, such as Adam Taylor, spelled it as "Connection."

19. As will be noted in chapter 2, a typical example is the depiction of evangelicalism in Edward P. Thompson, *Making of the English*, 738.

20. Bebbington, *Evangelicalism*, 20.

21. This was not the first time that Bebbington's approach had been criticized in this way. See, Stewart, "Did Evangelicalism Predate the Eighteenth Century?" 135–53.

22. This line of reasoning is examined later in the book.

23. Bebbington, "Response," 417–32.

but as having been deeply "embedded within it."[24] However, his conviction that the movement was primarily rooted in the eighteenth century, remains unchanged. The extent to which Taylor's pioneering evangelicalism serves to support Bebbington's argument is a central theme of this book.

The Study of Taylor

Taylor has received very little scholarly attention. Given his contribution to the life of eighteenth-century General Baptists and beyond, the lack of close examination of his theology and written works is surprising. Consideration of Taylor has rarely extended beyond the *Memoirs* of his life published in 1820 by his nephew Adam Taylor (1768–1832) who was a historian for the General Baptists and a London schoolmaster.[25] The earliest contributions on Taylor such as that found in James Wood's *A Condensed History of the General Baptists of The New Connexion* and William Underwood's *The Life of the Rev. Dan Taylor*, form little more than a recasting of Adam Taylor's biographical material.[26] This is important, for while *Memoirs* describes Taylor's life and ministry, it is almost entirely devoid of analysis and occasionally contains hagiography.[27] A near exclusive reliance on *Memoirs* and absence of critical appraisal has typified references to Taylor in Baptist works such as Henry Vedder's *A Short History of the Baptists*, William Whitley's *A History of British Baptists*, and Alfred Underwood's *A History of the English Baptists*.[28]

A failure to offer new insights on Taylor beyond those found in *Memoirs* is characteristic of most contemporary examinations of Baptist history. Examples include the descriptions of Taylor found in William Brackney's *A Genetic History of Baptist Thought* and James Leo Garrett Jr.'s *Baptist Theology*.[29] These publications offer no reflection on Taylor's works or the cultural influences which shaped him. While Tom Nettles in *The Baptists* devotes a whole chapter to Taylor, this also lacks depth as illustrated in his

24. Bebbington, *Evangelicalism*, 74; Bebbington, "Response," 427.

25. Adam Taylor also wrote a history of the General Baptists and a biography on the life of Taylor's younger brother—John Taylor. See Adam Taylor, *History* and *John Taylor*.

26. Wood, *Condensed History*; William Underwood, *Life of Dan Taylor*.

27. An example of hagiography was Adam Taylor's description of Taylor possessing a "remarkable" intellect in his infancy, which he claimed meant that "strangers frequently visited" to hear him read. See Taylor, *Memoirs*, 2.

28. Vedder, *Short History*, 247–48; Whitley, *History of British Baptists*, 219–22, 271; Underwood, *History of English Baptists*, 150–57.

29. Brackney, *Genetic History*, 147–49; Garrett Jr., *Baptist Theology*, 46–49.

repeated use of hagiographic quotations from Vedder's earlier cited work.[30] It should also be noted that the two publications by John Inscore Essick and Clint Bass which consider the ministry and theology of the influential seventeenth-century General Baptist minister Thomas Grantham (1633–92) contain no mention of Taylor.[31] The lack of theological attention that has been given to Taylor is particularly pronounced in *Pulpit and People*, edited by John Briggs and which contains only the briefest of references to Taylor.[32] Considering it specifically covers eighteenth-century Baptist life, the neglect of proper consideration of such an important figure as Taylor is significant. Similarly, despite Taylor's prominence as a leading evangelical in Yorkshire, John Walsh in his 1956 thesis on eighteenth-century evangelicals in Yorkshire refers to him only once, citing his name among others he designates as "some of the most effective Dissenting pastors."[33] Further typical of the lack of focus on Taylor is how the second volume of *Protestant Nonconformist Texts* edited by Alan Sell and others, concentrates on the eighteenth-century but contains no texts by Taylor, other than the New Connexion's *Articles of Religion*.[34] It is also notable that there are only three short references to Taylor in the twenty-two contributions that comprise the 2013 *T&T Clark Companion to Nonconformity* edited by Robert Pope.[35] Also, there is no mention of Taylor in the works on early evangelicalism by scholars such as Deryck Lovegrove, Bruce Hindmarsh and Ward.[36] This is symptomatic of a neglect of scholarly attention to Taylor.[37]

The limited consideration of Taylor that has extended beyond the narrative of his ministry has often focused on his establishment and oversight of the New Connexion.[38] By far the most significant example is Frank

---

30. Nettles, *Baptists*, 95–127.

31. Inscore Essick, *Thomas Grantham*; Bass, *Thomas Grantham*.

32. Briggs, *Pulpit and People*.

33. Walsh, "Yorkshire Evangelicals," 330.

34. Sell et al., *Protestant Nonconformist Texts*. For the inclusion of the *Articles of Religion of the New Connexion General Baptists*, see 136–37.

35. Pope, *T&T Clark Companion to Nonconformity*. The most significant reference is Peter Morden's drawing attention to Taylor's influence on Andrew Fuller, see Morden, "Nonconformists and the Work of Christ," 195–96.

36. See, e.g., Lovegrove, *Rise of the Laity*; Hindmarsh, *Evangelical Conversion Narrative*; Ward, *Protestant Evangelical Awakening*, and *Early Evangelicalism*.

37. It should also be noted that the limited number of web based articles on Taylor rarely rise above narrative description and have therefore not been relevant to this book.

38. See, e.g., Welch, "Origins," 59–70; Ambler, "Church, Place and Organization," 238–48; Hayden, *English Baptist History*, 50–58.

Rinaldi's 1996 PhD thesis, entitled "The Tribe of Dan."[39] This examines the evolutionary transition of the Connexion. While Rinaldi's research highlights Taylor's envisioning leadership and organizational skills, it offers little reflection on his theological understanding. There is no delineation of his works and he refers only briefly to a few of his publications. Many of Taylor's most important works such as *The Scriptural Account of the Way of Salvation, Fundamentals of Religion in Faith and Practice* and those written during his engagement with Andrew Fuller, are omitted.[40] Neither is there any serious examination of Taylor's spirituality, soteriology, or approach to subjects such as the atonement, conversion, and worship.[41] A large proportion of his book focuses on the Connexion during the seventy-five years after Taylor's death. For these reasons, Rinaldi's research is only of limited use for the examination of Taylor's evangelicalism undertaken in this book. Occasionally, I have also criticized aspects of Rinaldi's judgments where his lack of detailed knowledge of Taylor's theological thinking is exposed.

The few reflections on Taylor that have not focused on his oversight of the Connexion, have nearly always been marked by a pronounced absence of analysis of his theology and neglect of attention to his works. Examples include the consideration of Taylor's contribution to Yorkshire Baptist life by W. E. Blomfield in 1912,[42] Frank Beckwith in 1939,[43] the brief references to the subject found within *Our Heritage* edited by Ian Sellers,[44] and also the way John Hargreaves draws attention to Taylor's evangelistic work in Yorkshire in his 1991 PhD thesis on "Religion and Society in the Parish of Halifax."[45] The same is true of Raymond Brown's examination of Taylor within the context of eighteenth-century Baptist life and Bebbington's highlighting of Taylor as an innovator in *Baptists Through the Centuries*.[46] Similarly, while Taylor's significance is noted in publications such as Michael Watts's *The Dissenters*,[47] Bebbington's *Evangelicalism in Modern Britain*,[48]

---

39. Rinaldi, "Tribe of Dan." Rinaldi's revised thesis was published in 2008, see Rinaldi, *Tribe of Dan*.

40. Dan Taylor, *Scriptural Account*; Dan Taylor, *Fundamentals*.

41. These considerations were beyond the scope of Rinaldi's thesis.

42. Blomfield, "Yorkshire Baptist Churches," 53–112.

43. Beckwith, "Dan Taylor," 297–306.

44. Sellars, *Our Heritage*, 16, 23, 34, 62.

45. Hargreaves, "Religion and Society," 111–12.

46. Brown, *English Baptists*, 98–114; Bebbington, *Baptists*, 85.

47. Michael R. Watts, *Dissenters*, 454–56.

48. Bebbington, *Evangelicalism*, 27, 33.

and Mark Noll's *The Rise of Evangelicalism*,[49] the brevity of the references add little to the study of Taylor.

Of the handful of commentators who have attempted to engage meaningfully with Taylor's works, one of the first to do so, albeit in a limited way, was Leon McBeth. Within *The Baptist Heritage*, McBeth provides a brief examination of Taylor's *A Dissertation on Singing*.[50] Although he highlights certain helpful subtleties of Taylor's approach, his wider commentary contains misinformation.[51] Of greater significance are Peter Morden's insights on Taylor's engagement with Andrew Fuller. Morden's examination of Fuller in *Offering Christ to the World* contains brief reflection on Taylor's works that were pertinent to their discourse and his influence on Fuller's revised understanding of the atonement.[52] Contributions on Taylor's theological engagement with Fuller are also found in *"At the Pure Fountain of Thy Word,"* edited by Michael Haykin, but several of these are marked by a lack of depth and accuracy.[53]

Overall, the published literature on Taylor is sparse and concentrates mainly on the narrative of his life and oversight of the New Connexion. With a few exceptions, they also lack academic rigor. The rare studies of his works have been limited in scope, prone to inaccuracy, and have failed to delineate the tenets of his theological understanding. There remains no substantial work dedicated to the study of his theology. This book seeks to address this vacuum of knowledge. I endeavor to make a significant contribution to the study of Taylor by providing an examination of the full range of his works, an exposition of the key facets of his evangelicalism, and their congruence with central aspects of eighteenth-century evangelicalism, and reflection on the influences that both shaped him and propelled him onwards.

Defining the Enlightenment

The attention given in this book to the influence of the Enlightenment on evangelicalism, as exemplified in the nature of Taylor's theological thinking, necessitates a working understanding of its meaning. The term is applied to the broad cultural movement and accompanying changes in outlook that were experienced in Europe and beyond from the closing decades of the

49. Noll, *Rise of Evangelicalism*, 152, 254.

50. McBeth, *Baptist Heritage*, 166–67; Dan Taylor, *Dissertation*.

51. This will be examined in chapter 6.

52. Morden, *Offering Christ*, 63–74.

53. Haykin, *"At the Pure Fountain"*. The most relevant of these contributions will be considered in chapter 4.

seventeenth century. The period ranges from the 1688 so called "Glorious Revolution" in England (a convenient early marker), to the last third of the eighteenth century (with many viewing the French Revolution as its climax), or at the very latest, to the early decades of the nineteenth century, after which the age of Romanticism emerged.[54] While many in the eighteenth century who engaged with the new "movement of ideas" as it was commonly understood to be, and which was described in Italy as *Illuminismo* (illumination), in France as *Lumière* (light), and in the German states as *Aufklarung* (enlightenment), were aware of its diverse emphases, the tendency has been to depict the Enlightenment as a monolithic phenomenon.[55] Most who have followed in the footsteps of German philosopher Immanuel Kant who addressed the subject "What is Enlightenment?" in 1784,[56] have presented it as a unified concept that was closely bound together with the leading thinkers in Western Europe, and especially France. Examples of this approach include Ernst Cassirer's 1932 *The Philosophy of the Enlightenment*[57] and Peter Gay's *The Enlightenment*.[58] Much recent scholarship has, however, revised the singularity of assumption that surrounds the Enlightenment. Many commentators now speak of a plurality of "enlightenments," whether national or regional, Catholic or Protestant, European or beyond.[59] Peter Hanns Reill's assertion that "it cannot be denied that there were a number of Enlightenments, that can, for example, be called the French, English, Scottish, German, Swiss, Italian, and American Enlightenments" illustrates this shift in perspective.[60] This approach is helpful, for instance the English Enlightenment certainly differed from the French Enlightenment and both differed from the Jewish and Russian Enlightenments. It is this variegated and contextually sensitive understanding of the Enlightenment that I have assumed throughout this book.

Given that the Enlightenment should not be understood as a single, unifiable phenomenon, some argue, as does John Pocock, that neither the definite article nor capital letter be used, but instead that reference be made only to "enlightenments."[61] However, I have used the term "Enlighten-

---

54. For further consideration of the dating of the Enlightenment, see, e.g., Reill, "Introduction," x.

55. Outram, *Enlightenment*, 1.

56. Kant, *What is Enlightenment?* 1–7.

57. Cassirer, *Philosophy of the Enlightenment*.

58. Gay, *Enlightenment: Modern Paganism* and *Enlightenment: Science of Freedom*.

59. See, e.g., Outram, *Enlightenment*, 8; Porter, *Enlightenment*, 11; Withers, *Placing the Enlightenment*, 4. Sorkin, *Religious Enlightenment*, 3–5.

60. Reill, "Introduction," x.

61. Pocock, "Historiography," 83.

ment"—both with and without the definite article. Although I have focused primarily on that which took place in England, my use of "Enlightenment" rather than "enlightenments" reflects a mindfulness that the shifts in outlook that occurred in England were not in isolation. As Pocock himself acknowledges, there is a sense in which the Enlightenment was a related "family of discourses."[62] While wanting to avoid the errors found within the earlier cited approaches to the Enlightenment that tended to overlook its complexity or even occasional apparent contradictions, it would be remiss to ignore its "core intellectual issues."[63] These included a move away from absolutism, divine right, dogmatism, and superstition, to an embracing of the conviction that the universe is fundamentally rational; that truth can be arrived at through the social scientific methods of empirical observation and use of reason; that human experience is the foundation for understanding truth; the value of universal principles over local ones; an optimism concerning human nature and progress; and a penchant for innovation and pragmatism (epitomized in the quest for personal happiness). These, and other characteristics, can be considered as the cross-fertilizing facets of the Enlightenment differing in intensity and importance from place to place.

The relationship between the developing Christian traditions and the Enlightenment varied in different regions and cultures. For example, while focusing on Voltaire's championing of atheism has traditionally led many, such as Gay, to refer to the Enlightenment as a "war on Christianity," the reality of the relationship between Christianity and the Enlightenment was far more complex.[64] In many situations, as Helena Rosenblatt notes, "the Enlightenment was more about reinvigorating and redefining religion than destroying it."[65] David Sorkin is typical of many who now speak of the religious Enlightenment, pointing to its "intellectual similarities while recognizing national differences."[66] It is in this respect that Taylor and the evangelicalism he espoused is of relevance, as he was shaped within the context of the English Enlightenment by both the epistemological breakthroughs associated with those such as John Locke (1632–1704) and by the Enlightenment as a "revolution in mood" and its accompanying sensibilities.[67]

62. Pocock, "Enthusiasm," 7.

63. Israel, *Enlightenment*, 863.

64. Gay, *Enlightenment: Modern Paganism*, 203.

65. Rosenblatt, "Christian Enlightenment," 283. For an overview of the reassessment that has taken place regarding an understanding of the Enlightenment and religion, particularly in the context of England, see also Gregory, "Religion," 25–54.

66. Sorkin, *Religious Enlightenment*, 11.

67. Porter, *Enlightenment*, 3.

Sources Used

This book works mainly with primary data. Taylor's writings have proved indispensable in establishing the dominant facets and more subtle nuances of his evangelicalism. Use has been made of virtually all of his forty-nine publications.[68] Significant aspects of over one third of these works have been carefully delineated in view of their relevance to the study of his evangelicalism. His writings cover a range of subjects and literary forms. These include expositions on aspects of faith such as *An Humble Essay on Christian Baptism*;[69] tracts and pamphlets on matters such as *The Absolute Necessity of Searching the Scriptures*;[70] newspaper submissions on the atonement; sermons—some of which formed the content of *Fundamentals*; ordination addresses where he frequently highlighted the importance of mission; funeral tributes, catechisms; and his publication of a hymn book.[71] His works were often written as a consequence of issues he engaged with in his ministry. Irrespective of his form of writing or complexity of subject matter, he wrote in an accessible style with the literary limitations of the poor often at the forefront of his mind.

In addition to Taylor's published works, his wider writings have been useful. Extracts from his diary have proved valuable in acquiring an understanding of his spirituality and closely related inner impulses of his evangelicalism. His diary entries are included in *Memoirs* which also contains some of his letters. The only known source of unpublished material Taylor wrote has also provided notable insights. This is a collection of letters to his fellow General Baptist minister George Birley (1746–1824) and which, along with his published works, are located in the Angus Library, Regent's Park College, Oxford.[72] While Taylor's letters to Birley are generally short in length and many concern specific matters such as the editing of Taylor's works prior

68. The Angus Library, Regent's Park College, Oxford lists forty-nine publications by Taylor in its catalog. In addition, it lists thirteen letters to the Connexion's churches that Taylor wrote on behalf of the annual Association.

69. Anon. [Dan Taylor], *Humble Essay Christian Baptism*.

70. Dan Taylor, *Absolute Necessity*.

71. [Dan Taylor], *Hymns*. The evidence that Taylor was the editor of this hymn book will be considered in chapter 6.

72. Letters from Dan Taylor to George Birley, 1771–1808, (D/HUS 1/6). As is evident, "Revd" does not include a full stop in the title of this collection. George Birley assisted at Taylor's school in Wadsworth, West Riding between 1765–1768. He then worked as a teacher at the boarding school of the Particular Baptist minister John Ryland Sr. in Northamptonshire. He was ordained as a General Baptist minister in 1786, serving as a minister at the General Baptist church in St Ives, Huntingdonshire which became part of the New Connexion in 1789. See Wood, *Condensed History*, 243.

to publication which was a role that Birley assumed, sixteen of them have been particularly useful in my examination of Taylor's evangelicalism. In addition, I have drawn on some of his letters to Birley that are located in *Memoirs*, but which are not found in the entirely unpublished collection of his letters to Birley in the Angus Library. Taylor's letters to the Connexion's member churches have also been important in helping to establish an understanding of Taylor's thinking on matters such as the need for pastors and church members to work together in the interests of mission,[73] the merits of churches associating together,[74] and duties of church membership.[75] Taylor's contributions recorded in the unpublished and published minutes of the New Connexion's annual Association have also proved instructive.[76] In addition, consideration has been given to some of Taylor's articles in the *General Baptist Magazine* that he established and edited from 1798 to 1800.[77]

One of the ways that the main characteristics of Taylor's evangelicalism emerged was when he functioned as an apologist when responding to wider works. For this reason, I have given attention to publications from a range of others. These include Unitarians such as the theologian and scientist Joseph Priestley (1733–1804) and Halifax minister William Graham (1721–96); Particular Baptists such as Robert Hall Sr. (1728–91) and Andrew Fuller; leading General Baptists who resisted the Evangelical Revival such as Gilbert Boyce (1712–1800); and the Universalist American Baptist minister Elhanan Winchester (1751–97). An assortment of writings by eighteenth-century evangelicals such as John Wesley, William Grimshaw (1708–63), George Whitefield, and John Newton (1725–1807) have also been used. These have been useful, providing insight into particular features of evangelicalism. An example is my use of some unpublished letters by William Grimshaw, located in The John Rylands Library, Manchester.[78] The records of the West Yorkshire Archive Service in Wakefield have also been useful in identifying certain facts concerning Taylor's earliest years, beyond those provided by Adam Taylor.

Evaluation of the distinctive aspects of Taylor's evangelicalism, has necessitated an examination of both the theological emphases and ways in which the faith was articulated within Puritanism. Various publications by

73. See, e.g., Dan Taylor, "Concurrence of People," 15–22.
74. See, e.g., Dan Taylor, "Nature and Importance," 12–19.
75. See, e.g., Dan Taylor, *Duties of Church Members*, 9.
76. These are also located in the Angus Library.
77. Dan Taylor, *General Baptist Magazine*.
78. The John Rylands Library also contains some of Taylor's published works but the collection is smaller than that located in the Angus Library.

Puritans such as John Goodwin (1594–1665), Thomas Goodwin (1600–1680), Richard Baxter (1615–91), and John Owen (1616–83) have been drawn upon. Consideration has also been given to the writings of earlier General Baptists such as Thomas Helwys (1575–1616) and Thomas Grantham. The General Baptist creeds and confessions of faith from this earlier period have been scrutinized.[79] Given Taylor's Arminianism, some attention has been given to the writings of Dutch theologian James Arminius (1560–1609) and Remonstrant leader Hugo Grotius (1583–1645). Certain works by key Enlightenment figures such as Locke have also been examined, due to their influence on Taylor.

This book works with a substantial amount of primary evidence. Central place is given to the writings of Taylor which are diverse in range—from published sermons, theological expositions, catechisms and confessions, to tracts and unpublished letters. This is supplemented by wider primary material that provides further help in evaluating all notable aspects of his evangelicalism.

A Biographical Sketch of Taylor's Life and Ministry

Taylor was born on 21 December 1738 in Northowram—a village just outside Halifax in the West Riding of Yorkshire.[80] He was the second son of Azor and Mary who had eight children, including Taylor's younger brother John (1743–1818) who also became a General Baptist minister.[81] From the age of four to twenty-four, Taylor worked with his father in a local coal mine. This was arduous and dangerous, and on at least one occasion he nearly lost his life.[82] He received no formal education other than that taught by his mother. Family life was marked by material austerity, hard work, and a regard for moral living. The Bible was read to him from an early age and the family regularly attended Halifax Parish Church, with Taylor having been confirmed during this period.[83] At fifteen years of age, he began

---

79. Examples include, the 1660 *Brief Confession* and 1679 *Orthodox Creed*. See Lumpkin, *Baptist Confessions*, 224–35, 297–334.

80. Taylor, *Memoirs*, 2.

81. Ibid.

82. Ibid., 2–4. Adam Taylor describes how Dan Taylor narrowly escaped with his life when the mine flooded in 1753.

83. Ibid., 2–5. While Adam Taylor did not provide the name of the parish church that the family attended, my examination of records at the West Yorkshire Archives Office indicate that it was Halifax Parish Church. This will be examined further in chapter 1.

to participate in the Evangelical Revival. He traveled across the moors to listen to preachers such as George Whitefield, John Wesley, Charles Wesley (1707–88), and William Grimshaw—in whose Haworth churchyard he often stood among many thousands of others.[84] He was so affected by what he heard that he joined the Methodists where, for nine years, he was actively involved and gained substantial spiritual understanding.[85] For various reasons, he declined the opportunity to become a traveling Methodist preacher and withdrew from the Methodist movement in 1762.[86] Later that year, he assumed leadership of a small group of fellow Methodist seceders in Hepstonstall, near Halifax.[87] He acquired premises for the fellowship in nearby Wadsworth where he found lodgings and developed a school.[88] At the close of the year, he left his employment in the coal mine to commit more fully to the fellowship's development.

In early 1763, Taylor helped the fellowship establish core ecclesiological and theological principles they would unite around.[89] These included a commitment to a general view of the atonement. At this time he also made the significant decision to embrace the doctrine of believers' baptism.[90] Having persuaded the believers at Wadsworth to do likewise, he then sought to be baptized. After he was declined baptism by local Particular Baptists due to his belief in the doctrine of general redemption, he was grateful when informed that there were General Baptists in Lincolnshire who shared the same outlook on the universal scope of Christ's death.[91] Taylor had presumed that "he and his few friends at Wadsworth were the only Baptists in existence who denied the doctrine of personal election."[92] Despite having never left the West Riding and it being "the depth of winter," he set off immediately on foot.[93] The journey was dramatic when he was lost in the flooded countryside of Nottinghamshire and forced to spend the night sheltering under a haystack. The next day he was surprised to

84. Ibid., 5.

85. Ibid.

86. Ibid., 9. The reasons for this will be considered in chapter 1.

87. Ibid.

88. Ibid., 10. In 1774 Taylor relocated the school to some buildings on the site of a nearby farm named "Hirst" that he rented. This enabled him to accept pupils who wanted to board and provided him with some limited revenue. He also farmed the land and sold its produce, see, e.g., ibid., 90.

89. Ibid.

90. Ibid., 10–11.

91. Ibid., 11–12.

92. Ibid., 12.

93. Ibid.

discover some General Baptists in Gamston. It was there that he was baptized in the River Idle by the church's pastor Joseph Jeffery on 16 February
1763.[94] During the ensuing months, Taylor facilitated the process by which
the Wadsworth fellowship joined the General Baptists, becoming the first
General Baptist church in Yorkshire. Taylor was then ordained as a General
Baptist minister by Gilbert Boyce, Messenger of the Lincolnshire General
Baptists, on 30 July 1763.[95]

As Taylor implemented various innovative initiatives and structures,
the church soon began to grow in number. One of the "first fruits" was his
first wife Elizabeth Saltonstall who he met when she joined the church in
1763.[96] They were married in November 1764, had thirteen children, and
enjoyed twenty-nine years together until Elizabeth's death in 1793.[97] During 1764 Taylor was fully occupied with his involvement in the building of
a larger place of worship for the fellowship.[98] The work was completed in
December 1764 with Taylor carrying the pulpit from the old meeting house
to the new premises, situated on the side of a hill in Wadsworth called Birchcliff.[99] The fellowship subsequently became known as Birchcliff Baptist.[100]
Soon afterwards, Taylor became increasingly aware of the influence of Socinianism and Unitarianism on the wider General Baptists, and how this had
led to the adoption of certain beliefs that differed considerably from those
he had embraced within the Evangelical Revival.[101] These involved subjects
such as the deity of Christ, nature of sin, justification, and atonement. His
response was to contest these contrary outlooks in his preaching and published works. By the late 1760s he had become a figurehead for those few
General Baptists who wanted to remain faithful to orthodox understandings

94. Ibid., 13.

95. Ibid., 15. The role of General Baptist Messenger will be considered in chapter 2.

96. Ibid., 17.

97. Taylor's high regard for Elizabeth was particularly apparent when he mourned
her loss in a 1794 letter he wrote to George Birley, see Dan Taylor, "Letter to George
Birley," 17 March 1794. Page not numbered.

98. See Dan Taylor, "Letter to George Birley," [1764]. Although this letter is not
dated, Taylor's description that "it has been concluded proper to attempt the building
of a meeting-house," page not numbered, and that "the foundation is laid," page not
numbered, suggest that the letter was written in 1764 as this is when Adam Taylor
recorded that the work on the building of the new church began, see Taylor, *Memoirs*,
17. If, as suggested, this letter was written in 1764, this means that this collection of
Taylor's letters to Birley should be dated from 1764, not 1771.

99. Taylor, *Memoirs*, 17.

100. Throughout this book, I have used the spelling of "Birchcliff" which is the way
it was written by Taylor and his contemporaries. It later became known as "Birchcliffe."

101. This will be considered in chapter 2.

of the faith. A combination of factors led him to take the innovative step of creating the New Connexion of General Baptists in 1770.[102] This was a movement of ministers and churches committed to an evangelical understanding of the faith, as embodied in its six *Articles of Religion*.[103] It initially comprised nineteen founding ministers who represented sixteen churches, and a total of 1,635 believers.[104] His oversight of the Connexion required extensive input into matters of theological, missional, pastoral, and structural importance. He frequently upheld its evangelical convictions.

In the 1770s Taylor wrote extensively on subjects such as the importance of the Scriptures, divinity of Christ, and nature of salvation.[105] The content of these works, as well as his later publications, highlight a surprising feature of his theological development. This concerns how he made very few changes to his beliefs after the early 1760s. Once settled in his thinking on matters such as evangelicalism, Arminianism, and believers' baptism, his beliefs underwent few modifications. The subsequent developments that took place in his ministry were of a more practical orientation. This was particularly evident in endeavors such as his creation of the New Connexion (as previously noted), development of training and approaches to mission.

The 1780s saw Taylor act as an advocate for a general view of the atonement. This is apparent in his contributions to a Leeds newspaper and discourse with Andrew Fuller. During the 1780s and 1790s he also addressed many other issues such as baptism, the Lord's Supper, hymn singing, mission, and duties of church members. Alongside his continuing publications, strategic guidance for the movement's church planting, and regular visits to the growing number of churches, he remained committed to his responsibilities at Birchcliff. In 1783 he left to become minister of the newly founded General Baptist church in Halifax.[106] Only two years later he

---

102. Taylor, *Memoirs*, 72.

103. *Articles*, in Lumpkin, *Baptist Confessions*, 342–44. They were first recorded in *Assembly of Free Grace General Baptists, 1770*. Page not numbered. It should be noted that the annual minutes that comprise this collection are not individually referenced. The *Articles* are also found in Adam Taylor, *New Connection*, 139–42. As is considered in different chapters of the book, the six Articles were written by Taylor and provide brief consideration of the fall of humankind; the moral law; the person and work of Christ; salvation by faith; the Holy Spirit; and baptism.

104. The names of the ministers are found in *Assembly of Free Grace General Baptists 1770*. Page not numbered. The churches they represented are listed in Wood, *Condensed History*, 176. For wider statistical considerations regarding the size of the movement, see Rinaldi, *Tribe of Dan*, 213.

105. See, e.g., Philagathus [Dan Taylor], *Practical Improvement*; Taylor, *Scriptural Account*.

106. Taylor, *Memoirs*, 117.

took the decision to move to London, accepting the call to his final pastorate as joint minister at Church Lane General Baptist Church, Whitechapel.[107] He became sole minister after the death of his colleague John Brittain in 1794.[108] Taylor also opened a bookseller's shop in 1791 in Union Street, Bishopsgate. This provided a helpful supplement to his income.

From the mid-1790s he devoted much of his time to training ministers. He established the General Baptist Academy in 1797 and was its tutor until 1813.[109] During this time he was active within the General Body of Protestant Dissenting Ministers which, as noted earlier, provided him with the opportunity to speak before King George III.[110] Taylor also assumed an important role in the formation in 1816 of the General Baptist Missionary Society.[111] This period of Taylor's life involved regular changes in his personal circumstances. In 1794 he married Elizabeth Newton who died in 1809.[112] He married again in 1811 although his wife, Mary Toplis, died one year later.[113] A month before his death he was married for the fourth time, to Mrs. S. Saunders.[114] Taylor died at home on 26 November 1816 and was buried at Bunhill Fields.[115] He left the New Connexion with 6,624 members across seventy churches[116] and with a rich foundation of vibrant and pioneering evangelicalism that he had nurtured.

The Content of this Book

An examination of Taylor's evangelicalism is provided in seven main chapters. Chapter 1 considers his emergence into the movement through his participation in the Evangelical Revival and subsequent involvement in Methodism. Attention is given to how this proved crucial regarding the formation of his spirituality and future pattern of ministry. Chapter 2 focuses on Taylor's soteriology, and particularly the innovative ways in which he functioned as an apologist for his evangelical understanding of the gospel, as he responded to proponents of Socinianism and Unitarianism. The

107. Ibid., 169. The church at this time had 150 members, see ibid., 125.

108. Ibid., 207.

109. Ibid., 217.

110. Ibid., 169.

111. See, e.g., *Minutes of an Association 1816*, 10.

112. Taylor, *Memoirs*, 206.

113. Ibid., 237.

114. Ibid., 247. The first name of Mrs. S. Saunders is unknown.

115. Ibid., 249.

116. Rinaldi, *Tribe of Dan*, 213.

creative fusion of ideas that underpinned his partial adoption of a moral government theory of the atonement is also examined. Chapter 3 analyzes his commitment to general redemption, and how his theology of general atonement was novel. Primarily this was because of the way the doctrine was worked out, rather than the doctrine itself being novel. Nevertheless, something new was being done. Chapter 4 examines Taylor's understanding of the means and process of conversion as revealed in the context of his dialog on this subject with Andrew Fuller. Chapter 5 scrutinizes the combination of different emphases that underpinned Taylor's ecclesiology and how he acquired an influence throughout the New Connexion that was, in certain respects, comparable to John Wesley's influence over Methodism. Chapter 6 studies Taylor's approach to worship, the sacraments of the Lord's Supper and baptism, and examines the creative means by which he acted as a proponent for what he deemed to be the correct way of proceeding in each of these areas. Chapter 7 engages with his missiology, and how this led him to become a "religious entrepreneur," a term that Bebbington uses to describe him.[117] Reference to him as an entrepreneur, both by Bebbington and throughout this book, differs in meaning from the usual definition of an entrepreneur as a person who undertakes an enterprise or business with the hope of profit. Instead, the designation of Taylor as a religious entrepreneur refers exclusively to his propensity for theological and practical innovation. Mention also needs to be made that there are certain important themes in this book that cross chapters, such as Taylor's approach to the Bible and the influence of Enlightenment values on many aspects of his thinking and practice.

Each main chapter contributes to an understanding of Taylor as a person whose theological thinking and exercise of his ministry was marked by a vibrant evangelicalism that was pioneering. This was encapsulated in the overall objective he set for the Connexion, that it might serve "To revive experimental religion or primitive Christianity in faith and practice."[118] In addition, it will be argued that the core tenets of his thinking reflected key Enlightenment values. I will aim to demonstrate that the evangelical

---

117. Bebbington, *Baptists*, 85.

118. *Assembly of Free Grace General Baptists 1770*. Page not numbered. These minutes were written by Taylor who assumed the lead role in establishing the Connexion's objective.

It should be noted that in all quotations I have endeavored to follow the capitalization, grammar, and spelling of the original. I do not provide a footnote for the quotations which are at the beginning of each chapter, as these appear later in the chapter. A further point to note is that Taylor did not use inclusive language. While I have quoted Taylor accurately, I have sought to use inclusive language in my own writing in the book.

distinctions of his approach were particularly apparent when compared to certain commonplace emphases and methods used to articulate the faith by other believers. Consideration is given to both the many General Baptists of Taylor's day who resisted the Evangelical Revival, and to those of earlier generations who, despite being more orthodox, exhibited a theological outlook that in places differed notably from Taylor's. I will seek to highlight that the chief characteristics of Taylor's theological thinking were also apparent as he engaged with Particular Baptists who were evaluating how they could be liberated from the missiological constraints of High Calvinism. Comparisons are made, throughout the book, with the understanding of the faith that emanated from within Puritanism. While mindful of Puritanism's diversity, it will be contended that Taylor's evangelicalism contained certain important differences.

I will argue that the central facets of Taylor's evangelicalism reflected that which was new and distinct about eighteenth-century evangelicalism. Although notable elements of continuity remained, it will be argued that Taylor's evangelicalism gave rise to an outworking of faith that differed from that generally found among earlier bodies of believers such as the Puritans and seventeenth-century General Baptists. This included the constant primacy he placed on the practical and experiential above the cerebral, reason and observation above the metaphysical, conciseness above wordiness, entrepreneurship above apathy, liberty above prescriptiveness, and the interweaving of mission into all he taught. This significant combination of emphases provides a crucial integrating theme throughout this book. It also serves to affirm much of the "Bebbington thesis" regarding the distinguishing features and origins of evangelicalism.

Conclusion

This book makes a detailed examination of the evangelicalism of Dan Taylor. Previous studies of Taylor, who was of significance in eighteenth-century Baptist life, have failed to offer detailed insights into his theological thinking. Using a range of primary material, this book seeks to address this deficit of knowledge. As the chief characteristics and varied nuances of his evangelicalism are identified it will be seen that it was pioneering in nature. It will be argued that the central facets of Taylor's evangelicalism provide further evidence of important new expressions of faith and emphases that were dominant within eighteenth-century evangelicalism. The way in which Taylor demonstrated these tendencies compared to certain earlier groups of believers serves, in turn, to support much of what Bebbington posits concerning the emergence of evangelicalism. In this way, this book aims to contribute to the study of Taylor to an understanding of that which was new and distinct about eighteenth-century evangelicalism.

1

Emergent Evangelical

DAN TAYLOR FIRST ENCOUNTERED the Evangelical Revival at William Grimshaw's parish church in Haworth, West Riding. Through the preaching of Grimshaw and other evangelicals, he gained an understanding of the gospel that differed from that which he had acquired during his earlier years. All that Taylor found to be new, both within the preached message and how the gospel was communicated, will be considered. Attention will be given to his nine-year involvement in the structures of Methodism as he participated in society, class, and band meetings at the Methodist society in Halifax. The commitment with which he embraced much of what was distinctive about eighteenth-century evangelicalism will be examined and how this became evident in his later practical embodiment of evangelical values, his structural initiatives and teaching. The extent to which his evangelicalism was manifest in the dynamics of his personal spirituality and how this highlights something of the discontinuity between evangelicalism and earlier movements such as Puritanism, will be explored. Lastly, consideration will be given to certain reasons and influences that contributed to his decision to leave Methodism.

Taylor's Introduction to the Evangelical Revival

"meat and drink"

During the mid-1750s Taylor traveled many miles with his younger brother John to hear evangelical preachers. In particular, they made frequent visits to Haworth to listen to the preaching of William Grimshaw.[1] John Walsh,

1. Adam Taylor, *Memoirs*, 5. Haworth was twelve miles from the family home in

in his examination of eighteenth-century evangelical clergy in Yorkshire, describes Grimshaw as "the dominating figure of the period."[2] He became perpetual curate at Haworth Parish Church in 1742, previously serving eleven years as a curate at Todmorden where, he spent his first seven years enjoying a lifestyle of carefree indulgence.[3] A turning point came in 1738 when (among other factors) he read a sermon on justification by faith by the prominent evangelical Robert Seagrave.[4] Grimshaw then decided "to embrace Christ only for my all in all," abandoned his loose living, renounced his merit based understanding of salvation and dedicated himself to preaching faith in Christ crucified and risen as the only means of salvation from sin.[5] The twelve regular communicants at Haworth in 1742 soon grew to a gathering of over a thousand people during the summer months.[6] As John Laycock described, Grimshaw became "one of the greatest evangelists in the North of England."[7] At the time when Taylor traveled to hear Grimshaw, growth in numbers was still taking place. This was reflected in a 1754 letter from Grimshaw who wrote, "I bless the Lord. His work still spreads and flourishes on all sides of us."[8] Three years later, he similarly wrote "Our congregations . . . are larger," "several souls are added" and "some are seemingly just now awakening."[9] The Taylors' visits to Haworth, between 1753–62, also saw them introduced to the preaching of other leading evangelicals who were provided the "best hospitality" by Grimshaw.[10] These included John

---

Northowram.

2. Walsh, "Yorkshire Evangelicals," 330. For the significance of Grimshaw's ministry in Yorkshire, see ibid., 96–113. See also Baker, *William Grimshaw*.

3. For a biographical overview of Grimshaw's life, see Venn, *Christ the Joy*.

4. Ibid., 32. Robert Seagrave was a Church of England minister and close friend of George Whitefield. Between 1731–46 Seagrave published many letters and pamphlets through which he aimed to encourage clergy to a greater earnestness in their work.

5. William Grimshaw. Quoted [Hereafter Qtd] in Venn, *Christ the Joy*, 32. Primary source unknown.

6. Newton, *Memoirs*, 70. When the Wesleys and George Whitefield visited, the crowds numbered several thousand.

7. Laycock, *Methodist Heroes*, 32.

8. Grimshaw, "Letter to Mrs. Gallatin," 10 May 1754. Page not numbered. Mrs. Gallatin was married to Bartholomew Gallatin who was a naturalized Swiss army officer—reaching the rank of Lieutenant-Colonel in the British army in 1759. They both embraced the Evangelical Revival and offered friendship and support to Grimshaw, Whitefield, and the Wesleys. For brief reference to the significance of Mrs. Gallatin, see Charles Wesley, *Letters of Charles Wesley*, 433.

9. Grimshaw, "Letter to Mrs. Gallatin," 31 July 1757. Page not numbered.

10. Lowery, "William Grimshaw," 3. For Adam Taylor's description of these trips, see Taylor, *Memoirs*, 5.

and Charles Wesley, and George Whitefield whose ministries further contributed to how "the revival was expanding and consolidating in Yorkshire."[11]
Taylor was both a witness of this revival and willing participant.

The preached message of the need to place faith in Christ as the Son
of God, who died for the sins of the world and for each person individually, was "instrumental" in helping Taylor gain "clearer views of the plan of
mercy through a redeemer."[12] Taylor experienced that which David Hempton draws attention to as a characteristic of Methodist preaching during the
Evangelical Revival. Hempton states that while the message was "neither
uniform nor completely formulaic . . . it spoke of the possibility of salvation and a new start, not at the dictates of authoritarian divinity, but as the
result of divine love inspiring a willing human response."[13] Having been
exposed to this, Taylor considered his inherited understanding of the gospel
as deficient. A typical example of the criticism he expressed regarding his
earlier experience of faith was how he had "often been heard to say, that
if the gospel had been preached as it ought to have been, he should have
obtained liberty much sooner."[14] Neither his attendance of worship at Halifax Parish Church,[15] nor his parents' Bible teaching gave him the clarity of
gospel understanding that he gained from evangelical preachers. This was
despite his parents' best efforts. John Taylor noted that their mother had
diligently sought to instruct her children in the truths of Scripture and that
their father possessed "much more knowledge of the holy Scriptures than
working men generally have."[16] He, in turn, recorded that his brother Dan
began to teach the Bible to others, himself included, by his tenth year.[17]
However, Taylor viewed his earlier introduction to the faith as inadequate

---

11. Walsh, "Yorkshire Evangelicals," 144. Frank Baker demonstrates that the Wesleys preached frequently at Haworth, particularly during the first period of Taylor's visits there. Whitefield also preached there as many as seventeen times between 1748–62,
see Baker, *William Grimshaw*, 238–39.

12. Taylor, *Memoirs*, 6.

13. Hempton, *Methodism*, 206.

14. Taylor, *Memoirs*, 9. Adam Taylor's account of Taylor's entrance into evangelicalism is particularly important as neither Taylor's diary entries, surviving letters, nor
published works cover this period. It was not until 1764 that Taylor began writing his
diary and he was then occupied with more immediate concerns rather than recording
his experience of faith during his earlier years.

15. Consideration is given to Taylor's parish church later in this section.

16. John Taylor. Qtd in Adam Taylor, *John Taylor*, 5. The fact that Adam Taylor was
quoting from a particular manuscript that John Taylor wrote (and which is otherwise
unknown) accounts for why he provided no surrounding detail or dates regarding the
source of these quotations.

17. John Taylor. Qtd in ibid., 5.

compared to how the content of the evangelical message enabled him "with greater confidence, to lay hold on the hope set before him in the gospel."[18] Taylor perceived the evangelical depiction of the gospel as something new and with which he felt compelled to engage.

Adam Taylor claimed that the evangelical preacher who Dan Taylor "most highly esteemed" was Grimshaw.[19] Taylor's high regard for Grimshaw is further supported as his death was the catalyst for his first published work, a ninety-five line poetic elegy that he wrote as a tribute following his death in 1763.[20] Taylor noted that his death had "deeply affected him," and commended Grimshaw as a "man of eminence and worth," "brother and friend of human race" and "son of learning."[21] He further mourned his loss as he asked, "But why, my Lord, why didst thou call so soon? Why does thy people's sun go down at noon?"[22] Walsh cites this elegy as typical of how many "bewailed the death of Grimshaw."[23] While Walsh appears unaware that the poem was written by Taylor, his note regarding the elegy captures the sense of mourning that Taylor felt.[24]

Taylor paid tribute to Grimshaw as a "powerful preacher."[25] Grimshaw's preaching was also highlighted by Grimshaw's close friend, the Anglican minister and hymn writer John Newton who regularly visited him. Newton claimed that for many of those who had a Church of England background (such as Taylor), listening to Grimshaw preach was a very different experience. With such people in mind, he noted that they had "seldom heard any thing more from the pulpit, than cold lectures upon lean, modern morality" but that Grimshaw "commanded their attention. His heart was engaged, he was pressed in spirit, he spoke with earnestness and authority, as one who was well assured of the truth and importance of his message."[26] The Wesleys and Whitefield preached with a similar compelling

18. Taylor, *Memoirs*, 6.

19. Ibid., 5.

20. Anon. [Dan Taylor], *Thought on Wm. Grimshaw*. Adam Taylor confirmed that Dan Taylor was the author of this work, see Taylor, *Memoirs*, 16.

21. Taylor, *Memoirs*, 16; [Taylor], *Thought on Wm. Grimshaw*, 1.

22. [Taylor], *Thought on Wm. Grimshaw*, 1.

23. Walsh, "Yorkshire Evangelicals," 241.

24. Walsh correctly cites the work as anonymous, but fails to note that Dan Taylor was the author. He instead refers to the elegy as having been written by a "simple poet," see ibid., 241.

25. [Taylor], *Thought on Wm. Grimshaw*, 1.

26. Newton, *Memoirs*, 56. The formatting of "any thing" in the first of these quotations is as in the original. Further examples of words that have been quoted in this book where the spelling and grammar are as in the original include "any way," "tho,"

power, passion, and resolve. When Taylor listened to evangelical preachers he also heard a uniformity of message. As Laycock outlined, "substantially the same doctrines" were preached, irrespective of the evangelical who visited Haworth.[27] These comprised what Grimshaw referred to as the "main doctrines of all discourse" and included "man's fall and degeneracy, his redemption through Jesus Christ alone, the nature & necessity of the new birth, justification by faith alone, sanctification by the indwelling spirit of our redeemer."[28] These elements reflect David Bebbington's emphasis on the crucicentrism of evangelicals (see introductory chapter) and together formed the essential content of the evangelical message that Taylor heard. They became his new "meat and drink."[29]

While Taylor's introduction to evangelicalism centered around Grimshaw and other evangelicals who visited Haworth, the origins of the evangelical movement in Yorkshire lay elsewhere. It began with the evangelistic endeavors of Benjamin Ingham (1712–72) who in 1734 began his preaching ministry in his native Ossett.[30] This had the effect that "Numbers of persons were convinced of their lost condition as sinners."[31] Following his ordination training at Oxford where he became a member of the "Oxford Methodists" and after also having accompanied the Wesleys on their mission to Georgia, he resumed his labors in Yorkshire in 1737.[32] He was initially welcomed into parish churches in places such as Ossett, Wakefield, Leeds. and Halifax and there occurred "a great stirring up of the people to seek salvation by faith alone, in the merits of a crucified Saviour."[33] For much of the eighteenth century evangelicals were "generally despised by the bishops" and Ingham was subsequently prohibited from preaching in the Diocese of York.[34] He then embraced field preaching, functioning as an evangelical pioneer in Yorkshire, Lancashire, and Cumbria. Ingham also worked closely with Moravian believers who were active in Yorkshire.[35]

"every where," "commonsense," "shews," "dogmatical," "systematical," "powe'r," "possest," "whereof," and "similies."

27. Laycock, *Methodist Heroes*, 37.

28. Grimshaw, "Letter to John Gillies," 19 July 1754, 507.

29. Taylor, *Memoirs*, 9.

30. See Walsh, "Yorkshire Evangelicals," 86, 89–91. For more on the nature of Ingham's ministry, see Tyerman, *Oxford Methodists*, 57–154; Pickles, *Benjamin Ingham*.

31. Laycock, *Methodist Heroes*, 3.

32. See Tyerman, *Oxford Methodists*, 86.

33. Grimshaw, "Letter to John Gillies," 506.

34. Hylson-Smith, *Evangelicals*, 33.

35. See Valentine, "Significant Inroads," 142–43. Valentine makes passing reference to Taylor in this article although wrongly addresses him as "Daniel," see 142. Despite

Ingham's close association with the Wesley brothers and Whitefield meant that his work was originally under a Methodist mantle. There were also those who Henry Rack refers to as "freelance evangelicals," meaning that they were not connected to any particular movement.[36] One such example was stonemason John Nelson (1707–74), who embraced evangelicalism as a consequence of hearing Whitefield and John Wesley preach in London.[37] When he returned to his home town of Birstall in 1740, he preached a message of forgiveness of sins through faith in Christ.[38] The sense of novelty which greeted his teaching is evident in Nelson's journal reference that,

> the people of the neighbouring towns have frequently sent for me to hear of this new doctrine for they were quite sure no man could know of his sins being forgiven in this world. But I proved it from the written word of God, . . . In a little time many cried out, "Lord, grant this thing unto me!"[39]

Shoemaker William Darney ([1684/5?]–1774) held a similarly significant itinerant ministry. He was converted during the Scottish evangelical awakening of 1741 and commenced preaching in the West Riding in 1742.[40] Darney's preaching was influential on Grimshaw's conversion to an evangelical outlook, although Grimshaw originally dismissed it as "an error of Popery."[41] A common response to the teaching of Ingham, Nelson, and Darney was one of surprise concerning the perceived newness of the gospel message they preached. Taylor's near identical reaction to evangelicalism suggests that this response remained commonplace in the West Riding, even into the 1750s.

While Taylor and many others in the West Riding considered the content of evangelical gospel preaching as new, what Grimshaw cited as its "main doctrines" were found within the teaching of earlier movements such as the Protestant Reformers, Puritans and Separatists. It also shared certain commonalities with Latitudinarianism, which was dominant in the Church of England in the eighteenth century. Latitudinarianism emerged in the seventeenth century through individuals including the Archbishop

---

Moravians being found in Yorkshire, Taylor provides no evidence that he ever came into contact with them.

36. Rack, *Reasonable Enthusiast*, 214.

37. See Walsh, "Yorkshire Evangelicals," 91–93. See also, Nelson, *Journal*.

38. See Valentine, "Significant Inroads," 143–44.

39. Nelson, "Letter," 15.

40. See Goldhawk, "Darney, William," 629. For further references to Darney's ministry, see Laycock, *Methodist Heroes*, 39–44, 53–59, 228–34.

41. Laycock, *Methodist Heroes*, 40.

of Canterbury John Tillotson who drew upon the ideas of Cambridge Platonists such as Ralph Cudworth.[42] Similar to the evangelicalism that Taylor came to embrace, many Latitudinarians disliked theological controversy and instead promoted irenicism. A further commonality was the way in which their preaching and written works tended to be marked by plainness, absence of abstractionism and an emphasis on the practical duties of faith.[43] Despite these similarities, a crucial difference concerned the way in which Latitudinarians often understood salvation without reference to Christ's atoning work and as guaranteed for those who lived a moral life.[44] This was very different from the emphasis that Taylor heard evangelical preachers place on Christ's atonement as the only means of salvation.

It is likely that Taylor was influenced by Latitudinarianism as he worshiped in his parish church. While neither the name nor location of the church were provided by Adam Taylor, nor specified in Dan Taylor's writings, nor considered by any of the commentators cited in this book, it can be confidently assumed that it was Halifax Parish Church. The records of the West Yorkshire Archive Service in Wakefield show that Taylor's parents, Azor and Mary, were married at Halifax Parish Church in October 1736 and that Taylor was baptized there in December 1738.[45] This information is significant. It provides a means of gaining an understanding of Taylor's spiritual background beyond that recorded by Adam Taylor. It is helpful in this respect to consider the potential Latitudinarian tendencies of George Legh (1693–1775) who was minister of the church from 1731 until his death.

On the one hand, Legh was a friend to evangelicals. Ingham, Whitefield, and John Wesley all preached at Halifax Parish Church during Legh's ministry.[46] He also commended the preaching of the Anglican evangelical Henry Venn.[47] A monument at the church commends Legh's regard for the Bible. It notes how he viewed the Bible as the "only standard of faith and practice" and "ordered Bibles" to be given to the poor.[48] John Wesley

---

42. For an examination of Latitudinarianism and its central tenets, see Griffin, *Latitudinarianism*.

43. For consideration of this, see, e.g., Muller, *Latitudinarianism*, 79–82.

44. See, e.g., Griffin, *Latitudinarianism*, 39–40, 106, 126–48.

45. Halifax St John the Baptist, Register of Baptisms, Marriages, and Burials 1726–1756, WDP53/1/1/10. The church was known as Halifax Parish Church, or alternatively, Halifax, St John the Baptist.

46. Hargreaves, "Religion and Society," 71–72. Ingham preached at Halifax Parish Church in 1738, Whitefield in 1755, and Wesley in 1774.

47. Walsh, "Yorkshire Evangelicals," 379.

48. Hargreaves, "Religion and Society," 71.

referred to Legh as "a candid inquirer after truth."[49] This could imply that Legh was not settled in his theological convictions. It is noteworthy that the Anglican minister Thomas Dunham Whitaker described Legh as "a disciple of Bishop Hoadly."[50] The earlier cited monument notes Legh's "opposition to ecclesiastical tyranny" as he "defended the rights of mankind in that memorable Hoadlian controversy."[51] Benjamin Hoadly was a bishop of Latitudinarian persuasion.[52] Legh appears to have supported the view that Hoadly articulated before King George I in 1717 when he stated that the church lacked doctrinal and disciplinary authority.[53] This provoked much controversy, with advocates of ecclesiastical authority attacking Hoadly's position and over two hundred pamphlets issued.[54] Legh's support for Hoadly was evident in his 1718 publication of a letter to Thomas Sherlock who opposed Hoadly and, at that time, was Vice-Chancellor of Cambridge University.[55] Legh argued in favor of individual freedom from ecclesiastical authority and for people to be able to judge the Bible for themselves. He believed that "God's favour follows the sincerity of a Christian," irrespective of whether they worshiped in the Church of England or were Dissenters.[56] Hoadly was also widely known for his denial of doctrines such as justification by faith, insisting on "the mistake of relying upon faith" alone for salvation.[57] While Legh's support for Hoadly does not necessarily imply his agreement with

49. John Wesley, Journal entry, 2 June 1742, 271. It should be noted that throughout this book my dating of Wesley's Journal entries, sermons, and wider works follows that outlined in the appendices of each of the volumes that comprise *The Bicentennial Edition of the Works of John Wesley* [Hereafter *BE*], edited by Ward and Heitzenrater. When a full date is stated, this refers to when the text was composed or preached; a solitary year refers to the year of publication.

50. Whitaker. Qtd in Crabtree, *Concise History,* 130. Primary source unknown.

51. Hargreaves, "Religion and Society," 71.

52. For an overview of Hoadly's ministry and theological convictions, see Gibson, *Enlightenment Prelate.*

53. See ibid., 149–52.

54. For an examination of this controversy, see Starkie, *Church of England.*

55. Dalrymple [George Legh], *Letter from Edinburgh.* Sherlock later became a Bishop. He was firstly made Bishop of Bangor in 1728, then Salisbury in 1734, and finally London in 1748. It is evident from the postscript to this work that Gilbert Dalrymple was a pseudonym, see ibid., 52. Legh is widely regarded as the author, see, e.g., Starkie, *Church of England,* 44.

56. Dalrymple [Legh], *Letter from Edinburgh,* 24.

57. Hoadly, "Mistake," 549. For reflection on Hoadly's rejection of justification by faith alone, see Gibson, *Enlightenment Prelate,* 76–80.

him on other theological matters, the absence of any detailed reference to Christ's atoning work within Legh's works is notable.[58]

Given the nature of Legh's writings and his association with Hoadly, it seems best to concur with Walsh's view that it is "most doubtful if he can be claimed as an evangelical."[59] This also appears to be confirmed by Legh's fellow West Riding Anglican minister Samuel Knight who was an evangelical and referred to him as a person of "great liberality of sentiment, tho' not of much personal religion, yet he had a great respect for it in others."[60] Knight's view lends itself to John Hargreaves's designation of Legh as an "undogmatic Latitudinarian."[61] If, as seems likely, Legh had Latitudinarian leanings, then these would have contributed to that which Taylor found to be new as he listened to evangelicals emphasize the sufficiency for salvation of the exercise of faith alone in Christ's atoning work. Taylor never mentioned Legh in his writings, which further suggests his ministry was inconsequential to the evangelicalism Taylor came to embrace.

The difference between the key tenets of evangelicalism and Deism is another example of how evangelicalism differed from wider theological and philosophical frameworks of Taylor's day. Mindful of Wayne Hudson's caution against seeing Deism as a unitary phenomenon, deists were however in broad agreement that God was wholly transcendent, denied his immanence and generally believed he could only be known through reason and observation of the natural world.[62] It was first developed in systematic manner by Lord Herbert of Cherbury in the seventeenth century and then assumed its more customary form, through the writings of John Toland, Anthony Collins, and Matthew Tindal.[63] These British deists replaced Cherbury's notion of innate ideas of God's existence with frameworks of thought based, for example, on the empirical principles of the English philosopher John Locke, although not himself a deist.[64] They all maintained that the content

58. Other notable works that are attributed to Legh include; A Christian [George Legh], *Letter to the Reverend Mr. Stebbing*; A Christian [George Legh], *Answer to Reverend Mr. Stebbing's Remark on B. of Bangor's Doctrine of Religious Sincerity*; A Christian [George Legh], *Case of an Erroneous Conscience*.

59. Walsh, "Yorkshire Evangelicals," 378.

60. Knight. Qtd in ibid., 379. Primary source unknown. Samuel Knight was the son of Titus Knight who, as will be seen later in this chapter, Dan Taylor spent much time with during his involvement with the Methodists in Halifax.

61. Hargreaves, "Religion and Society," 71.

62. Hudson, *Enlightenment and Modernity*, 26. Hudson argues that there was a "plurality of different deisms," see ibid., 26.

63. For examination of these deists and the nature of English Deism, see ibid., 1–27, 79–114; Israel, *Radical Enlightenment*, 599–627.

64. For consideration of the significance of Locke, see, e.g., Aaron, *John Locke*.

of revelation must neither contradict nor transcend the dictates of reason and viewed salvation as assured for those who lived a moral life based on knowledge of the laws created by God. While Taylor frequently appealed to the merits of reason (see chapter 2) the central tenets of Deism differed considerably from his core evangelical understanding.

The view that the essential elements of Christian belief should reflect rational thinking was also held by the increasingly influential Socinians who were initially associated with the sixteenth-century Italian theologian Fausto Sozzini (1539–1604).[65] Socinian insistence on that which was reasonable meant that in contra-distinction to evangelicalism, doctrines such as the Trinity, Christ's deity, and justification by faith were all viewed as irrational. It was, therefore, with much vigor that Taylor later responded to the growing influence of Socinianism on the General Baptists.[66] Taylor's mindfulness of the criticisms made against the tenets of the evangelical message led him, in 1764, to write *The Absolute Necessity of Searching the Scriptures*.[67] He displayed a biblicism akin to that noted by Bebbington (see introductory chapter) as he defended doctrines such as the divinity of Christ, justification by faith, and belief in a triune God, all of which he had heard taught by evangelicals.[68]

To summarize, Taylor displayed considerable dedication as he regularly traveled to hear the gospel preached by evangelical ministers. He held the preaching of Grimshaw in the highest regard. As Taylor attended services at Haworth, he soon discovered that the thrust of the preached gospel message was different from that taught by his parents and at Halifax Parish Church. The core of the evangelical message also differed from the central emphases of prevailing frameworks of belief, such as Latitudinarianism which was very likely influential on his parish church under the ministry of George Legh, Deism, and Socinianism. Just as Taylor was awakened to a new perspective by evangelical preaching, he was also introduced to new styles of delivery and ways in which the gospel was articulated. This will be examined in the next section.

---

65. An examination of Sozzini's theological thinking and the wider development of Socinianism is provided by Sarah Mortimer, see Mortimer, *Reason and Religion*. See particularly ibid., 13–22. For wider consideration of Socinianism, see also Cottle, *Essays*; McLachlan, *Socinianism*. Further consideration will be given to Socinianism in chapter 2 of this book.

66. See chapter 2.

67. Dan Taylor, *Absolute Necessity*.

68. This publication will be examined more closely in chapter 2.

Taylor's Introduction to Evangelical Preaching

"enlightened clergymen"

When Dan and John Taylor listened to evangelical preachers at Haworth, they were struck by the clarity with which the gospel was preached. For instance, John Taylor noted that listening to evangelical preachers made him realize how, at his parish church, "I was not taught plainly enough by the preachers I then heard."[69] This echoed Dan Taylor's earlier cited regret that he had previously not heard the gospel preached as it "ought to have been."[70] In particular, the way in which evangelicals often framed their sharing of the gospel around an invitation to come to Christ would have been evident. This is apparent in Grimshaw's declaration that "My business is to invite all to come to Christ for salvation, and to assure all that will come of a hearty welcome."[71] It was the tendency of all evangelicals who preached at Haworth to provide their listeners with an opportunity to respond personally in faith to Christ, and to insist that "Jesus is our only Saviour, Surety, Mediator, Redeemer, and no other Person or Thing."[72] Both this invitational approach and core content of the gospel message were new to Taylor and contributed to the way John Taylor described how Dan and himself viewed those they heard preach at Haworth as "enlightened clergymen."[73] While it is argued throughout this book that evangelicalism was influenced by the Enlightenment as an intellectual and social phenomenon, John Taylor's use of the word "enlightened" pointed to evangelical preachers having been enlightened by God's Spirit. The Taylors believed this was particularly evident in the way evangelicals preached the gospel.

Taylor's repeated exposure to invitations to respond in faith to Jesus as the sole means of salvation was the likely catalyst through which he entered into the "liberty" of mind and heart that was highlighted earlier.[74] Prior to this, an emphasis on moral living appears to have comprised the thrust of the Christian message with which he had become familiar. This was again in keeping with Taylor having been influenced by Latitudinarianism whose

69. John Taylor. Qtd in Taylor, *John Taylor*, 7.

70. Taylor, *Memoirs*, 9.

71. Grimshaw, "Letter to Rev. Malachi Blake," 203.

72. Grimshaw, *Answer to a Sermon*, 20.

73. John Taylor. Qtd in Taylor, *John Taylor*, 9. In light of that noted earlier in respect of Dan Taylor's limited references to his early spiritual development, his brother John's recollections are significant and particularly so, given the shared nature of their upbringing in the faith, and early experiences of evangelicalism.

74. Taylor, *Memoirs*, 9.

proponents tended to emphasize practical morality. The Anglican Bishop Edward Fowler, in his defense of Latitudinarianism, noted how, for Latitudinarians, "the great end of the gospel was to make men good."[75] The priority of moral living was also instilled in Taylor by his parents. When Taylor preached at his father's funeral in 1782, his chosen text was "the great day of their wrath",[76] and he recounted how his father had impressed on him the need to live correctly in the light of this Scripture.[77] The way in which the Taylor brothers' earlier understanding of faith centered around the need for moral works is also intimated in John Taylor's description that, prior to his "conversion," he regularly practiced self-denial and "When I had behaved well in my opinion, I was encouraged; but when I had blundered, I was cast down."[78] John Taylor's statement that during this time "I had not obtained solid comfortable peace of mind from any proper believing views or knowledge of the precious Saviour," reflected Dan Taylor's earlier noted opinion about the inadequacies of his inherited faith.[79] Through their parents' influence, the Taylors possibly participated in the trenchant and legalistic religious system which emerged at the close of the seventeenth century as a reaction against the liberalizing attitudes to morals and religion that accompanied the Restoration of Charles II. As Michael Watts notes, this made "impossible demands on the moral and spiritual resources of the ordinary believer."[80] Both this and the general Latitudinarian emphasis on moral living help account for the liberty Taylor experienced as he embraced the gospel message taught by evangelicals.

Given that Taylor heard Grimshaw speak most frequently, it is significant that one widely recognized hallmark of Grimshaw's preaching was his use of what Newton referred to as "Market Language."[81] Similar to the other leading evangelicals of his day, Grimshaw stressed the need to be understood by those who, like Taylor, were of ordinary speech and lacked formal education. As Grimshaw remarked to Newton, "If they do not understand me, I cannot hope to do them good."[82] Grimshaw did not verbally employ the intellectual frameworks that had been part of his education at Christ's

---

75. E. Fowler, *Design of Christianity*, 218.

76. Rev 6:17 (NIV).

77. Taylor, *Memoirs*, 4.

78. John Taylor. Qtd in Taylor, *John Taylor*, 7–8.

79. Ibid., 7.

80. Watts, *Dissenters*, 427.

81. Newton, *Memoirs*, 65.

82. Grimshaw. Qtd in ibid., 64. Newton was quoting from that which he once heard Grimshaw say.

College, Cambridge, but with the poor in mind, "condescended to accommodate himself, in the most familiar manner, to their ideas, and to their modes of expression."[83] Methodist minister John Pawson, fifty years after first hearing Grimshaw, vividly recalled how he was struck by the way "he spoke in a most encouraging manner to the poor."[84] As Robert Hardy highlighted, Grimshaw succeeded even with Scriptures that appeared difficult to be made more graphic, such as replacing "a ram, caught in a thicket" (Gen 22:13) with the "moor-side paraphrase" of "a tup that had fastened its head in a bunch of briers."[85] Taylor's witnessing of how evangelicals such as Grimshaw communicated the gospel likely influenced developments in his written and spoken word. Despite Taylor having become increasingly learned through his acquisition of biblical Hebrew and Greek and study of various theological works,[86] he sought to communicate the Christian faith in a way that was readily understandable to the less educated. This was typified in the introduction to *Fundamentals of Religion in Faith and Practice*, where he specified that he had "kept in view, especially the advantage of the illiterate, and persons of inferior capacities, I have made it my great concern to write with plainness and simplicity."[87] This characterized nearly all of Taylor's works. It was also typical of other evangelicals. For example, Richard Heitzenrater, in his consideration of John Wesley's preaching, notes how Wesley "desired clearness of style and language."[88] Wesley stated this intention in the preface to his *Sermons on Several Occasions*, where he emphasized "I design plain truth for plain people."[89] The similarity to that asserted by Taylor in *Fundamentals* is evident.

A further characteristic of the nature of evangelical preaching that Taylor heard at Haworth was the way that doctrinal detail was generally not emphasized. Newton noted the absence of "scrupulous systematical accuracy" from Grimshaw's teaching.[90] Walsh's examination of the preaching of evangelicals in Yorkshire during the Evangelical Revival leads him to argue that "If they preached the old doctrines they preached them in dilution,

---

83. Ibid., 65.

84. John Pawson. Qtd in Hardy, *William Grimshaw*, 132. Primary source unknown.

85. Hardy, *William Grimshaw*, 124; Grimshaw. Qtd in ibid., 124. Primary source unknown.

86. Examples of these various works will be considered in the subsequent chapters of this book

87. Dan Taylor, *Fundamentals*, v.

88. Heitzenrater, "John Wesley's Principles and Practice of Preaching," 97.

89. John Wesley, *Sermons on Several Occasions*, 104. Qtd in Heitzenrater, "John Wesley's Principles and Practice of Preaching," 9.

90. Newton, *Memoirs*, 100.

simply, practically and moderated by commonsense and directitude."[91] This is one of the reasons Walsh refers to the "different ethos" of evangelicalism compared to Puritanism which was previously strong in the West Riding, but declined from 1662 onwards.[92] In general, Puritans demonstrated a greater tendency for precision in carrying out God's revealed will in moral and ecclesiastical matters. As the Puritan English church leader Richard Baxter noted, they were at first pejoratively "derided" as "precisians."[93] They produced what John Coffey and Paul Lim describe as a "vast quantity" of "formidable" doctrinal works.[94] It should also be noted that while Coffey and Lim recognize the imprecision of the term Puritanism as a historical category, as well as the movement's "multifaceted" nature and breadth of debate that surround attempts to define it, they provide a helpful starting place regarding its essential nature.[95] They locate its origins in the sixteenth-century and refer to it as

> a distinctive and particularly intense variety of early modern Reformed Protestantism which originated within the unique context of the Church of England but spilled out beyond it, branching off into divergent dissenting streams, and overflow-ing into other lands and foreign churches.[96]

A further distinctive feature of the evangelical preaching that took place at Haworth was how, as Newton recorded, evangelicals such as Grim-shaw tended to dismiss "metaphysical subtleties" and "speculative" aspects of the faith as superfluous to the core gospel message, and particularly to the task of helping people reach a point of conversion to Christ.[97] A char-acteristic example of Grimshaw's outlook is found in a 1753 letter where he stated "Let us determine then to know nothing . . . following nothing in heart, lip, or life, but JESUS, JESUS, JESUS and him crucified."[98] Hempton argues that Methodist theology was generally "too concerned with human

91. Walsh, "Yorkshire Evangelicals," 12.

92. Ibid. For the earlier strength of Puritanism in the West Riding, see Collinson, *English Puritanism*, 32. The decline of Puritanism followed the religious settlement that was agreed subsequent to the 1660 English Restoration. For an examination of this, see Spurr, "Later Stuart Puritanism," 89–105.

93. Baxter, *Practical Works*, 30.

94. Coffey, and Lim, *Cambridge Companion to Puritanism*, 11.

95. Ibid., 1.

96. Ibid., 1–2.

97. Newton, *Memoirs*, 99.

98. Grimshaw, "Letter to Mrs. Gallatin," 19 September 1753. Page not numbered, Grimshaw's emphasis.

experience to engage in meta-physical abstractions."[99] This later became a central characteristic of Taylor's approach.[100] It also reflected how intellectual thinking and social attitudes gave rise to pragmatism as part of the English Enlightenment.[101]

In the interests of his listeners, Grimshaw contended that he "did not think it to their profit to insist on subjects of controversy" in his preaching.[102] Taylor also came to embrace this conviction. For example, when writing to George Birley in 1778, he noted that ministers should "preach on plain subjects and in a plain manner" and "be little concerned in the pulpit about niceties of dispute, especially in nonessentials."[103] One of the consequences of Taylor having been introduced to this style of preaching at Haworth was that he was unlikely at that point to have been aware of the differing theological standpoints surrounding the scope of the atonement. While these differences had elsewhere caused contention between the Wesley brothers and George Whitefield and some discord between their partisans,[104] Walsh notes that "here on the moors individual quiddities, Election or Perfection, seemed insignificant while the great harvest stretched before the little band of reapers."[105] This was reflected in how Taylor held the Wesleys and Whitefield in equal regard.[106] It is also notable that Frank Baker points to Grimshaw, Taylor's favorite preacher, as "syncretistic" in the way that he defended both unconditional election and universal redemption.[107] It is

99. Hempton, *Methodism*, 84.

100. This will be examined in chapters 2 and 4.

101. See, e.g., Porter, *Enlightenment*, 22.

102. Newton, *Memoirs*, 99.

103. Dan Taylor, "Letter to George Birley," 6 February 1778. Page not numbered.

104. For example, in 1739 John Wesley published his 29 April 1739 sermon on *Free Grace* within which he challenged the doctrines of limited atonement and unconditional election. Annexed to this work was a poem on universal redemption by Charles Wesley, see John Wesley, *Free Grace*. In response, Whitefield wrote a reply to John Wesley where he strongly defended the sovereignty of God in salvation, see Whitefield, "A Letter to John Wesley," 571–88.

105. Walsh, "Yorkshire Evangelicals," 108. Walsh's reference to "Perfection" concerns John Wesley's doctrine of perfection which is considered later in this section.

106. Taylor, *Memoirs*, 5. It will be seen in chapter 3 that Taylor later became aware of disputes regarding the scope of the atonement in the West Riding, even in his own community. However, this was not his experience during his visits to Haworth.

107. Baker, *William Grimshaw*, 233. Baker points to how Grimshaw, in respect of unconditional election and universal redemption, noted, "It seems clear to me from the Holy Word of God, that both are true." See Grimshaw, "Experiences gather'd by Conversation with my own & the Souls of Others," page not numbered. Qtd in Baker, *William Grimshaw*, 233. Understandings of unconditional election and universal redemption will be considered in chapter 3.

likely that the particular nuances of Grimshaw's theological thinking were unknown to Taylor who did not hold an unconditional view of election.[108] Grimshaw's mindfulness of aspects of John Wesley's beliefs such as his rejection of unconditional election, initially caused him to consider carefully whether to invite him to Haworth.[109] His decision in favor of doing so was based on his recognition that John Wesley "preached repentance towards God, and faith in the Lord Jesus Christ" and that he had been "instrumental in turning many from darkness to light," and Grimshaw's refusal to be "fettered by a regard for names and parties."[110] These reasons demonstrate a mission-minded pragmatism, tolerance, and benevolence that were common features of eighteenth-century evangelicalism and which later epitomized Taylor's approach to ministry.

A further contributor to the Taylor brothers' designation of the evangelicals they heard as "enlightened" was almost certainly the prominence given to the experiential. Although the "weeping, roaring, and agonies" that had often accompanied evangelical preaching at Haworth were "rarely seen or heard" by the 1750s, the need to be experiencing God's power and presence was integral to the preached message.[111] As Ted Campbell notes, evangelicals such as the Wesleys "stressed the centrality of religious experience and the way of salvation punctuated by such experiences."[112] This emphasis was very different from elements of the Church of England which had, to some extent, become "mechanical, or dead."[113] Wesley referred to the Christian faith as "the religion of the heart."[114] Newton similarly noted that "the true religion that cometh from above, is seated rather in the heart than in the head; and depends not so much upon a set of new opinions, as on a new birth, and a new nature."[115] The Taylors would have been familiar with Grimshaw's repeated insistence that genuine believers were "those who are experientially born again, and pardoned, and know the Lord Jesus to be in them."[116] Grimshaw also emphasized the experiential as an ongoing dimension of the faith. For instance, when defining "Christian love," he stated, "It is the kingdom of God within you. It is heaven within you every

108. Taylor's beliefs regarding election will be examined in chapter 3.

109. Newton, *Memoirs*, 97.

110. Ibid., 98.

111. Grimshaw, "Letter to John Gillies," 507, 508.

112. Campbell, *Religion of the Heart*, 121.

113. Overton and Relton, *English Church*, 64.

114. John Wesley, *The Nature of Enthusiasm*, 46.

115. Newton, *Memoirs*, 77.

116. Grimshaw, "Letter to John Gillies," 508.

where . . . O that you may be always filled with this love, this Heaven, this Christ, this God!"[117] Grimshaw's animated preaching style and the way that he read liturgy with "great solemnity," in the hope that his listeners" hearts might be touched, would also have been apparent to them.[118] The Taylors' experience of worship under the ministry of Legh at Halifax Parish Church was likely typical of the way in which the Book of Common Prayer was often quickly repeated by rote but little understood, and therefore treated as "a mere prelude to something of another kind to afterwards be introduced."[119] Contrary to Grimshaw's style of preaching, Legh was also viewed by some as having a "very careless and languid manner" and prone to forgetfulness.[120] These variations in emphasis and approach of the evangelicals would have contributed to Taylor's appreciation of what he felt was their greater vitality of faith.

Adam Taylor emphasized that the preaching at Haworth fostered in Taylor more than an intellectual assent to the gospel. He noted that it was specifically "under the influence of the Holy Spirit" that Taylor's commitment rose to "that Saviour whom his soul had found precious."[121] This reflected Newton's description of Grimshaw's preaching as "a power from on high, applied to the heart, what he could only declare to the ear."[122] The way in which Taylor was emotionally stirred during his early engagement with evangelicalism was made apparent by the dedication he developed for prayer. He expressed "regret" at "the neglect of family worship in his father's house" and privately instigated the regular practice of praying and reading the Scriptures with his brother John.[123] The significance of this initiative was highlighted by Adam Taylor, who identified it as "the first time that he engaged in any religious exercise, in the presence of a fellow creature."[124] This development also illustrates Hardy's assertion that "communings of secret prayer began to prevail" as an outcome of Grimshaw's ministry.[125] A frequent consequence of Taylor's participation in prayer, and particularly of his attendance at revival prayer meetings at Haworth, was that they

117. Grimshaw, "Letter," (no addressee specified), 12 January 1762, (DDPR 2/65). Page not numbered.

118. Hardy, *William Grimshaw*, 127.

119. Ibid.

120. Whitaker. Qtd in Crabtree, *Concise History*, 130. Primary source unknown.

121. Taylor, *Memoirs*, 6.

122. Newton, *Memoirs*, 56.

123. Taylor, *Memoirs*, 5.

124. Ibid.

125. Hardy, *William Grimshaw*, 131.

"melted him to tears."[126] This was again illustrative of the commonplace nature of expressions of emotion among evangelicals and particularly how the hearts of many caught up in the revival were impacted. The evangelical insistence on justification by faith that was to be experienced in a spiritual new birth meant that, for many, there was a particular moment of conversion which was emotional in nature. Although Taylor's conversion was the consequence of a gradual process, where "By degrees he obtained clearer views of the plan of mercy through a redeemer,"[127] an accompanying emotionalism was an important aspect of his spiritual awakening. Just as Phyllis Mack argues that Wesley "never lost his conviction of the importance of emotion or of inward religion"[128] after his heart had been "strangely warmed" during a visit to the Fetter Lane society in Aldersgate Street, London in 1738, the same was true for Taylor.[129] A typical example is a routine 1767 diary entry when, following a time of prayer, Taylor noted that his "heart was sensibly warmed."[130] The similarity of language to that of Wesley's Aldersgate experience is apparent.

In summary, the Taylors did not limit their understanding of evangelicals as enlightened only by their grasp of the message of the gospel but also included how they communicated the good news. The framing of sermons around an invitation for people to put their faith in Christ, use of market language, limited attention to doctrinal detail, and the importance placed on the experiential, were influential on Taylor's evangelical development. As will be seen next, the way Taylor was impacted by all he had encountered led him to join a Methodist society where he was exposed to further distinctive facets of eighteenth-century evangelicalism.

---

126. Taylor, *Memoirs*, 6.

127. Ibid.

128. Mack, *Heart Religion*, 36.

129. John Wesley, Journal entry, 24 May 1738, 250. See also Tyson, "John Wesley's Conversion," 27–42. For further consideration of Wesley's Aldersgate experience and particularly its place within the wider context of Wesley's spiritual development, see Maddox, *Aldersgate Reconsidered*.

130. Dan Taylor, diary entry, 26 January 1767, in Taylor, *Memoirs*, 71.

Taylor's Exposure to Activism and Innovation

"I would set down in several classes,
the names of my dear brethren"

As Taylor embraced evangelicalism, he was not only introduced to its biblicism, crucicentrism, and conversionism, but also to the movement's fourth key characteristic as identified by Bebbington—its activism.[131] Although Bebbington, in *The Emergence of Evangelicalism*, accepts that there were examples of activism among earlier movements such as the Puritans,[132] Taylor likely encountered an activism among evangelicals that surpassed anything he had known among other clergy. While there is the need for some caution regarding the "traditionally hostile picture"[133] of the dedication of non-evangelical parish clergy exemplified in Elie Halévy's generalization of the Church of England as "apathetic, sceptical, lifeless" and William Lecky's definitive claim that evangelical ministers maintained "a far higher standard of clerical duty," the activism of many evangelical clergy was significant.[134] Taylor was, for example, familiar with Grimshaw's pattern of ministry which included extensive pastoral visiting and preaching four times on a Sunday and twice each week day.[135] This differed from how in the mid-1740s less than half the churches in the West Riding Diocese conducted two Sunday services and only half the parishes had incumbent clergy.[136] Grimshaw was keen that all believers displayed an "indefatigable industry" in their commitment to the gospel.[137] As he pointed believers to Christ, he urged them to demonstrate an "unquenchable zeal for the illustration of his glory, the prosperity of his church and the salvation of souls."[138] Grimshaw's commitment to this task saw him establish the "Great Haworth Round" of churches. He gained widespread notoriety as he broke the rules of parochial order and shared the gospel in parishes beyond his own—some as distant as sixty miles.[139] Such activism and accompanying vitality of faith were further

131. Bebbington, *Evangelicalism*, 3.

132. Bebbington, "Response," 418–19. Consideration will be given to evangelical activism in chapter 7 of this book.

133. Gregory, "Religion," 43.

134. Halévy, *History of the English People*, 410; Lecky, *History of England*, 37.

135. See Laycock, *Methodist Heroes*, 194.

136. See Beckwith, "Dan Taylor," 298.

137. Grimshaw, *Answer to a Sermon*, 17.

138. Grimshaw, "Letter to Mrs. Gallatin," 13 September 1755. Page not numbered.

139. See Hardy, *William Grimshaw*, 52–77.

important elements of that which Taylor witnessed as he participated in the Evangelical Revival at Haworth.

Taylor's initial exposure to evangelical activism did not involve any contact with the dissenting church. This is despite Frank Beckwith's reference to a "healthy leaven of dissent" in the West Riding Diocese in the 1740s,[140] and how Walsh notes that in 1743 there were eighteen Baptist chapels, seventy Presbyterian chapels, five Independent chapels, and over one hundred Quaker meeting houses.[141] However, John Taylor's assertion that his parents had "little knowledge then of any of the denominations of dissenters," is significant.[142] In addition, he stated that "few of the common people knew what a dissenter meant. I rather question, if the name *baptist* had ever been heard."[143] It was not until the Particular Baptists became active in Halifax in 1755 that Dan Taylor attended worship at a dissenting church. He then did so only "occasionally."[144] It should also be noted that the Dissenters, who at that time still only accounted for 6 percent of the population of England and Wales,[145] had generally lessened in their vigor for the gospel compared to the previous century. This vigor had been replaced, in many instances, by a missional lethargy and rational intellectualism that undermined confidence in key tenets of faith.[146]

Evangelicalism's proclivity for innovation was closely related to its activism.[147] It has already been demonstrated that Taylor was introduced to practices such as open air preaching, use of "market language," and ministers preaching the gospel in parishes beyond their jurisdiction. His exposure to evangelical innovation continued when he joined a Methodist society in Halifax in 1755.[148] A Methodist chapel had been built in the town in 1752.[149] It is not clear if Taylor, after he joined the society, ceased attending Halifax Parish Church, although Methodists were encouraged to attend Sunday worship at their churches.[150] The Methodists had a strong

140. Beckwith, "Dan Taylor," 298.

141. Walsh, "Yorkshire Evangelicals," 88. The Baptist chapels were affiliated to the Particular Baptists.

142. John Taylor. Qtd in Taylor, *John Taylor*, 4.

143. Ibid.; Adam Taylor's emphasis.

144. Taylor, *Memoirs*, 6.

145. See Watts, *Dissenters*, 3.

146. This will be examined further in chapter 2.

147. This will be considered in chapter 7.

148. Taylor, *Memoirs*, 6. At this time the society comprised thirty-one members, see Laycock, *Methodist Heroes*, 239.

149. Laycock, *Methodist Heroes*, 130.

150. See Royle, "When did Methodists?" 275–96.

presence in Yorkshire. Walsh notes that by 1760 almost a quarter of the national Methodist membership was found in the region.[151] The Halifax society was originally under the oversight of John Nelson, coming under Methodist jurisdiction following Nelson's entering into partnership with the Wesleys in 1742.[152] This provides an example of how the Methodists often engaged in "cannibalising a number of localised evangelical networks originated by others into a national organisation."[153] Following the preaching of the gospel during the Evangelical Revival many religious societies were established in the West Riding, such as those presided over by Nelson, Ingham, and Darney.[154] However, the localized and independent nature of these societies differed from the "connexional system" of Methodist societies.[155] As Baker notes, this inventive structure involved "a network of itinerant preachers moving from society to society throughout the nation ... keeping in constant touch with the Wesleys."[156] Taylor gained first-hand experience of this innovative system.

The nature of Methodist societies differed from the societies established in the 1690s for the Reformation of Manners, which, through their network of moral guardians and stewards, sought to compel people into moral living through enforcement of laws against vices such as drunkenness, prostitution, gambling, Sabbath-breaking, and general public immorality.[157] In contrast, at the Halifax society Taylor became familiar with methods that aimed to consolidate people into an intellectual understanding, heartfelt experience, and practical outworking of the spiritual truths they had heard preached at revival meetings. John Wesley was convinced that it was by these

151. Walsh, "Yorkshire Evangelicals," 144.

152. See ibid., 94; Rack, *Reasonable Enthusiast*, 218.

153. Ibid., 177.

154. See Walsh, "Yorkshire Evangelicals," 93–95; Laycock, *Methodist Heroes*, 39–121. The question of Taylor's continued attendance at Halifax Parish Church is briefly returned to in the last section of this chapter.

155. Baker, *John Wesley*, 114. Another difference was that the societies that developed in the 1690s were largely independent in the way they functioned. John Wesley occasionally sought to breathe fresh vitality into some of these societies and co-opted certain of them into his wider connexion of societies. For an account of the development of these earlier societies, see Woodward, *Religious Societies*. This book added to the popularity of these religious societies, which spread all over England and to Ireland.

156. Ibid.

157. The Society for the Reformation of Manners was formed in Tower Hamlets, London, in 1690. There quickly followed the development of subsequent societies. By 1701 there were nearly twenty societies in London and others in different parts of the country. An insight into their core values and ethos is found in a sermon by Lord Bishop Richard Smalbroke who was one of the societies' leading members, see Smalbroke, *Reformation*.

means that his objective for Methodism to revive the Church of England and spread scriptural holiness could be achieved.[158] The attention given by Methodists to inner transformation also meant that its societies stood apart from those societies that focused more exclusively on promoting moral living through better education. An example was the 1699 establishment of the Society for Promoting Christian Knowledge which further contributed to a High Church moral reform movement that often left people "burdened by the over-scrupulous performance of religious duties."[159] Such a duty-bound perspective had dominated Taylor's understanding of faith prior to his engagement with the Evangelical Revival. His decision to join the Halifax society then gave him the opportunity to delve more deeply into those elements of evangelical teaching that had fostered within him a new sense of liberation and understanding of the Savior.

When Taylor attended society meetings he was taught the key tenets of Methodism. John Wesley was keen that the core gospel elements he proclaimed were expounded at these occasions.[160] These included an emphasis on the doctrine of personal salvation by faith in Christ's atoning work. A general view of the atonement was also laid before Taylor who soon became "a warm advocate for the great truth that Christ died for every man."[161] It is noteworthy that at this point, John Taylor still held to the doctrine of limited atonement.[162] He did not attend a Methodist society and therefore was not exposed to the same teaching on the universal scope of Christ's death. It is possible that Dan Taylor also received instruction on the doctrine of perfection although, as will be examined later, he rejected this. The teaching Taylor listened to in the main meetings of the society also included practical elements. This was in part a consequence of Methodism's place within the Christian tradition of Arminianism which, contrary to the Calvinist priority on the absolute sovereignty of God and predestinarianism, attached greater importance to human freewill.[163] It was also a consequence of the

---

158. For Wesley's objective for Methodism, see John Wesley, "Minutes of Several Conversations," 299.

159. Watts, *Dissenters*, 428.

160. See Baker, *John Wesley*, 117.

161. Taylor, *Memoirs*, 6. Taylor's general view of the atonement will be examined in chapter 3.

162. It was not until 1769 that John Taylor adopted a general view of the atonement, see John Taylor, diary entry, 1769, in Taylor, *John Taylor*, 23–24. John Taylor's transition in his approach to the atonement will be considered in chapter 3. The nature of the doctrine of limited atonement will also be considered.

163. Although not Taylor's position, Arminians also commonly aligned the importance of holy living with the need to ensure that salvation was not lost (see chapter 4).

different social composition of Methodist societies compared to many other religious societies. Methodist societies comprised less people from the so called respectable classes, but more from "the lower ranks of life,"[164] such as manufacturing and industrial workers who generally lacked the capacity and inclination for sustained learning. Taylor learned much from how scriptural teaching was made accessible to the lives of ordinary people. He subsequently sought to emulate this throughout his ministry. When addressing a gathering of General Baptist ministers at Conningsby in 1766, he insisted that ministers when preaching should not only focus on the "minds of the hearers" but, so as to meaningfully connect, must also look to elicit a "practical and experimental" response.[165] Further typical was how Taylor, when speaking at a baptism in 1785, stated that non-believers should not be expected simply to believe the truth of Scripture, but that instead it must be set out in "such a light as that they, even the most ignorant of them" might see it to be true.[166] His reasoned approach, which sometimes involved him drawing on the merits of experience and observation (see chapter 2), reflected Enlightenment thinking.

Taylor's regard for his Methodist society was such that after his mother's death in 1758, he left the family home and moved to Halifax so he might "more conveniently attend the instructions of Mr. Titus Knight" (1719–93) who was prominent in the society and widely held as a "star of increasing magnitude."[167] Taylor's affinity with Knight was based not only on their coal mining backgrounds and having both been converted through Grimshaw's ministry, but also from Knight teaching him subjects such as Latin, Hebrew and Greek. He therefore referred to Knight as his "tutor."[168] This reflected Taylor's increasing appetite for evangelical teaching.

Taylor's participation in the Halifax society, as well as his attendance at large open air Methodist meetings, introduced him to hymn singing.[169] This involved the singing of hymns that comprised non-biblical poetry and which were written by Independent ministers such as Isaac Watts and Philip

---

164. Smollett, *History of England*, 280. Qtd in McInelly, "Method or Madness," 198.

165. Dan Taylor, *Faithful and Wise*, 23. This publication contains the content of that which Taylor preached at Conningsby.

166. Dan Taylor, *Our Saviour's Commission*, 14–15.

167. Taylor, *Memoirs*, 7. Knight was a founding trustee of the Methodist chapel that was built in Halifax. The chapel was erected following a generous gift from Grimshaw, see Laycock, *Methodist Heroes*, 130.

168. Ibid., 7.

169. For the prominence of hymn singing in Methodism, see, e.g., R. J. Watson, *English Hymn*, 205–64.

Doddridge, and others such as politician and writer Joseph Addison.[170] This form of hymn singing was new to Taylor. The approach to singing that Taylor was familiar with at Halifax Parish Church consisted of a "firmly entrenched" commitment to John Chetham's *A Book of Psalmody* which contained tunes for the singing of metrical psalms and for chanting.[171] In contrast, the hymns Taylor sung in the context of the Evangelical Revival possessed characteristics such as a "preference for experience over formality," "diversity of mood and spirit," and the "ability to address the Christian experience."[172] This style of singing was actively embraced by the Wesleys who appreciated the freedom it gave to express religious truth, thoughts, and feelings in rich and emotional language. It is estimated that Charles Wesley wrote between 6,000–9,000 hymns and sacred poems.[173] Many of the new aspects that Taylor found in the evangelical teaching he had embraced were reiterated in the hymns that were sung.[174] As Randall McElwain notes, hymns such as those written by Charles Wesley were "saturated with Scripture" and "were central to the theological and biblical understanding of early Methodists, especially the laity."[175] The deep impression that hymn singing left on Taylor is evident as, in contrast to most General Baptists, he became a committed advocate for hymn singing.[176]

Taylor's involvement in the Halifax society led him to become a regular attendee of a class meeting.[177] In doing so, Taylor provides an example of that which Jack Jackson describes was a typical process of spiritual formation whereby a person first heard the gospel proclaimed, joined a society and became a member of a Methodist class.[178] It was normal for Methodist societies to be divided into class meetings, with William Dean noting "The basic functions were evangelism and conservation—the *recruitment* and *as-*

---

170. For more on the significance and contributions of these writers, see ibid., 133–90.

171. Temperley, *Music*, 182; Chetham, *Book of Psalmody*. John Chetham became a schoolmaster in Skipton in 1723 and a curate in 1741. This hymn book was popular in the West Riding with eleven editions published.

172. Watson, *English Hymn*, 132, 225.

173. See Tyson, *Assist Me to Proclaim*, vii–viii.

174. Examples include concepts such as God's love for sinners, salvation for the individual, the liberating power of Jesus, the inner experience of the Holy Spirit, strength to withstand oppression, and the promise of future glory. See Watson, *English Hymn*, 205–64.

175. McElwain, "Biblical Language," 57, 70.

176. See chapter 6.

177. Taylor, *Memoirs*, 7.

178. See Jack Jackson, "Collecting and Preserving Disciples," 46–59.

similation of new members."[179] Taylor's decision to involve himself in this additional tier of the Methodist system was not surprising, as otherwise he would have been restricted from attending the society's sometimes "closed" main meetings.[180] Given his desire to grow in his evangelical understanding, this would have been an inconceivable prospect.[181] The intimate setting of a class meeting, with its twelve or so members, was the prime place where previous learning was reinforced and people assisted in their application of scriptural truth. As David Lowes Watson states, "the essential purpose of the class meeting" was discipleship.[182] It formed the "basic unit" of Methodism and aimed "to nurture godly language, temperance, honesty, plainness, seriousness, frugality, diligence, charity and economic loyalty within the connection."[183] As specified by Charles Perronet, who for a period of time was a Methodist itinerant preacher, a prime function of a class meeting with regard to its members was "To inspect their outward walking; to inquire into their inward state; to learn what are their trials; and how they fall by or conquer them?"[184] Wesley's determination that all class leaders followed these guidelines is evident in the postscript he added to Perronet's article. He stipulated, "I earnestly exhort all leaders . . . to put them into execution with all the understanding and courage that God has given them."[185] Through use of such means as the rules Wesley prepared for the Societies,[186] Taylor's class leaders would have regularly questioned him on different issues related to his practice of faith. Its lasting influence on him is apparent by his later willingness to confront and challenge whenever he saw evidence of sin and, as he stressed the need for correct patterns of Christian behavior.

An illustration of the all-encompassing nature of the evangelicalism that was instilled into Taylor through his attendance at class meetings was

179. Dean, "Methodist Class Meeting," 43; Dean's emphasis.

180. For the importance of attending a class meeting for membership of a society, see, e.g., A. C. Thompson, "To Stir Them up," 164.

181. See Taylor, *Memoirs*, 6.

182. D. L. Watson, "Origins and Significance," 15. See also D. L. Watson, *Early Methodist Class Meeting*.

183. Hempton, *Methodism*, 78.

184. Perronet, "Of the right method," 132. Charles Perronet was son of the evangelical Church of England minister Vincent Perronet and joined the Methodists in 1746. He accompanied Charles Wesley to Ireland in 1746 and entered the itinerant ministry in 1751. Perronet later withdrew from the movement due to his advocacy of separation from the Church of England.

185. John Wesley, "Of the right method," 132.

186. These rules were compiled in 1744 and contained specific patterns of behavior that the class meeting was intended to produce within its members, see, e.g., Baker, *John Wesley*, 79.

his hope that a person's "whole life and conduct be such as becometh, that is, answereth, or is agreeable to, and worthy of the gospel."[187] Taylor's participation in a class meeting was also significant as it was quite a "heterogeneous grouping" with membership not based on confession of any doctrinal statement, or even profession of faith, but on a person's desire for conversion.[188] This meant he found himself alongside people holding a range of perspectives. Class meetings sometimes included Anglicans, Dissenters, Presbyterians, and Independents.[189] If, as is probable, Taylor was exposed to such an eclectic group, this likely influenced the way he later demonstrated respect towards those of contrary ecclesiological perspectives.[190] The significance Taylor attributed to his participation in a class meeting was evident in his replication of this structure shortly after he commenced his ministry at Birchcliff. He carefully outlined in 1765 how "I would set down in several classes, the names of my dear brethren, that I may more regularly take them, a class at a time, and recommend them with their several circumstances and necessities, as far as I know them, to the Lord."[191] Within the context of General and Particular Baptist life, the formation of class meetings was a truly pioneering initiative. It provides an early indication of the innovation that characterized so much of Taylor's ministry.

The methodology of the class meeting became the framework for Taylor's enterprising formation of experience meetings. He initiated these at Birchcliff in the late 1760s and then later throughout the New Connexion.[192] Similar to class meetings, members were divided into groups that met weekly. Group leaders then recounted their recent experience of faith, including reference to their "struggles against inward and outward enemies" and "advancement or decline in the Christian course."[193] Members were then expected to do likewise. Adam Taylor described how leaders "requested each of the friends present, in rotation as they were seated, to give a similar statement of his experience; and made such observations, and offered such advice and cautions as the circumstances of each might

187. Dan Taylor, *Consistent Christian*, 91.

188. A. C. Thompson, "To Stir Them up," 164. For further consideration of the presence of non-believers in class meetings, see Jackson, "Collecting and Preserving Disciples," 56–59.

189. The presence of nonconformists in Methodist societies is emphasized by Maddox, *Responsible Grace*, 202.

190. See chapter 5.

191. Dan Taylor, diary entry, 4 October 1765, in Taylor, *Memoirs*, 22.

192. Adam Taylor, *New Connection*, 77.

193. Ibid., 78.

seem to require."[194] The innovative nature of this initiative was highlighted by W. E. Blomfield who drew attention to the way Taylor "introduced into Yorkshire the practice of Experience Meetings."[195] Given the lack of later mention of class meetings at Birchcliff, it is possible that these groups evolved into experience meetings. Such a transition would have reflected the importance Taylor placed on the experiential dimension of faith as a means of validating applications for individual church membership and for entrance into the Connexion.[196] Taylor's alignment of the experiential with membership was more akin to the Baptist and Congregationalist emphasis on evidence of conversion, than the Methodist membership criterion that was based on a desire for salvation, as demonstrated by attendance at public worship and accompanying good works.[197] This aspect of Taylor's understanding of membership again reflected the wider credence attached to personal experience within Enlightenment thought. Another feature of experience meetings was that, similar to Methodist class meetings, they were not restricted to believers. Instead, they were open to all "who desired to engage in the cause of Christ, and wished to obtain religious knowledge."[198] They therefore fulfilled the same function of "evangelism and conservation" that Rack attributes to class meetings.[199] The mixed composition of the groups and the singing of hymns point to an increasingly common facet of eighteenth-century evangelicalism, namely the belief that an experience of God was a catalyst to conversion.[200] It was perhaps for this reason that Taylor placed such priority on experience meetings. He even established them during the short period of two years when he was minister in Halifax.[201] Taylor's approach to experience meetings highlights the nature of his pioneering evangelicalism.

The third significant element of Methodist structure, after the society and class meetings, was the band. John Wesley referred to the bands and class meetings as together providing the "sinews" of the Methodist societies.[202] As Kevin Watson notes, "The band meeting was the crucial piece of

194. Ibid.

195. Blomfield, "Yorkshire Baptist Churches," 105.

196. See chapter 5.

197. See Watts, *Dissenters*, 444.

198. Taylor, *New Connection*, 78.

199. Rack, *Reasonable Enthusiast*, 242.

200. The importance Taylor placed on the singing of hymns in the process of conversion will be examined in chapter 6.

201. Taylor, *Memoirs*, 122–23.

202. John Wesley, "Letter to Thomas Maxfield," 194.

John Wesley's approach to "social holiness."[203] Watson's examination of the functioning of band meetings between 1743–65 includes his drawing of attention to how it was "a place where Methodists sought a direct encounter with God's grace that would enable them to become more holy."[204] Closely related was how the band leaders facilitated a context where "searching, blunt conversation occurred."[205] Despite the absence of categorical evidence for Taylor having been a band member, Adam Taylor likely referred to this when he noted that Taylor at twenty years of age was welcomed into "strict communion" with the Methodists.[206] While commentators such as Alfred Underwood and Beckwith applied this reference to when Taylor first joined the Methodists,[207] this could not have been the case for he had been active within the Halifax society and member of a class meeting for the previous four years.[208] Particular difficulty surrounds Adam Taylor's use of the expression "strict communion" which, although a commonplace Baptist term, was not one used within Methodism and therefore exposes his lack of finer understanding of the Methodist system. It is probable that he employed the expression to indicate the greater narrowness of the membership of the bands, with their composition of those who were more advanced in the faith necessitating that applicants formally applied to be admitted.[209] The intensity of purpose that surrounded the weekly functioning of bands meant, as Watts describes, that it was "a much more forbidding occasion" than the class meeting.[210] Its influence on Taylor is likely reflected in his frequent references in his works such as *The Consistent Christian* to the imperative that believers be vigilant and open with one another regarding such matters as their substance of conversation, private thinking, use of time, attitude to possessions, family life, and commercial activity.[211] Moreover, it is conceivable that Taylor's likely attendance at a band provided the inspiration for his further innovation of discipline meetings.

203. K. M. Watson, *Pursuing Social Holiness*, 62–63. See also, Perronet, "Of the right method," 130–32.

204. Ibid., 117.

205. Ibid.

206. Taylor, *Memoirs*, 6.

207. A. Underwood, *History of English Baptists*, 151; Beckwith, "Dan Taylor," 300.

208. The act of "joining" within Methodism was linked to membership of a class, see Rack, *Reasonable Enthusiast*, 238–39.

209. The *Rules of the Band Societies* that were established in 1738 included a list of proposed questions to be asked before people were admitted to a band, see K. M. Watson, *Pursuing Social Holiness*, 194.

210. Watts, *Dissenters*, 445.

211. Taylor, *Consistent Christian*, 88–121.

Taylor began discipline meetings early into his time at Birchcliff and continued them for the duration of his ministry.[212] They were held once every six weeks and, similar to bands, were restricted to members and focused on a particular aspect of Christian discipline. Just as Methodism was held together by what Baker refers to as "the life-blood of a disciplined evangelical impulse," so Taylor, by establishing discipline meetings, sought to reproduce this in the churches where he assumed direct personal oversight and throughout the New Connexion.[213] Taylor was, in part, motivated by his desire to model a different approach to ministry from what he viewed as the lackadaisical outlook of many of his General Baptist colleagues, reaching this opinion as he participated in General Baptist life in the 1760s.[214] His establishment of discipline meetings was another early marker of his entrepreneurship, which was also in keeping with the ethos of eighteenth-century evangelicalism.

In summary, Taylor's emergence into evangelicalism involved him gaining experience of the way in which it gave rise to activism. This in turn led to innovation which, within the structures of Methodism, was formatively experienced by Taylor as he became a member of the Halifax society, committed attendee of a class meeting, and very likely participated in a band. In these varied contexts, Taylor further developed his understanding of the evangelical gospel message and certain specific aspects of Methodist teaching, such as a general view of the atonement. The regard with which Taylor viewed both his period within Methodism and the innovation he encountered was apparent by his later establishment of class, experience, and discipline meetings. Next it will be argued that the influence of his years in Methodism and nature of the evangelicalism he embraced were reflected within the dynamics of his spirituality.

Taylor's Development of a Missional Spirituality

"cordial affection for the souls of men!"

Taylor's participation within Methodism influenced the development of his spirituality. Extracts from his diary show that he acquired a greater concern for personal piety. For example, his entry for 28 December 1764 stated "This morning I had some humblings of heart from a sense of my past sins and present imperfections and neglects. Lord! Humble me to the dust, give me

212. Taylor, *New Connection*, 97.
213. Baker, *John Wesley*, 113.
214. This will be examined in chapter 2.

to see all the odious and abominable nature of every sin."[215] His desire for holiness demonstrated the overriding ethos of his involvement in Methodist society, class, and band meetings. Just as important was the way in which his spirituality was marked by his concern for mission. His personal prayer life and the disciplines he followed such as self-examination, fasting, and scriptural meditation were overtly orientated in a missional direction. For example, his frequent practice of spiritual self-examination included a regular assessment of his contribution to the cause of mission. He often prayed that God might grant him a greater "cordial affection for the souls of men!" and consequently see "the church still grow in number."[216] In a similar way he stressed the importance of fasting. Though recognizing its importance as a means of promoting personal holiness, he more commonly applied it to the task of mission. For instance, in 1765 he urged the believers at Birchcliff to commit to more days of "fasting and prayer" so they might witness even greater numbers of "quickenings of soul."[217] The interests of mission similarly governed his thinking regarding the practice of scriptural meditation. He insisted that believers concentrated less on the detail of Scripture, and instead meditated on Scripture's grand plan concerning God's desire for the salvation of the world.[218] He urged them to make this "familiar to yourselves by frequent meditation" and to consider the precise "work of the Lord" to which God had called them.[219] Whereas John Wesley's priority within the practice of spiritual disciplines and growth of believers in the faith concerned the spread of scriptural holiness, Taylor was more precisely focused on the need to assist believers to share the gospel with others.

The importance Taylor attached to the need for believers to engage in regular self-examination so as to maintain and develop their responsibility for evangelism was evident as he endeavored to foster a missional spirituality throughout the New Connexion. One such example is found in his 1789 letter to the churches. As he encouraged people to share the gospel, he stated "We earnestly beseech you, brethren, frequently to examine yourselves" and specifically to consider whether "your families and neighbours see the evidence of it?"[220] With similar directness, he asked them to consider the extent to which they were evangelistically prepared before the Lord—as

215. Dan Taylor, diary entry, 28 December 1764, in Taylor, Memoirs, 47.
216. Dan Taylor, diary entry (date not specified), in Taylor, Memoirs, 197.
217. Dan Taylor, diary entry, 10 May 1765, in Taylor, Memoirs, 40.
218. Dan Taylor, "Concurrence of People," 22.
219. Ibid.
220. Dan Taylor, "Letter to the Churches," in Minutes of an Association 1789, 4.

gaged by their willingness to be "ready to every good work."[221] Taylor stated that members should not only pray for their own needs. but ask God to empower their efforts regarding their sharing of the gospel with others. He stipulated in his 1794 letter to the churches that they should "pray for the Holy Spirit and for the operations and increase of the Spirit" on their evangelistic endeavors so that the work of God might advance in their communities.[222] He challenged all members to engage in spiritual examination, hoping this would result in their secular concerns becoming of secondary importance when compared to what he viewed as the greater priority of sharing the gospel with others. In respect of issues arising in their places of work, he asked them to consider "Do we not bestow too much time upon them? Do we turn from them as soon as our respective duties and obligations will permit?"[223] He was similarly probing when he addressed ministers. In 1800 he spoke at his son-in-law's ordination and called on the ministers present to ensure that they regularly considered their inner "propensities, passions and tempers" and specifically "such *things* as are adapted for the purposes of conversion."[224] Whether writing to the New Connexion's churches, engaging individually with ministers or as a normal part of his own congregational oversight, Taylor constantly highlighted the need for spiritual self-examination to include evangelistic reflection.

The importance Taylor placed on a mission-orientated application of spiritual disciplines was such that it should be viewed as a further key distinguishing facet of his evangelicalism. It stood apart from the more introspective tendencies of many Puritans. Although never monolithic in their outlook, Puritans tended to have little regard for issues surrounding the sharing of the gospel when engaging in disciplines such as spiritual self-examination. It is, for example, notable that there is no mention of this within the reflections on the practices of Puritan piety provided by James Packer in *A Quest for Godliness* or in Charles Hambrick-Stowe's consideration of self-examination within his study of the exercise of spiritual disciplines by Puritans in seventeenth-century New England.[225] When Puritans approached spiritual self-examination they were generally more concerned with their own standing before God, particularly as they sought to identify the "signs of grace" that might indicate they were among those who they believed God had elected to be saved. It was in this respect that William

---

221. Ibid., 5.

222. Dan Taylor, "Letter to the Churches," in *Minutes of an Association 1794*, 17.

223. Taylor, "Letter to the Churches," 1794, 18.

224. Taylor, "Outline of a Charge," 211; 262; Taylor's emphasis.

225. Packer, *Quest for Godliness*; Hambrick-Stowe, *Practice of Piety*, 170–75.

Perkins, one of the foremost Puritan leaders in the Church of England, described a process of "descending into our own hearts."[226] Such an uncertainty was found within the declarations of other English Puritan preachers such as Thomas Brooks who viewed salvation as a "crown that few wear."[227] Likewise, Thomas Goodwin referred to it in equally ambiguous terms, as a "reward for faith."[228] Peter Morden draws attention to the "protracted struggle for assurance" of John Bunyan (1628–88) and how he tended to lack the "confidence and certainty" expressed by evangelicals.[229] Bunyan's worry that "I feared I was a reprobate" and that he might have committed "that sin unpardonable" of Mark 3:39 were typical examples.[230] There was, as Ian Randall states, a tendency for Puritans "to see a "settled, well-grounded" assurance of personal salvation as a blessing that was rare."[231] Taylor's position was different as he was convinced that all who placed their trust in Christ could be confident of their salvation.[232] His thoughts on this matter were central to a letter he wrote to George Birley in 1781.[233] With reference to many promises of Scripture and particularly an exegesis of Rom 8:24–25,[234] he noted his assurance of salvation. He expressed this in terms such as "my assurance of hope" and stated his delight regarding the "many precious promises for time and eternity" and how "my hope of these precious promises is excited and encouraged."[235] Such sentiments point to his evangelical understanding of assurance of salvation.

Some commentators, such as Campbell, who have sought to highlight a greater appreciation of the place of "heart religion" in Puritanism, have argued that it was "dominated by the quest for the assurance of one's election."[236] Mack, in her consideration of the nature of heart religion, states that "Unlike the Puritans who struggle for assurance throughout life, Wes-

226. Perkins, *Exposition of the Symbole*, 439. Qtd in Randall, *What a Friend*, 17.

227. Brooks, *Heaven on Earth*, 317.

228. Thomas Goodwin, *Objects and Acts*, 346.

229. Morden, "John Bunyan," 42, 51.

230. Bunyan, *Grace Abounding*, 35, 24. Mark 3:29: "but whoever blasphemes against the Holy Spirit will never be forgiven; they are guilty of an eternal sin."

231. Randall, *What a Friend*, 17.

232. This was an important aspect of Taylor's discourse with Andrew Fuller, see chapter 4.

233. Dan Taylor, "Letter to George Birley," 1 February 1781. Page not numbered.

234. Rom 8:24–25: "For in this hope we were saved. But hope that is seen is no hope at all. Who hopes for what they already have? But if we hope for what we do not yet have, we wait for it patiently."

235. Taylor, "Letter to George Birley," 1 February 1781. Page not numbered.

236. Campbell, *Religion of the Heart*, 40.

ley [John] believed that assurance was normal from the time of conversion onwards."[237] This was something that Grimshaw taught. For instance, he stated in one of his letters that an "experimental assurance" of "glorious privileges" such as "our faith, hope, confidence" should "inspire our souls with a personal love for him [Christ]."[238] Taylor shared the same conviction. In the second edition of *The Consistent Christian* he included a brief appendix on self-examination and was unequivocal that the Scriptures "suppose the readers to know their own condition" and that believers should be confident in "the reality of grace" regarding their assurance of salvation.[239] Taylor frequently declared his assurance of salvation in his, often daily, discipline of self-examination. Examples include his assertions that "I have though in a small degree, the marks of God's child" and "I have good evidence that my state is safe."[240] Taylor was convinced believers should have a "strong and assured faith" concerning their standing before God.[241] This confident platform of assurance meant Taylor did not use the practice of self-examination to help establish the inner reality of his conversion, but as a means of seeking to ensure that the orientation of his heart and daily living reflected a primacy on the cause of mission. This outlook was important within his evangelical approach to evangelism.

The importance Taylor attached to the practice of self-examination was again apparent in his 1795 *The Cause of National Calamities and The Certain Means of Preventing or Removing Them.*[242] Taylor highlighted "the necessity of universal self-examination," encouraging believers to consider whether they were catalysts or hindrances to the outworking of God's "smiles" on the nation.[243] To "help forward a reformation," he advocated that individuals give regular prayerful consideration to their willingness to be used by God as "the instruments of converting" others.[244] His hope that a spiritual reformation might take place was a common feature of evangelicalism.[245] While the history of Protestant revivalism can be traced back to the seventeenth century, it was among the eighteenth-century evangelicals that a widespread longing

237. Mack, *Heart Religion*, 34–35.

238. Grimshaw, "Letter to Mrs. Gallatin," 13 September 1755. Page not numbered.

239. Dan Taylor, *Consistent Christian Appendix*, 98, 99.

240. Dan Taylor, diary entry, 8 September 1764, in Taylor, *Memoirs*, 36; Dan Taylor, diary entry, 13 December 1765, in Taylor, *Memoirs*, 43.

241. Dan Taylor, "Letter to George Birley," [1782]. Page not numbered. This letter is not dated but its contents suggest that it was written in 1782.

242. Dan Taylor, *Cause of National Calamities.*

243. Ibid., 27, 16.

244. Ibid., 32, 34.

245. This will be examined in chapter 7.

for revival became popular.[246] It is in this respect that the reflections of David Ceri Jones on John Wesley and George Whitefield are relevant to Taylor, namely that they were "confident and secure in their spiritual standing" and that this "freed them from protracted bouts of morbid introspection to concentrate on ambitious schemes of evangelism, reformation and revival."[247] The same was true of Particular Baptist minister Andrew Fuller who made the transition from a High Calvinist introspection to confident assurance.[248] As Taylor linked the discipline of spiritual self-examination to "the necessity of a reformation" and his hope that this would involve "thousands and tens of thousands in one place and another," it is likely that his thoughts returned to all he had witnessed at Haworth.[249]

An implication of the way in which Taylor advocated and modeled a way of engaging with spiritual disciplines that was outward focused and predicated on salvific assurance, is that it exposes the misconceived nature of certain claims made by some commentators who argue only for the continuity from Puritanism to eighteenth-century evangelicalism. One such example is Garry Williams who, contending for such a continuum, cites the adoption by evangelicals of the Puritan practice of spiritual examination.[250] Williams points to Wesley's practice of the discipline and, in sweeping manner, lays claim to it as sufficient evidence "to counter Bebbington's argument that the Methodists were freed for their activism by leaving the self-examination of the Puritans behind them."[251] While Bebbington argues that "the dynamism of the evangelical movement was possible only because its adherents were assured in their faith," the ongoing practice of spiritual self-examination among evangelicals in no sense undermines his argument.[252] Crucially, Williams fails to acknowledge that evangelicals sometimes applied it in a different way—as Taylor demonstrated. Although not acknowledged by Williams, Bebbington does make mention of its continued practice among evangelicals whose different use of the discipline causes him to argue that it should be included among the "symptoms of discontinuity" of evangelicalism from Puritanism.[253] As evidence, Bebbing-

---

246. For both a reflection on the history of Protestant revivalism and its place within evangelicalism, see Coffey, "Puritanism," 273–75.

247. D. Jones, "Calvinistic Methodism," 103, 111.

248. See chapter 4.

249. Taylor, Cause of National Calamities, 34.

250. Williams, "Enlightenment Epistemology," 351.

251. Ibid., 353.

252. Bebbington, Evangelicalism, 42.

253. Ibid., 36.

ton highlights the eighteenth-century preacher and theologian Jonathan Edwards, drawing particular attention to how Edwards advocated an examination of the validity of a person's conversion that aimed "to hearten new believers rather than throw them back into painful introspection" in his 1741 *The Distinguishing Marks of a Work of the Spirit of God*.[254] Bebbington also points to the Particular Baptist minister Abraham Booth (1734–1806) who detailed how issues of wrestling with God no longer involved fears over the assurance of personal salvation but were concerned with the effects of sin.[255] It is therefore apparent that the outward thrust of Taylor's approach to self-examination provides a further significant instance of a changed evangelical application of this spiritual discipline from the way it was commonly embraced within Puritanism.

It should be noted that Williams's response to Bebbington is characteristic of how some commentators have been reluctant to accept the eighteenth-century origins of evangelicalism, as this necessitates an appreciation of the influence of Arminianism. This is explicit in how Williams expresses his concern that such an acknowledgment "serves to give a strong foothold to Arminianism within the evangelical movement."[256] He instead emphasizes that if evangelicalism is understood as a primarily "Reformational and Puritan phenomenon," then "With such a historical perspective, Reformed theology becomes the authentic evangelical mainstream of three centuries, and the historical case for the foundational status of Arminianism is undermined."[257] Such thinking, in part, accounts for why considerations regarding the extent of the continuity between Puritanism and evangelicalism have sometimes been marked by a lack of detailed scholarly attention to those who did not hold Calvinist beliefs, such as Taylor. This is apparent within many of the contributions that comprise *The Emergence of Evangelicalism*.[258]

Some such as Hambrick-Stowe have argued that an indicator of the continuity between Puritanism and evangelicalism was that evangelicals were often keen readers of Puritan literature.[259] The fact that Taylor read

254. Ibid., 47. See also Edwards, *Distinguishing Marks*.

255. Ibid., 36. See also, Booth, *Reign of Grace*, 57, 239. Taylor's friendship with Booth will be examined in chapter 7.

256. Williams, "Enlightenment Epistemology," 374.

257. Ibid.

258. With the exception of Bebbington's "Response," the other contributors to this work focus primarily on the emergence of evangelicalism from the perspective of the influence of Calvinism.

259. Hambrick-Stowe, "Spirit of the Old Writers," 280–91.

the works of Puritans, such as John Reynolds,[260] George Walker,[261] Philip Doddridge,[262] and almost certainly John Owen,[263] and yet arrived at certain distinct points of emphasis does however suggest the need for caution regarding this claim. The greater emphasis Taylor placed on assurance of salvation and application of spiritual disciplines in a mission-orientated direction provides an effective case in point.

To summarize, the distinct aspects of Taylor's personal spirituality not only demonstrated his desire for holiness, but the importance he placed on sharing the gospel with others. His engagement with spiritual disciplines such as prayer, fasting, meditation, and self-examination was strongly mission-orientated. This differed from how these practices were generally engaged with in a more introspective way within Puritanism. In turn, this further suggests the need for caution regarding those who perceive the relationship between Puritanism and evangelicalism only in terms of continuity. Taylor also sought to foster a missional spirituality throughout the New Connexion. Consideration will be given next to how further developments in Taylor's theological and ecclesiological thinking led him to leave Methodism.

Taylor's Withdrawal from Methodism

"independent spirit"

Taylor's Methodist involvement provided him with his first opportunity for Christian service. For example, he regularly led public prayer and visited the sick.[264] There is no evidence that such opportunities were available to him as he worshiped at Halifax Parish Church. The absence of reference from the 1760s onwards to Taylor attending worship at his parish church allows for the possibility that, in contrast to "official" Methodist practice, he had considered it as so inconsequential to the development of his faith that he had ceased attending. As Taylor embraced opportunities for service within Methodism, James Wood noted that he was viewed as "a zealous young man of good natural abilities and an intrepid temperament, whose occasional labors were highly appreciated by the leading men among Yorkshire

---

260. See Taylor, diary entry, 13 December 1765, 43.

261. Ibid.

262. See Dan Taylor, diary entry, 16 July 1765, in Taylor, *Memoirs*, 40.

263. Taylor's engagement with Owen's works will be examined in chapter 3.

264. Taylor, *Memoirs*, 8.

Methodists."[265] In 1761 he had a successful preaching trial in front of a panel of judges which included the Methodist District Superintendent, and he subsequently became a recognized local preacher.[266] He delivered his first sermon that same year to some believers in a meeting house in Hipperholm, near Halifax.[267] It was in keeping with the nature of his evangelical awakening that he spoke on what it meant to be saved by grace.[268]

The "great acceptance and success" that followed Taylor's early attempts at preaching led some of his friends, in 1762, to suggest that he should contact John Wesley with a view to becoming a traveling preacher.[269] This was an important role within Methodism. Traveling preachers were appointed by the Methodist Conference to particular circuits where they preached and provided pastoral support.[270] Given the ways that Taylor already served within the movement and his attendance at society, class, and band meetings, it is likely that his friends expected him to concur with their suggestion. Yet Taylor not only declined, but chose to withdraw from all Methodist involvement.

A notable factor in Taylor's withdrawal from Methodism was his disquiet regarding aspects of doctrine. As Adam Taylor recorded, "Though he agreed with Mr. Wesley in many leading points, yet, he doubted of the propriety of his mode of explaining several other important parts of doctrine."[271] Baptism was one such area of Taylor's concern. After he became aware that some local Particular Baptists baptized believers by immersion, he grew increasingly unsure about the scriptural veracity of infant baptism and regularly "teased" his Methodist friends with his "queries and doubts."[272] The way in which believers' baptism was adopted as early as 1763 at Taylor's Wadsworth fellowship, attests to the importance he attributed to this practice.[273]

It is highly likely that Taylor experienced difficulties with Wesley's commitment to the doctrine of Christian perfection,[274] and that this was

265. Wood, *Condensed History*, 173.

266. Taylor, *Memoirs*, 8.

267. Ibid.

268. Ibid. He chose Eph 2:8 as his text—"For it is by grace you have been saved, through faith—and this not from yourselves, it is the gift of God."

269. Ibid.

270. See Baker, *John Wesley*, 114.

271. Taylor, *Memoirs*, 8–9.

272. Ibid., 10. Taylor's understanding of baptism will be considered in chapter 6.

273. Ibid., 14.

274. For consideration of Wesley's understanding of the doctrine, see, e.g., Lindstrom, *Wesley and Sanctification*; Maddox, *Responsible Grace*, 179–90. Maddox

pertinent to his decision to leave Methodism. It is evident from Grimshaw's letters that the doctrine received much attention in the West Riding in the early 1760s. Grimshaw stated in a letter to Charles Wesley in 1760 that "the doctrine of perfection seems very high just now in these parts," and voiced his personal conviction that "my perfection is to see my imperfection . . . This is my perfection. I know no other."[275] A year later Grimshaw noted, in his correspondence with John Wesley, that it remained "much discussed" in the Haworth Round, referring to how it was "a grating term to many of our dear brethren."[276] Taylor's likely membership of a Methodist band is also significant, as Watson argues that band meetings were "a focal point for disputes about entire sanctification."[277] Opposition to the doctrine stemmed from the fanaticism of some of its proponents and the widespread perception that the possibility of living sin-free lives was being advocated.[278] As Laycock highlighted, even among "some of Wesley's preachers it was not fully accepted."[279] Taylor was very likely aware of this, given his Methodist involvement.

As well as Taylor probably sharing the fears of others that Wesley advocated the possibility of living in a condition of sinless perfection,[280] there is no evidence in any of Taylor's writings that he subscribed to Wesley's view that sanctification involved a second stage of holiness beyond justification. Wesley referred to this as "Entire Sanctification" or "Christian Perfection" and urged all believers to attain it.[281] He described it as "neither more nor less than pure love—love expelling sin, and governing both the heart and life of a child of God. The Refiner's fire purges out all that is contrary to love."[282]

---

delineates Wesley's understanding of the doctrine, his continued progression of thought on the subject and draws attention to certain modifications that Wesley made to his position. He also argues that Wesley's understanding of sanctification came to comprise broader elements beyond his emphasis on Christian perfection. Some of the works within which Wesley outlined his thinking on the doctrine of Christian perfection can be found in John Wesley, "Treatises on Christian Perfection".

275. Grimshaw, "Letter to Charles Wesley." Page not numbered.

276. Grimshaw, "Letter to John Wesley," 21 July 1761. Qtd in Laycock, *Methodist Heroes*, 220.

277. Watson, *Pursuing Social Holiness*, 133.

278. Examples of fanatics included Thomas Maxfield and George Bell who were part of a group of London Methodists and taught that perfection could be attained instantaneously, see Maddox, *Responsible Grace*, 185–86.

279. Laycock, *Methodist Heroes*, 214.

280. For the development of this aspect of Wesley's thinking, see Maddox, *Responsible Grace*, 181–84.

281. John Wesley, "Letter to Walter Churchey," 223.

282. Ibid. See also, John Wesley, *Christian Perfection*.

Similar to the dominant viewpoint among his evangelical contemporaries, Taylor viewed sanctification as a continuous process that was not punctuated by the receiving of a special gift of perfect love or entire sanctification. Taylor's understanding of perfection was evident in his insistence that Paul's instruction that the Corinthian church "be perfect" was not addressing "the purity of their minds and conduct as individuals" but the church's general sinful state.[283] He also avoided Wesley's differentiation of sin as "a voluntary transgression of a known law" and labeling of involuntary or subconscious transgressions as "mistakes" or "infirmities" rather than sins.[284] Taylor explicitly referred to sins of "behaviour, of the tongue, of the thought, of the temper, and of the desire; both of omission and commission."[285] Neither could Taylor dismiss the doctrine of Christian perfection as a peripheral matter, for Wesley designated it "the grand depositum" that God had entrusted to the Methodists.[286] Taylor's rejection of the doctrine means that the judgment of some commentators, such as Rack, that Wesley's adherence to perfectionism meant he was "never to be quite a typical evangelical," should not be applied to Taylor.[287]

Taylor's disapproval of the way he felt Wesley exercised discipline was influential on his decision to withdraw. In somewhat forceful language, Adam Taylor noted Dan Taylor's refusal to submit to "that dictatorship which Mr. Wesley then assumed over the conduct and faith of his preachers."[288] While Taylor's familiarity with aspects of Methodism such as its class and band leaders, stewards, exhorters, trustees, visitors to the sick, and lay and local preachers saw him introduced to what Bruce Hindmarsh identifies as "the rise of an articulate and involved laity in eighteenth-century evangelicalism," Wesley exerted a strong influence.[289] Taylor would have been aware of the allegiance that Wesley expected from those active in Methodism. There was, for instance, a widespread awareness of how Wesley had removed William Darney from the list of Methodist itinerant preachers for three years after he had spoken out against the doctrine of Christian perfection.[290] Wesley's penchant for control was evident in his as-

283. Dan Taylor, *Discourse on 2 Cor. xiii.II*, in Dan Taylor, *Memoirs of William Thompson*. 20.

284. John Wesley, *On Perfection*, 79, 73.

285. Dan Taylor, *Scripture Directions*, 7. Further consideration will be given to this publication in chapter 6.

286. John Wesley, "Letter to Robert Brackenbury," 238.

287. Rack, *Reasonable Enthusiast*, 104.

288. Taylor, *Memoirs*, 9.

289. Hindmarsh, "Reshaping individualism," 67.

290. See, e.g., Laycock, *Methodist Heroes*, 179.

sertion concerning his conflict with Darney that "if local preachers who differ from us will keep their opinions to themselves then they may preach in our societies, otherwise they may not."[291] As Gwang Seok Oh asserts in his examination of Wesley's ecclesiology, "His authority was supreme."[292] Watts similarly notes that "Wesley kept the discipline of the societies in his own hands, or in the hands of assistants appointed by him" and that his visits to societies were often followed by "expulsions."[293] While factors such as Taylor's later organizational skills, commitment to the spread of the gospel, pioneering tendencies, and authority granted him by the New Connexion mean it is appropriate to refer to him as the "Baptist Wesley," differences in certain aspects of their leadership style were apparent.[294]

Taylor's unease with Wesley's "scheme of discipline" reflected his growing concern towards what he felt was the hierarchical nature of Methodism and particularly its location within the Church of England.[295] He was convinced that "the New Testament gave no countenance, either by precept or example" to its model of governance and that he should "call no man master."[296] In 1805 Taylor wrote on the subject of dissent and stated that "national churches," as opposed to dissenting "gospel churches," did not rest under the authority of Christ's headship.[297] They were "established by civil laws, which are enforced by human penalties" and therefore were "under the direction and government of men."[298] He designated this basis alone as sufficient reason for dissent, as otherwise believers were forced to serve two masters.[299] It is likely that the process by which Taylor reached this judgment began prior to his withdrawal from Methodism. His involvement in the Halifax society meant he was probably aware of the ongoing debates considering whether the movement should separate from the Church of England. For instance, in 1760 when he was at the peak of his Methodist involvement, the issue of separation again attracted much

---

291. John Wesley, "Letter to Matthew Lowes," 270. Matthew Lowes was one of Wesley's preachers who served on the "Newcastle Round" between 1757–71.

292. Oh, *John Wesley's Ecclesiology*, 172.

293. Watts, *Dissenters*, 404.

294. The extent to which Taylor can be referred to as the "Baptist Wesley" will be considered in chapter 5.

295. Taylor, *Memoirs*, 9.

296. Ibid.; Dan Taylor. Qtd in ibid., 8. Primary source unknown.

297. Dan Taylor, "Reasons of Dissenting," 25.

298. Ibid.

299. Ibid.

attention due to a violation, elsewhere, of agreed Methodist abstention from administering the Lord's Supper.[300]

When Taylor assumed oversight of the believers at Wadsworth, it is significant that he immediately functioned in a collaborative way that differed from the Methodist system of governance. Taylor's collective approach was evident even before the fellowship was constituted into a General Baptist church and members' meetings established. For example, the elders asked Taylor to provide foundational theological principles, but he refused to do this in isolation. Instead, "Mr. T. and his friends" together considered "on what principles they could unite to carry on the cause of their blessed redeemer."[301] While Taylor's interpretation of Scripture influenced the way he believed ecclesiological governance should be exercised (see chapter 5), Enlightenment influences were also evident. Just as Taylor valued people's individual views, so it was the case, as Hindmarsh outlines, that "more weight devolves on the individual as time passes from the late Renaissance into the seventeenth and eighteenth centuries."[302] Although the exact origins of individualism are debatable, the progression of the Enlightenment in England saw increasing credence given to the societal involvement of all individuals and significance placed on their accompanying personal perspectives, experiences, and liberty.[303] Taylor's rejection of hierarchical governance and resolve to embrace the viewpoints of others should, at least in part, be understood from the paradigm of Enlightenment influence.

It is ironic that the nature of the evangelicalism that was consolidated within Taylor during his period of involvement within Methodism likely contributed to his inclination to withdraw. This is something that has not been considered by those who have examined Taylor's departure from Methodism.[304] Evangelicalism's propensity for innovation and experimentation was a catalyst and source of influence on the decision processes of many who left the movement. As in Taylor's case, those who had experienced an evangelical awakening frequently became active within a society and were suitably equipped to take more responsibility and direction over

---

300. See Rack, *Reasonable Enthusiast*, 300.

301. Taylor, *Memoirs*, 10. Taylor's commitment to collective decision making was also evident in his leadership of the New Connexion, see chapter 5.

302. Hindmarsh, "Reshaping individualism," 74.

303. See O'Hara, *Enlightenment*, 66–115.

304. Raymond Brown's brief reference to Taylor's departure from Methodism only in terms of his having been "unhappy about some of the features of Wesleyan doctrine and pastoral practice" is typical of those who have considered the reasons for Taylor's withdrawal. See Brown, *English Baptists*, 68.

the outworking of their faith.[305] When they found that their own particular theological or ecclesiological emphases fell outside the fairly regimented Methodist system, the next step was sometimes to consider withdrawal from the movement. Added to this was the "profoundly radical individualism," which, as Isaac Kramnick asserts, was central to Enlightenment thinking.[306] It is probable that all these factors were significant in accounting for Taylor's departure. It is also likely that they were influential on the reasoning behind the believers from Heptonstall who left Methodism and formed an independent fellowship which subsequently became the nucleus of Taylor's church in Wadsworth.[307] They were also likely influential on the split that took place at the Halifax society where, subsequent to Taylor's departure, half the members left to begin an Independent congregation under the leadership of Titus Knight.[308] Taylor did not subscribe to the Calvinist theology that was often embraced by those who left Methodism and founded or joined Congregationalist and Independent fellowships (such as Knight), but would probably have been aware of what James Miall noted regarding their frequent vibrancy and numerical growth.[309] He would, in turn, have treated with caution Wesley's sometimes "bitter and prejudiced" attitude to nonconformity,[310] and Grimshaw's warning that if Methodism separated from the Church of England then "the work of God which has hitherto been greatly blessed in our hands, I fear, will then be greatly impeded."[311] The impact of this, along with the evolution of his enlightened evangelicalism, meant that Taylor became an "independent spirit" whose strong evangelical foundations propelled him to leave the security of Methodism and venture onwards in faith.[312]

305. While sometimes there was a reverse movement of believers into Methodism from nonconformist backgrounds, Taylor's experience was commonplace.

306. Kramnick, *Portable Enlightenment Reader*, xv.

307. See Taylor, *Memoirs*, 9. The specific reasons why these believers left Methodism is not stated.

308. See Laycock, *Methodist Heroes*, 239.

309. Miall, *Congregationalism in Yorkshire*, 138.

310. Gregory, ""In the Church," 175.

311. Grimshaw, "Letter to Mrs. Gallatin," 2 May 1755, in Laycock, *Methodist Heroes*, 149.

312. Taylor, *Memoirs*, 9.

Conclusion

As Taylor traveled to Haworth to listen to the preaching of Grimshaw and other evangelicals, he was strongly influenced by them. The substance of their teaching such as salvation by faith in Christ alone, the necessity of a new birth, and the sanctifying work of the Spirit, appear to have been absent from the Christian instruction Taylor received at his parish church and from his parents. He acquired an understanding of Christ as his Savior that he had not previously known. For the first time, he experienced a powerful inner sense of spiritual freedom and assurance of salvation. As the Taylor brothers traveled to hear evangelicals they viewed as having been enlightened by God, they noted the way in which the gospel was delivered. The repeated invitations to come to Christ, use of market language, lack of emphasis on the precise details of doctrine and validity that was granted to the experiential, were all new to them. Taylor had particular respect for Grimshaw and it was a tribute to his life and ministry which formed the first of Taylor's published works. Taylor was also influenced by the zeal, activism, and innovation that frequently accompanied the expressions of evangelicalism he encountered. He was further exposed to all these key facets of eighteenth-century evangelicalism when he joined a Methodist society in Halifax. His participation in society, class, and probably band meetings strengthened his understanding and appreciation of evangelicalism's core theological convictions, entrepreneurial practices, and Enlightenment-inspired values and emphases. These were soon replicated in Taylor's ministry, a notable example being his introduction of class, experience, and discipline meetings, as well as being apparent throughout his teaching.

Taylor's emergence into evangelicalism was evident in the development of his personal spirituality as he demonstrated an overriding regard for the task of mission. The mission-orientated nature of Taylor's spirituality was particularly apparent in the ways he engaged with spiritual disciplines such as self-examination, prayer, fasting, and scriptural meditation. It was later reflected in his successful fostering of a missional spirituality throughout the New Connexion. This approach differed from the often introspective expressions of personal spirituality that were espoused by earlier movements such as the Puritans. Although Taylor became active in Methodism, he reached convictions on issues such as baptism, Christian perfection, Wesley's system of discipline and the place of Methodism in the Church of England which led him to withdraw from the movement. Evangelicalism's predilection for innovation, and the influence of Enlightenment values such as a regard for experimentation and expression of individual freedom, also helped foster a pioneering spirit within Taylor which likely contributed to his decision to leave the Methodist movement. It will be shown in the next chapter that Taylor soon felt compelled to act as an apologist for the evangelicalism he had embraced, as he encountered perspectives on the faith which significantly differed from that which he had been introduced to in the Evangelical Revival.

2

Innovative Apologist

TAYLOR'S MINISTRY AS A pastor and his oversight of the New Connexion saw him assume the role of apologist. He frequently felt compelled to defend his soteriological beliefs. Firstly, consideration will be given to Taylor's response to the prevalence of Arian, Socinian, and Unitarian thinking within the General Baptists. In particular, the creative means by which he upheld his evangelical beliefs will be examined. As he defended his understanding of the gospel he placed importance on God's moral governance and this will be closely considered. The inventive way in which Taylor sought to apply an Enlightenment-inspired regard for reason and empirical thinking to his apologetic advantage and how this differed from the approaches of some earlier believers will also be examined. It will be argued that Taylor's consistent refusal to engage in reasoning of a metaphysical and speculative nature was an important distinction of his theological thinking. As will be seen, his resolve to articulate and embrace a commitment to the plain meaning of the Scriptures and accompanying simplicity of faith was another notable example of the particular way he defended his soteriological convictions. Throughout the chapter, emphasis will be placed on how the main characteristics and underpinning values of Taylor's apologetic framework reflected facets foundational to evangelicalism.

Taylor's Defense of the Gospel

"preach the gospel, the whole gospel"

In 1762, Taylor assumed oversight of a group of fellow Methodist seceders in Heptonstall, near Halifax, and immediately began to preach the gospel in

the fields of the surrounding villages.[1] A consequence of the fellowship joining the General Baptists in 1763 was that Taylor also recognized the need to
provide a defense of his soteriological convictions.[2] Only five months after
his ordination in July 1763, he referred to the "many strange notions" he had
encountered within the wider body of General Baptist believers.[3] Later that
year he noted that while preaching in other General Baptist churches he had
been repeatedly forced "to defend his principles and practice against every
attack."[4] This adversarial response was typical of the resistance often shown
by the General Baptists to the Evangelical Revival. For example, in 1745 the
General Baptist national Assembly addressed the subject of Methodism and
declared "their faith and practice to be contrary to the Holy Scriptures and to
the peace and welfare of their [General Baptist] societies."[5] Church members
who attended Methodist gatherings were frequently threatened with discipline by the church meeting.[6] When General Baptists embraced evangelical
convictions, they tended to leave the denomination and join congregations
which had responded positively to the revival, or Methodist societies that
had sprung up as a consequence. General Baptists who remained committed to doctrines such as the deity of Christ and his vicarious atonement
were therefore encouraged by Taylor joining their ranks. This accounted
for the enthusiastic way in which William Thompson (1735–94), pastor of
the General Baptist church in Boston, Lincolnshire, befriended Taylor at
the 1763 General Baptist Association gathering of Lincolnshire churches.
Thompson quickly realized their agreement on the "leading doctrines" of
the gospel and shared zeal to see people "awakened and converted."[7] He then
encouraged the process by which the fellowship in Wadsworth became a
General Baptist church.[8] When Taylor wrote Thompson's memoirs in 1769

1. See Adam Taylor, New Connection, 9.

2. The process by which the church joined the General Baptists was noted in the
introductory chapter.

3. Dan Taylor, "Letter to William Thompson," 10 December 1763, 73.

4. Adam Taylor, Memoirs, 13. Taylor had undertaken a preaching tour of General
Baptist churches in Derbyshire, Lincolnshire, and Leicestershire as he sought to raise
funds for the building of a meeting house in Wadsworth.

5. [Anon.]. Qtd in Taylor, New Connection, 110. It is not clear who Taylor was here
quoting as what he recorded is not found in the minutes of this meeting, see Whitley,
Minutes of General Baptist Assembly, 1731–1811, 75–77.

6. See, e.g., Taylor, New Connection, 110.

7. Taylor, Memoirs, 14, 77. For an examination of William Thompson's life and
ministry, see Dan Taylor, Memoirs of William Thompson. Thompson's high regard for
Taylor presumably accounts for why he was very keen that Taylor wrote his memoirs,
see Dan Taylor, "Letter to George Birley," 17 February 1794. Page not numbered.

8. Ibid., 14.

he noted their close friendship, stating that "few intimacies, considering the distance of situations, could be more cordial or less interrupted, for so many years."[9] However, Thompson did not initially warn Taylor of the "spurious liberality and laxity of principle" that had "gained the ascendancy" in the denomination.[10] Thompson's keenness for fellowship with a kindred spirit probably led him to ensure that he said nothing that might deter Taylor from joining the General Baptists. Given that Thompson later became a leading protagonist for the creation of the New Connexion, he likely recognized that Taylor would both ably defend an evangelical understanding of salvation and provide needed innovation.

General Baptist antagonism towards the Evangelical Revival was caused by a variety of factors. These included their different approaches to baptism and worship,[11] the Anglican origins of Methodism, and, in keeping with that noted by Brett McInelly as a common criticism of Methodism, some were resistant to its "emotional forms of religious expression."[12] There was also opposition to some of the content of evangelical preaching. The soteriology of many General Baptists had become increasingly influenced by Arianism and Socinianism. These anti-Trinitarian perspectives flourished in eighteenth-century England,[13] with both articulating a subordinate view of Christ in relation to the Father. Arians took their name from the Alexandrian priest Arius whose beliefs were condemned by the Council of Nicaea in 325. While Arians viewed Christ as in some sense divine and held on to his pre-existence, Socinians rejected both these viewpoints as well as Christ's substitutionary atonement.[14] Socinianism's origins lay with Fausto Sozzini (as noted in chapter 1) whose most "striking claim," as Sarah Mortimer notes, was that "Christ saved men by his teaching and his

---

9. Taylor, *Memoirs of William Thompson*, 3.

10. Taylor, *New Connection*, 470.

11. General Baptists were committed to an understanding of believers' baptism by immersion whereas leading figures of the Evangelical Revival such as the Wesley brothers and Whitefield held to infant baptism. These differences will be considered in the examination of baptism in chapter 6. Regarding worship, it will, for example, also be considered in chapter 6 how most General Baptists were opposed to hymn singing.

12. McInelly, "Method or Madness," 197. It will be seen in chapter 6 how an example of this was the different stances of Dan Taylor, and General Baptist Messenger Gilbert Boyce who was largely resistant to the evangelical revival, to the expression of emotion in worship.

13. For consideration of this see, e.g., Israel, *Radical Enlightenment*, 22–27; Watts, *Dissenters*, 371–82. As Watts notes, Arianism and Socinianism were also influential among other Dissenters such as the Presbyterians and Congregationalists.

14. See ibid., 371–72.

example, not by atoning for their sins on the cross."[15] Sozzini was the chief architect of the 1605 Racovian Catechism.[16] Its fourth section was entitled "The Person of Christ" and designated Christ's divinity as "repugnant to sound reason" and contrary to the Scriptures.[17] Salvation was viewed in terms of following the teachings of Jesus and the example he set in his life and death, not by trusting in his substitutionary sacrifice. This belief was reinforced by those such as the Gloucestershire schoolmaster John Biddle and Anglican Rector Stephen Nye who, in the late seventeenth century, distributed material in favor of this viewpoint.[18] Taylor soon reached the judgment that "the Socinians, as well as the ancient and modern Arians" had led many believers away "from the plain truths of the gospel."[19] It was this that he felt compelled to address.

Taylor's 1763 visit to a General Baptist church in Lincoln was typical of that which he frequently encountered. He was opposed by "a very great crowd of rude people" who were more concerned with good behavior than orthodox belief.[20] This is evident in Taylor's consternation that they were convinced "God will accept sincere, though imperfect obedience" as a means of salvation.[21] He was "astonished" that General Baptists could embrace such "destructive principles" that brought "dishonour upon the merits of the blessed Jesus" and which he emphatically dismissed as "the master-piece of all the schemes that ever were hatched in hell."[22] Their thinking was far removed from Taylor's commitment to Christ as "the *only* true foundation" of salvation which was a doctrine central to earlier General Baptist confessions of faith.[23] It is, for example, found in *A Brief Confession or Declaration of Faith* which was published in 1660 and after subsequent modifications was accepted, as Barrington White notes, as the "standard

---

15. Mortimer, *Reason and Religion*, 15.

16. Rees, *Racovian Catechism*.

17. Ibid., 58. While this catechism never assumed the authority of a public confession among the Socinians, it did embody its chief tenets.

18. Biddle published an English translation of the Racovian Catechism in 1652. For consideration of Biddle, see, e.g., Mortimer, *Reason and Religion*, 161–63. While Mortimer notes the influences of Socinianism on Biddle, she refers to him as a Unitarian. Stephen Nye's *Brief History of the Unitarians* was also popular. See also McLachlan, *Socinianism*.

19. Dan Taylor, "Letter to William Thompson," 9 July 1770, 139.

20. Taylor, "Letter to William Thompson," 10 December 1763, 73.

21. Ibid.

22. Ibid.

23. Dan Taylor, diary entry, 26 January 1767, in Taylor, *Memoirs*, 71, Taylor's emphasis.

for virtually all General Baptists."[24] Its sixth Article specifies that "the way set forth by God for men to be justified in, is by faith in Christ."[25] Similarly, Article eleven states that to "preach the gospel" involves leading people to "profess repentance towards God and faith towards our Lord Jesus Christ."[26] A further example is the 1678 *Orthodox Creed* which did not stem from the General Baptist General Assembly but was written on behalf of a group of General Baptist churches with the influential General Baptist Messenger Thomas Monk ([?]–[1685]) having assumed a leading role in its compilation.[27] Article sixteen contains unequivocal reference to how "man is justified by faith" in "God's free grace through Jesus Christ, whom God has set forth to be a propitiation . . . for the remission of sins."[28] Although Taylor did not refer to these confessions of faith, the contents of these cited Articles accorded with what he designated as "the great truths" of the faith and which he became "earnest in his efforts" to promote.[29] He also drew attention to what he considered as the "pernicious consequences to poor souls" of the alternative doctrines that many General Baptists had embraced and which he believed would hinder the spread of the gospel.[30] This demonstrates that his decision to assume the role of apologist did not emanate from a duty to uphold doctrine for its own sake, but to safeguard the interests of mission that were central to his evangelical stance.

It is significant that Taylor produced his first apologetic work only a few months after his distressing experience in Lincoln. It was entitled *The*

24. White, *English Baptists*, 97. See *Brief Confession*, in Lumpkin, *Baptist Confessions*, 224–35. After its first modification in 1663 the *Brief Confession* became known as the Standard Confession of the General Baptists. I therefore refer to it as the Standard Confession from here onwards. It should be noted that I have not italicized the name Standard Confession as this was not its formal title. For the wider context within which the Confession was written, see Crosby, *History of the English*, 3:74–75.

25. *Brief Confession*, Article six, 228.

26. Ibid., Article eleven, 228.

27. *Orthodox Creed*, in Lumpkin, *Baptist Confessions*, 297–334. This creed was compiled in January 1678 by fifty-four Messengers and elders of the Buckinghamshire, Hertfordshire, Bedfordshire, and Oxford Associations, see White, *English Baptists*, 120–21. Thomas Monk led the Berkhamstead congregation of General Baptists and from 1654 onwards served as Messenger for the General Baptist churches in mid-Buckinghamshire and Hertfordshire. The role of General Baptist Messenger is considered later in this section. For Monk's influence on the writing of the *Orthodox Creed*, see Adam Taylor, *English General Baptists*, 361. Uncertainty surrounds Monk's date of birth with even approximate estimates proving difficult. It should also be noted that occasionally commentators refer to Thomas Monck, although most omit the letter "c."

28. *Orthodox Creed*, Article sixteen, 310.

29. Taylor, "Letter to William Thompson," 10 December 1763, 73.

30. Ibid.

Absolute Necessity of Searching the Scriptures.[31] In keeping with how the production of tracts and pamphlets formed a distinctive feature of evangelicalism, he wrote *The Absolute Necessity* as a tract which comprised different elements of sermons that he had preached during the first months of 1764.[32] The soteriological concerns that prompted him to write were apparent in his opening sentences where he expressed unequivocally, "Nothing is more certain, than that we are 'Justified by faith, not of works, lest any man should boast.'" This is a doctrine fully maintained in the Scriptures."[33] He insisted that believers "be led and directed by the Scriptures, and by them alone."[34] This was indicative of his belief that many General Baptists had departed from a correct interpretation of the Bible. He further impressed that "The Scripture is the touchstone whereby we ought to try every word we hear, every doctrine we receive, every work we are found in the practice of."[35] More broadly, he emphasized that the Bible was humankind's "only rule, both in faith and practice."[36] This assertion likely reflected a mindfulness, as Gerald Cragg outlines, that the near universal acceptance of the supremacy of human reason gave rise to a situation across eighteenth-century society where "old forms of authority were being challenged" and some "very disconcerting questions" asked of the Scriptures.[37]

Part of Taylor's response, to what he felt was an undermining of the authority of Scripture, was to advocate the embracing of a greater simplicity of faith. This was something he repeatedly emphasized such as in his encouragement to George Birley that he should "preach the essentials of gospel truth, and the Ordinances and Commands of Christ, in a plain, serious, spiritual, experimental and practical manner."[38] The essential elements of this assertion reflect what Taylor referred to as "Primitive Christianity in faith and practice," although this was never explicitly defined by him.[39] He was convinced that such an approach would prevent soteriological error. In *The Absolute Necessity* he declared that Jesus should be obeyed because "if he hath said it, it ought, without a moment's hesitation, to be diligently at-

---

31. Dan Taylor, *Absolute Necessity.*

32. The distribution of tracts by Taylor and other evangelicals will be examined in chapter 7.

33. Taylor, *Absolute Necessity*, 4. Taylor was quoting from Eph 2:8–9.

34. Ibid., 7.

35. Ibid., 15.

36. Ibid., 7.

37. Gerald R. Cragg, *Reason and Authority*, 19, 4–5.

38. Dan Taylor, "Letter to George Birley," 6 February 1778. Page not numbered.

39. *Assembly of Free Grace General Baptists, 1770.* Page not numbered.

tended to, by all that hear or read it."[40] This alone was reason enough and no further argument was deemed necessary. This simple approach was different from the way Puritans tended to defend the gospel, as will be shown in more detail in the final section of this chapter. Although Puritan defenses of the gospel were similarly practical in their goal of eliciting a true obedience to Christ, they were characteristically founded on rigorous doctrinal reflection, extensive scriptural citation, and often metaphysical reasoning. Even when Taylor, on future occasions, demonstrated his theological competence as he engaged in complex soteriological matters, an emphasis on the merits of simplicity remained interwoven throughout his works.[41]

As Taylor defended his evangelical convictions, he attached importance to declaring the depravity of the natural human condition. This was in contrast to one of the key tenets of Socinianism and accounted for much of the criticism he faced during his early preaching excursions to General Baptist churches. For example, he received considerable "opposition" when he preached at an unnamed church in 1767 on the subject of the inability of non-believers to please God as they were controlled by the sinful nature.[42] Such a response reflects Dorinda Outram's assertion concerning the "older orthodox religious beliefs that sat uneasily with Enlightenment thought" which instead affirmed humankind's natural goodness.[43] As Taylor encouraged others to recognize "the misery of man by nature," his concern for the spread of the gospel was again a powerful stimulus.[44] He insisted that this doctrine was a crucial element of what it meant "to preach the gospel, the whole gospel."[45] To do otherwise was to fail to demonstrate a "real love to precious souls," for it conveyed the impression that humankind's natural state did not require redemption by Christ.[46] When he laid out his soteriological convictions in *The Absolute Necessity* he was therefore unequivocal about the "deplorably wretched and ruined condition, which all our souls are in by nature."[47] In characteristic manner, he provided no delineation of his thinking. It was not until twenty years later, in his discourse with Particular Baptist minister Andrew Fuller, that Taylor provided more insight

---

40. Taylor, *Absolute Necessity*, 18.

41. An example of this was the nature of Taylor's theological engagement with Andrew Fuller, see chapter 4.

42. Dan Taylor, diary entry, 26 February 1767, in Taylor, *Memoirs*, 22.

43. Outram, *Enlightenment*, 120.

44. Dan Taylor, diary entry, 1 January 1765, in Taylor, *Memoirs*, 55.

45. Ibid.

46. Ibid.

47. Taylor, *Absolute Necessity*, 4.

into his understanding of the nature of imputed sin, guilt, and the basis on which he maintained that the sinful human condition did not prevent people from freely responding to the gospel.[48] The incisive nature of Taylor's written works and approach to core aspects of his soteriology, such as his understanding of God's moral governance, demonstrates that his reluctance to engage in detailed doctrinal examination did not stem from a slow development of his theological acumen. It instead emanated from his belief that believers would be kept from "innumerable" theological "mischiefs" when the Scriptures were simply viewed as a "rule" and reasoned consideration given to their surrounding context of "scope and intent."[49] In *The Absolute Necessity* Taylor also referred to "him that made the world, coming to atone for the transgressor" as "a revelation purely from heaven."[50] This assertion is typical of how Taylor sought to maintain a primacy on revelation and did so even when he commended the need for reason in theological thinking, as will be shown later in the chapter.

Taylor's May 1765 visit to the General Baptist church in Gamston, Nottinghamshire was another notable occasion during the earlier years of his ministry when he provided a defense of his salvific thinking.[51] When opposed by church members at the close of his sermon, he entered into "long contests about original sin, justification, atonement."[52] His exasperation was apparent as he declared, "how far do we differ in judgment with respect to all these things! What can be done? Lord, teach thou me!"[53] Taylor's upholding of his evangelical convictions caused lasting disquiet. This soon came to the attention of Gilbert Boyce, Messenger of the Lincolnshire General Baptist Association.[54] While the office of Messenger was established in the 1650s for the chief purpose of evangelism,[55] the role of Messengers shifted significantly during the second half of the eighteenth

---

48. See chapter 4.

49. Taylor, *Absolute Necessity*, 14, 9, 10.

50. Ibid., 20.

51. As noted in the introductory chapter, it was after Taylor met believers from this church in 1763 that he was baptized by one of its ministers, Joseph Jeffery. For an overview of the history of the General Baptist church in Gamston, see Harrison, "Nottinghamshire Baptists: Rise and Expansion," 60–61.

52. Dan Taylor, diary entry, 19 May 1765, in Taylor, *Memoirs*, 21.

53. Ibid.

54. See Taylor, *Memoirs*, 22.

55. Adam Taylor in his description of the early function of Messengers, noted that their "chief task" was "preaching the gospel where it was not known," see Taylor, *English General Baptists*, 413. The importance of the task of evangelism within the work of the earlier Messengers was also emphasized by William Whitley, see Whitley, *History of British Baptists*, 87–88.

century.[56] General Baptist minister William Evershed stated at an ordination service for Messengers in 1783 that their principal function was "to visit the churches"; "set in order things that are wanting and out of order"; and to "ordain elders."[57] It was with a view to the second of these duties that Boyce invited Taylor and all affected parties to a meeting in Gamston in August 1783.[58] The agenda items that were discussed included,

> If, or how far we are affected by Adam's sin; What is meant by the terms regeneration and justification and the way by which a sinner becomes regenerated and justified; Whether we allow, and if so, what we mean by Christ's atonement; Whether and how far the Spirit's operations are necessary to a sinner's conversion.[59]

While evangelicals sometimes disagreed in their precise understanding of these issues, the non-presumptuous qualifiers that precede even a basic belief in each of these points indicate the theological distance that existed between the evangelicalism that Taylor espoused and the convictions of General Baptists of Socinian persuasion. Taylor expressed his frustration that "while no solid arguments are produced, wise men can satisfy themselves with impertinent quibbles."[60] He likely witnessed the "temptation to intellectual arrogance" that Cragg identifies as a common characteristic of Enlightenment-inspired attempts to make the Christian faith reasonable.[61] Taylor was explicit regarding his hope that the believers at Gamston might return to "the plain truth of the gospel."[62] Although Taylor deemed the outcome of the meeting "unsatisfactory,"[63] Fred Harrison notes that he maintained "strong links" with the church.[64] This almost certainly accounts for

56. For an overview of the origin and evolution of the office of Messenger, see Nicholson, "Office of 'Messenger,'" 206–25. Helpful consideration of the function of Messengers is also provided by Clint Bass within his examination of the seventeenth-century General Baptist minister Thomas Grantham and the wider General Baptist life of this period, see Bass, *Thomas Grantham*, 46–60.

57. Evershed, *Messenger's Mission*, 27, 28, 30.

58. Taylor, *Memoirs*, 21. As noted in the introductory chapter, Taylor was already acquainted with Boyce as he had officiated at his ordination in 1763. Boyce also presided at Taylor's first visit to the Lincolnshire Assembly of General Baptists that was mentioned earlier in this section.

59. Taylor, diary entry, 19 May 1765, 22. It is unfortunate that there is no surviving record of Taylor's response.

60. Ibid.

61. Cragg, *Reason and Authority*, 18.

62. Taylor, diary entry, 19 May 1765, 21.

63. Ibid., 22.

64. Harrison, "Nottinghamshire Baptists. Church Relations," 180. It should be

the significant theological transition the church later made and which enabled it to be welcomed into the New Connexion in 1779.[65] Taylor's enduring commitment to the church, despite the initial opposition he received, reflected his desire to see all people embrace the soteriological convictions that he resolutely defended.

The significance of Taylor's early apologetic efforts in places such as Gamston should not be overlooked. It was over seventy years since a General Baptist minister had provided a truly substantive and coherent defense of tenets of the faith such as Christ's divinity and vicarious atonement. The occasion was the 1691 General Baptist Assembly, where Kent Messenger Joseph Wright accused his fellow Messenger Matthew Caffyn of denying the deity of Christ.[66] As Raymond Brown notes, the denomination had failed to replace those ministers who, in the second part of the seventeenth century, had provided "inspiration for decades" as they endeavored to keep their contemporaries on an orthodox theological footing.[67] Notable examples included the loss of influential Association Messengers such as Thomas Grantham whose 1678 *Christianismus Primitivus* was widely considered the "touchstone of General Baptist orthodoxy,"[68] Thomas Monk who opposed the christological thinking of Matthew Caffyn,[69] and the aforementioned Joseph Wright. Although Taylor's succinct and pragmatic apologetic approach contrasted with the detailed style of those such as Grantham,[70] he praised the "vigour and earnestness" of his General Baptist forebears as they had contended against "the sentiments of Arius and Socinus" and maintained that "Christ atoned for the sins of men, and that none can be saved

---

noted that Harrison fails to recognize the theological tensions that had been evident in the church at Gamston.

65. See Taylor, *New Connection*, 451. Further illustrative of the significant theological change that the church experienced is that there is also no evidence of a church split having taken place.

66. Wright argued for Caffyn to be excommunicated. However, Caffyn's defense satisfied the Assembly, as it did when the matter was raised again in 1693, and later in 1698, 1700, and 1702. For an overview of the controversy see Taylor, *English General Baptists*, 463–80; Bass, *Thomas Grantham*, 181–85, 195–207; Hayden, *English Baptist History*, 40–42.

67. Brown, *English Baptists*, 25.

68. Hayden, *English Baptist History*, 42. See Grantham, *Christianismus Primitivus*. For an examination of Grantham's ministry and theological thinking, see Inscore Essick Jr., "Messenger, Apologist, and Nonconformist"; Inscore Essick, *Thomas Grantham*; Bass, *Thomas Grantham*.

69. For more on the ministry of Monk, see Taylor, *English General Baptists*, 226–29; Hayden, *English Baptist History*, 39–40.

70. For the thoroughness of Grantham's approach to doctrine, see Bass, *Thomas Grantham*, 30–31.

but through that atonement."[71] This was apparent in the 1696 decision of Caffyn's opponents to secede from the General Baptist Assembly and form the General Association of General Baptists.[72] However, this resolve steadily diminished during each of the decades of the early eighteenth century. By the second half of the century, there were only a few General Baptists, such as William Thompson, who were prepared to defend orthodox principles of faith. It is in this respect that Taylor's strong defense of orthodox soteriological principles was, to some extent, an innovation within the context of General Baptist life in the second half of the eighteenth-century.

Taylor's vigorous articulation of the faith accounted for Gilbert Boyce's request that he address the 1766 gathering of the Lincolnshire General Baptist Association in Conningsby. Taylor accepted the invitation and addressed the complacency he detected towards those who were not saved.[73] In keeping with his preferred apologetic style, his reasoning was not rooted in a close examination of doctrine nor extensive scriptural citation. Instead, he lamented over the everlasting damnation of those dying without knowledge of the Lord. He referred to "the myriads of myriads who go to the place which is lower than the grave, who eternally perish" and urged those present to acquire a "tender regard for their precious and immortal souls."[74] The fervor with which Taylor upheld the imperative of evangelism was intrinsic to every aspect of his evangelicalism. This contributed to why, as Clive Jarvis highlights, Boyce had been "quick to see the potential in Taylor" and taken him to the national General Baptist Assembly in London in 1765 and again in 1767.[75] Boyce was particularly concerned about the numerical decline of the General Baptists. He was therefore encouraged that Taylor's vitality of faith had led to a situation where, from the mid-1760s onwards, "The Congregations at Birchcliff were numerous, frequently overflowing, and many were affected by the word."[76] However, as James Wood recorded, Taylor's visits to the Assembly saw him again become "intimately acquainted with the diversity of opinion which had caused him so much altercation" as he

71. Dan Taylor, "Letter II to Gilbert Boyce," 25 May 1793, in Taylor, *Memoirs*, 273. Despite Taylor's praise, it will be noted throughout this book, such as in chapter 3, that some of his theological beliefs differed from those held by earlier General Baptist proponents of orthodoxy.

72. See Wood, *Condensed History*, 145–50. Reconciliation was reached in 1704 but this lasted only a few years. The General Association was then re-established and the two bodies functioned separately until their coming together in 1731.

73. See Dan Taylor, *Faithful and Wise*.

74. Taylor, *Faithful and Wise*, 16.

75. Jarvis, "Gilbert Boyce," 76.

76. Taylor, *Memoirs*, 27.

preached the gospel.[77] This in turn contributed to his continued determination to uphold the core tenets of his soteriology.

To summarize, when Taylor joined the General Baptists he was exposed to a range of soteriological beliefs that differed from his evangelical convictions. Most striking was how some believers had replaced a commitment to Christ as the only means of salvation with an emphasis on moral obedience. In line with the nature of his evangelicalism, it was Taylor's concern at the implications that this belief might have on effective evangelism that motivated him to provide a defense of his understanding of the faith. Rather than engage in detailed doctrinal examination, his commitment to preaching what he viewed as "the whole gospel" saw him instead prioritize the adoption of a simplicity of faith where believers occupied themselves with the plain message of the Scriptures. These emphases were crucial to his foundational apologetic position and accorded with both the innovative and pragmatic nature of evangelicalism. As will be argued next, these tendencies were also evident in Taylor's understanding of God's moral governance.

Taylor's Advocacy of God's Moral Governance

"to appease divine justice and remove that wrath
which was otherwise our desert"

Taylor first attempted to outline his soteriology in his 1772 *The Scriptural Account of the Way of Salvation*.[78] His motivation was apologetic. This was reflected in his stipulation that "The opposition which has lately been made against the plainest and weighty truths of the gospel" meant that "If ever there was a time for the servants of Jesus, to contend for the faith once delivered to the saints, it is surely needful at present."[79] He was particularly concerned by the teachings of William Graham—a Unitarian minister in the West Riding and close friend and provider of religious counsel to the influential Joseph Priestley.[80] Graham embraced Unitarianism in the 1750s while minister at Warley near Halifax, and then moved to Halifax in 1763 to assist the minister of Northgate End Unitarian Chapel.[81] In 1771,

---

77. Wood, *Condensed History*, 175.

78. Dan Taylor, *Scriptural Account*.

79. Taylor, *Scriptural Account: Important Doctrines*, 2.

80. It was during Priestley's theological transition from Calvinism to Unitarianism in the early 1750s that he came into contact with Graham whose open defense of Unitarianism commanded his respect, see Wykes, "Joseph Priestley," 23.

81. The background and significance of Graham is noted by John Hargreaves in

he preached a notorious sermon entitled *Repentance the Only Condition of Final Acceptance* to a gathering of dissenting ministers at Priestley's Unitarian chapel in Leeds.[82] Graham rejected Christ's identity as the Son of God, and viewed repentance as demonstrated in "personal virtue" as the only means of salvation.[83] These beliefs were similar to those held by the General Baptists who Taylor judged as having embraced Socinianism. Taylor held Unitarianism and Socinianism as synonymous.[84] He read Graham's sermon soon after its publication and unhesitatingly declared it as symptomatic of "the virulence with which Mr. Graham has attacked the defenders of some fundamental gospel truths."[85] He also attached a specific response to Graham's sermon as a second part of *The Scriptural Account*.[86] Taylor was emphatic that "one can never enjoy eternal life by your own works," and that to believe otherwise was "contrary to the immaculate holiness of God."[87] These convictions reflected Taylor's understanding of grace and faith that he had acquired in his embracing of evangelicalism, and which had led him to make a transition from a merit based understanding of salvation to the crucicentrism that lay at the movement's core.

As Taylor commenced *The Scriptural Account* he was determined to expose what he viewed as the fallacy of trusting in approaches to salvation that depicted Christ as no more than an example to be followed. He immediately expressed the need for a grasp of what "the Scripture teaches concerning yourself and your only Saviour."[88] With this in mind, he outlined that people's depravity and situation of guilt before God meant humankind was a naturally "helpless creature."[89] Therefore salvation was only acquired as a free gift through faith in the atoning work of the fully human and yet fully divine Christ.[90] He emphasized how people's natural propensity "to desire, think, or

his examination of religious life in Halifax, Hargreaves, "Religion and Society," 112–13, 125, 127.

82. Graham, *Repentance*.

83. Ibid., 35.

84. The continuity between Socinianism and Unitarianism is a point of debate, although many contemporary commentators would contest Taylor's understanding of them as synonymous. Mortimer provides a good overview of the positions assumed by different scholars on this matter, see Mortimer, *Reason and Religion*, 4–10.

85. Taylor, *Scriptural Account: Important Doctrines*, 2.

86. Taylor, *Scriptural Account: Examination of a Sermon*.

87. Ibid., 7, 9.

88. Taylor, *Scriptural Account: Important Doctrines*, 6.

89. Ibid., 6.

90. Ibid. The way in which Taylor defended Christ's deity is considered in the final section of this chapter.

indulge" fell far short from the demands of God's law.[91] He reasoned that it was this which the apostle Paul pointed to when describing people as "by nature children of wrath."[92] In Taylor's 1775 *Fundamentals of Religion in Faith and Practice* which, after *The Scriptural Account*, provides the most detailed insights into his soteriology, he reinforced his understanding of a person's natural inability to live fully in accordance with God's law by claiming this was even impossible for believers.[93] As an example, he cited Paul's description in Romans chapter seven of his struggles with sin as a believer.[94] Taylor's interpretation of this passage highlights the inaccuracy of claims by those, such as Andrew Fuller, that Taylor's thinking was in accordance with the influential Dutch theologian James Arminius.[95] In contrast to Taylor, Arminius understood Paul to have been referring to his experience before he was a Christian, with the passage therefore only applicable to non-believers.[96] Despite it having become a common characteristic of Arminianism that believers could lose their salvation, there is no indication in any of Taylor's soteriological works that he doubted the doctrine of the final perseverance of the saints. As implied throughout *The Scriptural Account*, Taylor instead wrote in terms of a believer's passage to glory being a certainty.[97] The way Taylor demonstrated his independent soteriological thinking by holding convictions not commonly associated with non-Calvinists was in keeping with the propensity for innovation that was found within evangelicalism and the wider context of the English Enlightenment.

It was in *The Scriptural Account* that Taylor, for the first time in his published works, employed his favorite metaphor of God as moral governor.[98] Both here, and in all his wider writings, it was this which formed

91. Ibid., 8.

92. Ibid., 9. Taylor was referring to Eph 2:3.

93. Dan Taylor, *Fundamentals*, 81.

94. Ibid., 81.

95. For Fuller's associating of Taylor with the thinking of Arminius, see Fuller, *Reply*, 2.

96. Arminius delineated his understanding of this passage in his dissertation on Rom 7. He was specific that "the apostle, in this passage, is not treating about a man that is already regenerate through the Spirit of Christ, but has assumed the person of a man who is not yet regenerate," see Arminius, *Dissertation*, 221.

97. Arminius was generally not explicit on this matter. This was evident when in his examination of certain controversial passages of Scripture he asked "is it possible for true believers to fall away totally and finally." In his response, he stipulated that to view this as impossible should not be considered "heretical opinion," but that to consider it as possible "has always had more supporters," see Arminius, *Certain Articles*, 502–3. This aspect of Taylor's soteriology will be examined further in chapter 4.

98. Taylor, *Scriptural Account: Important Doctrines*, 10.

his overarching soteriological motif. His first written reference to God's moral governance was in a 1771 letter to his fellow New Connexion minister George Birley, where he stated that "all men are considered simply as the creatures of God as the creator of all and as the subjects of his moral government."[99] Taylor delineated his understanding of this in *The Scriptural Account*. He emphasized that the "only standard of moral good and evil" was God himself as "moral governor" of humankind.[100] He in turn argued that God therefore had the right to be served by all people as his subjects. This required that,

> Every power, passion and faculty of the inner man, should be only, wholly, and at all times, fixed on, and engaged for God; and that we should always feel the same tender concern, and warm affection, for the person, possessions, interest, reputation, and every thing dear and valuable to our neighbour, as if it was our own.[101]

God as a righteous and just governor was not able to overlook sin. Any deviation from God's law therefore necessitated that humankind was "liable to the curse, condemnation and punishment" which was prescribed for law breakers.[102] With this in mind, Taylor designated the "end and design" of Christ's sufferings and sacrifice as "to appease divine justice, and remove that wrath which was otherwise our desert."[103] In specific response to Graham's view that repentance independent of Christ's salvific work could atone for past offenses, Taylor was unequivocal that such a belief was "absurd and contrary to all rules of good and just government."[104] He also sought to substantiate his position by pointing to the functioning of civil society. In particular, he noted that if it were no longer necessary to punish an offender who had repented and reformed, then respect for all laws would diminish.[105] Such an approach was typical of how Taylor's apologetic reasoning was characterized by a pragmatic rather than metaphysical orientation. Taylor's rejection of metaphysical reasoning in favor of pragmatism was a common feature of evangelicalism.

Taylor's understanding of God's moral governance as a focal point of his soteriological thinking was again evident as he encouraged the believers

99. Dan Taylor, "Letter to George Birley," 24 June 1771. Page not numbered.

100. Taylor, *Scriptural Account: Important Doctrines*, 10.

101. Ibid., 7.

102. Ibid., 18.

103. Ibid., 19.

104. Ibid., 11.

105. Ibid.

at Birchcliff to resist understandings of salvation which were contrary to that stipulated in the Scriptures. This is evident within *Fundamentals* which comprises an extension of the main subjects he taught at the church between 1762–75. After Taylor dismissed as "mere nothings" methods of obtaining salvation such as a reliance on the piety of parents; possessing a Christian name; professing the Christian faith; having extraordinary gifts; abstaining from crime; and strict observance of all religious or moral duties, he outlined his core framework of salvific understanding.[106] Again, his starting place was God's representation in the Scriptures as "the moral governor of the world, who has given a law to man, by which his temper and conduct are to be regulated."[107] He in turn likened humanity's rejection of this law to "rebellion against the best of kings" and, drawing on the image of an earthly monarch, considered the punishment that befit such a rebellion.[108] His conclusion was that the punishment should be in proportion to the monarch's supremacy. He reasoned that the only reprimand appropriate for sin committed against the eternal God was an "infinite duration of pain and anguish."[109] Crucially, God's compassion was such that "he gave his own dear Son, to be a sacrifice in our stead" with his death serving "to appease the divine anger," and thereby providing "a compensation for our offences" so that all might enjoy a free pardon.[110] Taylor emphasized, that this solution to humankind's condition meant "that God might be just, and maintain the most inviolable regard to his law and governing authority, and yet justify every believing sinner."[111] In his letter to Graham, Taylor also highlighted the appropriateness of God's method of salvation reflecting his divine attributes of justice and mercy. He urged Graham to recognize that God's gift of his Son was both "the fullest and richest display of mercy that the human mind can conceive of" and yet provided "the most complete satisfaction to divine justice."[112] Taylor's sense of marvel at how this means of salvation served to honor God's moral governance was apparent every time he addressed the subject.

While theologians, such as fourth-century Archbishop of Constantinople, Gregory of Nazianzus and the thirteenth-century Franciscan John

---

106. Taylor, *Fundamentals*, 119.

107. Ibid., 170.

108. Ibid., 171.

109. Ibid.

110. Ibid., 171, 173, 171.

111. Ibid., 180.

112. Taylor, *Scriptural Account: Examination of a Sermon*, 49.

Duns Scotus, provided reflections on the nature of God's governance,[113] its influence on modern atonement thinking was primarily extended through the writings of the Dutch jurist, statesman, and early Remonstrant leader, Hugo Grotius.[114] His principal work, *A Defence of the Catholick Faith Concerning the Satisfaction of Christ*, saw him use the language and semantics of government acquired during his training in law, to articulate an atonement standpoint that was founded on an understanding of God as moral governor.[115] Taylor's awareness of Grotius's teaching was evident from his diary. For example, on 10 November 1769 he spent all day "reading of the learned Grotius."[116] He also referred to Grotius in his wider works. For instance, when arguing in his letter to Graham that Jesus's suffering for sin was caused by the evil of humanity's sins, he included a footnote where he directly quoted Grotius in Latin from an unnamed source.[117] A form of Grotius's governmental theory was adopted by some New England theologians and former pupils of Jonathan Edwards such as Joseph Bellamy and Samuel Hopkins (later known as the New Divinity movement).[118] One of the reasons why moral government thinking resonated with these theologians from New England and those they influenced was because it was congruent with cultural trends.[119] Others such as Utilitarian philosopher Jeremy Bentham and influential Italian philosopher and jurist Cesare Beccaria adopted a similar intellectual framework.[120] However, there is no evidence that Taylor was influenced by any of these writers. While the New Divinity movement influenced Andrew Fuller in his modification of his soteriology in the 1790s, as highlighted by Peter Morden, the same was not true for

---

113. Gregory of Nazianzus believed that the sufferings of Christ were necessary to God's governance. He declared, "Is it not plain that the Father received the ransom, not because He Himself required or needed it, but for the sake of the Divine government of the universe, and because man must be sanctified through the incarnation of the Son of God?" Gregory of Nazianzus. Qtd in Gordon Olson, *Truth Shall Make You Free*, 99. Primary source unknown. For an examination of the moral governance thinking of John Duns Scotus, see Richard Cross, "Duns Scotus," 48–76.

114. For an overview of the life of Grotius, see C. Butler, *Life of Hugo Grotius*. See also, Nellen and Rabbie, *Hugo Grotius*. The contributors to this work examine a range of Grotius's works and consider the scope of his theological influence.

115. Grotius, *Defence of the Catholick Faith*.

116. Dan Taylor, diary entry, 10 November 1769, in Taylor, *Memoirs*, 71.

117. Taylor, *Scriptural Account: Examination of a Sermon*, 39.

118. For more on the New Divinity movement, see Conforti, *Samuel Hopkins*. See also, Foster, *Genetic History*, 107–223.

119. See, e.g., Bebbington, "British Baptist Crucicentrism," 230–31.

120. Ibid.

Taylor.[121] Despite Taylor's works containing reference to many theological and historical publications, none appear to have emanated from within the New Divinity movement.

While it is possible that Taylor read Grotius's *A Defence of the Catholick Faith*,[122] he more likely became familiar with Grotius's governmental theory through secondary publications. For instance, in his letter to Graham he mentioned the English scholar Anthony Blackwall's 1725 *The Sacred Classics Defended and Illustrated* which included numerous references to the "learned," "excellent" and "esteemed" Grotius.[123] Given that Taylor's earlier cited diary reference to Grotius appears to allude to a biographical work, it is possible he read *The Life of the Truly Eminent and Learned Hugo Grotius* by Jean Lévesque de Burigny which was printed in English in 1754 and was the leading work of its kind.[124] If, as seems probable, Taylor in the early 1770s was unaware of the governmental theory of the atonement propounded by the New England theologians, yet chose to utilize Grotius's metaphor of God as moral governor from what he read, then this demonstrates significant initiative.[125]

When compared to Grotius's theory of the atonement, Taylor's governmental perspective contained certain parallels of theme, emphasis, and language. Grotius for example insisted on the impossibility of God overlooking sin as this would have contravened his status as moral governor.[126] Similar to Taylor, Grotius described Christ's death as a manifestation of God's displeasure against sin and as the means by which his forgiveness was rendered consistent with the interests of his governance.[127] However,

---

121. Morden, *Offering Christ*, 89–92.

122. That it was written in Latin does not preclude this possibility as Taylor was taught Latin through the tutelage of Titus Knight, see chapter 1.

123. Blackwall, *Sacred Classics*, 19, 20, 141. For a typical instance of Taylor's utilization of this work by Blackwall, see Taylor, *Scriptural Account: Examination of a Sermon*, 70.

124. Lévesque de Burigny, *Life of Hugo Grotius*.

125. Taylor's attention may have been drawn to Grotius's *Defence of the Catholick Faith* due to a knowledge that Grotius was also responding to the challenge posed by Socinianism, particularly Fausto Socinus's contention that Christ's atonement was unnecessary as God could have chosen to overlook sin. For more reflection on the context that motivated Grotius to write and the nature of his engagement, see Blom, "Grotius and Socinianism," 243.

126. Blom argues that Grotius "skilfully combines a critique of Socinianism with a defense of his own Remonstrant position," see Blom, "Grotius and Socinianism," 124–25.

127. H. D. McDonald noted Grotius's concern that, "if the law were completely abrogated, then its authority would be endangered and the forgiveness of sin regarded as too easy an affair," see McDonald, *Atonement*, 77.

while Taylor shared Grotius's core belief that God's moral government was vindicated by Christ's death, a crucial difference was that Taylor did not view Christ's atonement as necessary for this reason alone. Whereas Grotius had stood apart from the penal substitution view of the atonement which, particularly through the influence of John Calvin, had dominated the thinking of the Reformers, Puritans, and large sections of Separatism, Taylor argued that Christ had been punished for sin. Taylor urged Graham to recognize that when the Scriptures spoke of Christ having "suffered" for humanity's sins and being "wounded," "bruised," and "stricken," that they "naturally convey to us the idea of punishment for our sins."[128] He similarly stated that the biblical language of Jesus having "borne our sins, died for our sins, and having been made a propitiation and curse for humankind" served further to "illustrate and corroborate" the "generally received idea of punishment."[129] This view contrasted with Grotius's understanding of Christ's sufferings and death as not the actual punishment of the law, but as a representative non-penal substitute.[130]

It is important to recognize that whereas Grotius rejected propitiatory understandings of Christ's atonement as a sacrificial ransom that paid humankind's debt before God,[131] Taylor insisted that to preach Christ was to make clear that "he came to give his life a ransom for many."[132] In his earlier cited 1771 letter to Birley in which he mentioned God's moral governance, he also noted that "Jesus Christ has died for them to deliver them, to save them from their misery and to deliver or ransom them from the hand of inflexible justice."[133] Again extending beyond what Grotius posited, Taylor asserted that as well as Christ's death maintaining the honor of God's law and governance, it was also "vicarious and efficacious."[134] He cited Scriptures such as Rom 5:19,[135] and drew attention to how a person who responds in faith to Christ has the "well-grounded assurance, that God imputes unto

128. Taylor, *Scriptural Account: Examination of a Sermon*, 37. Taylor's assertion was in response to Graham's claim that Christ's being punished when he had committed no wrong was a "horrid and blasphemous" doctrine, see Graham, *Repentance*, 17.

129. Taylor, *Scriptural Account: Examination of a Sermon*, 39.

130. Grotius, *Defence of the Catholick Faith*, 315.

131. Taylor, *Scriptural Account: Examination of a Sermon*, 29. For consideration of Grotius's rejection of propitiatory understandings, see R. Olson, *Arminian Theology*, 230.

132. Ibid.

133. Taylor, "Letter to George Birley," 24 June 1771. Page not numbered.

134. Taylor, *Scriptural Account: Examination of a Sermon*, 29.

135. Rom 5:19: "For just as through the disobedience of the one man the many were made sinners, so also through the obedience of the one man the many will be made righteous."

you righteousness without works" and that "Christ's righteousness, and not his own, shall screen him from the wrath that is to come."[136] While Taylor creatively crafted his soteriological thinking around Grotius's central point of God as moral governor, his understanding of God's governance was underpinned by a far broader atonement perspective.

Rather than Taylor fully embracing the governmental theory of the atonement as postulated by Grotius, he instead fused elements of the governmental view to substitutionary and penal understandings of the atonement. This approach was in keeping with the way in which other leading eighteenth-century evangelicals creatively held together different elements of atonement thought. For example, Randy Maddox demonstrates John Wesley to have embraced a "blend of traditional explanations" regarding the atonement.[137] Maddox's examination of the primary material leads him to conclude his summary of Wesley's understanding of the atonement, with the assertion that "One is tempted to describe this as a Penalty Satisfaction *explanation* of the Atonement which has a Moral Influence *purpose*, and a Ransom *effect!*"[138] Some Methodist scholars have also pointed to the influence of Grotius's advocacy of God's moral governance on Wesley, although others have contested this.[139] While the fact that the governmental theory was based on a general view of the atonement meant that forms of the doctrine were often popular among those labeled "Arminians," its use was not restricted to evangelicals of this persuasion.[140] As noted earlier, the Calvinist Andrew Fuller engaged creatively with the theory. Taylor's eclectic outlook regarding governmentalism should therefore be understood as reflecting wider tendencies of evangelical thinking regarding the atonement. However, within the context of eighteenth-century Baptists (both General and Particular), Taylor appears to have been the first to have fused governmentalism with a penal approach to the atonement. Although not proven, it is conceivable that Taylor's viewpoint influenced Fuller.[141]

136. Taylor, *Scriptural Account: Examination of a Sermon*, 23, 32.

137. Maddox, *Responsible Grace*, 103.

138. Ibid., 109; Maddox's emphasis.

139. Ibid., 108, 308n88. While Maddox does not consider there to be explicit evidence of its influence on Wesley, he cites some scholars who have suggested otherwise.

140. It should be noted that Arminius, despite having taught Grotius at the University of Leiden, does not appear to have held to the theory. He instead maintained a strong commitment to an atonement perspective in which he believed, as John Hicks asserts, that "Christ suffered both the temporal and eternal punishments of sin for all sinners and satisfied those penalties." See Hicks, "Theology of Grace," 75. Qtd in Olson, *Arminian Theology*, 230.

141. Taylor's influence on Fuller will be considered in chapter 4.

Taylor's pragmatic inclination was important in his adoption of his catholic soteriological position. This accounts for why he did not recognize there to be any tension in embracing particular aspects of certain doctrinal positions while disregarding other supposed "standard" elements of the same theological outlooks. His apparent rejection of the view that believers could lose their salvation alongside his belief in a general view of the atonement is an example of this. It was likely that Taylor's pragmatic awareness of Socinian and Unitarian views surrounding the perceived injustice of Christ being punished for humankind's sin accounted for why it was only in his response to Graham's rejection of penal substitution that he specifically referred to punishment. Instead, in the first part of *The Scriptural Account*, in *Fundamentals* and on most other occasions, he used the language of Christ's "sufferings," with this term less likely to dissuade people from engaging with his wider evangelical convictions. This pragmatism accorded with the general nature of evangelicalism.

In summary, Taylor in *The Scriptural Account* strongly refuted the Socinian inspired doctrines of salvation that advocated a person's sincerity or moral character as a basis on which people could be saved. With reference to the depravity of the human condition, Taylor firstly highlighted the hopelessness of trusting in means of salvation outside of the atoning work of Christ. His reasoning demonstrated examples of innovative thinking as he outlined certain beliefs that were distinct from those of Arminius and were commonly embraced by non-Calvinists. Taylor's understanding of how Christ's atoning work vindicated God's moral governance was pivotal to his defense of his soteriological convictions. He understood God's giving of his Son as a sacrifice for sin as preserving the authority of God's government and law, and therefore demonstrating his rule of justice to his subjects. In employing this governmental metaphor, Taylor was indirectly influenced by the works of Hugo Grotius. Compared to Grotius, Taylor exhibited a greater breadth of perspective, particularly in the pragmatic and creative fusion of his governmental approach with a substitutionary penal understanding. The next section will demonstrate that an Enlightenment-inspired respect for the dictates of reason underpinned Taylor's defense of these convictions.

Taylor's Advocacy of Reason

"grand office of reason"

A notable feature of David Bebbington's *Evangelicalism in Modern Britain* is the cogency with which he argues against customary portrayals of evangelicalism as a fundamentalist reaction to the pre-eminence placed on reason within the Enlightenment.[142] While many such as Edward Thompson have depicted evangelicalism as "self-consciously anti-Enlightenment" and "strongly anti-intellectual,"[143] Bebbington instead claims that "its emergence was itself an expression of the age of reason."[144] Even some who contest Bebbington's portrayal of the extent of evangelicalism's distinctiveness have commended this aspect of his framework. An example is Michael Haykin who highlights Bebbington's "clear evidence of positive cross-fertilization and interaction between our eighteenth-century evangelical forebears and their culture."[145] Bebbington's claim is substantiated by an endorsement of reason across the spectrum of eighteenth-century evangelicalism. For example, John Wesley cited the "fundamental principle" that "religion and reason go hand in hand."[146] Similarly, Henry Rack, in his examination of Wesley's response to the Enlightenment, draws attention to how he commended reason for "laying the foundation of true religion, under the guidance of the Spirit of God."[147] Other examples include the Independent minister Thomas Gibbons's poem on the subject of *A Religious, the Only Reasonable Life; or Reason and Religion the Same,*[148] and Andrew Fuller's affirmation that "Faith and right reason are not at variance."[149] As will be demonstrated, Taylor's soteriological framework also included a high regard for the use of reason.

An example of the primacy Taylor placed on reason was his understanding that God's moral governance (as delineated in the previous section) was based on the premise that God's working in the world was always ordered and logical and therefore able to be reflected on rationally. Taylor's perception of God creating a natural order that was designed to function

---

142. Bebbington, *Evangelicalism*, 50–69.

143. Thompson, *Making of the English*, 738.

144. Bebbington, *Evangelicalism*, 53.

145. Haykin, "Evangelicalism," 48.

146. John Wesley, "Letter to Dr. Thomas Rutherforth," 364. For further consideration of Enlightenment influences on Wesley, see Gregory, "Religion," 19–54.

147. John Wesley, *Reason Impartially Considered*, 599. Qtd in Rack, "Man of Reason and Religion?" 6–7.

148. This work is highlighted by David Bebbington, see Bebbington, *Evangelicalism*, 53.

149. Andrew Fuller, "XXXV.—The choice of Moses," 658.

on the principles of reason was evident whenever he referred to God's governance. This is apparent in *Fundamentals* where, in reference to God's workings, he notes "as he is a righteous governor of his *rational* creatures, it appears *very proper* that he should keep up the authority of his government and law, by punishing transgressors."[150] The ordered nature of God's conduct was such that Taylor believed his manner of governance could be predicted with near certainty. This conviction was central to his *Cause of National Calamities and the Certain Means of Preventing or Removing Them.*[151] A typical example was his confident generalization that "God, in his judicial proceedings, towards nations, as the Sovereign, and moral Governor of the world, smiles upon any Kingdom" where there can be found a "generosity of temper," and "piety, and benevolence" but "frowns" on the wicked.[152] Taylor's consistent representation of God's governance in almost mechanical "cause and effect" terms, points to the influence of Newtonian laws of universal order and reason which were dominant in eighteenth-century society.

Despite Taylor's belief that rational tendencies unfettered by scriptural parameters contributed to the embracing of theological error among General Baptists, this did not prevent him from commending humankind's rational abilities. While he stipulated that people "Must have a greater light than reason to direct us to a Saviour," he was unreserved in his praise for the "grand office of reason."[153] This was explicit in *The Absolute Necessity* where he contended that "reason and the common notion we have of things" should help people to conclude that they fall short of God's holiness.[154] He also urged that it should promote an understanding of how "Irrational is it to imagine" that those who offended God's law were not guilty of causing him offense, and that they therefore required a Savior.[155] Taylor believed that the process of submission to divine revelation was complemented by a rational means of approach. This differed from the position commonly assumed by Puritans. Even among what John Spurr refers to as the "Arminian Puritanism" that was expounded by those such as the seventeenth-century poet and polemicist John Milton, and preacher and theologian John Goodwin, a sensitivity concerning the corrupting effects of sin led to a refusal

---

150. Taylor, *Fundamentals*, 170; italics added.

151. Dan Taylor, *Cause of National Calamities.*

152. Ibid., 6, 26, 25, 26.

153. Taylor, *Absolute Necessity*, 19–20; Taylor, *Scriptural Account: Important Doctrines*, 8.

154. Taylor, *Absolute Necessity*, 19.

155. Ibid.

to commend the benefits of rational thinking in the salvific process.[156] For example, while Milton resisted strictly deterministic understandings of salvation, his emphasis on the corrupting influences of the "general depravity of the human mind and its propensity to sin" meant that he did not attribute specific credence to humankind's rational abilities.[157] Although Taylor, as noted earlier, recognized the "misery of man by nature," his positive endorsement of humankind's rational capacity reflected his refusal to accept that a person's depraved nature restricted their ability to respond in reasoned manner to the message of the gospel.[158]

The importance Taylor attributed to humankind's faculty for effective reasoning was apparent in *The Scriptural Account* where he declared,

> God has made you a rational creature; capable of thinking, reasoning and judging. No proof of this appears necessary. Your own conscience bears testimony to the truth of it, as you daily feel yourself possest of a capacity for these exercises.[159]

He provided further insight into his understanding of the link between reason and revelation as he emphasized that the most natural orientation of humankind's extensive capability for reasoning was "to receive and embrace" divine revelation as found in the Scriptures.[160] His position was encapsulated effectively in his stipulation that,

> *Reason* itself shews, that a man who sets up his HOWS, and his WHYS, when the Scriptures assert and declare, instead of meekly submitting to, and humbly embracing divine truth acts in a manner quite inconsistent with the character of a *rational* being.[161]

Taylor then brought his thoughts on this subject to a close by emphasizing his conviction that "the revelation of God, is superior to the reason of man."[162] As noted earlier, when Taylor wrote this work he primarily had in mind those of Socinian and Unitarian persuasion, who he accused of placing too high an authority on reason as distinct from revelation. There-

---

156. Spurr, "Later Stuart Puritanism," 101.

157. John Milton, *Treatise on Christian Doctrine*, 348. It appears that this work was not published during Milton's lifetime but a manuscript of the text was found in 1823 and it was then published.

158. Taylor, diary entry, 1 January 1765, 55.

159. Taylor, *Scriptural Account: Important Doctrines*, 6.

160. Ibid., 5.

161. Ibid., 8; Taylor's emphasis.

162. Ibid.

fore, it might have been expected that he would begin with an endorsement of his belief in the primacy of revelation. Instead, it is significant that he first sought to apply to his apologetic advantage his understanding of God having designed humankind with rational faculties that Leaned themselves to an embracing of revelation.

Taylor's distinctive approach to reason and revelation is apparent when compared to the way certain Latitudinarian scholars attempted to uphold the reasonableness of divine revelation. Most notable were the eighteenth-century religious apologist Bishop Joseph Butler and philosopher Samuel Clarke. Through rational means they refuted the claim of deists such as John Toland, Anthony Collins, and Matthew Tindal that the attributes of God could be so exhaustively ascertained from the natural world that the necessity of supernatural revelation was superseded. Butler maintained that natural and revealed religion were so intertwined that the truths of natural theology provided a basis for aspects of the Christian faith, such as miracles, the Incarnation, and redemption.[163] Similarly, Clarke contended that the wisdom, power, and even the goodness of God were demonstrable by the processes of natural theology.[164] The moral philosophy, theological abstractionism, and sense of the Scriptures as only a supplement to natural knowledge that dominated the rationalistic perspectives of Butler and Clarke, differed from Taylor's advocacy of reason as an aid to an appropriate response to God's revelation found in the Scriptures and person of Christ. Maddox's description of John Wesley's understanding of reason is equally applicable to Taylor, "It was not another source of revelation supplementing that of creation or the Bible, it was 'the candle of the Lord' given to help us appropriate revelation."[165] This evangelical approach to reason was distinct from the Latitudinarian outlook.

The compatibility between reason and revelation advocated by Taylor in his soteriological framework was underpinned by his references to influential Enlightenment writers. For example, when he emphasized in *The Scriptural Account* the need to submit to that which the Scriptures taught concerning salvation, he pointed his readers to the "celebrated Poet" Alexander Pope.[166] He highlighted Pope's description within his 1734 *Essay on Man* that "to reason RIGHT, IS TO SUBMIT" to God.[167] Taylor heaped

163. See J. Butler, *Analogy of Religion*. See also, Duncan-Jones, *Butler's Moral Philosophy*.

164. See Clarke, *Discourse*. See also Whiston, *Historical Memoirs*.

165. Maddox, *Responsible Grace*, 109. Maddox is quoting a phrase used by John Wesley, see John Wesley, Sermon 70: *Case of Reason*, 599.

166. Taylor, *Scriptural Account: Important Doctrines*, 5.

167. Pope, *Essay on Man*, 32. Qtd in Taylor, *Scriptural Account: Important Doctrines*,

even greater praise on John Locke whose works made possible some of the most radical and progressive advances of the seventeenth century.[168] Given Locke's centrality to the English Enlightenment and influence on Voltaire and Rousseau, it was appropriate that Taylor hailed him as the "consummate Philosopher."[169] In his letter to Graham, Taylor drew upon Locke's 1695 *The Reasonableness of Christianity* which became the "unofficial lexicon of the Christian Enlightenment."[170]

The catalyst to this work was Locke seeing a pre-publication copy of Toland's *Christianity not Mysterious*.[171] Different from the Deism of Toland and the thinking of Taylor's Socinian opponents, Taylor was struck by Locke's insistence that the message of Scripture could not be contrary to reason but that some truths lay beyond the unaided power of reason. As Cragg notes,

> Locke did not restrict knowledge to the things which the human mind can grasp; he acknowledged that some truths are above reason—though never contrary to it. He allowed a place for the supernatural order and for divine revelation. But he was a rationalist in that he insisted that all truths must be ultimately judged by reason.[172]

Taylor employed a Lockean framework when explaining to Graham that "we ought to exercise reason and common sense to the utmost of our power, in passing a judgement on the truth revealed in Scripture."[173] He argued that claims of biblical truth must be rooted in whether "God has revealed" them and if there "be a divine fitness in them."[174] Taylor, in turn, cited Locke's instruction that "it is enough to justify the fitness of any thing to be done, by resolving it into the wisdom of God who has done it; where-of our narrow understandings and short views may utterly incapacitate

---

5; Taylor's emphasis.

168. For the influence of Locke, see Aaron, *John Locke*, 302.

169. Taylor, *Scriptural Account: Examination of a Sermon*, 5.

170. Rosenblatt, "Christian Enlightenment," 285. Locke, *Reasonableness of Christianity*. For Taylor's first reference to this work, see Taylor, *Scriptural Account: Examination of a Sermon*, 46.

171. Toland, *Christianity not Mysterious*. For an examination of the context that gave rise to Locke's *Reasonableness of Christianity*, see Jacob, "Enlightenment Critique of Christianity," 269.

172. Cragg, *Reason and Authority*, 8. The accuracy of Cragg's assertion is suggested by my subsequent provision of references from certain of Locke's works in this section.

173. Taylor, *Scriptural Account: Examination of a Sermon*, 45.

174. Ibid., 46.

us to judge."[175] There were differences between Locke and Taylor, such as how Locke did not embrace a fully Trinitarian perspective,[176] and Locke's dismissal of religious enthusiasm as "the conceits of a warmed and over-weening brain."[177] However, Locke's exaltation of reason alongside an attempt to uphold the primacy of divine revelation was of undoubted influence on Taylor.

Taylor again placed importance on Locke in his 1790 *An Essay on the Truth and Inspiration of the Holy Scriptures*.[178] Taylor's recent engagement with the Universalist American Baptist minister Elhanan Winchester gave him a new determination to challenge what he held as "bold and assiduous attempts" to undermine the divine authority of the Scriptures.[179] Taylor directed his readers to Locke's "masterwork"—his 1690 *An Essay Concerning Human Understanding*.[180] As Isaac Kramnick observes, this saw Locke "set forth what would become the Enlightenment's dominant conception of the mind: a blank state on which the sensations provided by sensory experience produce ideas."[181] Taylor found Locke's delineation of knowledge and opinion in Book IV of his *Essay* particularly helpful, especially that deemed by Locke as sufficient for a particular matter to be considered a fact.[182] Taylor accurately summarized certain factors that Locke stated as essential, such as "A sufficient number of witnesses—the integrity of those witnesses—their skill and understanding—their design—the consistency of the parts, and circumstances of the relation—and the evidence of contrary testimonies."[183] With reference to the Bible, Taylor was firm that these particulars gave rise to "all the evidence of authenticity which can be reasonably desired."[184] Such

175. Locke, *Reasonableness of Christianity*, 134. Qtd in Taylor, *Scriptural Account: Examination of a Sermon*, 46.

176. For consideration of Locke's position on the Trinity, see, e.g., Jacob, "Enlightenment Critique of Christianity," 269. Taylor's Trinitarian understanding is considered in the next section.

177. Locke, *Essay Concerning Human Understanding*, 514.

178. Dan Taylor, *Truth and Inspiration*, 47–49.

179. Taylor, *Memoirs*, 192. Taylor first spoke on this subject at the New Connexion's 1789 annual Association. His discourse with Winchester will be examined in chapter 3.

180. Porter, *Enlightenment*, 60.

181. Kramnick, "Explanatory note, John Locke," 185.

182. Taylor, *Truth and Inspiration*, 48. Taylor was referring to chapter 16 of Locke's *Essay Concerning Human Understanding*, which is entitled "Of The Degrees of Assent," see Locke, *Essay Concerning Human Understanding*, Book IV, 502–10.

183. Ibid.

184. Ibid.

an assertion provides insight into the confidence with which Taylor applied this aspect of Locke's thinking.

The heralding of sensory perception, experience, and "constant observation" as the basis for knowledge which lay at the heart of Locke's empiricism influenced other elements of Taylor's soteriological thinking.[185] A typical example was his use of Lockean terms as he sought to convince Graham that it was through Christ's obedience that believers are made righteous, and that God therefore imputes righteousness as a gift rather than in response to good works.[186] Taylor argued that the appropriateness of God choosing to act in this way was confirmed if people "judge according to the nature of things, or consult our own experience in the matter" as "gratitude is the most animating spring of obedience" and therefore "the most effectual means of promoting obedience to God."[187] This was similar to how Locke, for example, established truth by upholding the merits of "the regular proceedings of causes and effects in the ordinary course of nature" (Locke referred to this as an argument from the "nature of things") and "my own experience, and the agreement of all others that mention it."[188] Taylor's embracing of key elements of Locke's epistemological framework, which in the context of its day was such an original framework of philosophical thinking, should be viewed as a further important aspect of his evangelicalism.

Taylor's examination of the nature of humankind's depravity in his 1785 *Our Saviour's Commission to His Ministers* shows how an empirical outlook was interwoven throughout his salvific thinking.[189] As he substantiated his claim that there was "undeniable proof" for the inherent deviation of the natural human condition away from God, he was explicit that this was evident "from constant observation, from universal experience, and from the current language of Scripture."[190] This statement is again significant. His attempt to affirm his beliefs with reference not only to the Scriptures but to the merits of observation and experience was an approach that was rare within Puritanism. As evident from Charles Hambrick-Stowe's reflections on Puritan spirituality, Puritans tended to rely on the sufficiency of Scripture and associated biblically based spiritual practices as the sole means to be convinced of truth.[191] Reference to observation and experience were

---

185. Locke, *Essay Concerning Human Understanding*, 506.

186. Taylor, *Scriptural Account: Examination of a Sermon*, 20.

187. Ibid., 23, 24.

188. Locke, *Essay Concerning Human Understanding*, 506.

189. Dan Taylor, *Our Saviour's Commission*.

190. Ibid., 7.

191. Hambrick-Stowe, "Practical divinity," 195. An emphasis on observation and

commonplace among evangelicals. For instance, it is notable that William Grimshaw included reference to "the holy Scriptures, reason and *experience*" in his personal creed.[192] John Wesley's approach provides another example. A particular aspect of his emphasis on reason was how, as Robert Wall notes, "He considered close observation of life as foundational for understanding human nature and divine revelation."[193] The readiness with which evangelicals embraced such an understanding can, at least in part, be explained by the influence of the empiricism of those such as Locke, David Hume, and Francis Bacon. In the practice of science and theory of knowledge, this influence gave rise to the new concept of ideas and knowledge originating from within human senses and experiences.[194]

Taylor's position had much in common with what Jonathan Lowe identifies as a prominent aspect of Locke's intention in his *Essay*, namely his determination "to reconcile faith . . . with empirical knowledge and rational inquiry."[195] It was for this reason that Taylor, in *An Essay on the Truth and Inspiration of the Holy Scriptures*, cited Rousseau's pronouncement that "the history of Socrates, which nobody presumes to doubt, is not so well attested, as that of Jesus Christ."[196] Within the same work, Taylor commends as "ingenious" the critique of the religious skepticism of Scottish philosopher David Hume, written by James Beattie in his 1770 *An Essay on the Nature and Immutability of Truth*.[197] Despite Taylor recognizing the apologetic strength of intentionally appealing to observations beyond those recorded in Scripture, there was also a very real sense in which his empiricism was so engrained in him, that it naturally undergirded his theological outlook. It is pertinent to note Bebbington's reflections in respect of John Wesley, that while rejecting the "sceptical Enlightenment" of the continent, "the whole cast of his mind was moulded by the new intellectual currents of his time. Supremely he was an empiricist."[198] David Hempton similarly notes Wesley's "indebtedness to

---

experience is absent from among that which Hambrick-Stowe identifies as central to Puritan spirituality.

192. Grimshaw, "Mr. Grimshaw's Creed," in Newton, *Memoirs*, 183; italics added.

193. R. Wall, "Wesley as Biblical Interpreter," 115.

194. See, e.g., Outram, *Enlightenment*, 93–109.

195. Lowe, "Locke," 370. See also, Lowe, *Locke*.

196. Rousseau, *Expostulatory Letter from J.J. Rousseau*, 48.

197. Taylor, *Truth and Inspiration*, 48; See Beattie, *Nature and Immutability of Truth*. Beattie's *Essay* was very popular, and led to an audience with King George III. For more reflections on the influence of Beattie, see Forbes, *Beattie and His Friends*.

198. Bebbington, *Evangelicalism*, 52.

Lockean empiricism."[199] As has been demonstrated, the same can be said for Taylor and the evangelicalism he espoused.

To summarize, a crucial facet of Taylor's defense of his soteriological convictions was his endorsement of reason and his contention that this complemented an active embracing of divine revelation. Such a position was in keeping with the nature of evangelicalism. It was Taylor's Enlightenment-inspired belief that the natural order was designed to function along the principles of reason, which underpinned his understanding of God's governance. He stated his belief that the workings of human reason should lead people to recognize their situation of guilt before God. The way in which he held the process of submission to divine revelation as aided by a rational means of approach differed from the position typically assumed by Puritans, whose convictions concerning the natural depravity of the human mind often prevented such an outlook. His perspective was also at variance with the near exclusive focus on natural theology which lay at the core of Latitudinarian defenses of divine revelation. Taylor's thinking was influenced significantly by key Enlightenment thinkers such as Locke. The empirical way in which Taylor placed the importance of "observation and experience" alongside the Scriptures, further demonstrated his inventive apologetic outlook. As will be examined next, the frequency with which he stressed the need to view the Scriptures in a straightforward and practical way was a further central aspect of his theological framework.

Taylor's Advocacy of Simplicity

"O give me the spirit of simplicity"

A distinct feature of Taylor's functioning as an apologist was the consistency with which he maintained a succinctness of theological reflection. This contrasted with the style of approach commonly assumed by his General Baptist forebears. An example was the close attention to detail and exhaustive systematic manner adopted by Thomas Grantham in his 1678 publication of *Christianismus Primitivus*. This "mammoth work" is over 600 pages in length with Grantham having "canvassed the whole of Christian doctrine."[200] At his most impassioned, Taylor declared in 1767 "I have now done with preaching on doctrinal points" and instead resolved to be "diligent in illustrating, enforcing and promoting experimental and practical religion."[201] When his

---

199. Hempton, *Methodism*, 41–42.

200. Bass, *Thomas Grantham*, 30.

201. Dan Taylor, diary entry, 31 July 1767, in Taylor, *Memoirs*, 53.

role as overseer of the New Connexion necessitated he engaged with doctrine, the underpinning sentiments of his 1767 declaration still influenced his thinking. This was commonly expressed in his yearning that God would grant him the ability to articulate the core tenets of his soteriology in a straightforward and concise way. The climax of his 1791 prayer "O give me the spirit of simplicity" was typical.[202]

Taylor was committed to focusing on the plain message of the Scriptures. He emphasized this in the preface to *The Absolute Necessity*, stressing that unless there was "plainness" in his text "I cannot think this discourse worthy the notice of the wise."[203] While he was keen to be understood fully by the poor and uneducated, Enlightenment influences were also pertinent. For example, Taylor's approach to the Bible contained similarities to that outlined by Locke in *The Reasonableness of Christianity* where Locke emphasized that the Scriptures were "to be understood in the plain, direct meaning of the words and phrases."[204] There is a similarity between Taylor's stance and Cragg's drawing of attention to Locke's insistence that "Christianity was basically simple in character" and that believers must not therefore search the Scriptures for "abstruse principles" as "the obvious sense is the true one."[205] As will be shown, this remained Taylor's primary way of proceeding even when engaging with complex issues, such as Christ's deity and the nature of the Trinity.

Taylor's early experience of Socinian inspired opposition to Christ's divinity often led him to uphold Christ's deity within his apologetic writings. His commitment to Jesus as "both God and man" was integral to his understanding of the atonement, and specifically to how it enabled God's justice as moral governor to be satisfied.[206] However, his principal defense of Christ's divinity did not stem from its appropriateness in his overarching soteriological framework. It emanated from what he believed was "plainly spoken of" in the Scriptures.[207] This is evident in *The Scriptural Account* where, in characteristically brief manner, he affirmed Christ's deity by focusing exclusively on the Scriptures. In particular, he highlighted certain scriptural titles and terms describing Christ,[208] and drew attention to

202. Dan Taylor, diary entry, 1791 (date not specified), in Taylor, *Memoirs*, 197.

203. Taylor, *Absolute Necessity*, iv.

204. Locke, *Reasonableness of Christianity*, 2.

205. Cragg, *Reason and Authority*, 14.

206. Taylor, *Scriptural Account: Important Doctrines*, 13.

207. Ibid., 13.

208. These included Jesus as Immanuel "GOD with us"; "my Lord and my GOD"; that there dwelt within him "all the fullness of the Godhead, bodily"; Christ's having been described as the "true" and "mighty" God who was "manifest in the flesh," and

Christ's assumption of divine prerogatives unique to God.[209] On the basis of these Scriptures, Taylor was unequivocal that Christ was "absolutely God" and that there was "no God-head, or Divinity, separate from, or superior" to that which Jesus possessed.[210]

Taylor dismissed those who just designated Christ a "mere man" as having "done the Lord of Glory an infinite dishonour" and of being "infinitely short of what the Scripture relates concerning him."[211] While Taylor frequently commended the dictates of reason (as examined earlier) his apologetic approach was underpinned by a belief in the "literal truth and authority of Scripture" which Leanne Van Dyk notes was central to evangelicalism.[212] This conviction differed from Socinian practice where, despite rigorous scriptural study being frequently undertaken (as evident in Graham's writings), an ascendant rationalism meant Socinians were unwilling to accept such a literal biblical hermeneutic. It is conceivable that this point of differentiation was at least, in part, attributable to how the embracing of evangelicalism often involved a notable experiential element, whereas the Socinian platform of faith tended to be almost exclusively cerebral.[213] It is likely that Taylor's experiences as he entered into evangelicalism (see chapter 1) such as his assurance of Christ's closeness, and of the sufficiency of grace for his salvation contributed to his subsequent willingness to accept beliefs that lay beyond the scope of human understanding.

Taylor's evangelical approach to the Scriptures also differed from how Puritans tended to defend the veracity of core gospel truths. Whereas evangelicals, as exemplified by Taylor, upheld the truth of the Scriptures by seeking to convince people of the plainness of the Bible's essential teaching, Puritans characteristically assumed a more detailed and doctrinally rooted apologetic. John Owen's widely respected 1679 *Christologia* was a typical example.[214] Although Owen sought to demonstrate the relevance of Christ's deity to practical Christian duty, he did so from a platform of extensive doctrinal reflection. Through his own insights, and those of a plethora of scholars from the earliest centuries of the church, Owen ad-

---

"over all," see ibid., 14–15. Taylor was respectively quoting Matt 1:23; John 20:28; Col 2:9; 1 John 5:20; Isa 9:6; 1 Tim 3:16; and Rom 9:5.

209. For example, Taylor drew attention to Christ's declaration "I am he who searches hearts and minds," see ibid., 16. Taylor was here referring to Rev 2:23.

210. Ibid., 15.

211. Ibid., 4.

212. Van Dyk, "Church in Evangelical Theology," 128.

213. This was, for example, apparent among many of the General Baptists referred to earlier who had been influenced by Socinianism and opposed Taylor.

214. Owen, *Christologia*.

dressed in precise manner subjects such as Christ's divine nature, how Christ as the Word of God sought to restore the image of God in human-kind, Christ's designation as the foundation of the Father's determined blessing for his elect, the nature of Christ's victory in his human nature, and an examination of Christ's exaltation and priestly mediation in heaven.[215] While Sinclair Ferguson draws attention to how Owen, in his response to Socinianism as propounded by John Biddle, never presented Christ as "a subject for technical analysis," his doctrinal thoroughness was to an extent that was not found among Taylor's works.[216]

Puritans who were regarded by their peers as adopting less rigorous apologetic styles were often more expansive in approach than evangelicals such as Taylor. An example was Thomas Goodwin who was viewed by the Puritan Divine Edmund Calamy (1600–1666) as having a "plain and famil-iar" apologetic style.[217] Yet while Goodwin, similar to Taylor, responded to Socinian opposition to Christ's divinity by focusing on Christ's titles within his publication *Of the Knowledge of God the Father and His Son Jesus Christ*, he did so in exhaustive manner.[218] His examination of Christ as the "Word" and "son" of God involved extensive theological, historical and philosophi-cal reflection.[219] It was this which led Calamy also to acknowledge that Goodwin sometimes assumed a "diffuse" and "tedious" approach.[220] The editors of Goodwin's 1681 works noted that "He had a genius to dive into the bottom of points . . . not contenting himself with superficial knowledge, without wading in the depths of things."[221] This tendency was often evident within Puritanism. Hambrick-Stowe argues that Owen's and Goodwin's works provide examples of how Puritans frequently engaged in "rational expositions of theology," "an examination of doctrines" and that their sermons were often "painstakingly prepared."[222] This differed significantly from Taylor's approach.

Taylor's reluctance to enter into protracted soteriological reflection did not stem from a lack of intellectual interest in wider aspects of theology. His "congenial taste for literature" was apparent from the referenced works

215. For Owen's further development of many of these themes in *Christologia*, see Owen, *Meditations and Discourses*.

216. Ferguson, "John Owen," 72.

217. Calamy, *Nonconformist's Memorial*, 186.

218. T. Goodwin, *Knowledge of God*, in *Works*, vol. 4.

219. Ibid., 404–53.

220. Calamy, *Nonconformist's Memorial*, 219.

221. Owen and Barron, "Preface to the Reader," in T. Goodwin, *Works*, 4:xxix..

222. Hambrick-Stowe, "Practical divinity," 195.

within his publications, and participation in ventures such as his creation of a book society with his close friend Particular Baptist minister John Fawcett Sr. (1740–1817).[223] Taylor's diary contains instances where he self-chastised due to his concern that "I indulge too much curiosity in reading."[224] However, he recognized the need to ensure that "I am not too nice and curious in the pulpit" and to avoid all "unnecessary enquiries, and subtle disquisitions, respecting subjects not to be known, or of little use when they are known."[225] He was convinced that the chief focus of all defenders of the faith should be that "clearly revealed" concerning "the infinite importance of that salvation which is exhibited to man in the gospel."[226] This remained the focal point of all Taylor's apologetic engagements.

Taylor's reluctance to engage in protracted doctrinal reflection was particularly apparent in his 1772 *A Practical Improvement of the Divinity and Atonement of Jesus* which he wrote using the pseudonym Philagathus ("lover of good").[227] He did not state his reason for writing under the guise of Philagathus although the adoption of pseudonyms was common practice. This publication stemmed from his concern that believers might be led astray through the doctrines published in "several small pieces" by "the ingenious writer" Clemens who he identified as Joseph Priestley.[228] While Taylor did not specify the names of Priestley's works that he was referring to, Clemens was a pseudonym that Priestley frequently adopted.[229] Examples include many essays that Priestley contributed to *The Theological Repository* which was a journal he established in 1768.[230] After twelve years away from the West Riding, Priestley returned in 1767 and became minister of Mill Hill

223. Taylor, *Memoirs*, 31. The significance of Taylor's friendship with Fawcett will be considered in chapter 3.

224. Dan Taylor, diary entry, 29 October 1765, in Taylor, *Memoirs*, 43.

225. Ibid; Taylor, *Memoirs of William Thompson*, 79.

226. Taylor, *Memoirs of William Thompson*, 79.

227. Philagathus [Dan Taylor], *Practical Improvement*. Taylor identified himself as Philagathus in a letter to George Birley, see Dan Taylor, "Letter to George Birley," 20 March 1772, 81.

228. Philagathus [Taylor], *Practical Improvement*, 11. Taylor stated in a letter to George Birley that Clemens was a fictitious name for Priestley, see Taylor, "Letter to George Birley," 20 March 1772, 81.

229. For Priestley's use of the pseudonym Clemens, see Schofield, *Joseph Priestley: 1733 to 1773*, 195. For consideration of the later years of Priestley's life, see Schofield, *Joseph Priestley: 1773 to 1804*.

230. For Priestley's commencement of *The Theological Repository* and examples of the contributions which he wrote under the name of Clemens, see Schofield, *Joseph Priestley: 1733 to 1773*, 193, 195.

Chapel, Leeds until 1773.[231] It was during this period that, in addition to his works on electricity and the functioning of government, Priestley completed and published his *Institutes of Natural and Revealed Religion* where he laid out his rejection of Christ's divinity and the virgin birth.[232] This work emphasized the necessity of a strict accord between revelation and natural law and became standard within English Unitarianism. As Taylor responded to Priestley, his characteristic concern that the issues surrounding Christ's divinity should not be reduced to "speculative notions" again caused him to resist providing a full delineation of his thinking.[233] Instead he simply reiterated what he believed the Scriptures taught concerning Christ's divinity, and expressed his hope that this would bring his readers to a place of worship and exaltation of Christ. This included attention to Christ as "the MIGHTY GOD" and "IMMANUEL," and wider aspects of his divine status.[234] He issued an impassioned plea that Priestley might recognize that Christ's "work is all divine," and that he might hear "no more of human dignity and pow'r, but, instead, only a regard for Christ as the sole means through whom sin could be forgiven and sinners brought close to God."[235] Despite writing in verse, these assertions fully encapsulate Taylor's position.

It was a measure of Taylor's stature as a General Baptist minister that when Priestley, in 1788, required a historical account of the General Baptists for his wider writings, it was Taylor he invited to his Birmingham home.[236] Taylor gladly accepted and, despite their theological differences, they enjoyed a cordial time. Priestley "expressed great satisfaction in receiving the information" Taylor provided.[237] They drank wine together and Priestley stated that he had wanted to accompany Taylor to the New Connexion's annual Association meeting in Birmingham, which Taylor chaired on the same visit.[238] Taylor did not use this occasion to challenge Priestley's Unitarianism, thereby showing his reluctance to exploit Priestley's invitation to his own advantage. Taylor's willingness to place respect above doctrinal disagreement was a further notable feature of his evangelicalism. It

---

231. Ibid., 157.

232. Priestley's writings on Christ's divinity and the virgin birth are both found in volume 1 of this publication, see Priestley, *Institutes*, vol. 1.

233. Philagathus [Taylor], *Practical Improvement*, 2.

234. Ibid., 4; Taylor's emphasis.

235. Ibid., 11, 4.

236. See Dan Taylor, "Letter to George Birley," 30 April 1788, 253.

237. Ibid., 254.

238. See ibid. Priestley's wider commitments meant that he was not able to accompany Taylor.

also reflected the greater tendency for irenic debate that was evident within the Enlightenment.

The key distinctions of Taylor's apologetic style were seen in his approach to the doctrine of the Trinity which, as the concomitant of the deity of Christ, was frequently cited in his soteriological writings. From the very outset, his Trinitarian thinking was marked by modesty towards the enormity of the subject. This is evident in a 1767 diary entry where he noted "Much of this day I have spent in thinking concerning the Trinity and the person of the blessed Jesus. But what a subject! How suited to humble our natural pride! Lord humble me more."[239] He adopted the same tone in his largest piece of writing on the subject in a 1770 letter to William Thompson.[240] Thompson had asked for guidance regarding how to explain the precise "personality of the Father, Son and Holy Ghost" to the detractors of his Trinitarianism.[241] While Taylor concurred that the Scriptures "attribute Godhead to each" and yet present a "distinction" between them, he warned against offering prescriptive explanations.[242] He stated,

> I am inclined to believe that it is a matter above human comprehension; and what God has not revealed in his word. Hypotheses may be formed, schemes may be drawn, reasons assigned, supposed representations invented, and parallels run; but I am free to declare, that those who seem most positive and dogmatical seem to me to know the least about the matter.[243]

Bebbington points to this letter, in addition to Taylor's surprising failure to mention the Trinity in his delineation of God's attributes in his 1805 *Catechism*, as indicative of his belief that "there was no need to wrestle with complex and mysterious questions."[244] Bebbington proceeds to highlight the stance taken by Taylor as evidence of "a striking dissimilarity between the prevailing ethos among the seventeenth-century Puritans and the atmosphere of the eighteenth-century Evangelical Revival."[245] The position assumed by Taylor provides a good case in point.

---

239. Dan Taylor, diary entry, 13 February 1767, in Taylor, *Memoirs*, 44.

240. See Taylor, "Letter to William Thompson," 9 July 1770, 139–41.

241. William Thompson. Qtd in Taylor, "Letter to William Thompson," 9 July 1770, 139. Primary source unknown.

242. Taylor, "Letter to William Thompson," 9 July 1770, 139.

243. Ibid., 140.

244. Bebbington, "Response," 431. For the absence of mention of the Trinity in Taylor's *Catechism*, see Dan Taylor, *Catechism*.

245. Ibid.

Taylor was particularly disapproving of those who sought to "invent similies" to explain the Trinity.[246] He was critical of the way that the prominent seventeenth-century Puritan scholar and pastor Richard Baxter drew upon the workings of motion, light and heat as an explanatory aid.[247] Taylor also cited his concern with Puritan John Howe's description of there being "three distinct intelligent hypostases" and Owen's delineation of "the Father as the fountain of deity" from whom the Son and Spirit derived their divine natures.[248] Although Taylor acknowledged that these Trinitarian understandings "set my brains to work," he exercised a strong caution.[249] He asserted, "I am not very willing, in these sacred mysteries to coin new words, lest I should join more or fewer ideas to these words, than my Bible warrants."[250] Taylor accepted that his position could be perceived as a weakness by his opponents who might "accuse me of giving up any part of gospel truth because I pretend not to comprehend incomprehensibles."[251] However, the way in which his evangelicalism comprised such a strong commitment to proclaiming the Scriptures in their simplest form meant that he remained firm in his standpoint.

It is significant that Taylor's defense of the doctrine of the Trinity included reference to the insights of Jeremy Taylor who, as chaplain to Archbishop Laud and Charles I, had opposed Puritanism.[252] It is likely that Dan Taylor was introduced to elements of Jeremy Taylor's teaching during his period within Methodism. Jeremy Taylor's devotional works were respected by the Wesley brothers and aspects of his thinking influenced leading Methodists such as John Fletcher.[253] Both Fletcher in his 1790 defense of Christ's divinity and Taylor in his 1770 letter on the Trinity to Thompson cited Jeremy Taylor's view that,

246. Taylor, "Letter to William Thompson," 9 July 1770, 140. As noted in a footnote in the introductory chapter, the spelling in this quotation is one of many examples where I have followed the spelling found in the source that is quoted from.

247. Ibid. For Baxter's reference to the Trinity as motion, light and heat, see Baxter, *Practical Works*, 374.

248. Howe, *Calm and Sober Inquiry*, 1:149. Qtd in Taylor, "Letter to William Thompson," 9 July 1770, 140; John Owen, *Communion with God*, 61. Qtd in Taylor, "Letter to William Thompson," 9 July 1770, 140.

249. Taylor, "Letter to William Thompson," 9 July 1770, 140.

250. Ibid.

251. Ibid.

252. For Jeremy Taylor's role as an opponent of Puritanism, see New, *Anglican and Puritan*, 56.

253. Jeremy Taylor's influence on John Wesley is highlighted by Bebbington, see Bebbington, *Evangelicalism*, 37–38. For further consideration of Jeremy Taylor, see Streiff, *Reluctant Saint?*

> He who goes about to speak of the mystery of the Trinity, and does it by words, and names of man's invention, talking of essence and existences, hypostases and personalities, priorities in co-equalities, and unity in pluralities, may amuse himself and build a tabernacle in his head; and talk something—he knows not what; but the good man, that feels the power of the Father—to whom the Son is become wisdom, sanctification, and righteousness—and in whose heart the love of the Spirit is shed abroad,—this man, though he understand nothing of what is unintelligible, yet he alone truly understands the Christian doctrine of the Trinity.[254]

Taylor similarly emphasized the limitation of Scripture for understanding the "deep things of God" and particularly its inadequacy for explaining "the nature of that union which subsists in the sacred three."[255] He was firm that it was not God's intention for people to "enter into curious and nice distinctions concerning the manner of his existence."[256] He adopted the same position in his *Essay on the Truth and Inspiration of the Holy Scriptures* where, in reference to the question of how the Father, Son and Spirit were three and yet one, he stated that he was not "called to define it, nor to believe any thing concerning it, further than is asserted in Scripture."[257] Such a minimalistic stance was again distinct from the Trinitarian approach often assumed by Puritans. For instance, Owen in his 1655 *Vindiciae Evangelicae* responded to the perceived threat of Socinianism by providing a detailed exposition of the nature of the communion between the persons of the Trinity and their precise roles within the process of a person's salvation.[258] Compared to Puritan delineations of the Trinity, the narrow confines of Taylor's evangelical approach were a significant feature.

Conclusion

Taylor began as an apologist soon after he joined the General Baptists. A concern regarding Arian, Socinian, and Unitarian influences led him to uphold the evangelical soteriological beliefs he had embraced during his

254. Jeremy Taylor, *Via Intelligentiae*, 39. Qtd in Taylor, "Letter to William Thompson," 9 July 1770, 139. It was also quoted in Fletcher, *Rational Vindication*, 46.

255. Taylor, *Our Saviour's Commission*, 35.

256. Ibid.

257. Taylor, *Truth and Inspiration*, 172.

258. John Owen, *Vindiciae Evangelicae*, in Owen, *Works*. See also Trueman, *Claims of Truth*.

period in Methodism. Through his published works such as *The Absolute Necessity* and wider preaching ministry, he showed the need for both the plain message of the Scriptures to be embraced, and for the gospel to be shared with others. Such emphases were innovations when compared to that demonstrated and articulated by most of his General Baptist colleagues. They were also typical of the central facets of evangelicalism. A creativity of theological thought was interwoven throughout Taylor's upholding of his soteriological convictions. As he responded to the teaching of the Unitarian William Graham in *The Scriptural Account of the Way of Salvation*, he posited several beliefs that were, for example, distinct from tho se commonly embraced by non-Calvinists. The importance Taylor attached to God's moral governance was central to his salvific framework. His understanding of how God's giving of his Son as an atoning sacrifice demonstrated the authority of God's law and justice, contained a breadth of perspective which extended beyond that posited by Hugo Grotius, whose works were indirectly influential on Taylor's thinking. The way in which Taylor fused a governmental approach to the atonement with a substitutionary penal understanding reflected the creative and pragmatic tendencies that lay at the core of eighteenth-century evangelicalism.

Another innovative aspect of Taylor's apologetic position was the way he argued that the workings of human reason should lead people to recognize their guilt before God and to embrace Christ as savior. In accordance with Enlightenment values, it was Taylor's comprehension of how the natural order was designed to function along the principles of reason that undergirded his understanding of God's governance. In a way commonly found throughout the evangelical movement, Taylor emphasized how human reason should facilitate the embracing of divine revelation. This conviction differed from the perspective of earlier movements, such as Puritanism, where an understanding of the total depravity of the human mind typically prevented such a position from being embraced. Further highlighting the distinctness of Taylor's evangelical apologetic position was the empirical way in which, through the influence of Locke, he upheld the importance of "observation and experience" alongside the Scriptures. Such an outlook again demonstrated his progressive tendencies. A prominent dimension of Taylor's defense of his soteriological beliefs, which also differed from the approach of Puritans such as John Owen and Thomas Goodwin, was his constant succinctness of theological reflection. Even when Taylor engaged in more complex theological matters such as the deity of Christ and nature of the Trinity, he refused to enter into metaphysical and speculative reasoning. This is evident in his theological engagement with William Graham and Joseph Priestley, as well as in his wider writings.

Taylor's emphasis on the need for all believers to adopt a simplicity of faith, and to occupy themselves with the straightforward message of the Scriptures, again reflected ascendant emphases within evangelicalism. It will be highlighted in the next chapter that a creative outlook was again apparent in the way Taylor designated Christ's death for all as the supreme motivation for the spread of the gospel.

3

Novel Advocate

TAYLOR'S ADVOCACY OF A general view of the atonement occupied a pre-eminent position within his theological thinking. It will be argued that the readiness with which he upheld the doctrine, and the way it was the motivating thrust to his entire ministry, differed from the outlook of certain notable earlier proponents of general redemption as well as some of his contemporaries. Through examination of Taylor's response to Particular Baptist minister Robert Hall Sr.'s *Help to Zion's Travellers*, it will be seen that the evangelical basis of Taylor's Arminianism led him to apply some established Arminian arguments in favor of a general view of the atonement in a pioneering way.[1] It will be contended that within the context of the General Baptists, Taylor's approach to Christ's death was novel in the way that his unequivocal dismissal of divine election, as based on God's foreordaining purposes, differed from that posited by many earlier General Baptists. Through consideration of a series of articles that Taylor contributed to a Leeds newspaper on the scope of Christ's death, it will become evident that certain important facets of his evangelicalism underpinned his thinking. It will be argued that these gave rise to several important differences in outlook compared to the approach to the subject typically adopted by Calvinist and Arminian Puritans. Examination of Taylor's discourse with the Universalist American Baptist Elhanan Winchester will show that the evangelical platform of understanding from which Taylor advocated a general view of the atonement became an increasingly novel theological stance among General Baptists outside of the New Connexion.

---

1. Hall Sr., *Help to Zion's Travellers*.

Christ's Death for All

"the very glory of the gospel"

A belief in the doctrine of general redemption was intrinsic to Taylor's un-derstanding and articulation of the gospel. Taylor proclaimed this as his "darling theme" and "all in all of my soul's hope."[2] He embraced this belief during the earliest days of his participation in Methodism.[3] It formed a uniform component of the gospel invitations he had heard preached by evangelical Arminians, such as the Wesley brothers, who contended that God made salvation available to all who believed. During Taylor's theo-logical engagement with Particular Baptist minister Andrew Fuller, he stated that he considered the same message to have been reinforced by the preaching of moderate Calvinists such as George Whitefield, who he had heard preach at Haworth.[4] An early indication of the unrivaled importance of the doctrine of general redemption within Taylor's theological schema was his priority that the fellowship in Wadsworth connect with other be-lievers who shared the same belief. For example, while he briefly contem-plated uniting with the Independents, whose approach to church order and governance he respected, their commonly held belief that Christ died only for certain people was a significant barrier. Taylor was adamant that their joining together was "forbade" by their "difference of opinion respecting the extent of the atonement."[5] It was therefore with much relief that he learned of the existence of General Baptists and committed the fellowship in Wadsworth to their cause.[6]

A distinctive facet of Taylor's upholding of general redemption was his readiness to make it central to almost any subject he addressed. For instance, it was foundational to his understanding of the subject of "some Principal Parts of the Duty of Ministers" which he outlined at the 1775 ordination of General Baptist minister Benjamin Worship.[7] Taylor insisted ministers invite all sinners to repent and believe, and specifically that they "don't tell them that Jesus died *only* for part of mankind, for his people, his

2. Lover of All Mankind [Dan Taylor], *Observations*, 98, 88. As will be examined in chapter 4, Taylor was writing under a pseudonym.

3. See chapter 1.

4. Lover of All Mankind [Taylor], *Observations*, 61. This aspect of Taylor's rea-soning will be examined in chapter 4.

5. Adam Taylor, *Memoirs*, 10.

6. See introductory chapter.

7. Dan Taylor, "Principal Parts," in Dan Taylor, and William Thompson, *Respective Duties*, 5–78.

elect, his sheep" but that "he died for all—gave himself a ransom for all—tasted death for every man—and was the propitiation for the sins of the whole world."[8] Critical of those who believed God unconditionally elected only a limited number to salvation, Taylor urged ministers to teach from the Scriptures "that those who are the elect or chosen of God, are chosen, not to, but 'through sanctification of the spirit and belief of the truth.'"[9] A further typical example of the centrality within Taylor's works of his efforts to develop a widespread regard for the general extent of Christ's death was in his 1777 publication of a tract entitled *Entertainment and Profit* where he focused on *Some of the Chief Subjects of Christianity for the Use of Poor Children and Youth*.[10] Its centerpiece was that which he posited on "Christ and his great Salvation" and particularly his declarations concerning the universal scope of Christ's atonement.[11] He was emphatic that "*whoe'ver* believes is now forgiven," that there was "Pardon for *all*" and that "ev'ry creature" should therefore praise "Our Redeemer's name."[12] Even when Taylor offered pastoral support on the most sensitive of subjects, he still maintained an overriding importance on Christ's death for all. A notable instance was his 1768 *Mourning Parent Comforted* which was written for the benefit of bereaved parents who, similar to himself, had suffered the loss of a child.[13] His desire for people to draw strength from Christ's death for all was apparent, even though, as reflected in his earliest works, he did not labor the point.[14] He insisted that God's "everlasting strength" and "rich, powerful and efficacious grace" was available to all who trusted in "their only remedy, the only saviour, Jesus Christ."[15] The way in which Taylor drew attention to Christ's death for all was a striking feature of his approach to a whole range of subjects and aspects of ministry.

8. Ibid., 24; Taylor's emphasis.

9. Ibid. Taylor did not specify who he was quoting. As will be seen in the next section, Taylor was adamant that God's electing purposes emanated from his foreknowledge of who would respond to him in faith rather than God having indiscriminately foreordained those who would be saved.

10. Dan Taylor, *Entertainment and Profit*. Adam Taylor recorded that this work was published in 1777, see Taylor, *Memoirs*, 96.

11. Ibid., 9.

12. Ibid.; Taylor's emphasis.

13. Dan Taylor, *Mourning Parent Comforted*. Two of Taylor's children died in 1768, the same year as this publication, see Taylor, *Memoirs*, 25.

14. The reason for Taylor's caution when he first addressed the scope of the atonement is examined later in the chapter.

15. Taylor, *Mourning Parent Comforted*, 36.

The innovative way in which Taylor seized all opportunities to promote an understanding of a general view of the atonement is apparent when compared to John Wesley's approach. While Wesley addressed the subject such as in his sermon on *Free Grace* in Bristol in 1739,[16] and provided a refutation of unconditional election in his 1752 *Predestination Calmly Considered*,[17] he generally did not uphold the universal extent of Christ's death in his public speaking as routinely as Taylor. Unlike Taylor, Wesley did not always utilize the doctrine as such a dominant theological motif. Distinct from Taylor's approach, Wesley spoke on subjects such as *Scriptural Christianity* and *The Way to the Kingdom* without drawing significant attention to the importance of general redemption.[18] Explicit reference to Christ's death for all was also absent from Wesley's 1748 account of what Charles and he "chiefly insisted upon" as the Methodist movement came into being—namely "inward righteousness," repentance, justification by faith, and a walk of holiness.[19] When seeking to account for the greater regularity of emphasis Taylor attached to the doctrine, it should be noted that the overarching aim of Wesley's ministry was different from Taylor's. Wesley's prime focus was his belief that "God's design in raising up the Preachers called Methodists" was "to spread scriptural holiness over the land."[20] This was "the aim of his life, the organizing centre of his thought, the spring of all action, his one abiding project."[21] While Taylor also held the need for holiness in high regard, his overriding concern was "To revive experimental religion or primitive Christianity in faith and practice."[22] A crucial aspect of this aim was his resolve that all might grasp the importance of what he referred to as "the very glory of the gospel"—Christ's death for all.[23] It was therefore central to all that Taylor taught.

The importance Taylor placed on a general view of the atonement was evident in his leadership of the New Connexion. As stated in the title of the

16. See John Wesley, *Free Grace*. Wesley heralded salvation as "free for all," and asserted that all "preaching is vain" if it is held that Christ only died for a limited number, see ibid., 5, 10.

17. John Wesley, *Predestination Calmly Considered*.

18. John Wesley, *Scriptural Christianity*, 159–80; John Wesley, *Way to the Kingdom*, 218–32.

19. John Wesley, *People Called Methodists*, 254.

20. John Wesley, "Minutes of Several Conversations," 299. Wesley was here responding to the question—"What may we reasonably believe to be God's design in raising up the preachers called Methodists?"

21. Jennings, *Good News*, 140.

22. *Assembly of Free Grace General Baptists*. Page not numbered.

23. Lover of All Mankind [Taylor], *Observations*, 86.

1770 New Connexion annual Association minutes, its members originally referred to themselves as an *Assembly of Free Grace General Baptists*. This conveyed Taylor's aim that their belief in Christ's death for all should lead them to offer God's grace freely to all people.[24] It was also central to the Connexion's *Articles of Religion*.[25] In the third Article on *The Person and Work of Christ*, Taylor drew attention to how Christ,

> suffered to make a full atonement for the sins of *all* men—and that hereby he has wrought out for us a compleat salvation; which is received by, and as a free gift communicated to, *all* that believe in him.[26]

This was reiterated by Taylor in his 1785 *Confession of Faith*, with its twenty-four Articles adopted by the Connexion as an extension of its chief beliefs.[27] Taylor emphasized in Article eleven that Christ "provided a complete and free salvation for miserable sinners and for all sinners without exception," and that all people could therefore have complete confidence that Christ was "the justifier of him that believeth in Jesus."[28] The unequivocal nature of these pronouncements should not be overlooked. For example, its firm promise of assurance of salvation for all who exercised faith in Christ's atoning work extended beyond that stipulated in the 1660 Standard Confession and the 1678 *Orthodox Creed*.[29] While the inference of the Standard Confession, through references to Christ's death as a "ransome for all,"[30] and "propitiation for our sins,"[31] and that "God is not willing that any should perish,"[32] is that all who place their faith in Christ will be saved, this is not categorically stated.[33] Neither is it unequivocally asserted in the *Orthodox Creed*, despite what Nigel Wright refers to as its "robust" declaration that "Christ died for all men, and there is a sufficiency in his death and merits for the sins of the whole world."[34] There is a difference, albeit by degree, between what is stipulated in the Standard Confession and *Orthodox Creed*,

24. *Assembly of Free Grace General Baptists 1770*. Page not numbered.

25. See *Articles* in Lumpkin, *Baptist Confessions*, 342–44.

26. *Articles*, Article three, 343; italics added.

27. Dan Taylor, *Confession of Faith*. Taylor wrote this *Confession* in June 1785, see Taylor, *Memoirs*, 129.

28. Ibid., Article eleven, 5, Article ten, 5.

29. These creeds are found in Lumpkin, *Baptist Confessions*, 224–35, 297–334.

30. *Brief Confession*, Article three, 225.

31. Ibid., 225.

32. Ibid., Article four, 225.

33. Ibid., Article three, 225.

34. Wright, "Election and Predestination," 27; *Orthodox Creed*, Article eighteen, 310.

compared to what Taylor specifically emphasized regarding the promise of salvation for all who exercised faith in Christ.

The universal scope of Christ's atonement did not have the same pre-eminence in many of the works of General Baptist defenders of orthodoxy in the second part of the seventeenth century, as it did in Taylor's approach. For example, while Thomas Monk wrote on subjects such as the Incarnation, the Trinity, and religious tolerance, Christ's death for all was not as promi-nent a theme as it was in Taylor's writings.[35] This was similarly apparent within the examination of doctrine provided by the General Baptists' fore-most seventeenth-century apologist Thomas Grantham in *Christianismus Primitivus.*[36] Although Grantham addressed subjects such as how "Christ the saviour of the world" was "man by nature," and the mystery of Christ as the "God-man in one person" who suffered for "the sins of the world," he did not focus exclusively on the scope of Christ's salvation as a separate topic.[37] It is therefore not cited among that which Clint Bass lists as the central doctrinal elements of *Christianismus Primitivus.*[38] This omission of emphasis differed from Taylor's regular focus on how Christ's death for all "shines with an awful glory on every other part" of the gospel message.[39]

In summary, the universal scope of Christ's death was of pivotal importance within Taylor's theological thinking. After embracing the doctrine as he participated in the Evangelical Revival, the frequency with which he explic-itly highlighted its primacy of importance surpassed that of certain other prominent proponents of the doctrine. Taylor's emphasis on Christ's death for all also exceeded that stipulated in certain General Baptist creeds. con-fessions, and works such as Grantham's *Christianismus Primitivus.* It will be seen next that the novel nature of Taylor's advocacy of the universal scope of Christ's death was apparent in the way some of his arguments in favor of

35. See, e.g., Monk, *Cure for the Cankering Error.* See also, Monk et al., *Sions Groans.*

36. Grantham, *Christianismus Primitivus.*

37. Grantham examined each of these subjects in the first part of *Christianismus Primitivus.* His reflections on Christ as the "God man" are found in chapter 3.3; being "man by nature" chapter 3.4; and his suffering for sin in chapter 3.6.

38. Bass, *Thomas Grantham,* 30–31.

39. Scrutator [Dan Taylor], "To Mr. Responsor," *Leeds Intelligencer,* 19 September 1780, in Aequus [Author unknown], *Scrutator's Query,* 7. This publication comprises Taylor's 1780 contributions to the *Leeds Intelligencer* newspaper on the subject of the scope of the atonement and is examined later in this chapter. Adam Taylor identifies Taylor as Scrutator, see Taylor, *Memoirs,* 106–7. While the title of the publication iden-tifies Aequus as its author, the role of this otherwise unknown individual was that of editor. The publication comprises no actual contribution from Aequus, although he was the direct recipient of Taylor's first contribution.

a general view of the atonement extended beyond those commonly posited by some earlier General Baptists.

General Atonement: A Representation of God's Love

"the most glorious display of the Father's love"

A dominant feature of Taylor's defense of a general view of the atonement was his conviction that the nature of God's character necessitated a universal rather than limited provision of atonement. He repeatedly drew attention to Christ's sacrifice for all as the complete revelation of God's love. A typical example was his description of general redemption as "the most glorious display of the Father's love, as well as the love of his Son" in a 1793 letter to Gilbert Boyce.[40] While such an emphasis was commonplace among the arguments of earlier proponents of general redemption, such as Church of England minister Samuel Hoard and Puritans such as Laurence Saunders and Thomas Moore Sr., Taylor applied it in a particularly novel way.[41] Instead of focusing solely on the incongruence of aligning God's universal benevolence with a limited view of the atonement, he attached significance to how God's love, as supremely exemplified in Christ's death for all, should serve as the chief motivation for sharing the gospel with others. For example, in his previously cited letter to Boyce, he stated that the only appropriate response to God's love as demonstrated by the universal extent of Christ's death was that all might "sincerely love and praise him for his great goodness."[42] With particular regard to evangelism, he also urged that all believers might "gratefully serve him for such a display of love."[43] The way in which this assertion was so closely bound to his advocacy of a general view of the atonement reflected the missional thrust of his evangelicalism. This link was also apparent in a 1791 letter Taylor wrote to William Thompson where he noted the prevalence of "a laxness of mind, with respect to some important doctrines" and with specific reference to Christ's death for all, expressed his concern that "where these doctrines are slighted, the work of God declines."[44] In accordance with his desire that God would "revive his ministers; and thereby revive his truth and his work," Taylor hoped this

---

40. Dan Taylor, "Letter I to Gilbert Boyce," 25 May 1793, in Taylor, *Memoirs*, 268.

41. See, e.g., Hoard, *God's Love to Mankind*; Saunders, *Fullnesse of Gods Love*; T. Moore Sr., *Universality of Gods Free Grace*.

42. Taylor, "Letter I to Gilbert Boyce," 25 May 1793, 268.

43. Ibid.

44. Dan Taylor, "Letter to William Thompson," 13 May 1791, in Taylor, *Memoirs*, 267.

would be demonstrated by General Baptists advocating Christ's death for all, and sharing the gospel with renewed vigor of purpose.[45]

The importance Taylor attached to an understanding of a general view of the atonement as the greatest representation of God's love, and as the prime basis from which to proclaim the gospel to all, not only underpinned his atonement thinking at a general level, but was also evident on certain specific occasions. An example was his response to Particular Baptist minister Robert Hall Sr.'s 1781 reflections concerning the spread of the gospel. Hall had been minister of the Particular Baptist church in Arnesby, Leicestershire since 1753, and in 1781 published his influential *Help to Zion's Travellers*. This was an enlargement of a sermon he preached in 1779 at a meeting of the Northamptonshire Particular Baptist Association. In line with the changes in theological approach that were increasingly embraced by many Particular Baptists over the last few decades of the eighteenth century, he promoted an expansive expression of Calvinism. He advocated that a full measure of human endeavor regarding the effective preaching of the gospel be placed alongside an understanding of God's sovereign direction over matters of salvation.[46] This formed an important distinction from those Particular Baptists who, through the influence of High Calvinism, emphasized the workings of God's sovereignty rather than human responsibility.[47] As a forerunner of the moderate Calvinism of Andrew Fuller, Hall argued that gospel invitations should be offered to non-believers. He declared that "The way to Jesus is graciously laid open for everyone who chooses to come to him."[48] Taylor was sent a copy of *Help to Zion's Travellers* by George Birley, and responded in the form of seven letters written between August 1783 and January 1784. Some significant extracts of these letters are found in Adam Taylor's *Memoirs of the Rev. Dan Taylor.*[49]

Although Taylor complimented Hall for endorsing the preaching of universal gospel invitations, he considered its significance to have been undermined by Hall's continued commitment to a particular view of atonement. Taylor was adamant that this lessened the intensity of conviction with which Christians could share with non-believers the promises

45. Ibid.

46. This is found in the second part of Hall's publication.

47. Through the research of those such as Roger Hayden, an increasing number of scholars now contend that the influence of High Calvinism on the eighteenth-century Particular Baptists was not as all-pervading as once thought. See Hayden, "Evangelical Calvinism," 305–6, 360. See also, Hayden, *Continuity and Change.*

48. Hall, *Help to Zion's Travellers*, 124.

49. See, e.g., Dan Taylor, "Letter to George Birley," 31 January 1784, 161–68. It is unfortunate that there appears to be no surviving full copies of these letters.

of "real comfort and hope of any man alive" that stem from the "spring" of Christ's death for all, and which form the very "essence of the gospel."[50] He highlighted what he understood as the contradiction between the many scriptural promises concerning "the love, pity and goodness of God" that believers were called to proclaim "to all mankind," and Hall's conviction that Christ died for only a limited number.[51] Taylor was firm in his declaration that "Mr. Hall's view of the matter, to me, seems opposite to all these Scriptures," and proceeded to ask "How can I tell good tidings to any persons alive, if I cannot assure them that Christ died for them?"[52] The depth of Taylor's conviction on this matter, and specifically his regard for Christ's death for all as the pre-eminent mandate for sharing the good news with others was tangible, and assumed importance in his later theological engagement with Andrew Fuller.[53]

Taylor rejected Hall's Calvinistic understanding of election. Hall placed importance on an "election of grace," which involved God unconditionally "choosing persons in Christ Jesus, or setting them apart as in connexion with him to salvation."[54] Taylor was adamant that to believe that God, since before creation, had chosen a limited number for salvation and determined to bring them to glory while consigning the remainder to eternal damnation, was to leave people only in a place of "hard thoughts" towards God.[55] He was convinced this gave rise to confusion as to why God should pass by the rest of humanity "without providing any salvation for them, or ever intending to do any thing for them that might contribute to their recovery from the fall, or make them happy in the next world."[56] The depth of Taylor's conviction on this matter was unmistakable. He viewed it as inconceivable that God would not have taken every measure that all might be saved and that this was confirmed by the universal scope of Christ's death, and how it represented God's love for all.

Taylor believed that God's electing purposes were predicated only on his foreknowledge of who would exercise a saving faith in Christ's atoning sacrifice.[57] This was in line with that commonly taught within Methodism

50. Ibid., 164.

51. Ibid.

52. Ibid.

53. See chapter 4.

54. Hall, *Help to Zion's Travellers*, 57.

55. Taylor, "Letter to George Birley," 31 January 1784, 165.

56. Ibid., 163.

57. Taylor cited Scriptures such as Rom 8:29–31; 1 Pet 1:2; and 2 Thess 2:1, see ibid. From that which Taylor writes to Birley it appears that he embraced this understanding of election during his participation in the Methodist society in Halifax.

and was articulated in Article sixteen of Taylor's *Confession of Faith*. He stated,

> The Scripture does not say, that they are chosen to faith, but through sanctification of the Spirit and belief of the truth. As God foreknew all things, therefore his choice was made according to his foreknowledge: and, this is what I understand by the election of grace.[58]

Taylor was convinced that this understanding of election exonerated God from any charge of indifference towards his creation. In accordance with God's mercy, love, and grace, it demonstrated him to have taken all "such methods to bring sinners to himself."[59] Taylor similarly argued that because whoever placed their faith in Christ could be assured of salvation, this meant that people need "never suspect his readiness to save the most unworthy sinner who comes to him by Jesus Christ."[60] The way Taylor held a compassionate concern for the interests of those who were not saved in greater regard than God's sovereign right to act in an indeterminate manner, reflected the underlying nature of his evangelical Arminianism and an Enlightenment-influenced understanding of what was reasonable. Taylor's commitment to vindicate God from any charge of injustice as he stressed God's salvific provision for all was a closely related point of emphasis.

The significance of Taylor's rejection of particular election within his defense of a general view of the atonement should not be overlooked. It differentiated his position from that commonly embraced by many earlier General Baptists. Particular election became the dominant outlook among General Baptists from the mid-1640s. It was maintained by the ministers of the two principal General Baptist churches of this period—soap boiler Thomas Lambe, minister at Bell Alley, Whitechapel and Edward Barber who led a church in Bishopsgate.[61] In 1642, Lambe wrote *A Treatise of Particular Predestination*.[62] Baptist historian Thomas Crosby emphasized that Lambe was widely known for his "reconciling of *particular election* with universal redemption."[63] The prominent evangelist Henry Denne was also typical of those who embraced general redemption and particular election.

58. Taylor, *Confession of Faith*, Article sixteen, 6.

59. Taylor, "Letter to George Birley," 31 January 1784, 163.

60. Ibid., 168.

61. In 1643 Edward Barber went beyond Lambe's position and rejected universal redemption. For consideration of this, see Bebbington, *Baptists*, 53.

62. Lambe, *Treatise of Particular Predestination*.

63. Crosby, *History of the English Baptists*, 3:56; Crosby's emphasis. For consideration of the ministry of Thomas Lambe, see S. Wright, *Early English Baptists*, 115–16.

He professed a commitment to "the doctrine of personal election, and the special efficacy of grace to some."[64] What Crosby described as this "middle way, being neither Calvinist nor Arminian" was also apparent in the General Baptist Standard Confession.[65] Its eighth Article states that "the purpose of God according to election, was not in the least arising from fore-seen faith" but from God's unconditional "decree of mercy" which "reaches only the godly man, whom . . . God hath set apart for himself."[66] Taylor strongly contested such an understanding of election.[67] Similarly, he was opposed to the belief, as stipulated in Article nine, that there are some who God "of old ordained to condemnation."[68] The names that are listed among the Confession's forty signatories suggest that this view of election was mainstream among seventeenth-century General Baptists.[69] The signatories include respected proponents of the gospel such as Joseph Wright (a Messenger in Kent), William Jeffrey author of the widely read *The Whole Faith of Man*,[70] and bookseller and publisher Francis Smith. The confession also claimed to represent "many others unto whom they belong in London and in several counties of this nation."[71] When Thomas Grantham edited the Standard Confession in 1678, it is noteworthy that he left its declarations regarding particular election unchanged.[72] This was contrary to the central position that Taylor's critique of particular election occupied within his upholding of a general view of the atonement.

Taylor's distinctive approach to the doctrine of election is apparent when compared to the contents of the General Baptist *Orthodox Creed*. Although it outlines Christ's death for all (see previous section), the ninth Article states that God "foreordained and so predestinated" people to salvation, and that this was not predicated on any "foreseen holiness," but on

64. Crosby, *History of the English Baptists*, 1:305. See also S. Wright, *Early English Baptists*, 116.

65. Ibid.

66. *Brief Confession*, Article eight, 227. It is for this reason that Lumpkin refers to the creed as only "mildly Arminian," see Lumpkin, *Baptist Confessions*, 221. That which the Standard Confession states regarding election differed from how earlier General Baptists such as Thomas Helwys and John Murton had understood election in terms of God's knowledge of foreseen faith.

67. Further consideration will be given to Taylor's stance on this matter in chapter 4.

68. *Brief Confession*, Article nine, 227.

69. For a list of its signatories, see *Brief Confession*, 235.

70. Jeffrey, *Whole Faith of Man*.

71. *Brief Confession*, 234–35.

72. See Lumpkin, *Baptist Confessions*, 223. Lumpkin notes how Grantham made only very minor changes to the Standard Confession.

God's "mere grace."[73] A further difference compared with Taylor's perspective is the way that it emphasizes an effectual grace for salvation that was only given to the elect.[74] It should also be noted that both of these beliefs, as well as some content of Articles addressing other subjects,[75] provide evidence of the way in which the *Orthodox Creed* was to some extent modeled on *The Westminster Confession of Faith* that was written by the 1646 Westminster Assembly which worked in the Reformed theological tradition.[76] For example Chapter 3 of the *Westminster Confession* speaks of believers having been "predestinated and foreordained,"[77] and its tenth Chapter draws attention to the workings of election and effectual grace.[78] While it is understandable that a desire to protect the General Baptists from the charge of heresy, and awareness of the shared context of persecution faced by all Dissenters, led Thomas Monk and others to stress their common theological ground with other persecuted Dissenters,[79] the nature of these Articles remains significant. This is particularly so, given that the General Baptists on whose behalf the creed was written were known for their zealous commitment to an orthodox understanding of the faith.[80] The extent to which a creed would have been produced which differed from their essential beliefs is therefore questionable. Also Monk, similar to Taylor a century later, was renowned as a key protagonist of the need for churches to remain faithful to central tenets of the gospel.[81] For example, the unequivocal nature of the pronouncements within the *Orthodox Creed* regarding the divinity and humanity of Christ were, in part, motivated by Monk's desire to repudiate unorthodox christological teaching.[82] It is therefore doubtful that Monk

---

73. *Orthodox Creed*, Article nine, 302.

74. Ibid., Article twenty, 312; ibid., 313.

75. Examples of these are provided in chapters 5 and 7 of the book.

76. For consideration of this point, see, e.g., Lumpkin, *Baptist Confessions*, 296. See also *Westminster Confession of Faith*, in Jones, Long, and Moore, eds., *Protestant Nonconformist Texts*, 165–90.

77. *Westminster Confession of Faith*, chapter 3, 168.

78. Ibid., 173–74.

79. This is, for example, reflected in part of the Creed's title—*Being an Essay to Unite and Confirm all True Protestants in the Fundamental Articles of the Christian Religion, against the Errors and Heresies of Rome*. See also Bebbington, *Baptists*, 59; White, *English Baptists*, 120.

80. See Taylor, *English General Baptists*, 225. See also Hayden, *English Baptist History*, 40; White, *English Baptists*, 121.

81. Hayden, *English Baptist History*, 40.

82. For consideration of this, see Brown, *English Baptists*, 21; Hayden, *English Baptist History*, 40.

would have included elements of belief in the *Orthodox Creed* with which he and the other fifty-four signatories were not in agreement.

The differences in outlook regarding election between that found in the *Orthodox Creed* and Taylor's position can, in large part, be attributed to how Taylor's evangelicalism was rooted in a Wesleyan rejection of beliefs such as particular election, unconditional salvific decrees, and elevation of God's sovereignty over human responsibility. This meant that his thinking did not allow for an advocacy of a general view of the atonement which, as detailed in the *Orthodox Creed*, viewed God as selectively "wooing" (a word not found in the *Westminster Confession*) his elect, who were chosen on the exclusive basis of the workings of his grace and for whom he had provided an efficacious grace.[83] Taylor's position was also underpinned by his Enlightenment-inspired regard for equality, justice, and full exercise and protection of human responsibility which grew increasingly apparent in his later discourses on the atonement.[84] Given the nature of the differences in outlook between Taylor and Monk, it is not surprising that an upholding of a general view of the atonement occupied a less commanding place within Monk's written works, and those of other seventeenth-century General Baptists such as Grantham, than it did in Taylor's publications.

To summarize, a key dimension of Taylor's endorsement of general redemption was his judgment that it provided a more accurate reflection of the universal nature of God's love than depictions of the atonement that limited the scope of Christ's death to only a particular few. Intertwined with this viewpoint was his conviction that the revelation of God's love as manifest in Christ's atoning sacrifice was the prime motivation for inviting all people to respond in faith to the good news of the gospel. The way this aspect of his thinking was so central to his defense of general redemption was distinct from the approach of many seventeenth-century proponents of the doctrine, and reflected the outward focused nature of his evangelicalism. It also formed an important part of his response to Robert Hall Sr.'s *Help to Zion's Travellers*. Taylor's rejection of particular election set him apart from the position assumed by many earlier General Baptists and from that stated in the Standard Confession and *Orthodox Creed*. The next section will examine certain distinctive aspects of Taylor's reasoning that were apparent in his 1780 defense of Christ's death for all in a Yorkshire newspaper.

83. *Orthodox Creed*, Article 21, 313.

84. See chapter 4.

The Straightforwardness of the Scriptures

"a plain matter of fact"

A distinctive facet of Taylor's advocacy of a general view of the atonement was his determination to model an approach that was predicated on a reasoned examination of Scripture. Taylor was aware of how proponents of general redemption had frequently responded with belligerence and antagonism towards Calvinists. The disrespect that surrounded a local theological controversy between the Methodists and Independents on the scope of the atonement, which Taylor witnessed in 1780, was typical. He referred to this in a letter to Birley where he expressed frustration that "There is a hot dispute begun lately between the Methodists and Calvinists on predestination etc. in this neighbourhood. When or how it will end, I know not."[85] His resolve to demonstrate a more considered, respectful, and scripturally based approach to the atonement led him in 1780 to write an article on the scope of Christ's death in the *Leeds Intelligencer* newspaper.[86] Writing under the pseudonym Scrutator, he stated that he had been disturbed by the theological content and general tone of certain writings that had fueled the local controversy. He specifically cited the works of Philathethes, Calvinisticus, and Polyphemus.[87] While it is not possible to establish with certainty the identity of Polyphemus or his contribution to the debate, Philathethes is widely considered to have been the Methodist itinerant preacher Thomas Taylor who, in 1780, wrote *A Solemn Caution Against the Ten Horns of Calvinism*.[88] The unknown Calvinisticus responded that same year with *Calvinism Defended and Arminianism Refuted*.[89] Both these works were highly polemical, inflammatory, and accusatory. This was reflected in the way Philalethes structured his defense of Christ's death for all on the theme of Calvinism's "ten blasphemous absurdities."[90] Dan Taylor accused them of having "departed from the Spirit of Christianity" and adopting "the method

---

85. Dan Taylor, "Letter to George Birley," 9 November 1780. Page not numbered.

86. Scrutator [Taylor], "To Mr. Responsor," 7–10.

87. Scrutator [Taylor], "My Dear Friend Aequus," in Aequus [Author unknown], *Scrutator's Query*, 3.

88. Philalethes [Thomas Taylor], *Solemn Caution*. It is evident from the biographical nature of the preface to this work that the judgment was reached that its author was Thomas Taylor. While it has not proved possible to locate who first identified Thomas Taylor as the author, the work was widely attributed to him, such as in Osborn's *Outlines of Wesleyan Bibliography*, 185.

89. See Calvinisticus [Author unknown], *Calvinism Defended*.

90. Philalethes [Thomas Taylor], *Solemn Caution*, 6.

of Satan."[91] In contrast, he hoped his newspaper contribution would "introduce a method of proceeding more directly suited" to "the God of love" who
called on believers to be "gentle towards all men."[92] He therefore proceeded
with much care towards the central thrust of his article where he posed
the question, "What Christian writer first maintained, that Jesus Christ, the
blessed Son of God, did not lay down his life for the sins of all mankind?"[93]
Although he believed there to be "no evidence" for this, it was with an enlightened regard for irenic debate and respect that he expressed his hope
that his question would "excite a discussion of the subjects in question, in a
natural, easy and instructive manner."[94] Given the animosity and fractious
attitudes that were evident towards this subject in his local ministry, his
approach and objective were, at least to some extent, pioneering.

Taylor's article was published on 15 August 1780, and a reply followed
three weeks later. It was written by "Responsor" whose identity is unknown.
Responsor argued that Christ's apostles maintained the doctrine of limited
redemption and that they had acquired it from Psalms, the teachings of
various Old Testament figures, and the pronouncements of Jesus.[95] Taylor's
desire to promote an understanding of a general view of the atonement from
a different platform from that which he had observed locally was evident in
his reply to Responsor. Firstly, he expressed his "grateful acknowledgements,
for the pains you have taken in answering my query," and then respectfully
engaged in a reasoned biblicism.[96] He emphasized that the sole reason Responsor had failed to convince him that the biblical writers ever limited
Christ's death to a part of humanity was his failure to provide even "one
single text where such a limitation is plainly expressed."[97] If Responsor had
done this satisfactorily, then Taylor stated that he would have been able "to
embrace the doctrine with humble pleasure."[98] Regarding those Scriptures
that Responsor did supply, Taylor argued that they bore no relation to Jesus's
death, contradicted their wider contexts, and were interpreted in too broad
or limited a way. For instance, Taylor accused Responsor of too narrow an

91. Scrutator [Taylor], "My Dear Friend Aequus," 3, 4. Taylor's opening address
to Aequus was not a contribution he submitted to the *Leeds Intelligencer* but instead
served as the introduction to the whole publication.

92. Ibid., 3.

93. Ibid., 5.

94. Ibid., 4.

95. Responsor, "For the Leeds Intelligencer," 5 September 1780, in Aequus [Author
unknown], *Scrutator's Query*, 5–7.

96. Scrutator [Taylor], "To Mr. Responsor," 7.

97. Ibid.

98. Ibid.

interpretation in the way he questioned Christ's assertion that he would give his life specifically for his sheep. Responsor had asked "if he had laid down his life for all men. What occasion would there have been for mentioning his sheep in particular?"[99] Taylor instead urged Responsor to recognize that "if he died for all, he certainly died for his sheep."[100] Taylor's approach was marked by its succinctness and depth of conviction.

Responsor claimed that the apostles, through "the Spirit's infallible direction," had demonstrated Christ's death to be limited only to his church.[101] He cited the apostle Paul's stipulation to the Ephesian elders "to care for the church of God which Christ bought with his own blood."[102] It was on this basis that Responsor asked Taylor, "will Mr. Scrutator aver, that all mankind belong to the church of Christ?"[103] In response, Taylor argued that Responsor's interpretation of Acts 20:28 was too broad, stating "the occasion,—the design,—the persons addressed" pointed to Paul's reference to the "church" as the specific church at Ephesus.[104] Taylor therefore deemed it inappropriate to use this Scripture to justify a limited understanding of Christ's death. Taylor also drew attention to how the Scriptures were written for the "the lowest of mankind" and that it would therefore be "shocking" if they were not "plain" in their meaning concerning a doctrine of "such solemn consequence" as the scope of Christ's death.[105] This was indicative of the pragmatically orientated nature of his evangelicalism. Offering no reflection on Responsor's wider Calvinist framework of thought, but exhibiting a measured and focused examination of the scriptural evidence alone, Taylor concluded with the assertion that Responsor had failed to convince him of the validity of a limited view of the atonement.

To Taylor's surprise, Responsor submitted another reply to the *Leeds Intelligencer* in 1781 although it was not published and no surviving copy can be located.[106] This reply led Taylor to engage for the first time with some arguments against a general view of the atonement advanced by John Owen. Taylor noted that Responsor drew upon Owen's thinking in order to con-

99. Responsor, "For the Leeds Intelligencer," 5.

100. Scrutator [Taylor], "To Mr. Responsor," 8.

101. Responsor, "For the Leeds Intelligencer," 6.

102. Ibid. Responsor was quoting Acts 20:28.

103. Ibid.

104. Scrutator [Taylor], "To Mr. Responsor," 9.

105. Ibid.

106. See Taylor, *Memoirs*, 107. My examination of both the microfilm of the *Leeds Intelligencer* in Leeds Central Library and the British Library's British Newspaper Archive has led me to conclude that Responsor's further reply was not published due to its absence.

solidate his position. This is not surprising, as Owen was widely viewed as the most articulate defender of orthodox Calvinism. While Owen upheld the doctrine of a limited atonement in publications such as *Of the Death of Christ*,[107] and *Dissertation on Divine Justice*,[108] his most exhaustive treatment of the subject is found in his 1647 *The Death of Death in the Death of Christ*.[109] This work contains his most definitive insights into the nature and extent of Christ's atoning death, and soon acquired seminal influence. It is evident from Taylor's reply that Responsor's thinking was shaped by Owen's "Arguments against the universality of redemption" in *The Death of Death*.[110] Responsor specifically drew attention to Owen's view that it was problematic to regard Christ as dying for all, as this necessitated he died for them "either absolutely or conditionally."[111] Owen had argued that if it was absolute, then it must be agreed that all people would "be made actual partakers of that eternal redemption so purchased," and yet contended that such a view was at variance with the wider teachings of Scripture.[112] On the other hand, if it was conditional on a person's exercise of faith in Christ, then he considered this as problematic due to his belief that people cannot choose to believe by their own free will, but that faith "must be bestowed on them and wrought within them by the free grace of God."[113] It was this reasoning that Responsor drew upon.

Taylor dismissed Responsor's use of Owen's arguments, as found within *The Death of Death*, as too abstract and convoluted. He asserted that "absolutely, conditionally and many other *human* phrases, . . . have no use, but to confound the minds of the simple."[114] Taylor was unequivocal that "I chuse not to meddle" with such questions.[115] This response should not be dismissed as a convenient basis on which he avoided the challenge of

107. Owen, *Death of Christ*, in Owen, *Works*, 10:429–79.

108. Owen, *Dissertation on Divine Justice*, in Owen, *Works*, 10:481–624.

109. Owen, *Death of Death*, in Owen, *Works*, 10:139–428. In 1642 Owen also published *A Display of Arminianism* where he compared his understanding of Arminianism with the teaching of Scripture, see Owen, *Display of Arminianism*, in Owen, *Works*, 10:1–129.

110. See Owen, *Death of Death*, 236–94.

111. Responsor. Qtd in Scrutator [Dan Taylor], "Letter I. To Mr. Responsor," *Leeds Intelligencer* (date not specified), in Scrutator [Dan Taylor], *Scrutator to Responsor*, 7. Responsor took this argument from chapter II of Book III of Owen's *Death of Death*, 240–46.

112. Owen, *Death of Death*, 240.

113. Ibid., 241.

114. Scrutator [Taylor], "Letter I. To Mr. Responsor," 7–8; Taylor's emphasis.

115. Ibid.

the issues raised. Instead it demonstrated his conviction, found throughout his works, that an important indication of whether an expressed belief was biblical truth was its capacity to be understood plainly by the less educated. When Taylor viewed arguments concerning the scope of the atonement as insufficiently straightforward, as he believed to be the case with Responsor's utilization of Owen's reasoning, they were readily dismissed. This was a central facet of his evangelical approach.

As Responsor contested Taylor's advocacy of Christ's death for all, he drew upon Owen's belief that the limited scope of the "merits" of Christ's death were "irreconcilable" with a general view of the atonement.[116] Responsor demonstrated an affinity with Owen's argument that, had God intended the "fruits and effects" of Christ's death such as the reconciliation, peace, healing, and deliverance that he "procured" for those for whom he died to have been universal, then his intention would have been universally made known.[117] Yet it was the case that "these things are not communicated to and bestowed upon all."[118] Taylor responded by rejecting the term "Christ's merits" as an "unscriptural ambiguous phrase."[119] This was harsh, for while Owen had acknowledged that "the word *merit* is not at all to be found in the New Testament," it was with some justification that Owen did not conceive this as problematic but considered that to which it pointed as evident in the Scriptures.[120] Taylor also expressed his dislike of Owen's and Responsor's shared conviction that if Christ's death was universal in scope then all people ought to have been made aware by God of the blessings bestowed on them. Taylor argued that it was "too high for mortals to say what God *ought* to do."[121] However, it should be noted that on other occasions Taylor did not hesitate to appeal to the appropriateness of how he felt God should function.[122] This inconsistency and his refusal to engage with Owen's understanding of "Christ's merits" illustrate Taylor's reluctance to accept that his advocacy of Christ's death for all required him to engage with theological questions which he held as superfluous in their importance, compared to what he believed the Scriptures taught. The theologically concise way in which Taylor's evangelicalism was outworked here has parallels with the

116. Responsor. Qtd in Scrutator [Taylor], "Letter I. To Mr. Responsor," 7. Responsor took this argument from chapter X of Book III of Owen's *Death of Death*, 286–90.

117. Owen, *Death of Death*, 287, 288.

118. Ibid., 288.

119. Scrutator [Taylor], "Letter I. To Mr. Responsor," 7.

120. Owen, *Death of Death*, 287; Owen's emphasis.

121. Scrutator [Taylor], "Letter I. To Mr. Responsor," 7; Taylor's emphasis.

122. This was particularly evident during his engagement with Andrew Fuller, see chapter 4.

narrow confines through which he approached other issues, such as the Trinity and Incarnation (see chapter 2). Taylor provided most insight into his atonement convictions during his theological engagement with Fuller who, similar to Responsor, had a positive regard for Owen.

Taylor's succinct approach was again evident as he challenged Responsor to abandon his preoccupation with the wider reasoning that he held as relevant to establishing the scope of Christ's atonement. Taylor invited him to focus solely on the issue of "whether Christ died for the sins of all men, or not."[123] For the first time in his published works, Taylor, in a further letter to Responsor, proceeded to demonstrate what he considered "a little of that Scripture evidence" in favor of Christ having died for all.[124] After claiming the evidence was so overwhelming that he "felt rather at a loss where to begin my proof," he settled on an exegesis of 1 John 2:1–2.[125] With reference to the words "ours" and "whole world," he demonstrated an awareness of various interpretations.[126] Although he recognized that the most "common exposition" was the understanding that Christ had died for the "whole world of the elect," he was convinced that it pointed to Christ not only providing "propitiation for our sin, who now believe . . . but also for the sins of all mankind."[127] He believed that the word "anybody" in the first verse was further proof that the "we" in the same verse and "our" of verse two, referred to all people.[128] With reference to "the language and doctrine of the epistle," Taylor was keen to assert his view that it contained no other examples where the words "we" or "our" could legitimately be construed as limited in their application.[129] Taylor's considered and concise biblicism remained free of the antagonistic language and accusations that frequently characterized Arminian and Calvinist discourses.[130] His fervor for the doctrine was evident

123. Scrutator [Taylor], "Letter I. To Mr. Responsor," 7.

124. Scrutator [Taylor], "Letter II. To Mr. Responsor," *Leeds Intelligencer*, 16 July 1781, in Scrutator [Taylor], *Scrutator to Responsor*, 15–16.

125. Ibid., 16. 1 John 2:1–2: "My dear children, I write this to you so that you will not sin. But if anybody does sin, we have an advocate with the Father—Jesus Christ, the Righteous One. He is the atoning sacrifice for our sins, and not only for ours but also for the sins of the whole world."

126. Ibid.

127. Ibid.

128. Ibid.

129. Ibid., 18. Taylor also noted that failure to recognize these verses as incorporating all people in their scope of reference was a mistake, as it served to remove what he felt was the only biblical reference to Gentiles being included within Christ's saving work, see ibid., 18.

130. As previously noted, the earlier cited publications by Thomas Taylor and Calvinisticus were examples of such an approach.

in his declaration that "the glorious truth" of Christ's death for all was "like a golden thread interwoven throughout a great part of the Scripture."[131] With a similar focus on the Scriptures, he responded to the accusation in a contribution to the *Intelligencer* under the pseudonym Observator, that his articles had served "to lay a foundation for endless dispute."[132] Taylor was adamant that there was "no ground" to this charge, as universal atonement was "a plain matter of fact, recorded in a plain book, designed to instruct plain people, in a plain way to heaven."[133] This assertion encapsulated the thrust of his overall approach to the doctrine.

Taylor's novel defense of a general view of the atonement is further apparent when compared to the way it was upheld by the few Puritan advocates of the doctrine such as Laurence Saunders and Thomas Moore Sr. (mentioned earlier in this chapter), and the Anglican minister John Goodwin. The most significant of these, was Goodwin, whose written works and public debates earned him the reputation as "the great Spreader of *Arminianism*."[134] By 1647 Goodwin had moved from an adherence to orthodox Calvinism to being an ardent proponent of general redemption, with an accompanying belief in conditional election based on divine fore-knowledge and the sufficiency of natural ability as an initial catalyst to salvation. Although Taylor shared these beliefs, Goodwin's expansive theological framework of thought was in sharp distinction. His detailed delineation of "free-will" and "free-grace" in *The Remedie of Unreasonableness*,[135] and his consideration of predestination in *An Exposition of the Nineth Chapter of the Epistle to the Romans*, were both typical.[136] The far reaching and scrupulous nature of his approach was exemplified in his seminal 1651 *Redemption Redeemed*.[137] Its six hundred pages formed the most extensive defense of Arminianism ever published in the English language. In contrasting style to Taylor's, the first four chapters saw Goodwin engage in much philosophical theology as he reflected on humankind's dependence on God, the workings of free will, divine foreknowledge, and the nature of divine decrees. Such an approach differed from Taylor's insistence that debate surrounding the

131. Scrutator [Taylor], "Letter II. To Mr. Responsor," 23, 6.

132. Observator [Author unknown], "To Scrutator," 26 September 1780, in Aequus [Author unknown], *Scrutator's Query*, 10.

133. Scrutator [Taylor], "Letter I. To Mr. Responsor," 5. Taylor reflected in his first letter to Responsor on that which Observator had written.

134. Toland, *Life of John Milton*, 125. Qtd in Coffey, *John Goodwin*, 199; Toland's emphasis.

135. John Goodwin, *Remedie of Unreasonableness*.

136. John Goodwin, *Exposition*.

137. John Goodwin, *Redemption Redeemed*.

atonement be restricted to "the plain, practical parts of Scripture."[138] Far beyond that ever provided by Taylor, Goodwin wrote over 200 pages examining the doctrine of perseverance of the saints.[139] Goodwin also devoted five chapters to an exegesis of Scriptures concerning the scope of atonement as he "endeavoured to close every loophole exploited by Calvinist theologians who wished to dodge the full force of Arminian proof texts."[140] Taylor's exegetical efforts were minimalistic compared to Goodwin's exhaustive manner. While the academic prowess of some of Goodwin's opponents, such as John Owen, contributed to his thoroughness, his liking for philosophical reasoning and precision demonstrated a natural tendency that differed from Taylor's almost sole focus on Christ's death for all as a fact of Scripture. The emphasis on simplicity and pragmatism within Taylor's evangelical outlook contrasted with the expansive defense of a general view of the atonement provided by Puritans such as Goodwin.[141]

Taylor's 1780 newspaper articles on the scope of Christ's death have been shown to confirm the novel nature of his advocacy of Christ's death for all. He successfully fulfilled his intention of modeling a way of engaging with the subject that was firm in its convictions but showed no animosity to those holding contrary beliefs. This contrasted with his observations in his local ministry. He focused in reasoned manner solely on the plain facts of Scripture, as understood by him, in favor of a general view of the atonement. He displayed a pragmatic outlook, and dismissed the insights of John Owen as too abstract and of little practical use. Taylor's conciseness also formed a contrast with the scrupulous efforts to prove Christ's death for all undertaken by Puritan Arminians such as John Goodwin. As will be examined next, the distinct way in which Taylor upheld general redemption was apparent within other aspects of his approach.

Taylor's Generous Spirited Approach

"the excellent of the earth"

Given Taylor's commitment to a general view of the atonement, it is necessary to consider why the doctrine received little extended attention in his

138. Scrutator [Taylor], "To Mr. Considerator," (date not specified), in Scrutator [Taylor], *Scrutator to Responsor*, 24. Considerator's letter (which cannot today be located) reached Taylor as he was finishing his final reply to Responsor. The identity of Considerator is unknown.

139. Goodwin dedicated seven chapters of *Redemption Redeemed* to this purpose.

140. Coffey, *John Goodwin*, 218.

141. I have found no evidence that Taylor ever cited Goodwin in any of his works.

earliest works. Prior to his affirmation of Christ's death for all in his 1775 "some Principal Parts of the Duty of Ministers" (as examined earlier), his ten previous publications, spanning a nine-year period, contain no detailed examination of the subject. Although, as highlighted earlier, mention was made of Christ's death for all in nearly all of Taylor's early works, it was not something that at this stage he chose to labor on. Help in accounting for this is found in a footnote attached to Taylor's brief assertion of belief in the universal scope of Christ's death in *Fundamentals of Religion in Faith and Practice*.[142] Taylor made clear his concern that his reference to Christ's death for all in the main body of his text might offend some of his readers. He hoped the footnote would provide a "sufficient apology" to those who "for conscience sake" differed from him in their opinion.[143] He specified that it was not his intention "to enter into any kind of controversy" or to cause anyone even "a moment's pain."[144] The "very weighty" nature of the doctrine did however mean that he felt compelled to address it.[145] He stated, "I could not well see my way clear, to open the gospel method of salvation, according to my apprehensions of it, without expressing my sentiments concerning the universal extent of our redeemer's design in dying for sinners."[146] Given that his engagement with controversial issues was not normally marked by a timidity of spirit, the sensitivity expressed in the footnote regarding those who held contrary understandings of the scope of the atonement likely accounts for why he had not delineated his thinking on this subject in his earliest works.[147] This sensitivity should be viewed as a significant feature of his approach to the subject. It was only after he assumed oversight of the New Connexion and recognized that a defense of what he held as core gospel truths was an important part of this responsibility that he began to advocate a general view of the atonement in a more substantial way. Even then, his advocacy of the doctrine retained a primacy on the need to be sensitive and considerate to the views of others.

The care with which Taylor upheld a general view of the atonement in his publications reflected his approach as a pastor. He regularly experienced local difficulties on this matter which, in turn, influenced the way

142. Dan Taylor, *Fundamentals*, 211. Taylor referred in the main body of the text to how "The sacred penmen very expressly inform us that the Lord Jesus Christ did not die for a part of mankind only, but for all men, without exception.," see ibid., 209–10.

143. Ibid., 211.

144. Ibid.

145. Ibid.

146. Ibid.

147. Whether Taylor also recognized the importance of the footnote in this respect is unknown.

he wrote. A typical example was his reaction to some theological quarreling that took place in the late 1760s. Some of Taylor's church members at Birchcliff disagreed with those of the neighboring Particular Baptist church at Wainsgate. The minister of this church was Taylor's good friend John Fawcett Sr. who was also influential in the establishment of an Association of Particular Baptist churches in Yorkshire and Lancashire.[148] The "squabbles" of their respective church members included considerable disagreement regarding the extent of Christ's atonement.[149] General and Particular Baptists had long been suspicious of each other. Their separate histories led to different organizational and theological emphases, of which the most contentious surrounded the scope of the atonement. A particular instance of discord between the two congregations occurred in July 1769.[150] While the precise issue is unspecified, it was central to the ongoing dispute. It is notable that Taylor and Fawcett agreed to address their churches on the same Sunday about their inappropriate divisive behavior, rather than defend the theological position of their members. Taylor joyfully recorded that this venture "succeeded as instrumental in making peace" and that he was very grateful for "so good-natured and peaceable a neighbour as Mr. Fawcett."[151] The way Taylor and Fawcett impressed on their congregations the need for mutual respect was indicative of the evangelical unity and generosity of spirit they shared as ministers.

The strong evangelical bond between Taylor and Fawcett led them to meet together regularly. Soon after Fawcett's arrival at Wainsgate in 1764, they began meeting and continued this practice as frequently as three or four times a week until Fawcett left to begin a new church in 1777.[152] They were sometimes also joined by Henry Foster (1745–1814) from Heptonstall who was training for the Anglican ministry in Oxford.[153] Despite Taylor and Fawcett's contrary views on the scope of the atonement, they realized they enjoyed many similarities such as their "congenial taste for literature" and strong organizational abilities.[154] However, it was their shared spiritual heritage in the Evangelical Revival that was key to their unity. Fawcett had been

148. Dan Taylor, diary entry, 9 July 1769, in Taylor, *Memoirs*, 32. For John Fawcett's involvement in the establishment of Yorkshire Baptist Association, see Haslam, "The Yorkshire Baptist Association," 273. See also Sellars, *Our Heritage*, 18–19, 21–22, 100. For an account of Fawcett's whole ministry, see Anon. [John Fawcett Jr.], *Account*.

149. Taylor, *Memoirs*, 32.

150. See Taylor, diary entry, 9 July 1769, 32.

151. Ibid.

152. Fawcett left Wainsgate to begin Ebenezer Baptist Church in Hebden Bridge.

153. See Taylor, *Memoirs*, 32.

154. Ibid.

strongly shaped through the preaching of George Whitefield.[155] Although
Taylor did not embrace Whitefield's Calvinist theology, he held him in high
regard, hearing him preach on different occasions at Haworth.[156] Taylor and
Fawcett together reflected on their faith and studied "to improve their knowledge of divinity, read the classics and cultivate other branches of learning."[157]
They recognized their agreement on evangelical imperatives such as the inspiration of the Scriptures, justification by faith, Christ's identity as the Son
of God, and the primacy of mission.[158] The way they chose to lay aside the
potential obstacle of their different persuasions on the scope of the atonement, and instead to unite around the other aspects of their evangelicalism,
was pioneering within Baptist life—both locally and beyond.

   A further example of Taylor's willingness to join with Particular Baptists was the close relationship he formed with John Sutcliff (1752–1814),
minister from 1775 of the Particular Baptist church in Olney, Buckinghamshire.[159] Sutcliff was born in the West Riding and became a member
of Fawcett's church in 1769. Presumably following an introduction by Fawcett, Sutcliff periodically assisted at Taylor's school in Wadsworth between
1769–72.[160] Despite Sutcliff's commitment to the limited scope of Christ's
atonement, an enduring friendship developed. The significance of Taylor's
influence on Sutcliff should be recognized. Taylor not only taught him Latin
but, even more importantly, what Adam Taylor referred to as that which was
"useful in the concerns of religion."[161] John Fawcett Jr. made similar mention
of Taylor having taught Sutcliff "the best things" of the Christian faith.[162]
Michael Haykin therefore argues that Taylor's insight into "spiritual matters"
and "tireless zeal for Christ" certainly "left their mark on Sutcliff."[163] Given
Sutcliff's later significance as an evangelical who was influential in promoting a more moderate Calvinism among the Particular Baptists, Taylor's early
influence should not be overlooked. Although not acknowledged by Haykin,
their friendship continued after Sutcliff's commencement of theological

155. Blomfield, "Yorkshire Baptist Churches," 98.

156. See chapter 1.

157. Taylor, *Memoirs*, 31.

158. Ibid.

159. For an examination of Sutcliff's life and ministry, see Haykin, *One Heart and One Soul*.

160. See Taylor, *Memoirs*, 33.

161. Ibid.

162. [Fawcett], *Account*, 162.

163. Haykin, *One Heart and One Soul*, 44.

study at Bristol Baptist Academy in 1772. They exchanged letters,[164] and following Taylor's move to London they met together regularly, with Taylor noting that he enjoyed "passing sweet and useful hours with his excellent friend, Mr. S."[165] Sutcliff also preached at least once at Taylor's church in London.[166] Taylor certainly valued his friendship with Sutcliff.

While Taylor trailblazed a more generous spirited approach to the scope of Christ's atonement than had been the norm within Particular Baptist and General Baptist relations, commonplace attitudes to this subject led to some who were close to him being treated very robustly. For example, his brother John was harshly treated when his doubts about the merits of Calvinism increased during the period he worshiped at Titus Knight's Independent congregation in Halifax.[167] As John Taylor recounted the events which led him to become a General Baptist, he expressed his disappointment that Knight had sought "to reprove me," and insisted "I must be quiet or take myself away."[168] Perhaps with the approach of his brother Dan in mind, he expressed his strong regret that Knight had not assumed a "more temperate conduct."[169] Dan Taylor was also aware of the difficulties experienced by William Thompson, his close colleague in General Baptist ministry.[170] When he wrote Thompson's memoirs, he referred to the early years of his ministry in Hull where his church was "divided and contentious" concerning the scope of the atonement.[171] As Thompson himself noted, "part of them were for Particular; and part of them for Universal Redemption."[172]

164. See Taylor, *Memoirs*, 33.

165. Dan Taylor, "Letter," (addressee and date not specified), in Taylor, *Memoirs*, 34.

166. Ibid.

167. It was noted in chapter 1 that Knight was Taylor's tutor during his years within Methodism. Knight then assumed Calvinist beliefs and began the Independent congregation in Halifax.

168. John Taylor, diary entry, 1769, in Adam Taylor, *John Taylor*, 24. While John Taylor recorded in his diary that he had been a Calvinist since he was young and had frequently sought to defend it, his doubts steadily increased. In 1769 he cited his chief stumbling block to his continued embrace of Calvinism, "I knew that the Scripture taught, in the plainest manner, the universality of the love of God and of the death of Jesus Christ, and that it did not restrict or confine these to any certain number. I therefore found it difficult for me to continue a Calvinist." See ibid., 23.

169. Ibid., 25. John Taylor was subsequently baptized by his brother (Dan Taylor) on 7 March 1770 and then became a member at Birchcliff, see ibid.

170. The background of Taylor's friendship with Thompson was examined in chapter 2.

171. William Thompson. Qtd in Dan Taylor, *Memoirs of William Thompson*, 72. Primary source unknown.

172. Ibid., 71. Primary source unknown.

This situation escalated with Thompson regretfully noting how "the prejudices of some grew so strong, that they could not be reconciled with any thing short of my removal."[173] Given Taylor's increased familiarity with these situations during the 1760s, it might have been expected that his 1770 publication of *Fundamentals* which, as stated in the title, examined *the Most Important Subjects of Doctrinal, Experimental, and Practical Divinity* would have included a lengthy defense of Christ's death for all. But as highlighted earlier, he made only brief reference. His desire to respect those who did not embrace a general view of the atonement was again apparent as he noted his "honour of being familiar, with several whom I reckon among the excellent of the earth, and who do, I doubt not, for conscience sake, differ from me in this particular."[174] This was indicative of the graciousness of spirit modeled by Taylor and other mission-minded evangelicals, such as Fawcett Sr.

A further important dimension of the approach Taylor advocated was his insistence that those seeking to establish the scope of Christ's atonement step aside from their "party" affiliations. This is apparent in his earlier examined engagement with Responsor in the *Leeds Intelligencer*. As Taylor highlighted Scriptures that he held as demonstrating Christ's death for the sins of the "whole world," he argued that they would not have been applied along the narrow confines that some in favor of a limited view of the atonement stipulated, "had it not been to serve a party scheme, which is generally the cause of Scripture being perverted."[175] Instead, he stated that "every honest, plain, unprejudiced reader, unacquainted with controversial niceties and party refinements, would not most naturally understand the words 'whole world,' as denoting 'all mankind.'"[176] Taylor appears to have been influenced by the prominence given within the Enlightenment to the espousal of a belief in objectivity.[177] He urged believers to step aside from preconceived attachments to the claims of Calvinist or Arminian atonement perspectives, and to focus on the Scriptures in objective manner. When writing on the scope of the atonement to Boyce, he emphasized that "the religion of the New Testament . . . does not consist in names, or notions, or forms, or impulses of any kind."[178] Similarly, when he referred to universal redemption at General Baptist minister John Deacon's

173. Ibid.

174. Taylor, *Fundamentals*, 211. John Fawcett Sr. is a likely example of one of those to whom Taylor was pointing.

175. Scrutator [Taylor], "Letter II. To Mr. Responsor," 19.

176. Ibid., 20.

177. It will be seen in chapter 4 that this aspect of Taylor's reasoning was even more pronounced during his engagement with Andrew Fuller.

178. Dan Taylor, "Letter II to Gilbert Boyce," 25 May 1793, 271.

(1757–1821) ordination, he warned against "the scandalous practice of calling *names* in the pulpit, or of *stigmatizing* others with the appellations of Socinian, Arian, Arminian or Calvinist. These names have no place in the Bible, and therefore have no business in your sermons."[179] This reflected the convictions expressed by other leading evangelicals such as Whitefield who, for example, when preaching in Philadelphia, urged that "God help us all to forget party names and to be Christians in deed and truth."[180] Although examples of such a stance were sometimes present within movements such as Puritanism,[181] the widespread resolve to such a commitment among evangelicals, although not uniform, was a notable characteristic of eighteenth-century evangelicalism. Its spirit was epitomized in what has been outlined here with regard to Taylor.

Given Taylor's outlook, it is not surprising he rejected Responsor's charge that his defense of a general view of the atonement relied on the reasoning of theologian James Arminius and that this caused him to go "too far" beyond the boundaries of Scripture.[182] Taylor was unequivocal that he was "far from approving the expressions of Arminius, and am not, therefore, accountable for them."[183] This pronouncement was justified, for while he shared some of Arminius's beliefs, such as in Christ's death for all, a conditional understanding of election, and adherence to the resistibility and sufficiency of God's grace so that all who freely exercised faith in Christ might be saved, there is no evidence that Taylor directly studied the specifics of Arminius's atonement perspective.[184] Although Taylor's awareness of the antagonism felt by most Calvinists towards Arminius and Arminians in general likely cautioned him against referring to Arminius in specific manner, it has already been demonstrated that Taylor's understanding of a general view of the atonement as a straightforward fact of Scripture was where he placed most importance. This served as a further stimulus to the priority Taylor placed on the need to relinquish preconceived affiliations to particular frameworks of atonement thinking.

179. Dan Taylor, *Charge and Sermon at Ordination of John Deacon*, 94, Taylor's emphasis. John Deacon was a son of Samuel Deacon Sr.—one of the founders in 1745 of the church at Barton-in-the-Beans whose significance in the formation of the New Connexion will be considered in chapter 5. For a brief overview of John Deacon's ministry, see Wood, *Condensed History*, 242.

180. Whitefield, "From the London Evangelical Magazine," 308.

181. This point will be considered further in chapter 7.

182. Responsor. Qtd in Scrutator [Taylor], "Letter II. To Mr. Responsor," 7.

183. Scrutator [Taylor], "Letter II. To Mr. Responsor," 7.

184. For an examination of the theological convictions of James Arminius, see Bangs, *Arminius*.

The less partisan approach to the atonement that Taylor aimed to model accounted for the respect he showed when he disagreed with those of Calvinist persuasion. An example was his treatment of John Owen. While Taylor, as noted earlier, rejected Owen's commitment to a limited view of the atonement and his related understanding of faith, predestination and reprobation, he maintained an attitude of deference that befitted Owen's esteemed scholarly status. He typically referred to Owen as one "whose memory I much venerate" and emphasized his "reverence to the Doctor."[185] Given Owen's opposition to the doctrine of universal redemption, Taylor's respect was significant. Taylor likely had Owen in mind when he declared, regarding the question of the extent of the atonement, that he had undertaken "a close and repeated study of the best authors on the opposite side of the question."[186] He also praised other aspects of Owen's theology such as his writings on indwelling sin.[187] The magnanimous nature of Taylor's manner of proceeding was epitomized in his earlier examined response to Robert Hall's *Help to Zion's Travellers*. Although Taylor contested Hall's understanding of election and endorsement of gospel invitations while believing that Christ only died for a limited number, he complimented wider aspects of Hall's approach. This is evident in his acknowledgment that other than "some very few expressions which seem to imply a limitation that I think the Scriptures does not countenance," he was adamant that "I must confess myself strongly inclined to Mr. H's views of the doctrine of atonement, in every branch."[188] Given the dimensions of Taylor's soteriology, which were outlined in the previous chapter, his praise for Hall was likely directed to chapter six of *Help to Zion's Travellers* which covered penal substitution and the necessity and efficacy of the atonement.[189] Taylor's wholehearted commendation of the broader dimensions of Hall's atonement thinking underlined the way in which Taylor's outlook differed from earlier expressions of Arminianism. Examples include both the way in which the seventeenth-century Dutch Remonstrants minimalized the effects of sin on the human condition to an extent that went beyond that stipulated by Taylor and Arminius, and the humanistic moralism that was the predominant orientation

---

185. Scrutator [Taylor], "Letter II. To Mr. Responsor," 7.

186. Taylor, *Fundamentals*, 211.

187. See Dan Taylor, diary entry, 18 May 1766, in Taylor, *Memoirs*, 70. From what Taylor acknowledged in his diary it is likely he was familiar with Owen's works such as his *Of the Mortification of Sin*, in Owen, *Works*, 6:1–86; and *Nature, Power, Deceit*, in ibid., 153–323.

188. Taylor, "Letter to George Birley," 31 January 1784, 167.

189. Hall, *Help to Zion's Travellers*, 92–115.

of the Arminianism embraced by many High Church Anglicans.[190] Taylor's evangelical Arminianism was of a different nature.

In summary, Taylor's upholding of the universal extent of Christ's death was marked by a determination to model an approach that was very considerate regarding the contrary beliefs of others. This accounted for his reluctance to delineate his thinking on the subject in his earliest works. It was also evident in his uniting with Fawcett Sr. around wider evangelical imperatives, ways in which they together sought to promote harmony between their respective churches concerning the scope of Christ's atoning work, and his rejection of "party" affiliations. It will be seen next that the evangelical platform of understanding that underpinned Taylor's appreciation and articulation of a general view of the atonement became increasingly uncommon among General Baptists outside of the New Connexion, in part due to the popularity of the teachings of Universalism.

Taylor's Discourse with Elhanan Winchester

"an alarming omen"

In 1793 Gilbert Boyce, in his capacity as a General Baptist Messenger, asked Taylor for his reflections concerning the numerical decline experienced by General Baptist churches that were not part of the New Connexion. Significantly, Taylor's answer was to emphasize the need for a vigorous preaching of the "fundamental doctrine" of Christ crucified for the sins of all.[191] He insisted this was "the sum and substance of the gospel," and that "all mankind" should be called to "a dependence on him as our great atonement."[192] Although not noted by Taylor, the way he linked the doctrine of a general view of the atonement with the task of mission was in some ways akin to earlier proponents of general redemption. An example was Thomas Helwys, whose 1611 *A Short and Plaine Proofe* sought to prove that Christ by his death had "redeemed all men."[193] A similar commitment to the doctrine was demonstrated by John Murton, who succeeded Helwys as leader of the General Baptist church in Spitalfields and whose 1617 *Truth's Champion* defended the need for all people to place their faith in Christ who died for

---

190. For more on the various strands of Arminianism, see Packer, *Honouring the People of God*, 279–307.

191. Taylor, "Letter I to Gilbert Boyce," 25 May 1793, 268.

192. Ibid., 268, 273; Taylor, "Letter I to Gilbert Boyce," 25 May 1793, 269.

193. Helwys, *Short and Plaine Proofe*, in Early, *Life and Writings of Thomas Helwys*, 89.

all.[194] However, many of the General Baptists of Taylor's day who belonged to the older body of believers did not hold the doctrine in the same missional regard. One of the reasons for this was the increasing credence given to the proponents of Universalism who were teaching that the universal scope of Christ's death was sufficient for all to be saved, irrespective of whether a person exercised faith in Christ.

Taylor's exposure to the teaching of Universalism increased following the attention given by many General Baptists outside of the New Connexion to the Universalist teachings of Elhanan Winchester during his visit to England between 1787–94.[195] Winchester was ordained as a Baptist minister in 1771 in Massachusetts, and in the mid-1770s changed from a Calvinist understanding of the limited scope of the atonement to a belief in its universal scope.[196] In 1781 he began to preach the doctrine of universal restoration.[197] Universalist works such as *The Everlasting Gospel* by Paul Siegvol (pseudonym for George Klein-Nicolai) and Sir George Stonehouse's *Universal Restitution* influenced his changed perspective and his founding in 1781 of the Society of Universal Baptists in Philadelphia.[198] Indicative of the attention Winchester commanded from English General Baptists was how, between 1790–92, he preached nearly every morning at Glass-House Yard General Baptist Church which then met at Worship Street, London, and was where the annual Assemblies of the denomination were held.[199] During this same period, Winchester gave evening lectures at White's Alley General Baptist Church which, from 1781, also met in Worship Street.[200] The significance of his ministry was noted by Adam Taylor who described how "the novelty of

194. Murton, *Truth's Champion*. Murton was a member of the original Gainsborough congregation of 1607 who traveled to Amsterdam. He was instructed in the faith by John Smyth while in Holland and then returned to London with Helwys and his congregation.

195. See Taylor, *Memoirs*, 189. For further consideration of Winchester, see Stone, *Biography of Rev. Elhanan Winchester*, 104–14. See also Parry, "Between Calvinism and Arminianism." Parry makes a very brief reference to Taylor's engagement with Winchester as he notes the respectful nature of their discourse, see ibid., 163.

196. Winchester details the chronology of his theological transition in the preface of *Universal Restoration*. See Winchester, *Universal Restoration*, Preface, iii–xxxvii.

197. Winchester's understanding of this is considered subsequently.

198. Siegvolk [George Klein-Nicolai], *The Everlasting Gospel*; Stonehouse, *Universal Restitution*. For the importance Winchester placed on these works, see Winchester, *Universal Restoration*, Preface, v–xix.

199. See Stone, *Biography of Rev. Elhanan Winchester*, 106; Vidler, *Sketch of the Life of Elhanan Winchester*, 80.

200. Stone, *Biography of Rev. Elhanan Winchester*, 106. Winchester also preached in other places, such as in Kent, Cambridge, Birmingham and Lincolnshire.

the sentiments" of his teaching "excited the attention of the religious public" and "gained proselytes among professors of various denominations."[201] The popularity of Winchester's teachings was such that by the end of 1792 he had formed a Baptist congregation with Universalist theological convictions at Parliament Court, Artillery Lane, Bishopsgate.[202]

Shortly after Winchester arrived in London, he published his most influential work *The Universal Restoration, Exhibited in Four Dialogues Between a Minister and His Friend*. Winchester taught the core material of this publication in London and other places. The thrust of his argument was that the doctrine of universal restoration for all sinners was far more in accord with the nature of God's love and justice than a belief in endless punishment. With reference to "the great number of heathen people that die without ever hearing the gospel, infants, idiots, persons born deaf," Winchester argued that it was unreasonable to believe that God created so many only to then condemn them.[203] He viewed it as similarly illogical to contend that a finite human creature was capable of sin meriting infinite punishment.[204] Taylor was concerned by much of what Winchester taught. This is apparent in a letter Taylor wrote to Birley in December 1788 where he noted, "It is amazing to me that the sentiment prevails in the manner it does. I think it an alarming omen with respect to the state of religion and the following age. Several churches in London are hurt by it."[205] Taylor's response was very different from the greater generosity of spirit that he extended to evangelicals who held to a limited view of the atonement. This serves as a reminder, as David Sorkin notes, that while toleration was a strong Enlightenment value, "This toleration was decidedly selective: every thinker and denomination had their respective limits."[206] Referring to Winchester's teachings, Adam Taylor recorded that many in the New Connexion "viewed its progress with sorrow, and wished that some attempt could be made to check its course."[207] Dan Taylor was himself approached by "numbers of his brethren in the ministry in London" who "earnestly solicited" him to make a response.[208] These included the influential Particular Baptist minister Abraham Booth

201. Taylor, *Memoirs*, 189.

202. Stone, *Biography of Rev. Elhanan Winchester*, 106.

203. Winchester, *Universal Restoration*, Contents Page, xlv.

204. Ibid., 265–71.

205. Dan Taylor, "Letter to George Birley," 30 December 1788, 189–90.

206. Sorkin, *Religious Enlightenment*, 15.

207. Taylor, *Memoirs*, 189.

208. Ibid.

and Henry Foster who was now a Church of England minister in London.[209] Although it is likely that their appeals to Taylor stemmed from a concern at the possible effects of Winchester's teachings on their own contexts of ministry, they also suggest that they respected Taylor's grasp of a general view of the atonement and particularly the way he held to it with such firm evangelical convictions. The holding together of these two theological strands had become an increasingly novel outlook among the General Baptists.

Taylor took seriously those who implored him to make a response to the teachings of Winchester. He was mindful that "All seem to think that something ought to be written in opposition to it, yet no one seems willing to undertake it," and therefore wrote two sermons on *The Eternity of Future Punishment*.[210] These were subsequently extended and published in pamphlet form in 1789.[211] This included an examination of matters such as the correct translation of the word "everlasting"; scriptural references to punishment lasting "forever and ever"; passages which imply that the wicked will never be restored to happiness after death; the eternal plight of particular sinners such as Judas Iscariot; and Jesus's references to the everlasting nature of the torments of hell.[212] Taylor's conclusion was that the eternal punishment of sinners was "a plain Scripture doctrine, positively and repeatedly asserted" and that nobody should therefore "be deluded with vain hopes of deliverance from punishment, if you continue in sin."[213] He considered those who taught otherwise as having failed to appreciate the true "filthiness" of sin and extent to which it "spoiled all the creation of God" and "separated the soul from God."[214] Taylor was adamant that nonbelievers could only be free of punishment if they had been "purified by faith" in Christ's saving work and therefore received the blessing of God's "great transaction," whereby Christ bore the sins of all people so that all might enter into "the *everlasting* enjoyment of God."[215] The firmness and

209. Ibid. The nature of Taylor's friendship with Booth will be considered in chapter 7. Foster's friendship with Taylor was noted earlier in the chapter. Foster served at several different churches in London, for a brief overview of his ministry, see [Anon.], "Additions to Obituary: The Late Rev. Henry Foster," in Urban [Edward Cave], *Gentleman's Magazine* 84 (July–December 1814) 704. Sylanvus Urban was a pseudonym for Edward Cave who founded *The Gentleman's Magazine* in 1731.

210. Taylor, "Letter to George Birley," 30 December 1788, 190.

211. Dan Taylor, *Eternity of Future Punishment*.

212. Ibid., 33, 34.

213. Ibid., 34.

214. Ibid., 40.

215. Ibid., 43, 43, 44; Taylor's emphasis.

clarity with which Taylor held to a general view of the atonement, within a framework of evangelical understanding, was apparent.

Taylor informed Birley, with much pleasure, that many ministers had found his publication helpful. He wrote, "As to the London ministers, many of them, of various denominations have expressed their approbation of my small thing, in terms too strong for me to repeat."[216] Given Taylor's general humility, this assertion is significant. Taylor proceeded to note how Henry Foster bought "half a guinea's worth to give away" and wrote to his contacts in Yorkshire recommending they purchase it.[217] A further indication of the respect Taylor's publication commanded is how Winchester stated that a friend "earnestly" asked him in a letter "to answer Mr. TAYLOR in every part."[218] Winchester duly obliged, noting that he spent an afternoon writing his brief thoughts on Taylor's *The Eternity of Future Punishment*.[219] These were sent to his unnamed friend and attached to his publication of *The Holy Conversation, and High Expectation of True Christians*. Winchester was firm that Taylor had not succeeded in persuading him to change his stance. Instead, Winchester drew attention to different Scriptures that he understood as pointing to the limited duration of punishment, and meaning that "all men must be included" in Christ's ultimate restoration of the world to a perfect state of happiness.[220] In addition, he defended his position by highlighting points of emphasis, such as how he believed Taylor had advanced an incorrect understanding of the word "everlasting," that endless misery would contradict scriptural promises of blessing and honor being available to all, and that Taylor had failed to appreciate the greater capacity of mercy to overcome any corrupting factors of sin. Although Winchester was entrenched in his thinking, he was full of praise for how Taylor had caused him to "rejoice at his taking up the pen, because he appears to be influenced, not by a malicious party spirit, but by nobler motives."[221] As is noted throughout this chapter, such an observation was a significant feature of Taylor's evangelicalism.

---

216. Dan Taylor, "Letter to George Birley," 4 April 1798 [1789?], 190. It would seem that Adam Taylor made a mistake with the dating of this letter. It was more likely to have been written in 1789. 1798 neither fits into the chronology of the material that comprises this section of *Memoirs* nor the timing of Taylor's immediate response to Winchester's work.

217. Taylor, "Letter to George Birley," 4 April 1798 [1789?], 190.

218. Winchester, *Letter to a Friend*, 40; Winchester's emphasis.

219. Ibid., 56.

220. Ibid., 42.

221. Ibid., 55.

Winchester's response did not bring their discourse to a close, as Taylor wrote a reply in late 1789. As implied in the title of the work *The Eternity of Future Punishment Re-asserted*, this publication saw Taylor re-cast and re-emphasize the chief material that had formed the substance of his previous work.[222] It consisted of six letters to Gilbert Boyce who was keen that Taylor issued a further response to Winchester due to his concern at how the doctrine was being embraced by General Baptists.[223] Taylor's desire to help rectify this situation was a key factor in his willingness to oblige, despite sharing his frustrations with Birley that Winchester's reply had included much that was "foreign to the subject" as well as certain "misrepresentations."[224] Winchester responded to Taylor later in the year with his publication of *The Restitution of All Things* which, as noted in the title, included *An Attempt to Answer the Reverend Dan Taylor's Assertions and Re-Assertions in Favour of Endless Misery*.[225] While Winchester reiterated his "personal respect for Taylor," he provided only an extension of the points he had made in his reply to Taylor's *The Eternity of Future Punishment*. Taylor's resolve was again apparent as he issued yet another response, although for some unknown reason this was not printed.[226] His willingness to respond to Winchester for a third time was again indicative of the importance he placed on an evangelical understanding of a general view of the atonement, and of his concern that many General Baptists were being influenced by what Winchester taught.

Following Winchester's return to America in 1794 his congregation at Parliament Court was led by William Vidler (1758–1816) who prior to becoming a Universalist after reading Winchester's works and then serving as Winchester's assistant, was minister of a Particular Baptist church in Battle, Sussex.[227] Andrew Fuller, beginning in 1795, wrote a series of letters, challenging Vidler's theological thinking.[228] After these were collectively published in 1802, Taylor expressed "considerable pleasure."[229] In 1802

222. Dan Taylor, *Eternity of Future Punishment, Re-asserted*.

223. See Taylor, *Memoirs*, 191.

224. Dan Taylor, "Letter to George Birley," 26 July 1790, 191.

225. Winchester, *Restitution of All Things*.

226. See Taylor, *Memoirs*, 192. It is unfortunate that there appears to be no surviving copy.

227. For consideration of Vidler's ministry and the evolution of his theological convictions, see Butt-Thompson, "William Vidler," 42–55. See also Parry, "Between Calvinism and Arminianism," 145.

228. See Fuller, *Letters to Mr. Vidler*, in Fuller, *Works*, 133–49.

229. Dan Taylor, "Letter to George Birley," 20 April 1803. Page not numbered.

Vidler was admitted into the Assembly of the older General Baptists,[230] having also embraced Unitarianism the previous year.[231] This met with Taylor's deepest disapproval and in 1803 he consequently withdrew from the Assembly, which he had remained nominally a part of since the establishment of the New Connexion.[232] His commitment to an evangelical understanding of the gospel was paramount.

Conclusion

As Taylor participated in the Evangelical Revival, he became convinced of the truth of a general view of the atonement. His understanding of the doctrine was further consolidated during his time spent within the structures of Methodism. The novel nature of Taylor's approach did not concern his actual doctrine but the way in which it was outworked. Although not delineating his thinking on the subject until the mid-1770s, the distinctive nature of Taylor's advocacy of Christ's death for all was apparent in the readiness and frequency with which he pointed to it as he addressed a variety of different issues. The regularity with which he drew attention to it in his works was beyond that of renowned proponents of the doctrine such as John Wesley, and influential General Baptists such as Grantham and Monk. There were also differences between the way Taylor confessed his belief in the assurance of salvation for all who exercised faith in Christ's atoning work and election, compared to that stipulated in the General Baptist Standard Confession and *Orthodox Creed*. A further difference was the way in which his affirmation of the doctrine was to the extent that it shaped the direction of his ministry. In particular, the connection he posited between God's love as supremely manifest in the universal scope of Christ's death and way that he, in turn, heralded it as providing the prime motivation and mandate to share the gospel with others, reflected the outward thrust of his evangelicalism. This is evident in his response to Robert Hall Sr.'s *Help to Zion's Travellers*. Hall's publication caused Taylor to outline carefully the basis on which he rejected understandings of election that were based on God, in determinate manner, having foreordained only a limited number to be saved. His rejection of this belief differed from the viewpoints held by some earlier prominent General Baptists, and that expressed in certain Articles within the Standard Confession, and *Orthodox Creed*.

230. See Whitley, *Minutes of General Baptist Assembly, 1654–1728*, xxv.
231. Butt-Thompson, "William Vidler, Baptist and Universalist," 52.
232. See Whitley, *Minutes of the General Assembly, 1654–1728*, xxv.

The novel nature of Taylor's advocacy of general redemption was evident in his 1780 articles to a Leeds newspaper. Keen to demonstrate a different way of approaching the subject to what he had observed locally, his submissions were free of animosity regarding those who did not share his convictions. His repeated focus on that which he understood as the straightforward facts of Scripture in favor of a general view of the atonement, and pragmatic dismissal of John Owen's insights as too abstract, were both in keeping with the nature of his evangelicalism. His succinctness also differed from the meticulous efforts to prove Christ's death for all that were undertaken by Puritan Arminians, such as John Goodwin. Similar to certain other evangelicals, Taylor's rejection of entrenched "party" affiliations was a further prominent feature of his approach and underpinned his sensitive articulation of the doctrine. The wider context of Taylor's discourse with the Universalist teachings of Elhanan Winchester demonstrated that Taylor's advocacy of an evangelical understanding of Christ's death for all had become an increasingly novel position among the General Baptists who remained outside of the New Connexion. Taylor's response to Winchester epitomized the pre-eminent position that his evangelical framework of a general view of the atonement assumed within his theological schema. At the same time that Taylor entered into dialog with Winchester, the distinctiveness of his evangelicalism and influence of the Enlightenment on his thinking, were again evident as he engaged in theological discourse with Andrew Fuller. This will be examined next.

4

Enlightened Critic

TAYLOR THROUGHOUT HIS MINISTRY entered into many theological discourses, but none was of greater significance than his 1786–90 engagement with Particular Baptist minister Andrew Fuller. As will be examined,
the catalyst was Fuller's publication of *The Gospel of Christ Worthy of All
Acceptation.*[1] This became a renowned statement of eighteenth-century
evangelical Calvinism. Particular consideration will be given to how
Taylor's critique of the basis from which Fuller advocated universal gospel
invitations led Fuller to make important modifications to his thinking. It
will be seen that the way Taylor persuaded Fuller to recognize the sufficiency of Christ's death for all (albeit applied in limited manner to the elect)
was of significance, especially since Fullerism became "the new orthodoxy"
among Particular Baptists.[2] Through a delineation of the central arguments
by which Taylor rejected Fuller's reasoning, such as Fuller's distinction between natural and moral inability, it will be argued that Taylor's perspective
was both shaped and fueled by important Enlightenment values. Taylor's
recognition of the common evangelical ground which existed between
Fuller and himself also influenced him to initiate certain pragmatically inspired changes to some of his convictions. Attention will be given to the
depth of insight Taylor provided into wider aspects of his understanding of
the means and process of conversion. Throughout their discourse, it will be
seen that elements of Taylor's thinking were pioneering. In addition, it will
be contended that, compared to older expressions of Arminianism, the new
form of evangelical Arminianism that Taylor embraced and embodied was

1. Fuller, *Gospel Worthy.*
2. R. Watts, *Dissenters,* 460.

less combative, more focused on the broad lines of argument, and always grounded in practical application.

Taylor's Rejection of the Basis from which Fuller Advocated Universal Gospel Offers

"universal invitations must be founded on universal provision"

It was Taylor's close friend and fellow New Connexion minister George Birley who presented him with a copy of Fuller's *The Gospel Worthy* in 1785, its year of publication.[3] This "epoch making work" formed Fuller's thinking into a vital "theological unity," as well as the more progressive and overtly missional emphases of other leading Particular Baptists, such as Robert Hall Sr., John Ryland Jr. (1753–1825) who was Fuller's official biographer, and John Sutcliff.[4] The publication was completed while Fuller was minister at the Particular Baptist congregation in Kettering known as the "Little Meeting." Prior to this he grew up in Soham, Cambridgeshire, becoming minister of its Particular Baptist church in 1775.[5] It was there that Fuller was exposed to the evangelicalism of certain colleagues in the Northamptonshire Particular Baptist Association. A subsequent fusion began to take place between his inherited High Calvinism and a fervent evangelicalism. Ryland noted how, theologically, "several of his brethren very cordially coincided with him, and had earnestly advised the publication" of what became *The Gospel Worthy*.[6] Fuller's immediate motivation was his frustration at the influence of High Calvinism within the Particular Baptists, which he considered as detrimental to mission and specifically to the gospel being preached to all people. Typically, High Calvinists preached only the facts of Christ's work, due to an interpretation of the Scriptures which denied that the invitation to come to him for salvation was extended to all sinners. Instead, salvation was understood as restricted to the elect, who God alone would bring to faith, through the sovereign outworking of his purposes. They also believed that faith in Christ should not be viewed as a duty for all, and that those advocating the free offer of salvation to all were therefore teaching that people were saved by their own efforts, rather

---

3. Adam Taylor, *Memoirs*, 173.

4. Clipsham, "Andrew Fuller," 269.

5. For the development of Fuller's theological thinking over these years, see Morden, *Offering Christ*, 7–30.

6. Ryland Jr., *Work of Faith*, 132. Ryland was Fuller's official biographer and had access to all Fuller's private papers, see Morden, *Offering Christ*, 2.

than by the grace of God.[7] In contrast, Fuller emphasized divine sovereignty and human responsibility.[8] Specifically, he sought to demonstrate that universal gospel invitations were in accordance with the Scriptures and that it was the duty of all to believe. This conviction was at the heart of the Evangelical Revival with both Calvinists and Arminians preaching it with equal conviction.

The publication of *The Gospel Worthy* elicited a strong reaction within the New Connexion. Some members approached Taylor and "besought him with tears" to publish a response, assuring him of their "fervent prayers for his success."[9] While the Connexion did not oppose the "profound revitalization" which the Particular Baptists experienced during the closing decades of the eighteenth century, there was a strongly shared conviction that all evangelistic endeavors should emanate from the theological premise that Christ died for all.[10] It was a source of much disquiet that those leading the new found Particular Baptist evangelistic impetus did not hold this view. This concern was further compounded by the fact it was being expounded by one as theologically able as Fuller, within whose writings "The stirrings of revival and recovery among Particular Baptists reached its zenith."[11] The widespread respect for Fuller's skill as a writer likely accounts for why earlier works such as Hall Sr.'s *Help to Zion's Travellers*, which was known to members of the Connexion and contains certain principles found in *The Gospel Worthy*, did not provoke the same intensity of response.[12] As far as Taylor was concerned, the fervency of the Connexion's reaction and the pivotal significance he attributed to Christ's death for all meant that he willingly acquiesced to the New Connexion's request that he issue a response.

Taylor's reply took the form of nine letters written to Birley between November 1785 and January 1786, collectively entitled *Observations on the Rev. Andrew Fuller's Late Pamphlet*.[13] Using the pseudonym Lover of All

---

7. See Daniel, "Andrew Fuller," 81.

8. See Morden, "Andrew Fuller," 137.

9. Taylor, *Memoirs*, 173.

10. Haykin, "Habitation of God" 306.

11. McBeth, *Baptist Heritage*, 181.

12. Hall Sr., *Help to Zion's Travellers*. As examined in chapter 3, Hall held to a determinative understanding of election while also advocating that the gospel be offered to all.

13. Lover of All Mankind [Dan Taylor], *Observations*. Given that the discourse between Taylor and Fuller led to the publication of other works where the word "observations" is central to their titles, I have sought to prevent any confusion by hereafter referring to Taylor's *Observations* in my main text as the *Nine Letters*.

Mankind/Philanthropos,[14] Taylor contested Fuller's belief that "Christ only died for some of the human race" and instead sought to prove the universal scope of the atonement.[15] It is significant that Taylor adopted a very respectful tone while being resolute in his aims. Although it is going too far to claim, as does Gerald Priest, that Taylor thought he had a "soul mate in Fuller," he appreciated the common ground they shared as evangelicals.[16] For example, he commended Fuller's endorsement of "so important a subject" as the proclamation of universal gospel invitations.[17] Taylor stated that this had caused him to "rejoice."[18] He expressed his hope that God would "give success to his [Fuller's] important undertaking" of seeking to convince other Calvinists of the validity of offering gospel invitations, and that it was the duty of all who heard to respond in faith.[19] Taylor was also complimentary regarding Fuller's "seriousness, impartiality and frankness of temper" and general "force of argument."[20] As will become evident, such an irenic way of proceeding was a uniform facet of Taylor's and Fuller's approaches to all aspects of their discourse. This was indicative of how they were nurtured as evangelicals in the context of the Enlightenment where the values of respect and cooperation were ascendant.

Taylor's respect for Fuller was apparent as he expressed his hope that his response would not cause him even "a moment's pain."[21] However, he was unequivocal that Fuller's advocacy of a particular view of redemption, alongside a conviction that the gospel be offered to all, was an "embarrassment to his hypothesis."[22] The language of Taylor's criticism reflected the high regard found within the Enlightenment for establishing and testing hypotheses. Taylor viewed Fuller's hypothesis as flawed because "universal invitations must be founded on universal provision."[23] This crucial difference in belief served as a focal point for Taylor throughout the Nine Letters. Taylor strongly rejected Fuller's stipulation that there was no need for a person "to have any particular interest in Christ's death, in order to make trusting

14. The publication is attributed to Lover of All Mankind and Taylor signed each of the nine letters with the Greek term Philanthropos which means love of humanity, or as Taylor put it—lover of all mankind.
15. Fuller, Gospel Worthy, 106.
16. Priest, "Andrew Fuller's Response," 67.
17. Lover of All Mankind [Taylor], Observations, 4.
18. Ibid.
19. Ibid., 37.
20. Ibid., 4.
21. Ibid.
22. Ibid., 15.
23. Ibid., 90.

in him his duty."²⁴ Taylor was firm that there could be no expectation that anybody would "rationally trust in him, as a Saviour, before he understand that he died for him" and that in the absence of such an assurance, "all the regards I can have to Jesus, are not the regards of faith, but of unbelief."²⁵ It was not possible to approach Christ with confidence, for he could not be viewed as "the friend of any for whom he did not die."²⁶ Taylor similarly dismissed Fuller's comparison of the conduct required by sinners in relation to Christ and the need for admittance of guilt, with trust in a prince by a person condemned for treason. Taylor insisted that it was impossible for a person to have confidence in a prince's clemency unless it was first directed towards them. He likewise argued that if Christ "manifested no clemency towards any for whom he did not die," then there was no "foundation to *trust* in him, till we have learnt that he died for us."²⁷ Taylor's critique of this aspect of Fuller's scheme was underpinned by a Lockean framework which, as examined in chapter 2, saw Taylor frequently urge that claims to truth must be judged with reason and common sense.

A consequence of *The Gospel Worthy* was that Fuller found himself, as John Morris described, "between two fires; the Hyper-Calvinists on the hills and the Arminians in the vallies."²⁸ As Fuller anticipated the response from Arminians that if the atonement was limited to only a few then the means and basis by which most could believe was removed, he referred to the arguments of the Puritan writer Elisha Coles. While he cited Coles's claim that though Christ only died for a limited number, there was hope for all as "you may be of that number,"²⁹ Taylor was emphatic that "may be" was "no foundation for faith."³⁰ He similarly dismissed Coles's urging of submission to God's mercy in the hope that "peradventure he will save me," as contrary to the early church's message that all are included in Christ's atoning work.³¹ Taylor also rejected the view of Dutch theologian Herman Witsius, as cited by Fuller, that the Scriptures do not teach that people are "commanded immediately to believe *that Christ died for them*; for that is a falsehood,"

24. Fuller, *Gospel Worthy*, 106. Taylor viewed this as a "fundamental paradox which served to invalidate his whole scheme of thought," see Lover of All Mankind [Taylor], *Observations*, 30.

25. Lover of All Mankind [Taylor], *Observations*, 31–32, 15.

26. Ibid., 16.

27. Ibid., 32; Taylor's emphasis.

28. Morris, *Memoirs*, 205.

29. Coles, *Practical Discourse*, 143. Qtd in Fuller, *Gospel Worthy*, 135.

30. Lover of All Mankind [Taylor], *Observations*, 33.

31. Coles, *Practical Discourse*, 142. Qtd in Fuller, *Gospel Worthy*, 134. For Taylor's rejection of this view, see Lover of All Mankind [Taylor], *Observations*, 33.

but that the process of faith begins when a person recognizes their state of condemnation before God and renounces all other means of salvation.[32] This view was dismissed by Taylor as failing to appreciate the different ways that people came to faith, and as being out of line with the teaching of the Scriptures and way that the gospel is to be received as good news.[33] As normal in his evangelical response to the works of Puritan scholars, Taylor emphasized the simplicity and plain message of the Scriptures.[34] He argued that if the basis for a person's coming to faith was not a confidence that Christ died for them, then he failed to understand how "we are to interpret the language of the apostles."[35] Also, he accused Fuller of failing to appreciate that the precedent of offering universal gospel invitations on the basis of Christ's provision for all was already established within the Calvinist tradition by those Taylor referred to as "INCONSISTENT CALVINISTS."[36] As was noted in chapter 3, he cited the preaching of George Whitefield (among others) as an example of how "it naturally appeared to their auditors, that God was willing they should all be saved; and that Christ had died for them all."[37] That he drew on the example of George Whitefield is not surprising, Whitefield himself noted in a letter to John Wesley that "Though I hold particular election, yet I offer JESUS freely to every individual soul."[38] Taylor was clearly impacted by this when he heard Whitefield preach at Haworth, during his participation in the Evangelical Revival.

Fuller's belief that Christ atoned for only a limited number and that it was therefore not possible for a person to believe that Christ had died specifically for them until they had actually partaken of that salvation, led him to contend that the universal obligation to obey the gospel was founded on the moral law. This was refuted by Taylor, who cited the contrary nature of the law and gospel as "two distinct covenants, built on two different foundations."[39] Taylor contrasted the "slavery and condemnation" of the "native tendency" of gospel invitations issued from the law's commands with the promises of grace emanating from "the most natural and eligible ground of universal

---

32. Witsius, *The Economy of the Covenants*, 44. Qtd in Fuller, *Gospel Worthy*, 137; Fuller's emphasis.

33. Lover of All Mankind [Taylor], *Observations*, 33–35.

34. This aspect of Taylor's approach was considered in chapters 2 and 3.

35. Lover of All Mankind [Taylor], *Observations*, 35.

36. Ibid., 62; Taylor's emphasis.

37. Ibid., 61.

38. Whitefield, "Letter CCCLXIII to John Wesley," 331; Whitefield's emphasis.

39. Lover of All Mankind [Taylor], *Observations*, 90.

invitations"—that of God's love and provision for all in Christ's death.[40] Fuller's advocacy of issuing gospel invitations from the platform of the moral law was held by Taylor as giving rise to a representation of God which sharply differed from a gospel framed understanding of his character, particularly his "free grace and mercy."[41] Taylor also underlined that he did not believe the gospel could be received as good news if offered on the basis of duty to the moral law. He asked, how could it be good news to tell people

> they are commanded of God, and obliged, by the moral law, to repent and believe in the Lord Jesus Christ, on pain of damnation; when yet they are not informed that Christ has died for them, and that salvation is provided for them![42]

He contended that this would be "bad news," and that it made God appear like an Egyptian task master who beat the Israelites "for that which they were not able to avoid."[43] As on other occasions, Taylor's disdain for such a notion was also undergirded by the influence of the values of justice and benevolence within the Enlightenment.

The importance Taylor placed on an understanding of God's actions towards humanity that was just and equitable was again apparent, as he emphasized the link between Christ's death for all and God's desire that all might know him. He argued that it was implausible for God to have given his Son for only a few, as this denied the possibility of salvation for any outside this number, and contradicted Scripture's depiction of God's goodness, mercy, and revealed will that all might repent and be saved.[44] Instead, he saw it as natural that God would do all he could so that all might respond in faith and none perish. Similarly, Taylor pointed to the theological coherence between a general view of the atonement and what he viewed as Scripture's depiction of a sinner's eternal misery being caused by unbelief. Taylor insisted that it would be unjust for a person's condemnation to be based on their unbelief, if Christ had not died for them. To do so would be to present God as "a cruel and merciless tyrant," as people could not believe if no provision of salvation had been made for them.[45] If Christ's death for all was accepted, then he concluded that all difficulty and inconsistency was eradicated. All humankind could then be judged accountable for its response to the gospel,

40. Ibid., 94, 94, 95.
41. Ibid., 91.
42. Ibid., 92.
43. Ibid.
44. Ibid., 74.
45. Ibid., 88.

with God's justice and grace able "to shine forth in all their awfully glorious lustre."[46] This assertion encapsulated the passion he felt on this matter.

    After Birley received Taylor's seventh letter of response to *The Gospel Worthy*, he criticized Taylor for only providing "general hints" as to why he held a general view of the atonement.[47] Birley felt that if Taylor was going to succeed in his aim of persuading Fuller "to embrace another gospel doctrine, which appears to me to lie at the foundation of that he has undertaken to vindicate," then this required "positive proof" from the Scriptures in favor of the universal extent of Christ's death.[48] Birley's intervention was merited. Considering Taylor's commitment to general redemption formed a vital point of inter-connection between all aspects of his reply, an absence of scriptural exposition was a significant omission. In response, Taylor attributed this to his dislike of controversy, thereby demonstrating a similar apologetic reserve to the subject as evident in the early years of his ministry (see chapter 3). He presumably anticipated inflammatory reactions such as that which appeared in the July 1787 edition of *The Monthly Review*, where his publication was deemed useful "in enlarging the conceptions of those narrow minded Christians, who think the kingdom of heaven no larger than the synagogue of their own little flock."[49] Taylor's caution reflected the irenic tendencies of his evangelicalism, yet for some within the Connexion, such as Birley, it was misconceived.

    It is evident that Taylor accepted Birley's criticism, as in his eighth letter he provided from the Scriptures what he viewed as "very good proof" in favor of the universal scope of Christ's death.[50] He drew attention to references that he believed "*must* be so explained and understood, as to teach us that Jesus died for all men, without exception."[51] He pointed to John 3:16 and claimed that distinguishing between Christ's death, and those who would choose to believe, would have been unnecessary if he only died for those who were saved.[52] In addition, he sought to convince Fuller of the need for a literal understanding of the word "all" in respect of the scope of Christ's

---

46. Ibid., 87.

47. Birley, "Letter to Taylor" (date not specified). Qtd in Lover of All Mankind [Taylor], *Observations*, 70.

48. Lover of All Mankind [Taylor], *Observations*, 38; Birley, "Letter to Taylor." Qtd in Lover of All Mankind [Taylor], *Observations*, 70.

49. [Anon.], "Art. 45. Observations on Fuller," 85.

50. Lover of All Mankind [Taylor], *Observations*, 71.

51. Ibid., 77; Taylor's emphasis. In an attempt to demonstrate the universal scope of Christ's death he cited passages such as 2 Cor 4:14–15, 1 Tim 2:6, Heb 2:9, and 1 John 2:2.

52. Ibid., 82. He also referred to passages of Scripture such as the wedding banquet of Matt 22:1–11 and John 6:32.

death, as recorded in passages such as 2 Cor 5:14–15.[53] Taylor was adamant that to understand these verses in any other way was illogical, and that "all" should therefore be interpreted in its broadest sense.[54] With accompanying scriptural citation, he again pointed to the gospel as "good news," insisting this description would not have been used if Christ's death had not been for "every creature."[55] Taylor urged Fuller to accept the contrast between the many passages that he felt demonstrated the universal extent of Christ's death, and absence of any clear scriptural evidence that Christ died only for a part of humankind. He also stated that it was inconceivable that "so weighty a doctrine would have been left to mere inference."[56] Fuller had not previously been directly exposed to such a considered provision of scriptural evidence in favor of a general view of the atonement.[57] Neither was Fuller used to being treated so respectfully when engaging in theological discourse. Peter Morden draws attention to how the "respectful tone" of his dialog with Taylor was very different from the "acrimonious" nature of Fuller's debate on the atonement with the High Calvinist John Martin.[58]

It is notable that Taylor's exposition of his basis for belief in Christ's death for all, and exhortation of the necessity that universal gospel invitations be founded on universal provision, contain a lack of reference to other publications which he might have used to corroborate his position. With the exception of several unreferenced quotes of minor significance, there is no mention of any individual or published work. This reflects Taylor's ownership of the subject that he had acquired after "many years consideration."[59] It is also indicative of how evangelicals, in contrast to

53. Taylor's reflections exceeded in detail that examined in chapter 2 regarding his earlier private correspondence on the same subject with Birley and within his 1780 submissions to the *Leeds Intelligencer* newspaper. His approach to 2 Cor 5:14–15 was typical. He emphasized how the second aspect of Paul's first clause in verse 14, "one died for *all* and therefore *all* died," referred to "all" people in its most expansive understanding. He argued that the second clause in verse 15, where Paul wrote "he died for all," should be interpreted as extensively as the "all" in the preceding verse, see ibid., 77, Taylor's emphasis.

54. Ibid., 84–85.

55. Ibid.

56. Ibid., 72.

57. This is a point emphasized by Morden in his consideration of Taylor's dialog with Fuller, see Morden, *Offering Christ*, 65–72. It was very likely George Birley's anticipation of how Taylor would be able to articulate effectively a defense of a general view of the atonement that caused him to view Taylor's provision of a basis for belief in general redemption as such an imperative.

58. Ibid., 65.

59. Lover of All Mankind [Taylor], *Observations*, 88, 98.

writers from the earlier scholastic period, were often more inclined to focus exclusively on the biblical text, without feeling the need to make reference to any wider authorities. As Taylor stated in his response to *The Gospel Worthy*, this way of proceeding was undergirded by that which was central to how he functioned as an innovative apologist—his belief that the Bible was "a book for the instruction of plain men."[60] This meant that the notion of God giving his Son for only part of humankind could not be true, as God would never express himself "in the *letter* of his word, different from his real *meaning*."[61] Taylor's resolve to demonstrate what he felt was the true meaning of the Scriptures concerning Christ's death for all, led him to advocate that those in sympathy with Fuller's position should step aside from preconceived systems of thought and prejudices. He provided numerous examples where he felt that the "natural construction" and historical and literary contexts of Scriptures pointed in favor of Christ's death being general, rather than limited in scope.[62] While such an approach was in accord with Taylor's understanding of the Scriptures as the revealed word of God, it also reflected how Enlightenment thinkers believed that the truth of a matter could be determined through the process of objective and measured reasoning. This likely further contributed to the way in which Taylor's publication meaningfully connected with Fuller, who was similarly influenced by Enlightenment values.[63]

In summary, a central element of Taylor's response to *The Gospel Worthy* included his attempt to expose what he held as Fuller's illogical and inconsistent alignment of universal gospel offers while embracing a limited view of the atonement. Although robust in his argument, the respect Taylor showed Fuller was an example of the tendency for irenic debate that marked evangelical dialogs between Arminians and Calvinists. Also notable was Taylor's Lockean insistence that Fuller's claims to truth must be measured in accordance with reason. This was underpinned by an affinity to the Enlightenment values of justice and benevolence, with Taylor arguing that Christ could not have died for only a particular few as this would have contravened these foundational aspects of God's character. Characteristic of Taylor's evangelicalism was that his proof for general redemption also focused on the plain message of the Scriptures, and that there was a corresponding absence of reference to wider works. It will next be seen that with

60. Ibid., 75. This aspect of Taylor's apologetic approach was examined in chapter 2.

61. Ibid.; Taylor's emphasis.

62. Ibid., 76.

63. For examples of the influence of the Enlightenment on Fuller's thinking, see Morden, *Offering Christ*, 66–67.

similar coherence, logic, and conviction, Taylor refuted Fuller's understanding of the process of conversion.

Taylor's Rejection of Fuller's Understanding of the Means of Conversion

"If I were to command a stone to walk, or a horse
to sing, they could not obey me"

Taylor's response to *The Gospel Worthy* included a rejection of the viewpoint that God's role in conversion was in any sense determinative. On this basis, he provided a robust rebuttal of Fuller's belief that the exercise of saving faith first required the creation of a divine principle of faith in the human heart.[64] While Taylor concurred with Fuller's opposition to reducing faith to intellectual acceptance of a fact or proposition, as taught by the Scottish Presbyterian minister John Glas and widely articulated by the non-conformist Robert Sandeman, he questioned the biblical basis for Fuller's understanding of the principle of faith and his differentiation of the principle from the act of faith.[65] Taylor was not convinced this principle was created before a person believed. He also argued that Fuller's representation of God as its sole architect portrayed God as unjust, for it was inappropriate for him to punish anybody "for not doing that which he never had any capacity for."[66] Neither did Taylor agree that non-believers required a divinely created disposition in order to turn to God. He felt this encouraged people to excuse their lack of response to the gospel by saying that without God's intervention "man is unable" to exercise faith.[67] Although Taylor upheld God's sovereignty, he constantly defended human responsibility and freedom.

Closely connected to Fuller's belief in the need for the creation of a divine principle of faith in a person's heart before salvation, was his view that regeneration preceded belief.[68] He insisted that "the enmity of men's

64. Lover of All Mankind [Taylor], *Observations*, 14. Fuller's approach to the creation of a divine principle of faith is outlined in Fuller, *Gospel Worthy*, 149.

65. Ibid. For Fuller's reference to Sandemanianism, see Fuller, *Gospel Worthy*, Preface, iv. Further background on Fuller's engagement with Sandemanianism is provided in Haykin, "Andrew Fuller," 223–36. See also Murray, "Robert Sandeman," 970–71.

66. Ibid., 59.

67. Ibid., 60.

68. Fuller, *Gospel Worthy*, 47. For a brief examination of Fuller's thinking on this subject, see Oliver, "Andrew Fuller," 206. Oliver describes how Fuller maintained "that regeneration takes place in a man with a view to faith although it is an act of God of which he is not immediately conscious," see ibid.

minds and enmity of their hearts" was such that "they must undergo an entire *renovation* of soul before they can be set right."[69] This accorded with High Calvinist understandings of salvation as an effect solely of God's regenerative work in an individual's life. However, he was adamant that this did not negate the need for the gospel to be offered to all. In Taylor's judgment, Fuller failed to demonstrate how these two dimensions of theological thought could be held together, but was willing to let Fuller's High Calvinist critics engage him on this subject. Instead, Taylor focused on the issue of regeneration as prior to belief, referring to it as "an embarrassment to Mr. F.'s grand design, which he cannot easily get rid of."[70] For Taylor, there was no scriptural foundation for the view that saving faith was an effect of regeneration. If it was true, he expected to find it clearly stated in the Bible. He also questioned why sinners were called to repent and believe so as to be saved, if they first needed to be regenerated. With reference to Scriptures such as John 1:12 and Gal 3:26, he stated that regeneration could not take place prior to a declaration of faith as this was irreconcilable with people becoming children of God by faith.[71] Again, this reflected his desire for primacy within the salvific process to be given to a person's freely chosen response to the gospel, as opposed to any notion of God's determinate operations. The Enlightenment emphasis on individual liberty was also a likely influence on the strength of Taylor's argument.

Taylor's view that the Holy Spirit is received subsequent to belief also led him to consider Fuller's depiction of regeneration as taking place before a person exercised faith, as problematic.[72] With reference to humanity's state of condemnation prior to faith in God, he accused Fuller of depicting people as "regenerated and condemned at the same time."[73] If faith was the effect of prior regeneration, Taylor suggested non-believers would view Fuller's conviction that they had a duty to believe the gospel as "very absurd."[74] In keeping with his Enlightenment outlook, Taylor reasoned that people would soon realize they could not "rationally attempt" to believe, since they knew it was impossible "till they be first regenerated."[75] Regarding this aspect of Fuller's approach, Taylor charged him with having taken

69. Fuller, *Gospel Worthy*, 47; Fuller's emphasis.

70. Lover of All Mankind [Taylor], *Observations*, 21.

71. Ibid. John 1:12: "Yet to all who did receive him, to those who believed in his name, he gave the right to become children of God"; Gal 3:26: "for in Christ Jesus you are all children of God through faith."

72. Ibid., 22.

73. Ibid.

74. Ibid.

75. Ibid.

the focal point of the gospel away from Christ as the "means of the sinner's recovery from his fall," thereby making Christ's work "only a consequence of that recovery."[76] Taylor further claimed that Fuller forced people who doubted their conversions not to look to Christ, but within themselves for evidence of their regeneration, therefore affirming the subjective warrant of faith which Fuller claimed to oppose.[77] Summarizing his opposition, Taylor referred to Fuller's depiction of faith in Christ as an effect of regeneration as

> repugnant to the state of man as a fallen sinner; to the gospel as
> a sovereign remedy, to the nature and design of faith in Christ;
> and to the beautiful harmony and connection of these several
> subjects as continued in the covenant of free grace.[78]

Taylor's rejection was emphatic.

Fuller's commitment to a pre-conversion creation of a divine disposition of faith in an unbeliever's heart, and regeneration as prior to belief, were encompassed within an understanding of divine election to salvation that Taylor opposed. Though Fuller suggested that the subject of election would not be prominent in any disputes that might ensue from his publication of *The Gospel Worthy*, Taylor viewed it as inseparable from the other elements of Fuller's framework. Taylor therefore referred to it in three of his nine letters. In line with the main thrust of Taylor's 1784 response to Robert Hall Sr.'s *Help to Zion's Travellers* (see chapter 3), he was particularly concerned about Fuller's depiction of God sovereignly determining "before the world began" who would receive salvation.[79] In a rational manner, Taylor argued that such an unconditional understanding of election undermined Fuller's chief emphasis on the duty of all to respond to the message of the gospel.[80] With the non-elect in mind, Taylor asked "why should they seek after salvation?" It could not be their duty "to do that which they were never able to do."[81] He also reasoned that it would be futile for them to seek salvation because there was no saving provision for them within Fuller's scheme. Although Fuller held that the eternal fate of the non-elect was de-

---

76. Ibid., 23.

77. The need for a subjective warrant of faith was part of Fuller's High Calvinist background. This viewpoint saw a person look within for assurance of salvation. It contrasted with the more objective position that Fuller later adopted and which viewed the gospel itself as sufficient warrant for faith in Christ. For more on this subject, see Oliver, "Andrew Fuller," 204–8.

78. Lover of All Mankind [Taylor], *Observations*, 24.

79. Fuller, *Gospel Worthy*, 123.

80. Lover of All Mankind [Taylor], *Observations*, 46.

81. Ibid.

termined only according to God's foresight and not his divine will, Taylor was convinced that this was not the logical outcome of Fuller's depiction of election and his particular view of atonement. In his critique of Fuller's understanding of election, Taylor's intention was to expose what he viewed as the misconceived nature of Fuller's approach to conversion.

Taylor was unconvinced by Fuller drawing on the writings of John Owen and Particular Baptist minister John Brine, as Fuller sought to uphold the validity of his doctrine of election.[82] Fuller pointed to the traditional Calvinist differentiation between God's purposes and people's duty, with the purposes never functioning as a rule governing the duty. While Owen was widely regarded as the bastion of Calvinist orthodoxy and Brine an influential High Calvinist, it was characteristic of the typically generous spirited nature of Taylor's evangelicalism that he referred to them as "great and good men."[83] However, he insisted that their arguments, regarding God's purpose and human duty, had no scriptural basis and could only be viewed "as their opinion."[84] For Taylor, the Calvinist tradition promoted by Fuller portrayed God's decrees and commands as opposite to each other. As an example, he cited Fuller's emphasis on God's command that all believe in Christ and yet Fuller's representation of God as knowing that "they are not; nor ever were; and determines they never shall be able to do it."[85] Taylor contended that there was no assurance for people to place confidence in God unless his word and decrees perfectly corresponded. He also dismissed Fuller's endorsement of Owen's view that ministers should not trouble themselves with "those secrets of the eternal mind of God" regarding who God had purposed to save.[86] Taylor was unequivocal that the issue of election was not principally about the mysteries of God, but that which the Scriptures clearly taught.[87] While Taylor stated his personal understanding of election elsewhere (see chapter 3), its absence from his response to *The Gospel Worthy* was to the theological detriment of the *Nine*

---

82. For Fuller's references to Brine, see Fuller, *Gospel Worthy*, 126–27. John Brine (1703–65) was a Particular Baptist minister whose most influential years within the life of the denomination were after he became pastor of the Baptist congregation at Curriers Hall, Cripplegate, London in 1730, where he remained until his death. Joseph Ivimey described him as "of great weight in the denomination," and "a very pious and useful minister," see Ivimey, *History of the English Baptists*, 367.

83. Lover of All Mankind [Taylor], *Observations*, 48.

84. Ibid.

85. Ibid., 49.

86. Owen, *Death of Death*, in Owen, *Works*, 10:300. Qtd in Fuller, *Gospel Worthy*, 127.

87. Lover of All Mankind [Taylor], *Observations*, 49.

Letters. It is likely that his failure to delineate his understanding of election stemmed from his tendency to minimize attention on matters of faith that could inflame controversy. This was particularly the case when Taylor, as in this instance, recognized he was engaging a fellow evangelical believer who was similarly convinced that the gospel be offered to all. Taylor's reluctance to state more than was strictly necessary stood apart, for example, from the more expansive approach to controversy that tended to characterize the nature of theological debate in the seventeenth century.[88]

A significant dimension of Taylor's critique of *The Gospel Worthy* was Fuller's differentiation between natural and moral inability. By contending that people possessed the natural ability to turn to God, but were morally unable to do so, Fuller hoped to defend his approach from what he anticipated to be the High Calvinist critique that people were unable to do what was spiritually good. Likewise, Fuller believed it would exonerate him from the Arminian accusation that his emphasis on God's sovereign electing purposes, and limited view of the atonement, meant people could not be held responsible for their lack of faith. Although not specific, Taylor recognized that this distinction had been embraced by "many others,"[89] such as Hall Sr. in *Help to Zion's Travellers.*[90] It is pertinent to consider whether Taylor read *Freedom of the Will*, by the New England Congregational preacher and theologian Jonathan Edwards, as Edwards extensively examined the nature of moral and natural inability.[91] However, there is no mention of this work in any of Taylor's writings. While Edwards's works influenced Fuller, Taylor only acknowledged Edwards's publications on two occasions. Firstly, a 1764 diary entry noted that he had benefited from a non-specified piece of Edwards's writing on the work of the devil.[92] Secondly, Taylor made an equally complimentary mention of Edwards in a 1788 letter to Birley, noting Edwards's work on original sin, although he had not read the primary source.[93] Given that Taylor regularly studied the works of writers offering a range of theological perspectives, his lack of consideration of such an influential theologian as Edwards is perplexing. It could be attributed to the cost of these works, which had to be shipped from America, but given Taylor's contacts it is likely he could have found an affordable means of accessing them. Alternatively, he may have viewed

---

88. Examples of this were provided in chapter 2.

89. Lover of All Mankind [Taylor], *Observations*, 43.

90. Hall, *Help to Zion's Travellers*, 198–218.

91. Edwards, *Freedom of the Will*, in Edwards, *Works*, vol. 1.

92. Dan Taylor, diary entry, 9 September 1764, in Taylor, *Memoirs*, 68.

93. Dan Taylor, diary entry, 30 August 1788, in Taylor, *Memoirs*, 257.

Edwards's theological importance as inferior to those who he chose to focus his attention on, such as John Owen. Also, he may have been aware
of what was sometimes regarded as Edwards's labored and philosophical
writing style, and therefore felt he lacked the time that such an examination
of these works would have necessitated.

While Taylor considered as "just and proper" Fuller's definition
of natural ability as "THE ENJOYMENT OF RATIONAL FACULTIES,
BODILY POWERS, AND EXTERNAL ADVANTAGES," he did not believe
that Fuller's employment of Edwards's distinction led to valid conclusions.[94]
His response to Fuller's understanding of moral inability was more guarded.
Although to "avoid unnecessary altercation" he admitted the definition "for
the present," he nevertheless endeavored to demonstrate that Fuller's depiction of moral inability was incorrect.[95] Taylor's chief judgment was that,
while Fuller had sought to differentiate it from natural ability, he had portrayed it as if it were natural and therefore undermined his argument. This
was reflected in Taylor's assertion that "though our author calls this vitiosity
of disposition *moral inability*; yet as it comes upon man, by generation, in
the course of nature, surely it is, in this sense, natural."[96] Taylor argued that
the sense of moral determinism which emanated from Fuller's scheme of
thought, was to the extent that he presented moral inability as synonymous
with humanity's "impurity of nature."[97] While neither Fuller nor Edwards
understood moral inability in this way,[98] this criticism indicates that Taylor
perceived Fuller's employment of the distinction as flawed.

According to Taylor, a "great deal of labour" and "ingenuity" had been
exerted by Fuller as he sought to overcome his "harsh idea" (as Taylor described it) of God punishing those who had neither the power nor capacity to respond to him.[99] Yet Taylor was convinced that Fuller's use of the
distinction between natural and moral inability gave rise to a profoundly
unjust representation of God.[100] If, in respect to moral inability, humankind
did not have the power to turn to God, then he viewed the idea proposed
by Fuller that God would punish people for their unbelief as immensely

94. Lover of All Mankind [Taylor], *Observations*, 64; Fuller, *Gospel Worthy*, 185.
Qtd in ibid., Taylor's emphasis.

95. Ibid.

96. Ibid., 65; Taylor's emphasis.

97. Ibid., 66.

98. For consideration of Jonathan Edwards's thinking on this subject see Holmes,
God of Grace, 125–67.

99. Lover of All Mankind [Taylor], *Observations*, 41.

100. Ibid., 43.

unjust.[101] Taylor asked whether anybody could be "justly charged as a *criminal*, for what he could not avoid."[102] He likened what he felt was its unfairness to how, "If I were to command a stone to walk, or a horse to sing, they could not obey me."[103] These assertions were underpinned by Taylor's belief that a person was declared guilty before God, not as a consequence of the impurity of their natural condition but only on the basis of sins actually committed—chiefly their failure to respond in faith to the gospel. This theological perspective was intimated in his pre-Fuller works, but nowhere more clearly expressed than in his seventh letter to Birley where he claimed that "no man will ever be sent to hell, for that impurity of nature, or that *moral inability* which he could never avoid."[104] Referring to Fuller's belief that God declared people guilty and punished them on the basis of their natural condition which they could not avoid, Taylor asked, "Would it not be equally unjust to blame or punish a man for being born blind, or deaf?"[105] Taylor's conviction was strongly apparent.

As Taylor rejected Fuller's understanding of moral inability, he stated that he did not believe the disposition of humankind's natural faculties to be inclined only to what was corrupt and evil. In line with that noted in chapter 2, he emphasized how humankind's rational capacity could foster an awareness of personal sin and need of a savior. While insisting on a person's "utter inability to recover himself,"[106] he was firm that "Man, though impure is a rational being, and capable of seeing that this impurity leads to sinful tempers and actions; and therefore ought not to be indulged."[107] Unlike Fuller, Taylor did not subscribe to the view that a person's impurity vitiated their rational capabilities regarding an understanding of salvation. As Morden notes, "Taylor clearly had a more optimistic view of human nature than Fuller."[108] This resonated with wider Enlightenment sympathies concerning the positive capacity of human nature. Although, compared to Fuller, Taylor outlined a more indeterminate understanding of salvation, he failed to offer any explanation of how he aligned his greater regard for the self-determining nature of the human will with his understanding of human depravity and the whole salvific process. This was a significant omission.

101. Ibid.
102. Ibid., 65; Taylor's emphasis.
103. Ibid., 44.
104. Ibid., 66; Taylor's emphasis.
105. Ibid., 65.
106. Ibid., 45.
107. Ibid., 66.
108. Morden, *Offering Christ*, 68.

While Taylor's imprecision might indicate his difficulty in reconciling these different aspects of his theological thinking, it was typical of his aversion to offering detailed insights on that which he viewed as the more speculative and metaphysical aspects of faith. Such a tendency was not unique to Taylor, but as noted on previous occasions, was common among evangelicals.

To summarize, Taylor rejected important aspects of Fuller's understanding of the process of conversion. Taylor dismissed both the necessity of a divine principle of faith in the human heart before salvation and regeneration prior to belief, as contrary to the Scriptures and God's granting of freedom and responsibility concerning responses to the gospel. Enlightenment values such as the promotion of individual liberty were influential on Taylor. His rejection of Fuller's differentiation between moral and natural inability was also of crucial importance. Among other reasons, Taylor viewed it as flawed because he was convinced that Fuller's use of the distinction, as a means of holding people accountable for their acceptance or rejection of Christ, failed to uphold an understanding of God as just and merciful. Taylor also offered insights into his own understanding of the human condition. As will be examined next, Taylor's response to *The Gospel Worthy* led Fuller to make significant modifications to his position.

Shifts in Perspective

"I tried to answer my opponent . . . but I could not"

Fuller received Taylor's response on 5 February 1786. He noted in his diary that "My mind has been generally much engaged in perusing different publications against my treatise on the gospel of Christ. This morning I received another, written by Taylor."[109] Although he categorized Taylor alongside others who opposed *The Gospel Worthy*, he was very complimentary. He affirmed Taylor's respectful way of writing, particularly welcoming his "amiable spirit."[110] Of even greater significance was his high regard for much of the content of Taylor's reply. He was unreserved in his praise for there being "a good deal of plausibility in some things he advances" and how his essential reasoning was "ingeniously wrought together."[111] Fuller's commendation is noteworthy as it suggests the need for caution regarding the inadequacy and misleading nature of certain criticisms leveled against Taylor by some who have considered his engagement with Fuller. For exam-

109. Andrew Fuller, diary entry, 5 February 1786, in Ryland, *Work of Faith*, 134.
110. Ibid.
111. Ibid.

ple Clint Sheehan, when writing on "Fuller's Defence of the Gospel against Arminianism," states,

> One cannot help but feel a certain heaviness of heart when reading about Taylor. He appeared to be sincere, motivated and diligent in his service to God; unfortunately this is marred by the errors he professed. The apostle's lament in Rom 10:2 could be applied to Taylor.[112]

Leaving aside the changes in outlook Taylor caused Fuller to undertake, Fuller's initial reaction to Taylor's *Nine Letters* is in itself sufficient to demonstrate that, unlike Sheehan's claim, "zeal without knowledge" (Rom 10:2) was not a description Fuller would have used in respect of Taylor. As noted by Ryland, it should not be forgotten that Taylor was by now regarded across the denominations as "a very respectable minister, among the more evangelical General Baptists."[113] The compliments Fuller extended towards him are indicative, as Morden notes, that this was "a respect that was certainly shared by Fuller himself."[114] It is important to recognize that Sheehan does not appear to have actually engaged with any of Taylor's works, which helps to account for his misconceived critique.

The extent to which Taylor's approach commanded Fuller's admiration was apparent within Fuller's 1787 publication *A Reply to the Observations of Philanthropos* which he hoped would provide a "solid and effective reply" to what Taylor had written.[115] This work constituted one section of Fuller's *A Defence of a Treatise Entitled The Gospel of Christ Worthy of All Acceptation*, with the other part comprising his response to the High Calvinist William Button. Taylor replied a few months later in the form of thirteen letters to Birley which were published under the title *Observations on the Rev. Andrew Fuller's Reply to Philanthropos*.[116] Taylor no longer used a pseudonym and revealed himself to be Philanthropos. His newly found eagerness to publish his thoughts openly was also evident in how his decision to respond was, this time, not influenced by the persuasion of some within the New Connexion.

While Fuller's reply to Taylor's initial response to *The Gospel Worthy* saw Fuller remain entrenched in certain important aspects of his thinking, such as his dismissal of Taylor's charge that he had presented moral

---

112. Sheehan, "Great and Sovereign Grace," 90.

113. Ryland, *Work of Faith*, 132.

114. Morden, "Andrew Fuller," 22.

115. Fuller, *Reply*, in Andrew Fuller, *Defence of Gospel Worthy*, 1–11; Fuller, diary entry, 6 February 1786, in Ryland, *Work of Faith*, 134.

116. Dan Taylor, *Observations on Fuller's Reply*.

inability as if were natural, he did make certain significant alterations to his position. For instance, when responding to Taylor's critique of his approach to regeneration, it is apparent that he changed his understanding of the principle of faith. He no longer referred to its divine workings in a person's heart but restricted it to a "bias of mind" that God sought to produce.[117] Contrary to Taylor's earlier criticism, Fuller asserted that he had not referred to God crafting the disposition in an unbeliever's heart. The validity of Fuller's claim is dubious, as he had specifically described the principle as being "wrought *in* us by the Holy Spirit."[118] Fuller's shift led Taylor to state that "with some limitations" he could accept Fuller's new position, and described it in terms of the Holy Spirit's influence on the minds of non-believers.[119] However, Taylor remained convinced that the specific principle could not be found in the Bible.[120] Yet in response to Fuller's assurance that he did not view the working of the principle as sufficient "to denominate any person a believer,"[121] Taylor accepted that this presented a very "different face" to the principle.[122] Correctly understanding Fuller as now referring to God causing a change in the bias of a person's mind regarding "the beginning of a person's journey of faith" rather than "the *completion* of faith, as it respects our justification," Taylor stated that the legitimacy of his position "may be granted."[123] Fuller's new stance was almost certainly attributable to the strength of Taylor's critique. It should be noted that Morden, in his noteworthy examination of the discourse between Taylor and Fuller, fails to recognize that Fuller made this notable shift in position.[124] However, unlike Sheehan, Morden does draw attention to other changes in Fuller's stance, as well as highlighting other nuances of his engagement with Taylor.[125]

As a consequence of Fuller qualifying his thinking concerning the divine principle of faith, and his evident willingness to engage with "the great question" of the precise nature of the Spirit's work in the lives of non-believers, Taylor initially thought Fuller might have abandoned the priority of regeneration to believing.[126] On further examination, he realized this was

---

117. Fuller, *Reply*, 6.

118. Fuller, *Gospel Worthy*, 152; italics added.

119. Taylor, *Observations on Fuller's Reply*, 9.

120. Ibid., 13.

121. Fuller, *Reply*, 8.

122. Taylor, *Observations on Fuller's Reply*, 11.

123. Ibid., 8, 11, Taylor's emphasis.

124. Morden, *Offering Christ*, 63–74.

125. Ibid., 68–74.

126. Fuller, *Reply*, 8. For Taylor's initial reflection on the possibility that Fuller

not the case.[127] Fuller caused Taylor to shift his own thinking on the matter. For instance, Taylor withdrew his charge that Fuller presented a person as regenerated and condemned at the same time. Taylor commended Fuller's clarification that he meant "no more than as a cause is prior to an effect which immediately follows."[128] Fuller's emphasis on "cause" and "effect" reflected an Enlightenment outlook. This very likely influenced Taylor's acceptance of Fuller's argument and the enthusiasm with which Taylor, on this specific point, referred to "the force of Mr. F's reply."[129] Taylor also accepted Fuller's statement that the Holy Spirit is given for purposes additional to regeneration.[130] Taylor's concessions illustrated his openness particularly to arguments rooted in an Enlightenment framework of understanding, and his awareness of the sometimes flawed nature of his own reasoning.

The most significant shift in Fuller's thinking in response to Taylor was his changed stance regarding the scope of Christ's atonement. Fuller now unequivocally declared Christ's death as sufficient for all humanity, so that whoever came to God could be saved.[131] He categorically stated "If we were to suppose, for argument's sake, that all the inhabitants of the globe should thus return, it is supposed not one soul need be sent away for want of a sufficiency in Christ's death."[132] This view was absent from the first edition of *The Gospel Worthy* and involved an accompanying depth of conviction that affected Fuller's theological outlook throughout the remainder of his ministry. Although Fuller remained insistent that the application of Christ's death, according to the "sovereign purpose and design of the Father and the Son," was restricted to a limited number, he was now convinced that "if every sinner who hears the gospel were to come to Christ for salvation, every such sinner would undoubtedly be saved."[133] He was unequivocal that Christ's death was of "infinite value, sufficient to have saved all the world, and a thousand worlds, if it had pleased God to have constituted them the price of their redemption, and made them effectual to that end."[134]

---

might have given up the priority of regeneration to belief, see Taylor, *Observations on Fuller's Reply*, 11.

127. See Taylor, *Observations on Fuller's Reply*, 12.

128. Fuller, *Reply*, 21. See also Taylor, *Observations on Fuller's Reply*, 13. It is conceivable that Fuller arrived at his understanding of there being no gap between regeneration and belief as a direct consequence of Taylor's questions.

129. Taylor, *Observations on Fuller's Reply*, 13.

130. Ibid., 12.

131. Fuller, *Reply*, 63.

132. Ibid., 64–65.

133. Ibid., 63, 53–54.

134. Ibid., 63–64.

Similarly, he affirmed that "supposing for argument's sake every man in the world should return to God in Christ's name, that they would all be accepted, I have no objection to it."[135] The position Fuller now embraced reflected that expressed by Edwards in *Freedom of the Will* and although never acknowledged by Fuller, likely aided his journey of thought.[136] As will be seen, however, Taylor's direct influence was of even greater importance as a catalyst to Fuller's changed stance. Given Fuller's high standing among the more progressive Particular Baptists, and his contribution to the theological rationale which underpinned the workings of the Baptist Missionary Society, his shift of position was very significant.

While Fuller within *Observations* did not openly acknowledge that Taylor had led him to change his position, his indebtedness to Taylor is clear. He explicitly referred to Taylor's influence on him in an 1803 letter to Ryland where, in respect of his theological discourse with Taylor, he wrote, "I freely own that my views of particular redemption were altered by my engaging in that controversy."[137] With specific reference to Taylor, he stated,

> I tried to answer my opponent without considering the suffi-
> ciency of the atonement in itself considered, and of its being
> the ground of gospel invitations; but I could not. I found not
> merely his reasoning, but the Scriptures themselves, standing
> in my way.[138]

This assertion provides categorical evidence of the influence Taylor successfully exerted on Fuller. It also exposes the inadequacy of argument of commentators who have denied this influence, or presented it in the most minimalistic way. For example, it negates Sheehan's claim that "Fuller maintains that, when taken to their logical conclusion, many of Taylor's principles are at best nugatory and at worst heresy."[139] Instead, as Morden suggests, Fuller "felt the force" of Taylor's arguments, particularly Taylor's "unanswerable point" that if Fuller maintained that the atonement was limited, then it was problematic to argue that the inability of at least some to

---

135. Ibid., 57.

136. For more on the similarities between Edwards's and Fuller's positions, see Morden, *Offering Christ*, 71. See also Chun, *Legacy of Jonathan Edwards*.

137. Fuller, "Letter IV to Dr. Ryland," 17 January 1803, in Fuller, *Works*, 322. This letter is from a series of six letters that Fuller wrote to Ryland in January 1803, see Fuller, "six Letters," in Fuller, *Works*, 317–25.

138. Fuller, "Letter IV to Dr. Ryland," 322.

139. Sheehan, "Great and Sovereign Grace," 89.

respond in faith was not natural, given there were some for whom there was no atonement provision.[140]

As one who was also shaped by the values of the Enlightenment, Fuller was sympathetic to Taylor's previous appeals to the interests of justice and benevolence. Influenced by Taylor's writing, Fuller acknowledged that understandings of the atonement must be "consistent with the rights of justice."[141] His commitment to the limited application of God's design within the sufficiency of Christ's atoning provision did, however, cause Taylor to argue that the gospel should not be indiscriminately offered from such a platform. To do so was still to proceed "on the ground of invitation without provision," and therefore make God seem "insincere" and contravene his "glorious perfections" of justice and love.[142] Fuller's declaration that his new position was "a sufficient ground for indefinite calls and universal invitations" was therefore dismissed by Taylor as "utterly inconceivable."[143] Taylor argued that if Christ's sufferings were sufficient to have saved all the world, but had not been extended in this way, then this would have been demonstrated in the Scriptures "where the whole design and plan of redemption are so fully and clearly laid open."[144]

Taylor's understanding of Fuller's changed position is akin to that articulated by Ernest Clipsham who describes Fuller as undergoing a "significant change of viewpoint," but that his "leading principles remained unaltered."[145] Yet this judgment fails to recognize the true extent to which Fuller's underpinning conviction concerning the scope of Christ's atonement altered. The profundity of Fuller's change of perspective and deference to Taylor was apparent in his admission to Ryland that "I conceded to my opponent that the death of Christ *in itself* considered, i.e. irrespective of the design of the Father and Son as to its application, was sufficient for all mankind."[146] This concession reflects the pioneering influence Taylor exerted on Fuller. With the exception of the writings of Jonathan Edwards, no one else was as influential in changing Fuller's views as Taylor. Although never fully acknowledged by Taylor, it was the case, as Morden argues, that the atonement perspective to which Fuller moved "could now properly be

---

140. Morden, *Offering Christ*, 70.

141. Fuller, *Reply*, 65.

142. Taylor, *Observations on Fuller's Reply*, 81, 82, 86.

143. Fuller, *Reply*, 64. Qtd in Taylor, *Observations on Fuller's Reply*, 81; ibid., 82.

144. Taylor, *Observations on Fuller's Reply*, 80.

145. Clipsham, "Andrew Fuller," 218.

146. Fuller, "Letter IV to Dr. Ryland," 322; Fuller's emphasis.

called general."[147] The shift in Fuller's core understanding regarding the scope of the atonement led him to reconstitute the section on the scope of Christ's redemptive work in his 1801 second edition of *The Gospel Worthy*.[148] Its contents then became consistent with his new position as delineated in *Observations*. Had Taylor been aware of the true depth of changed conviction that Fuller relayed to Ryland, he would likely have been more appreciative of Fuller's change of position.

In the course of their theological engagement, it was not only Fuller who experienced a change in his thinking. Taylor shifted in certain important aspects of his approach to the process of conversion. In contrast to his initial response to *The Gospel Worthy*, he declared, in unexpected manner, that he did not oppose Fuller's idea that "Christ absolutely determined to save any."[149] It is apparent that Taylor's use of the word "any" meant certain people. He similarly referred to the Spirit's operations as "not always irresistible."[150] These assertions were indicative of both the greater theological flexibility of Taylor's evangelical Arminianism, and an increased willingness to give tacit approval to aspects of Calvinism than was sometimes the case among seventeenth-century proponents of Arminianism. Taylor had evidently undergone a shift in his theological perspective, yet his affirmation of the possibility of an element of divine determination in salvation was never worked out in any systematic way. Furthermore, outside of his engagement with Fuller, he never even hinted at the possibility of his concurrence with such a position. It is very likely that Taylor's concession to Fuller was pragmatically motivated, with his hope being it might propel Fuller to accept, without any qualification, that Christ died for the sins of all. Taylor duly emphasized that "the truth which I am endeavouring to evince is perfectly consistent with such determination."[151] Mindful of Fuller's belief that God's determining purposes meant Christ's atonement was applied to a limited extent, Taylor pointed to Richard Baxter, Isaac Watts, and Archbishop Usher as examples of "many of the greatest and best of men who have admitted the *absolute determination* of Christ to save some," and yet who "maintained that he died for all."[152] On no occasion did Taylor affirm the determinacy of God's salvific workings without emphasizing that this was consistent with Christ's death for all. This again suggests that

147. Morden, *Offering Christ*, 70.
148. See Fuller, *Gospel Worthy*, 2nd ed. in Fuller, *Works*, 170–73.
149. Taylor, *Observations on Fuller's Reply*, 90.
150. Ibid., 25.
151. Ibid., 91.
152. Ibid.; italics added.

Taylor's change of theological stance was pragmatically inspired. Although pragmatism was a central facet of evangelicalism, it was rarely a catalyst to alteration of theological conviction expressed by those of earlier Puritan or scholastic persuasion.

Further evidence of the mutual influence that prevailed between Fuller and Taylor was Taylor's declaration that he allowed for an element of special design within Christ's death. While remaining committed to a general view of the atonement, he wrote somewhat ambiguously, "It is so plain that Christ might absolutely design the salvation of some."[153] He also contended that the "greatest number" of those who considered there to be a special design also believed that Christ died for all, and that the two beliefs were not mutually exclusive.[154] Again, it is likely that this concession was pragmatically motivated, particularly as he was wrestling with Fuller's charge that he had not given sufficient regard to the efficacy of Christ's death. It was on this basis that Fuller had previously stated that believing Christ died for the sins of all therefore offered no real advantage and even left open the possibility that "satan might, at last, have come off triumphant."[155] Fuller argued that people were "given to Christ prior to their believing in him," and that this therefore necessitated a "limitation of design" in the death of Christ.[156] While Taylor, in response, continued to reject any doctrine of election that denied parts of humankind the possibility of salvation, claiming such a view was "opposite to the spirit and design of the gospel," he again asserted his new view that Christ's death was not devoid of divine design.[157] Using language similar to Fuller's, he suggested that God's designs were "probably various, and far extended," and that there are "mysteries, to us, unaccountable."[158] This indicates a further broadening of Taylor's soteriological approach. It also illustrates his determination to remove, where appropriate, all obstacles that might prevent Fuller from unreservedly embracing the universal scope of Christ's atonement.

In summary, both Taylor and Fuller amended their thinking about the atonement as a result of their discourse. It seems that some of the shifts in Taylor's thinking were a consequence of his desire to find common ground with Fuller. Some of the views about conversion which he articulated in his engagement with Fuller do not feature again in his writings. Given Taylor's

---

153. Ibid., 90.
154. Ibid., 99.
155. Fuller, *Reply*, 14.
156. Ibid., 75.
157. Taylor, *Observations on Fuller's Reply*, 100.
158. Ibid., 19, 20.

integrity, these shifts of belief should be viewed as genuine, although it seems they were of minor significance to him. Of far greater importance for Baptist theology was the way Fuller changed his central understanding of the atonement.

New Insights

"no sinner would ever believe in Christ, without divine operations"

A new insight from Taylor, in his *Observations on the Rev. Andrew Fuller's Reply to Philanthropos*, was his doctrine of divine influences. He outlined his understanding of the Holy Spirit's role in conversion in a way that extended beyond anything he had previously written.[159] The catalyst was Fuller's accusation that Taylor "leaves out the agency of the Holy Spirit in the act itself of believing, maintaining that the Spirit is not given till after we have believed."[160] Fuller's criticism was a natural extension of his contention in *The Gospel Worthy* that Arminians denied the necessity of the Spirit's work in the process of salvation. For an unspecified reason, Taylor's *Nine Letters* included no response to this assertion, although Taylor did make passing reference to it in a 1785 letter to George Birley.[161] Mindful of Fuller's critique that to perceive a person's turning to Christ independent of the Spirit's work was as inconsistent as "a tree that is wholly evil to bring forth good fruit," Taylor recognized the need to clarify his position.[162] He unambiguously stated "no sinner would ever believe in Christ, without divine operations" and that it was impossible to have "any will, or power, or any concern about the matter, till the Holy Spirit work, awaken, and produce these in the mind."[163] In direct reference to the Holy Spirit, he declared that it was only "owing to his influence, that any are converted."[164] Taylor insisted Fuller was "greatly mistaken" to think he had ever considered the Spirit's operations as irrelevant in a person's coming to faith.[165] Fuller's judgment regarding Taylor's neglect of the Spirit's work was however understandable, considering Taylor maintained a near exclusive focus within the *Nine Letters* on humankind's rational

---

159. Ibid., 20–26.
160. Fuller, *Reply*, 8–9.
161. Dan Taylor, "Letter to George Birley," 11 October 1785. Page not numbered.
162. Fuller, *Reply*, 42.
163. Taylor, *Observations on Fuller's Reply*, 21.
164. Ibid., 25.
165. Ibid., 23.

capacity to respond positively to the gospel.[166] The way Taylor now emphasized humankind's inability to pursue God independent of the influence of the Spirit, who enabled a person to be "informed, convinced and awakened" of their need for Christ, was distinct from anything he had previously written.[167] Fuller's critique certainly led Taylor to reappraise his thinking on the necessity of divine influence in the salvific process.

Taylor also elaborated on what he called the "scriptural and important" differentiation between the Spirit's operations on the mind and indwelling presence within the heart.[168] He believed it was Fuller's failure to have appreciated his explanation of this in the *Nine Letters* that Taylor believed accounted for Fuller's accusation that he ignored the work of the Spirit. However, Taylor had not clearly outlined these different facets of the Spirit's work. Fuller's employment of this distinction probably influenced Taylor. It also encouraged Taylor that Fuller had changed his approach to the workings of the divine principle of faith. Fuller's critique of the limited attention Taylor attributed to the function of the Spirit in the process of salvation led Taylor to delineate his understanding of the Spirit's operations in a way that had continuing consequences. Taylor's changed approach was reflected in his 1802 second edition of *Fundamentals*, which he renamed *The Christian Religion*.[169] Compared to the first edition, the only significant change was the addition of a new chapter entitled "On the Operations of the Holy Spirit."[170] Taylor here affirmed his new found emphasis that nobody would pursue salvation "Till the Lord, by his word and Spirit, convince their consciences and awaken their desires after it."[171] Fuller's influence on Taylor was of enduring significance.

Significantly, Taylor's emphasis on the importance of the Spirit in a person's coming to faith, was reflected in his references regarding his understanding of grace and moral ability. Taylor was responding to Fuller's uncertainty whether he viewed grace as sufficient to overcome moral inability or likened it to natural ability.[172] While Taylor rejected Fuller's judgment that there was similarity between his depiction of power to receive the gospel and natural ability, he connected this power with the exercise of moral abil-

166. Ibid.

167. Ibid., 22.

168. Ibid., 23.

169. Dan Taylor, *Christian Religion*. For Taylor's recognition of the need for this publication, see Dan Taylor, "Letter to George Birley," 15 September 1801. Page not numbered.

170. Ibid., 191–208.

171. Ibid., 192.

172. Fuller, *Reply*, 41.

ity. Moving beyond that stated in the *Nine Letters*, Taylor referred to moral ability as "not a power to keep the law; but a power, by grace, to receive the gospel."[173] He asserted that it was people's duty as the subjects of God's moral government "to believe, receive or observe" the gospel and that the "ability to do this is also moral ability."[174] He emphasized that he did not suppose that "man in himself, as a fallen creature, without any divine operation or influence on his mind, has the immediate power of moral obedience."[175] Taylor's doctrine of grace, and particularly its workings in an unbeliever's life, should be understood as those divine influences which, when responded to rationally, enabled a person to exercise their moral ability to receive the gospel. His engagement with Fuller on this matter influenced the way his thinking evolved.

Taylor responded to Fuller's critique that he had described grace as a "debt" by making Christ's coming "the only thing which constitutes men accountable beings."[176] Instead, Taylor argued that he had always understood humankind's accountability before God to be a consequence of the actualization of sin.[177] Fuller's pronouncement that Taylor's approach presented Christ's sacrifice as the "greatest curse that could ever befall" humanity and placed humankind "into a capacity of sinning" was sarcastically dismissed by Taylor as "wonderful indeed!"[178] Fuller's misunderstanding of Taylor's view of grace was, at least to some extent, a consequence of Taylor's failure to clarify his thinking sufficiently in the *Nine Letters*. It also reflected Fuller's contention that Taylor's view of grace as "given to every man in the world or would be given, were he to ask for it" only served to exonerate God from being what Taylor called "a merciless tyrant."[179] Fuller argued that his own understanding of grace as "free favour towards the unworthy" demonstrated God's graciousness to a greater extent.[180] Contrary to Fuller's critique that Taylor advanced an understanding of the atonement that was limited in its effectiveness due to the possibility that nobody would come to faith, Taylor took the opposite view. He insisted that his approach should not be viewed as inferior, as it allowed for the possibility that all might be saved if they

173. Taylor, *Observations on Fuller's Reply*, 60.

174. Ibid., 59.

175. Ibid.

176. Fuller, *Reply*, 42.

177. Taylor, *Observations on Fuller's Reply*, 47–50.

178. Fuller, *Reply*, 43. Qtd in Taylor, *Observations on Fuller's Reply*, 49; Taylor, *Observations on Fuller's Reply*, 49.

179. Fuller, *Reply*, 43; Taylor, *Observations on Fuller's Reply*, 88. Qtd in Fuller, *Reply*, 43.

180. Fuller, *Reply*, 43.

submitted to the Spirit's workings on their minds, assumed responsibility, and actively chose to follow Christ. He contended that this contrasted with Fuller's framework, which he understood as continuing to reflect the view that only a restricted few could be saved.

While Taylor's response to Fuller saw him place new importance on the Holy Spirit and the workings of God's grace in the process of conversion, he also emphasized humankind's active involvement. Taylor was firm that the Spirit's urgings were "often resisted."[181] He described having met many people whose minds had been awakened through God's workings to an understanding of the truth of the gospel, but who had not responded in faith.[182] With reference to Heb 6:4–8, 10:26–30, and 2 Pet 2:20–22, he sought to demonstrate that the Spirit was often at work among non-believers in a way which "would have terminated in their salvation, if these operations had not been resisted."[183] Taylor's interpretation of these verses contrasted with what he had likely been taught within Methodism, where these Scriptures were ordinarily used to refute the Calvinist doctrine of the final perseverance of the saints.[184] However, Taylor never used these verses in this way. Indeed, there is no evidence he ever contested the doctrine of final perseverance. Fuller's reading of the *Nine Letters* also led him to conclude "If I am not misinformed, P. allows of the *certain perseverance of all true believers*."[185] While Taylor did not categorically affirm or deny Fuller's assumption, his limited response to Fuller on this matter was an unequivocal declaration that "nothing is more clear to me, than that God has made sufficient provision for the perseverance of all believers."[186] This suggests Taylor did hold a belief in the doctrine. His discourse with Fuller therefore provides a further indication of this distinctive aspect of Taylor's evangelical Arminianism.

Based on the premise that Taylor believed in the perseverance of the saints, it is pertinent to consider when he might have reached this conviction. It is almost certain he did not hold to the doctrine during his period within Methodism, for this would have likely provided an additional reason for his withdrawal from the movement and yet there is no evidence that this was the case.[187] Considering his first soteriological writings in the early

181. Taylor, *Observations on Fuller's Reply*, 25.

182. Ibid., 32.

183. Ibid., 25.

184. See Rack, *Reasonable Enthusiast*, 393.

185. Fuller, *Reply*, 99; Fuller's emphasis.

186. Taylor, *Observations on Fuller's Reply*, 131.

187. See chapter 1.

1770s contain no material at variance with the doctrine, it is probable that his change of perspective stemmed from his regular meetings, beginning in 1764, with Particular Baptist minister John Fawcett Sr. who advocated it.[188] Taylor's reluctance to record his thoughts on the subject may reflect some uncertainty regarding how he could harmonize his belief with the wider elements of his framework. At that time it was unusual for someone who subscribed to the doctrine of the perseverance of the saints to hold a general view of the atonement. However, it is also likely his reluctance to delineate his thinking stemmed from his frequently recurring concern that his publications should not fuel theological controversies which might distract the New Connexion from its wider work. It was perhaps for this reason that Taylor stated he would only engage fully with the subject when "the exposure of it was necessary."[189]

Taylor's conviction of the necessity for people to be converted was underpinned by his belief in humankind's guilt before God (see chapter 2). It is in this respect that his reply to Fuller was again of crucial importance. Taylor provided a new depth of insight into his conviction that humanity's culpability before God was based only on actual sins committed. Though he affirmed the union between Adam and humanity in respect of humankind being "BORN IN SIN" and inheriting "evil propensities," he stated that he did not believe people should be held as guilty concerning what was inherent and therefore unavoidable.[190] Instead, he advocated the blamelessness of the natural human condition. He argued that there was no "positive Scripture evidence" that Adam's posterity "could be blamed for his conduct."[191] His stance differed from how Fuller viewed people as subjects of God's condemnation due to the imputation of Adam's guilt. Taylor's understanding of the Scriptures and way in which he had been sensitized to an Enlightenment-influenced regard for benevolent justice meant that he felt unable to subscribe to such a viewpoint.

As Taylor sought to convince Fuller that humankind was the object of God's pity rather than blame, he challenged the scriptural evidence from which Fuller aimed to disprove the blamelessness of the human condition. For example, Taylor did not agree that David in Psalm 51 assumed blame for his original impurity, or that the apostle Paul's pronouncement of people as "by nature objects of wrath" concerned humanity's condition

---

188. For Fawcett's confident assurance that all believers would inherit salvation, see, e.g., Fawcett Sr., *Christ Precious*, 88–93. Taylor's friendship with Fawcett was examined in chapter 3.

189. Taylor, *Observations on Fuller's Reply*, 130.

190. Ibid., 37; Taylor's emphasis.

191. Ibid., 38.

before God at birth.[192] He also rejected Fuller's charge that if he judged the natural condition as blameless then he had no basis to attribute guilt to people's wrong actions. Taylor insisted that the exercise of "our wills had nothing to do with the state in which we were born."[193] For this reason, he objected to Fuller describing him as believing that humankind had an "evil disposition."[194] He referred to how Fuller "changes my words," since Taylor had actually referred to humanity's "impure propensities," with the implication instead being that sin was only a bias.[195] Taylor also contended that a belief in people's accountability for their actions must be maintained, because through the universal scope of Christ's sacrifice the option of deliverance "from the *indulgence* of sin" was available to all.[196] This assertion saw Taylor uniting some of his most fervently held theological principles. These included his general view of the atonement, his belief that all should assume personal responsibility in the process of salvation, and his hope that all might in turn embrace holiness.

Although a rejection of the doctrine of imputed guilt was a common characteristic of Arminian theology,[197] Taylor's position was distinctive. For example, whereas John Wesley believed that through Christ's death all were cleared from Adam's guilt with it "cancelled by the righteousness of Christ,"[198] it is significant that Taylor here made no mention of the work of Christ. Again typical of how Taylor was embedded in the thinking of the Enlightenment, his approach was rooted in a rational understanding of justice, whereby no person could be judged as guilty before any law had been broken. Taylor asked,

> Now, is there no difference in point of criminality, between our being born impure, in which we had no concern, of which we had no conception, and, as free agents, indulging sin, and slighting the salvation which God has provided?[199]

192. Eph 2:3. See Taylor, *Observations on Fuller's Reply*, 40.

193. Ibid., 39.

194. Fuller, *Reply*, 31. Qtd in Taylor, *Observations on Fuller's Reply*, 39.

195. Taylor, *Observations on Fuller's Reply*, 39; Lover of All Mankind [Taylor], *Observations*, 65.

196. Taylor, *Observations on Fuller's Reply*, 39; Taylor's emphasis.

197. See McGonigle, *Sufficient Saving Grace*, 158.

198. John Wesley, "Letter to John Mason," 239–40. Randy Maddox draws attention to this letter in his consideration of Wesley's rejection of inherited guilt, see Maddox, *Responsible Grace*, 74–75, 292n76.

199. Taylor, *Observations on Fuller's Reply*, 39.

He similarly dismissed as unjust and illogical Fuller's critique that his viewpoint undermined a correct understanding of God's law which "requires us to love God with all the heart, without making any allowance for our being born destitute of a disposition to do so."[200] Taylor urged that no law can "forbid us to be born in that state in which we were born, before we can read that law" and "before we could possibly be the subjects of government."[201] This reasoning reflected his characteristic approach of logical argument underpinned by a firm commitment to God's justice and mercy. In so doing, it further demonstrated that Taylor, in crucial aspects of his response to Fuller, acted as an enlightened critic.

To summarize, an important element of Taylor's discourse with Fuller was the way in which his response to Fuller's criticisms provides a greater understanding of certain notable areas of his thinking than that found in his wider works. Taylor's writings on the Spirit's operations, the nature of grace, and the basis for humankind's culpability before God, reveal noteworthy facets of his theological understanding. They highlight certain distinctive aspects of his evangelical Arminianism, such as his embracing of the doctrine of the perseverance of the saints. The pioneering nature of his evangelicalism was also apparent in how his rejection of imputed guilt was based on an Enlightenment-influenced understanding of justice. It is for this reason that his new insights should be considered a very significant aspect of his debate with Fuller.

The Close of Taylor and Fuller's Discourse

"The Friendly Conclusion"

In 1790, Taylor received a copy of *The Reality and Efficacy of Divine Grace* which comprised thirteen letters addressed to Fuller on the subject of Taylor's *Observations on the Rev. Andrew Fuller's Reply to Philanthropos.*[202] The

200. Fuller, *Reply*, 34.

201. Taylor, *Observations on Fuller's Reply*, 40.

202. Agnostos [Andrew Fuller], *Reality and Efficacy of Divine Grace*. Adam Taylor specified that this work was published in 1790, see Taylor, *Memoirs*, 175. This information is significant as Ryland only loosely referred to this work as having been written "some time after" *The Observations of Philanthropos*, see John Ryland, "Advertisement" to *Reality and Efficacy of Divine Grace*, in Fuller, *Works*, 234. While some academic citations give the date of publication as 1788, this is very doubtful. This date neither accords with that recorded by Adam Taylor nor the fact that Fuller immediately sent this publication to Taylor who received it in 1790 and immediately responded that same year. The reason Fuller waited nearly three years before making his response to Taylor's previous publication is unknown, although it is possible that he had not intended to respond but

author, who assumed the pseudonym Agnostos, was widely considered "a friend and admirer" of Fuller, such as Ryland.[203] However, subsequent to the deaths of Taylor and Fuller it emerged that Agnostos was, in fact, Fuller. The letters were included in the 1831 publication of *The Complete Works of the Rev. Andrew Fuller* with an attached "advertisement" by Ryland who stated that Fuller was the author.[204] This necessitated a revised understanding of some aspects of the material. For instance, Agnostos's praise for Fuller's engagement "on the side of truth," "integrity," and "piety" was nothing more than an expression of self-congratulation.[205] Adam Taylor's response was typical of most who knew Fuller. He asserted that it was never expected that "stern Mr. F. would have stooped" to such an action and, while it had been suspected that Fuller might have influenced the writer, it was never imagined "that Agnostos was a mere man of straw."[206] Ryland was similarly disquieted. This is evident in how, when including the letters in *The Complete Works*, he recognized they "could not with propriety, appear in their original form."[207] When necessary, he therefore changed the second person into the first person so they correctly became letters written by Fuller.

When seeking to account for Fuller's decision "to assume the mask" of Agnostos,[208] Ryland proposed that this was due to his hope that it would help not to prolong the debate.[209] This view was also held by Morris, although by the time he wrote the second edition of *Memoirs* he had become aware of Agnostos's true identity and so acknowledged that Fuller's adoption of the pseudonym was a consequence of his recognition of Taylor's strength as an opponent.[210] Morden also argues that Fuller's actions likely stemmed from how he felt "uncomfortable" at having to make alterations to his understanding of the atonement as a consequence of his discourse with Taylor.[211]

---

that the publication of the second edition of Taylor's *Observations on Fuller's Reply* in late 1788 rekindled his interest in their discourse, although the content of this second edition was identical to the first edition.

203. Morris, *Memoirs*, 205.

204. See Ryland, "Advertisement," 234.

205. Agnostos [Fuller], *Reality and Efficacy of Divine Grace*, 1.

206. Taylor, *Memoirs*, 175. Adam Taylor also contrasted Fuller's decision to "wrap himself in a veil which death alone could remove" with Taylor's willingness to abandon the pseudonym Philanthropos, see Taylor, *Memoirs*, 176.

207. Ryland, "Advertisement," 234.

208. Taylor, *Memoirs*, 175.

209. Ryland, "Advertisement," 234.

210. Morris, *Memoirs*, 205. The way that Morris highlighted Fuller's recognition of Taylor's theological strength was noted in the introductory chapter.

211. Morden, *Offering Christ*, 72.

Fuller's shift in perspective regarding the scope of Christ's death was now a central component of his theological apparatus. He unequivocally affirmed "the necessity of a universal provision, as a ground of invitation," and viewed Christ's death as providing "a foundation for sinners without distinction" to come to God.[212] Fuller had also adjusted other aspects of his atonement thinking. For example, whereas in *Observations* he regarded Christ's sacrifice as a ransom and propitiation only for those who were saved, he now designated these aspects of Christ's salvific work as "applicable to mankind in general."[213] This further modification of Fuller's understanding of Christ's death for all adds credence to the likelihood that his somewhat underhand decision to use the pseudonym Agnostos was contributed to by how he had felt the persuasive power of Taylor's reasoning.

It was actually Fuller who sent Taylor the "letters of Agnostos" (as Taylor called them) in June 1790, and attached "a few very respectful lines."[214] Taylor responded immediately with four short letters in a tract entitled *The Friendly Conclusion*.[215] After reading Agnostos's delineation of Fuller's position, Taylor recognized the depth of the shift Fuller had undertaken concerning the extent of Christ's death. He expressed his delight that he could "rejoice" at his agreement with Fuller on such a "momentous" subject.[216] Taylor asserted that they now shared "the same mind" on other matters that had formed part of their previous discourse.[217] This is illustrated by how he pronounced Fuller's changed approach to regeneration as of "vast importance."[218] Fuller now believed regeneration involved the "*whole change*" that a person underwent in the process of salvation, with its means being the "*word of truth*."[219] Taylor noted Fuller's important shift regarding faith in Christ. Fuller now saw faith as not "expressly" but only "remotely" required in the law.[220] This change was almost certainly a consequence of Taylor's earlier critique. Also, Taylor expressed his "pleasure" at Fuller's agreement that the final misery of sinners should not be attributed to a lack of divine influence, but that "sin alone" was the cause of a person's eternal

---

212. Agnostos [Fuller], *Reality and Efficacy of Divine Grace*, 56, 73.

213. Ibid., 74.

214. Dan Taylor, *Friendly Conclusion*, 3. It is unfortunate that it has not proved possible to locate the additional note that Fuller added.

215. Ibid., 9.

216. Ibid., 15, 14.

217. Ibid., 9.

218. Ibid., 11.

219. Agnostos [Fuller], *Reality and Efficacy of Divine Grace*, 6; Fuller's emphasis.

220. Ibid., 53.

misery.[221] As noted earlier, Taylor had previously emphasized the injustice of this aspect of Fuller's framework.

The generosity of spirit that marked Taylor's first response to *The Gospel Worthy* was again apparent in *The Friendly Conclusion*. This is illustrated in how Taylor viewed the slightly cautious way in which Fuller referred to Christ as "in some sense . . . dying for the whole world" as fully understandable.[222] Taylor emphasized that he recognized "the necessity of caution . . . when we make any revolution in our religious system."[223] Rather more surprising was Taylor's admission that he had no reason to dispute Fuller's doctrine of election.[224] Fuller had sought to assure Taylor that he did not view election as an "insurmountable bar" regarding a person's coming to faith.[225] However, Fuller's references to the limited number of elect, who through the workings of God's "predestinating grace" had been "ordained to eternal life," was a view that there is no evidence Taylor ever accepted.[226] Yet he offered no criticism of Fuller on this subject, referring only to their theological accord.[227] This was indicative of the tendency for pragmatism which was central to Taylor's evangelicalism. It was not his intention within *The Friendly Conclusion* to engage in protracted debate of the issues which Fuller and he had previously disputed, but to highlight areas where he believed they now walked "hand in hand."[228] He considered the subject of election as superfluous to this goal, and pragmatically elected to sidestep the subject. This is evident in Taylor's response to Fuller's claim that an "impartial judge" would find in favor of "the peculiarity of design in Christ's death,"[229] to which Taylor simply replied that this had "no connection with our present controversy."[230] The same pragmatic motivation likely accounted for the way he ignored Fuller's continued critique of his understanding of natural and moral inability and opposition to the blamelessness of humankind's natural condition. Instead, Taylor's priority was to highlight their common theological ground, hoping this might diminish the significance

---

221. Taylor, *Friendly Conclusion*, 11.

222. Agnostos [Fuller], *Reality and Efficacy of Divine Grace*, 57; see Taylor, *Friendly Conclusion*, 11.

223. Taylor, *Friendly Conclusion*, 11.

224. Ibid., 19.

225. Agnostos [Fuller], *Reality and Efficacy of Divine Grace*, 65.

226. Ibid.

227. Taylor, *Friendly Conclusion*, 19.

228. Ibid., 14.

229. Agnostos [Fuller], *Reality and Efficacy of Divine Grace*, 72, 72–73.

230. Taylor, *Friendly Conclusion*, 19.

of any remaining hindrances to Fuller's unreserved acceptance that Christ died for the sins of all.

Taylor's determination to focus solely on that which he considered relevant to Christ's general atonement very likely accounts for his failure to respond to Fuller's reflections concerning Taylor's apparent belief in the doctrine of the perseverance of the saints. If, as it appears, Taylor held to the doctrine, then Fuller stipulated that this contradicted Taylor's opposition to "a certain and effectual influence upon the mind being inconsistent with free agency," and instead demonstrated that Taylor believed there to be "an absolute purpose in God to accomplish an end."[231] Given Taylor's acceptance that God might have purposely designed to save some, Fuller argued that it was now logical for Taylor to accept that "God *could* have actually saved the whole world in the same absolute way, and not have suffered any of the human race to perish, and all this too, in consistency with justice."[232] Similarly, he urged Taylor to recognize that he now had a new platform of understanding from which he could "perfectly account" for people's different responses to the gospel.[233] It is conceivable that Taylor's failure to respond to Fuller's incisive observations was caused by him having been theologically challenged by their content. Theological tensions were sometimes experienced by those who held a general view of the atonement, yet also allowed for the truth of other doctrines such as the perseverance of the saints. Carl Bangs argues, for example, in his consideration of James Arminius's approach to the doctrine of the perseverance of the saints, that he sought "to skirt this issue throughout his career."[234] While to some extent this was true of Taylor, his concentration in *The Friendly Conclusion* on issues he considered pertinent to universal redemption, and characteristic brevity of approach to complex issues mean that his failure to provide Fuller with a delineation of his thinking is not absolute proof of any theological tension that he may have experienced. This was something Morris failed to appreciate when, in overly simplistic fashion, he designated Taylor's response to Fuller on these specific matters as showing his inability "to defend himself against the pugilistic efforts of such a gigantic adversary."[235] If Taylor had been aware of Agnostos's true identity, he might have felt compelled to respond more thoroughly.

---

231. Agnostos [Fuller], *Reality and Efficacy of Divine Grace*, 92.

232. Ibid., 58; Fuller's emphasis.

233. Ibid., 11.

234. Bangs, *Arminius*, 219.

235. Morris, *Memoirs*, 206.

Taylor's hope that his reply to *The Reality and Efficacy of Divine Grace* might conclude his engagement with the issues surrounding The *Gospel Worthy* was fulfilled. This was the last time he wrote on the subject. Although Fuller did not issue a reply, Morris recorded that Taylor's claimed examples of their theological agreement "appeared to him [Fuller] at the time, an instance of dis-ingenuousness."[236] Morris attributed this response to Taylor's "completely disgusting" and "unseasonable and unfounded triumph."[237] While Morris's assertions were misplaced and emotive, it appears that Fuller was aggrieved by Taylor's publication. When Adam Taylor became aware of Morris's comments, he sought to establish if *The Friendly Conclusion* had caused any offense to Fuller, and Dan Taylor confirmed that "a transient feeling of that nature had existed."[238] However, Fuller's sense of grievance soon passed, with Taylor outlining that it was "wholly removed by some mutual explanations at a personal interview, which took place not long afterwards."[239] This amicable outcome was in keeping with the respect they had previously demonstrated towards each other and their shared evangelical understanding of many aspects of the faith. Their resumption of "friendly terms" is evident from Fuller having preached at Taylor's Church Lane Sunday School in 1806 and its Friendly Society in 1807.[240] It is fitting that they developed an enduring friendship, particularly given the way in which, through the course of their theological engagement, they were shaped by each other's perspectives as they wrestled with soteriological issues of such importance.

Conclusion

Taylor's discourse with Fuller was of great significance. The substantial shift in understanding of the atonement that Taylor caused Fuller to undertake; the influence Fuller exerted on some of Taylor's beliefs; and the way in which their mutually irenic manner of debate reflected certain theological emphases and Enlightenment values shared by Arminians and Calvinists of evangelical persuasion were all very important. Taylor's critique of Fuller's *The Gospel Worthy* was the catalyst to their theological engagement. Most notably, Taylor challenged Fuller's assumption that the gospel could be offered universally while not believing there was provision for all in Christ's atonement. He contested Fuller's judgment that it was unnecessary for non-believers to have

236. Ibid.
237. Ibid.
238. Taylor, *Memoirs*, 177.
239. Ibid. The evidence suggests this was the first time they ever met.
240. Ibid.

assurance that Christ had specifically died for them. Taylor also dismissed Fuller's view that a duty to obey the gospel stemmed not from the universal nature of Christ's saving work, but from the moral law. In keeping with the nature of his evangelicalism, Taylor's provision of evidence in favor of general redemption saw him focus on the plain message of the Scriptures. In addition, Taylor's reasoning was underpinned by a Lockean emphasis that any claims to truth be judged by what was reasonable, particularly their need to uphold the Enlightenment values of justice and benevolence. Taylor also challenged aspects of Fuller's understanding of the means and process of conversion. These included Fuller's beliefs such as the necessity of the creation of a divine principle of faith within an unbeliever's heart, regeneration as prior to belief, and distinction between natural and moral inability. Taylor contended that these viewpoints lacked biblical justification, were illogical, and presented an unjust representation of God. Throughout, Taylor functioned as a critic who was steeped in the values of the Enlightenment.

Fuller's private reflections and published replies demonstrate that he was impacted by Taylor's critique. He recognized that if he held to a limited view of the scope of the atonement, then it was not tenable to argue that the inability of at least some to respond in faith was not natural, as there were some for whom there was no atonement provision. Instead, he shifted his position, recognizing that Christ's death was universally sufficient and that all who came to God would be saved. Although insisting God applied Christ's atoning work to a certain number, the atonement position Fuller assumed was "general" in its scope. This was a significant change of position and demonstrated Taylor's commanding influence on Fuller. Fuller also influenced Taylor, as evident in his acceptance that the salvation of at least some could be viewed as containing an element of absolute determinism and special design. Taylor's shifts in belief were partly pragmatically motivated, as he sought to remove obstacles from Fuller's acceptance that Christ died for all. Such a way of proceeding was a distinct facet of Taylor's evangelicalism. Their discourse also exposed creative aspects of Taylor's evangelical Arminianism. These included his belief in the doctrine of the perseverance of the saints, and how his Enlightenment-inspired understanding of justice formed the basis from which he rejected imputed guilt. It will be seen in the next chapter that the creative nature of Taylor's evangelicalism was again apparent in his oversight of the New Connexion.

5

The Baptist Wesley

TAYLOR'S ECCLESIOLOGY WAS OF crucial significance within his theological schema. While affirming long-standing tenets of a Baptist understanding of the church, his approach was pioneering. As the factors pertinent to the formation of the particular nuances of his ecclesiology are considered, it will become apparent that his embracing of evangelicalism, participation in Methodism, and influence of certain Enlightenment values, were all of importance. Initially, attention will be given to his understanding of Christ as head of the church. It will be argued that he applied this principle with a creativity which surpassed that demonstrated by earlier General Baptists. The distinctive facets of his understanding of the church as an embodiment of truth, holiness, and unity will also be considered. In keeping with the nature of eighteenth-century evangelicalism, it will be contended that a strong experiential, practical, and innovative emphasis was woven throughout each of these elements of his ecclesiological framework. This caused him to outwork his convictions in a way that set him apart from certain ecclesiological practices sometimes found among earlier believers such as within Puritanism. Examination will also be undertaken into how the key ecclesiological tenets that Taylor advocated were evident in his oversight of the churches of the New Connexion. It will be argued that the vibrancy of faith and creative practices that he introduced to the churches had an effect that was similar to John Wesley's influence on Methodism. Particular consideration will be given to Taylor's influence over the churches and the importance he placed on the development of centralized strategic initiatives. It will be contended that these aspects of his approach were significant within the history of English Baptist ecclesiological practice.

The Headship Of Christ

"Jesus Christ is the head of his body"

A focus on Christ as head of the church was supreme within Taylor's ecclesiology. It was of foundational importance whenever he addressed the subject of the church. A typical example is found in his 1795 publication of *A Good Minister of Jesus Christ* which he wrote in honor of the Particular Baptist minister Samuel Stennett (1727–95).[1] As he thanked God for Stennett's commitment to the church, he emphasized that the church should function solely for the purpose and glory of Christ, its "only Master."[2] A commitment to Christ's headship over the church was a crucial theme in early Baptist ecclesiology. It lay at the heart of discontent with the national church and underpinned the conviction that each congregation should be free to seek the will of Christ and acknowledge him as Lord. This was also affirmed in Baptist creeds and confessions. For example, Article five of the 1660 General Baptist Standard Confession refers to the church as "Christ's church,"[3] and Article twenty-nine of the 1678 *Orthodox Creed* notes that believers should be "gathered, in one body under Christ, the only head thereof."[4] It is significant that an exaltation of Christ as "the head and lawgiver of his church" was central to Taylor's first address to his General Baptist colleagues when he accepted General Baptist Messenger Gilbert Boyce's invitation to speak at the Lincolnshire Association of General Baptist ministers in 1766.[5]

Taylor's commitment to Christ's Lordship over the church was evident in how he highlighted its relevance to several issues. For instance, he emphasized its importance within his *A Catechism; Or Instructions for Children and Youth*.[6] He cited Scriptures such as Col 1:18 and Eph 1:22, and declared that "Jesus Christ is the head of his body, the church; and the head over all

---

1. Dan Taylor, *Good Minister*. Samuel Stennett succeeded his father Joseph as minister of the Particular Baptist church at Little Wild Street London in 1758 and remained there until his death in 1795.

2. Ibid., 17.

3. *Brief Confession*, in Lumpkin, *Baptist Confessions*, 226.

4. *Orthodox Creed*, Article twenty-nine, see ibid., 318. The language of this Article in the *Orthodox Creed* is another example, of that noted in chapter 3, regarding the similarity between aspects of the *Orthodox Creed* and *The Westminster Confession of Faith*, see *Westminster Confession of Faith*, chapter 25, in Jones, Long, and Moore, eds., *Protestant Nonconformist Texts*, 185.

5. Dan Taylor, *Faithful and Wise*, 8. The content of Taylor's address to this gathering has been considered elsewhere in this book, such as in chapter 2. See also Adam Taylor, *Memoirs*, 23.

6. Dan Taylor, *Catechism*.

things to the church."[7] His christological focus was also evident when he proceeded to define the church as "A society of persons professing faith in Jesus Christ, and love to him."[8] It was also central to his reasoning whenever he addressed the issue of Christian service. When speaking on this subject at the 1786 ordination of George Birley, he taught that Christian service was only meaningful if believers embraced their calling as servants of Christ their master. He insisted that "to talk of being a Christian, without such a surrender as this, is all a mere farce."[9] Taylor was similarly emphatic in his rejection of any exercise of ecclesiastical authority, which elevated ministers as "lords over God's heritage," and as exercising "dominion over the faith."[10] Instead, ministers were only to promote the honor and interests of Christ their master. It was this, he argued, that made the office of minister "the highest title borne on earth."[11] As was typical of the orientation of Taylor's evangelicalism, his pronouncements concerning Christ's headship were bound together with pleas that this should be evident within the life of the church. In this respect, it is appropriate to note Adam Taylor's description that, under Dan Taylor, the Birchcliff church "As far as they understood the will of the great Head of the church, . . . endeavoured to regulate the concerns of their society, according to his precepts: as to call no man master on earth."[12] This imperative was regularly emphasized by Taylor and, as will be examined later, influenced the way he exercised leadership over the churches of the New Connexion.

The zealous regard with which Taylor viewed the church as belonging to the Lord, led him to insist that ministers had "no right to dictate in it, according their own opinion, or their own will."[13] In line with customary General Baptist practice, he believed churches must have freedom to choose their own leaders. He stipulated that nobody possessed the authority "to impose, any person upon any people as a minister, before he's first join'd in fellowship with, and as a member, and person qualified for the ministry,

7. Ibid., 25. Col 1:18: "And he is the head of the body, the church; he is the beginning and the firstborn from among the dead, so that in everything he might have the supremacy."
Eph 1:22–23: "And God placed all things under his feet and appointed him to be head over everything for the church."
8. Taylor, *Catechism*, 25.
9. Dan Taylor, "Charge Delivered," in Dan Taylor, *Charge and Sermon at Ordination of George Birley*, 7.
10. Taylor, *Good Minister*, 9.
11. Ibid., 25.
12. Adam Taylor, *New Connection*, 79.
13. Taylor, *Faithful and Wise*, 8.

approv'd, and call'd to the work, by their unanimous consent."[14] Taylor's enthusiastic embracing of Christ's rule over the church was, to some extent, inspired by his study of church history.[15] This is apparent in the address he gave at the 1786 ordination service of General Baptist minister John Deacon. Taylor bemoaned the way in which he believed that the church's "simplicity, beauty, and liberty" had been lost during the fourth-century reign of emperor Constantine, and replaced with what he considered to have been a hierarchical pattern of governance where bishops assumed the authority of Christ and widespread biblical illiteracy and spiritual darkness prevailed.[16] He reflected soberly on how, after the "sacred sparks" of truth and dissent "shone gloriously" in the sixteenth-century Reformation, there continued in England the imposition of creeds to which obedience was enforced by imprisonment or death.[17] Even when he understood the cause of the Protestants as having benefited under Queen Elizabeth I, he argued that people were still denied the liberty of independent thought and action.[18] In line with Reformation principles and the emphasis on individual freedom within the Enlightenment, Taylor emphasized that "every individual has a right to judge for himself what he ought to believe and propagate" and that "every separate church has the same right."[19] While always seeking to ensure the Connexion's churches stayed faithful to the movement's evangelical basis of belief, he frequently sought to honor this principle in his involvement with the churches.[20] Taylor was convinced that ministers must not act as "a lord over others," as this prerogative belonged only to Christ.[21] This stood apart from the sometimes legalistic dogmatism of General Baptists outside of the Connexion.[22]

It is significant that Taylor's commitment to Christ as the church's only master was central to his decision to establish the New Connexion in 1770. When pressed by Gilbert Boyce, Taylor was explicit that he chose to withdraw from those to whom "he was affectionately attached" due to a regard

14. Ibid., 12–13.

15. Taylor studied church history as a daily discipline during the first few years of his ministry, see Dan Taylor, diary entry, 17 June 1770, in Taylor, *Memoirs*, 50.

16. Dan Taylor, *Charge and Sermon at Ordination of John Deacon*, 7.

17. Ibid., 14.

18. Ibid., 18.

19. Ibid., 44–45, 45.

20. Examples of this will be considered later in this chapter.

21. Dan Taylor, "Principal Parts," in Dan Taylor, and William Thompson, *Respective Duties*, 36.

22. The dogmatism of other General Baptists, such as towards the eating of blood, is examined later in this chapter.

for "the honour of his Redeemer, and the prosperity of his cause."[23] As examined in chapter 2, his concern was that the influence of Socinianism and Unitarianism had led to a disregard for the uniqueness of Christ's identity as the Son of God and trust in his atoning sacrifice as the only means of salvation. With this in mind, he gave his reasons for his decision to begin the New Connexion, stating, "It behoves us therefore to take the alarm; and, with all the little might we have, to militate against those pernicious tenets which our forefathers so much abhorred, and the word of God so expressly condemns."[24] While it will be argued later in this chapter that the formation of the Connexion was not Taylor's first response to the theological drift he encountered, his concern that Christ's Lordship was insufficiently honored throughout wider General Baptist life was an important catalyst to its creation. The way in which Taylor responded to what he felt was a diminished regard for Christ's Lordship by inventively beginning a new movement of churches was in keeping with Dorinda Outram's description of this period as "one of great religious creativity."[25] This not only involved attempts to prove the accordance between orthodox belief and human reason (see chapter 2) but also the development of "powerful religious movements."[26] Chief among these was Methodism which, in turn, influenced many aspects of Taylor's ecclesiological approach. The truth of this assertion will become increasingly evident throughout this chapter.

Taylor's high regard for innovation, as a response to situations where the authority of Christ as the sole master of the church was threatened, was evident within his earlier noted historical discourse at Deacon's ordination. He commended the efforts of "good and faithful" people throughout all ages, whose resolute adherence to Christ had "conscientiously differed" from national laws that had undermined their ability to place primacy on him as their master.[27] He referred to all such people as having followed in the footsteps of believers who were "Dissenters from the national religion" during the first three centuries of the church.[28] Expressing a clear affinity, he stated that their commitment to Christ's Lordship compelled them "to withdraw from the national church and to constitute different ones, according to the judgement of the directions and examples recorded in the

---

23. Dan Taylor, *Consistent Christian*, 83. See also, Taylor, *Memoirs*, 76.

24. Dan Taylor. Qtd in Taylor, *Memoirs*, 76. Primary source unknown.

25. Outram, *Enlightenment*, 113.

26. Ibid.

27. Taylor, *Charge and Sermon at Ordination of John Deacon*, 24.

28. Ibid., 7.

New Testament."[29] He also noted how his reading of church history had led him to be inspired by the pioneering endeavors and commitment to the authority of Christ as demonstrated by "valiant champions" such as the Petrobrussians, Albigenses, Waldenses, and Lollards.[30] Taylor's insights were again indicative of how his understanding of church history influenced his ecclesiological perspective. Given the Baptist context of Deacon's ordination, it is puzzling why Taylor failed to make any reference to Baptist history. It would not have been surprising if he had chosen to highlight earlier General Baptist ministers such as John Smyth (1570–1612), Thomas Helwys or Thomas Grantham who all championed the placing of an ecclesiological primacy on Christ's headship, despite opposition.[31] His failure to do so both here, and indeed throughout his published and private works, suggests that the history of the Baptists was not pivotal to the formation of his ecclesiological thinking. It cannot even be certain that he was aware of its intricacies. His time spent within Methodism, wider reading of church history, personal understanding of the Scriptures, and entrepreneurial tendencies were all of far greater influence on the development of his ecclesiological framework of approach.

In summary, Taylor regularly affirmed the importance of the church demonstrating Christ as its only master. This was underpinned by his reading of Scripture, understanding of church history, and years spent within Methodism. Certain creative ways in which he sought to honor Christ's rule over the church, such as his establishment of the New Connexion, served to set apart his approach from that of many wider General Baptists to this crucial aspect of his ecclesiology. Consideration will be given next to the importance he placed on truth and how this comprised certain distinct emphases.

Importance Of Truth

"pillar and ground of the truth"

Taylor's most frequently employed ecclesiological metaphor was the church as a pillar of truth. A typical example was a sermon he preached at Birchcliff in 1782 when he urged those present to love the truth, and made particular reference to Paul's instruction to Timothy concerning the church as the

29. Ibid., 25.

30. Ibid., 13.

31. The importance of Christ's headship to the seventeenth-century General Baptists was emphasized by James Wood, see Wood, *Condensed History*, 134.

"pillar and ground of the truth."[32] He proceeded to outline his understanding of truth as "the *real* and *genuine* revelation which the blessed God has been pleased to make of himself and his will to mankind. This he formerly revealed by his prophets; and afterwards, by his son Jesus."[33] On this occasion and throughout his writings, Taylor made clear that his primary approach to truth was not cerebral but experiential. It was rooted in a felt appreciation of God having personalized truth in the identity, words, and actions of Christ. He drew attention to how Christ as the "author and fountain" of all truth should be the church's "chief object of love."[34] Rather than conceptions of truth being determined by "party-zeal" to particular systems of thought, he argued that an embodiment of the church as a pillar of truth required a much warmer and relational embracing of the will of its master.[35] Consequently, throughout his ministry, Taylor emphasized the importance of experience meetings where believers gathered weekly in small groups to reflect on their present experience of God's truth in their lives.[36] His understanding of the synonymity between truth and personal experience of Christ accounts for why, in his most impassioned moments, he came close to undermining his teaching that ministers must not act as masters. For example, in *The Faithful and Wise Steward* he referred to ministers needing to "insist" that their understanding of the truth be acted on by the church.[37] There is no evidence that Taylor was himself aware of this tension. Consideration of the contexts where Taylor used such forceful language reveals it was rarely to do with points of doctrine but often concerned the church's embracing of truth, namely of Christ himself. As noted in the previous examinations in this book of Taylor as "Innovative Apologist" and "Novel Advocate," such an emphasis was a distinctive aspect of his evangelicalism.

While Taylor, in his understanding of the church as the pillar of truth, referred to the Scriptures and specifically the New Testament as a "perfect guide and directory in all matters of religion," he did not outwork this conviction in a doctrinally prescriptive way.[38] Instead, he preferred to focus on the practical implications of submission to the Scriptures, insisting that

---

32. Taylor, *Consistent Christian*, 43. Taylor was referring to 1 Tim 3:15.

33. Ibid., 20; Taylor's emphasis.

34. Ibid., 18, 19.

35. Taylor, "Charge Delivered," 33. Taylor's concern with "party affiliations" was also noted in chapters 3's examination of his approach to the atonement.

36. The function of experience meetings was examined in chapter 1 and is returned to later in this chapter.

37. Taylor, *Faithful and Wise*, 15.

38. Taylor, *Consistent Christian*, 22.

the Bible was "the perfect rule of faith and practice."[39] Taylor taught, in respect of Christ, that "his word alone must direct in all cases, and decide in all controversies."[40] One of the ways he sought to safeguard the function of the Scriptures as the "rule" of Christ within the church was by highlighting the dangers of interpretations of Scripture being imposed on people in an overbearing way.[41] At Deacon's ordination he emphasized that "every man has a right to read the Scripture for himself, and to act according to the best judgement he is able to form of it."[42] This conviction was in line with the emphasis on individual liberty within the Enlightenment.

The way in which Taylor endorsed a collective approach to scriptural interpretation was particularly notable. This was typified in what he wrote in *The Consistent Christian* regarding situations when churches encountered difficulties which were not resolvable from an immediate reading of Scripture. With an Enlightenment-influenced respect for reason, he stipulated that "no external compulsion ought to be made use of; for this can neither be vindicated by Scripture, nor by reason; nor is calculated to work conviction in the mind of any rational being."[43] Instead, he asserted that the matter should be referred to the judgment of all elders and office holders in the church, who would together "determine what is most scriptural and beneficial."[44] If unanimity could not be reached, he gave church members license to act according to how they felt best pleased God.[45] This judgment reflected Taylor's commitment to the principles of liberty and pragmatism regarding a person's approach to truth within the confines of the Christian community.

The ecclesiological primacy Taylor attributed to the experiential and practical dimensions of truth is an important factor when seeking to account for the brevity of the New Connexion's *Articles of Religion*.[46] These were written by Taylor at the founding of the movement in 1770 and consisted of six brief and general points regarding the fall of humankind, the moral law, the person and work of Christ, salvation by faith, the Holy Spirit, and baptism. The limited scope of the *Articles* is particularly surprising given that a pledge of commitment to them was the means through which

---

39. [Anon.]. Qtd in Taylor, *Charge and Sermon at Ordination of John Deacon*, 26.

40. Taylor, *Good Minister*, 16.

41. Dan Taylor, *Confession of Faith*, Article four, 3.

42. [Anon.]. Qtd in Taylor, *Charge and Sermon at Ordination of John Deacon*, 26.

43. Taylor, *Consistent Christian*, 135.

44. Ibid.

45. Ibid., 136.

46. *Articles*, in Lumpkin, *Baptist Confessions*, 342–44.

the Connexion came into being and its initial nineteen ministers accepted into membership.[47] Until 1775, no minister was allowed to join unless they subscribed to the *Articles* and, if they chose to abandon them, were "considered as no longer belonging to this assembly."[48] It is also pertinent to note that one of Taylor's chief reasons for establishing the Connexion was his belief that the influence of Socinianism and Unitarianism had caused many of his General Baptist colleagues to cease from preaching what he believed to be gospel truth. Therefore, it might be expected that Taylor would have sought to protect the doctrinal basis of the New Connexion by writing *Articles* which expansively outlined his complete understanding of the gospel. His decision not to do so was likely underpinned by his respect for the experiential and practical dynamics of truth fostered within him due to the nature of his evangelicalism. In turn, this led him to view the conciseness of the *Articles* as sufficient in helping to anchor the Connexion to the truth of the gospel.

The succinctness of the *Articles* is further pronounced when compared to earlier General Baptist creeds and confessions of faith. For instance, while the *Articles* in their entirety consist of only 652 words, the Standard Confession contains over 4,000 and, unlike the *Articles*, includes detailed reference to subjects such as election, the eternal destiny of children dying in infancy, and the laying on of hands.[49] Similarly, there is a contrast between the *Articles* and the 1678 *Orthodox Creed* which is 16,000 words in length. Its fifty Articles contain detailed reflection on subjects such as the nature of the Trinity, predestination, divine providence, free will, worship, and the Sabbath day.[50] The much smaller size of the *Articles* compared to these previous confessions reflects the lesser priority Taylor attached to the need to articulate truth in terms of doctrinal detail.[51] Whereas the tendency of Taylor's General Baptist forebears was to record all that was "profitable for Doctrine," Taylor was inclined to isolate core principles and offer only brief reflection.[52] The fact that he proceeded in this way in a document as significant as the *Articles* which was foundational to the Connexion's national movement of churches, which even at its smallest comprised sixteen

---

47. For a list of these signatories, see *Assembly of Free Grace General Baptists*. Page not numbered.

48. Ibid., page not numbered.

49. See *Brief Confession*, 224–35.

50. See *Orthodox Creed*, 297–334.

51. The exceptions to this were the occasions when Taylor was specifically called upon to defend particular aspects of the gospel.

52. *Brief Confession*, Article twenty-three, 232.

churches and 1,635 members,[53] reflects the extent to which this way of thinking was engrained within him.

As highlighted by Dan Taylor's nephew, James Taylor, the *Articles* were not intended to be "a perfect creed," but instead outlined only what were considered the "essential doctrines" of faith.[54] As Frank Rinaldi notes, they provided the movement's "theological glue."[55] This was again indicative of Taylor's practical approach to truth. Even when Taylor, for an unspecified reason, provided an extension of the *Articles* in his *Confession of Faith in Twenty-four Articles* written shortly after his 1785 move to London and which was then adopted by the Connexion (as noted in chapter 3), this lacked any detailed theological delineation. It provided only brief references to subjects, such as the importance of the Scriptures functioning as a rule over the church,[56] how the elect were chosen on the basis of God's foreknowledge,[57] the function of the Lord's Supper,[58] and a warning of God's future judgment.[59] Its contrast with the previously cited seventeenth-century General Baptist creeds and confessions remains apparent.

The way in which Taylor's leadership of the New Connexion involved less emphasis on a cerebral understanding of truth accorded with his aim that the movement might "revive experimental religion or primitive Christianity in faith and practice."[60] For Taylor, this necessitated that less attention be given to written confessions of truth, and more consideration placed on the protection of liberty and an active embodiment of truth that was personally experienced and practically outworked. This saw him attribute primary ecclesiological importance to building people up in the truth through relational means, rather than by creedal assent. Taylor's 1796 reminder to the Connexion's members that there was nothing they could be "more profitably engaged, than in endeavours to establish one another, in the belief of the truth," was typical.[61] From the outset of the Connexion's establishment, he desired to foster a practical and experiential regard for truth, akin to that introduced to Methodism by John Wesley. For this reason he imme-

53. These figures were noted in the introductory chapter, see also, Rinaldi, *Tribe of Dan*, 213.

54. James Taylor. Qtd in Wood, *Condensed History*, 178. Primary source unknown. See also Taylor, *New Connection*, 139.

55. Rinaldi, *Tribe of Dan*, 13.

56. Taylor, *Confession of Faith*, Article nineteen, 7.

57. Ibid., Article sixteen, 6.

58. Ibid., Article twenty-two, 7–8.

59. Ibid., Article twenty-three, 8–9.

60. *Assembly of Free Grace General Baptists 1770*. Page not numbered.

61. Dan Taylor, *Duties of Church Members*, 9.

diately prioritized the development of the relational means by which this could be achieved. One such example was his establishment in 1770 of a weekly meeting focused on "the exercise of gifts" among young people.[62] Some from this group, such as Birchcliff member Jeremy Ingham, became ministers of New Connexion churches.[63] By 1772, Taylor had also established a monthly meeting for pastors where he offered practical "instruction and advice."[64] The following year he began a "preachers meeting" where he advised and encouraged those preaching in Yorkshire and beyond.[65] Of further significance was Taylor's involvement as personal mentor to many of the Connexion's lay preachers and part-time pastors. For this reason, he frequently welcomed people to his home for extended periods of time, as he sought to strengthen them in what he considered the truths of the gospel and principles of effective ministry.[66] One such person who benefited in this way was John Deacon, whose 1782 stay with Taylor provided him with essential "preparatory studies" for ministry.[67] John Deacon's expressed delight at his ordination that "I am under no obligation whatsoever to subscribe to the creeds and follow the customs imposed by human authority" and free from "anathemas of establishments, councils, synods, or popes, who have usurped dominion over the consciences of men" certainly reflected the ecclesiological thinking of his mentor.[68]

To summarize, Taylor viewed the need to demonstrate the truth of the gospel as a matter of crucial ecclesiological importance. Particularly distinctive was how, compared to most of his General Baptist forebears, he had less regard for a cerebral appreciation of truth, but instead prioritized the need for it to be experientially embraced and practically demonstrated. Both these facets were foundational to his evangelical platform of belief. They also accounted for the brevity of the *Articles*, compared to earlier General Baptist confessions, and led Taylor to launch primarily relationally based means of increasing adherence to truth across the Connexion. Taylor's regard for the experiential is considered next.

---

62. Taylor, *Memoirs*, 78.

63. See Adam Taylor, *John Taylor*, 36–37.

64. *Association 1772*. Page not numbered.

65. Taylor, *Memoirs*, 88.

66. See, e.g., Taylor, *Memoirs*, 103.

67. Samuel Deacon Jr., *Memoirs*, 54. Samuel Deacon was John Deacon's brother and was particularly aware of the benefits that John Deacon received during the time that he spent with Taylor.

68. John Deacon. Qtd in Taylor, *Charge and Sermon at Ordination of John Deacon*, 42, 43. Primary source unknown.

Importance of the Experiential

"the genuine spirit of living Christianity"

The prominence of the experiential within Taylor's ecclesiology was evident in his understanding of holiness as an ecclesiological imperative. Referring to how the "native tendency" of the gospel is to promote "genuine holiness," Taylor taught that this could only be experienced once "the sinner becomes a new creation" and "the power of the gospel is experimentally known."[69] When Taylor began to participate in the Evangelical Revival he became convinced of the deficiency of moralistic approaches to issues of holiness which lacked an accompanying attention to the gospel's redemptive power.[70] From early in his ministry, he resolved to model a different way of proceeding. For example, he noted in a 1764 diary entry that when "speaking against particular sins" he must do so "in such a manner as to lead the sinner to look at the fountain, the heart. Otherwise if we prevail against that sin, yet the work of justification and purification are in danger of being neglected."[71] He also encouraged church members to remind each other that "all truth has a practical tendency, and is to be reduced to holy practical purposes."[72] His rejection of "moralism" on the one hand and antinomianism on the other was typically evangelical.

Taylor drew attention to how the origins of holiness lay with God's ability to transform. As apparent when addressing the holiness of the church in *The Consistent Christian*, he possessed a strong regard for the way in which "the gospel of Christ is a sacred and divine weapon in the hand of the Spirit."[73] He viewed holiness as only possible through God's active provision, and duly described that,

> The fellowship of professing Christians in a church relation, is a joint-interest in the various privileges and advantages which Jesus, their Lord and head, have graciously bestowed upon them, in order to their improvement in the divine life, and their advancement in holiness.[74]

---

69. Taylor, *Consistent Christian*, 152, 152, 99.
70. See chapter 1.
71. Dan Taylor, diary entry, 29 September 1764, in Taylor, *Memoirs*, 52.
72. Taylor, *Duties of Church Members*, 9.
73. Taylor, *Consistent Christian*, 101.
74. Dan Taylor, *Circular Letter 1778*, 2–3.

He, in turn, urged believers "to be earnest in prayer for the supply of the Spirit of Jesus Christ to be poured down upon us."[75] This was again indicative of his appreciation for the experiential roots of holiness. Taylor considered the church as then occupying a pivotal nurturing role regarding a believer's further growth in holiness.

Taylor's approach to holiness was an important aspect of the vibrancy of faith that he sought to foster within the churches he personally presided over and throughout the New Connexion. He regularly urged church members to be "faithful and free one with another" in the duties of exhortation, reproof and admonition.[76] His guiding principle, as detailed in his 1796 *The Duties of Church Members to Each Other*, was that "he who hath called you is holy, so be ye holy."[77] He emphasized the expansiveness of holiness, noting "It extends to every temper of the heart, to every connection and relation in life."[78] It was for this reason he encouraged believers "not to neglect meetings for keeping up order and discipline," but to establish gatherings such as the quarterly exhortation on "the duties connected with Christian Fellowship" which he began shortly after his arrival at Church Lane.[79] Even more significantly, Taylor successfully encouraged many of the Connexion's churches to adopt experience meetings. Fred Harrison's description of New Connexion churches in Nottinghamshire where "Experience meetings were held by many churches, when members made public statements of their spiritual experience," was typical.[80] As examined in chapter 1, Taylor's development of experience meetings saw him introduce an adapted form of the methodology and framework of the Methodist class meeting into the life of the New Connexion. Experience meetings met weekly, with the chief aspect of their focus on practical holiness being the way in which each member recounted their current experience of faith. Experience meetings were central to Taylor's aim that the churches consist of more than simply the "*form* of religion" which he bemoaned led to obedience in Christ becoming nothing more than "a piece of drudgery."[81] As he stated in a 1797 sermon, he wanted

75. Ibid., 9.

76. Ibid., 6. Such an emphasis is also evident throughout Samuel Deacon Jr.'s description of the nature of fellowship within the movement, see Anon. [Samuel Deacon Jr.], *Comprehensive Account*, 93. This publication was anonymously written but Samuel Deacon Jr. is widely considered as its author, see Rinaldi, *Tribe of Dan*, 17.

77. Taylor, *Duties of Church Members*, 3.

78. Ibid., 3.

79. Dan Taylor, "Letter to the Churches," in *Minutes Association 1789*, 8.

80. Harrison, "Nottinghamshire Baptists: Mission, Worship & Training," 314.

81. Dan Taylor, *Sermon Occasioned by Death of Elizabeth Taylor*, 20, Taylor's emphasis.

all churches to exhibit "the genuine spirit of living Christianity" that he believed emanated from believers experiencing a full "participation of the Holy Spirit."[82] Such an emphasis again epitomized the experiential thrust of Taylor's understanding of the holiness of the church. It was also very much in keeping with how Gwang Seok Oh notes that Wesley, particularly in the later years of his ministry, held that "the true members of the true church are not found in terms of sacramental rites, modes of worship or doctrines but in those who have living faith and live holy lives."[83]

Taylor's belief that the sharing of personal experiences of faith contributed to a growth in holiness led him to make this practice central to membership of the New Connexion. In 1771 he helped the annual Association reach the judgment that all potential members needed to provide an account of their "religious experiences in order to their being satisfied concerning the reality of each others conversion."[84] There was a desire for "full evidence" of the "genuineness of each other's piety."[85] In 1775 the Association (again chaired by Taylor) unanimously agreed that the validity of a person's experience of faith replaced commitment to the *Articles* as the key criterion for admission into membership. It became mandatory that those wishing to join the Connexion should "give their experience and when done withdraw in order that it may be debated whether he, or they shall be received."[86] While Rinaldi correctly highlights this judgment as evidence that "the essential nature of the Connexion lay in its reference point being spiritual experience and not credal assent," his view that this "shifted the basis of association away from theology to experience" is an oversimplification.[87] Although the Association's 1775 judgment reflected a development of the importance placed on the citing of experiences of faith, there remained a continuity with earlier approaches. For example, the Association continued to insist that a declaration of the movement's "most Fundamental doctrines," namely the *Articles*, be given to those wishing to join so as "it might be ascertained whether there was an agreement in our religious sentiments."[88] Taylor's position was very similar to the way in which Jeremy Gregory argues that John Wesley placed "great emphasis" on a person's experience of faith but, to ensure its genuineness,

82. Dan Taylor, "Sermon, Dec. 31, 1797," 25.

83. Oh, *John Wesley's Ecclesiology*, 204.

84. *Assembly 1771.* Page not numbered.

85. Taylor, *New Connection*, 143.

86. *Association 1775.* Page not numbered.

87. Rinaldi, *Tribe of Dan*, 190, 49.

88. *Association 1775.* Page not numbered.

also insisted that this "needed to be tempered by Scripture and by reason in a characteristically eighteenth-century balance."[89] The importance given to spiritual experience was certainly a distinct feature of the New Connexion and very much in keeping with Taylor's personal understanding of faith and ecclesiological practice.

It is important to note that the authenticity of Christian spiritual experience as a basis for membership of the Connexion was not lost subsequent to the 1777 decision that membership no longer be restricted to individuals, but that churches be allowed to become members.[90] Churches wishing to join the movement were required to submit reports of their experience of faith and only admitted upon the unanimous support of the annual Association. The seriousness with which this way of proceeding was embraced accounted, for example, for the one-year delay in the 1793 membership application from the General Baptist church in Fleet, Lincolnshire with its "cooler tone of church life . . . not in tune with the evangelical dynamic of the Connexion."[91] Taylor emphasized the importance of the experiential in *A Good Minister of Jesus Christ*, stating "Religion is a practical thing. Christianity influences and engages the heart and life, as well as illuminates and sanctifies the understanding."[92] In addition, all individuals wishing to join New Connexion churches were required to give a report of their faith. For instance, it was the "simplicity and apparent integrity" of the faith experience of Elizabeth Taylor (Taylor's first wife) that saw her welcomed into membership at Birchcliff.[93] Attention to spiritual experience was woven into nearly every aspect of the approach to holiness within the life of the Connexion.

The holiness of the church was emphasized by Taylor during his last address as minister at Birchcliff.[94] Its focal point was that the "scenes, relations and proceedings" of all believers, irrespective of their stage of life, should be marked by holiness.[95] If, in the future, he was to hear of the believers at Birchcliff being described in such a way, then he stated that this would bring him even greater pleasure than if the church were "attended

---

89. Gregory, "Religion," 52, 53.

90. For the context of this decision, see Taylor, *New Connection*, 212.

91. Ambler, "Building up the Walls of Zion," 22. Qtd in Rinaldi, *Tribe of Dan*, 38.

92. Taylor, *Good Minister*, 19.

93. Taylor, *Sermon occasioned by Death of Elizabeth Taylor*, 61–62.

94. Taylor highlights some of the contents of this sermon as he writes on the subject of gospel holiness in *Consistent Christian*, see Taylor, *Consistent Christian*, 88–121.

95. Ibid., 92.

with great numbers."[96] Given Taylor's commitment to the cause of mission, such a proclamation of the primacy of holiness is significant. However, it should be recognized that, just as Wesley held the need to spread scriptural holiness as synonymous with the mission of the church (see chapter 3), so Taylor viewed holiness and the call to share the gospel with others as inseparable. He impressed on believers the need "to the end of life, to be making advances in universal holiness; and to exert ourselves, according to our ability, in the promotion of it, among all with whom we have any connection."[97] Similarly, when he referred to the subject of holiness at the 1775 ordination of the General Baptist minister Benjamin Worship in Great Yarmouth, he insisted that "The great end of the gospel ministry is certainly to bring men to genuine holiness, and heaven hereafter."[98] Taylor stressed that "The operation, the tendency, the motives, the prospects of the gospel are all holy."[99] This interconnection between holiness and mission was a key aspect of Taylor's ecclesiological framework.

The link Taylor perceived between the spread of the gospel and holiness was apparent as he impressed on ministers the need to prioritize the protection of their churches from error and ungodly behavior. This was also something he demonstrated within the conduct of his own ministry. Both at Birchcliff and Church Lane he facilitated the process of church discipline regarding matters, such as personal holiness and what he felt were distortions of the gospel message.[100] While it could be argued that this points to a tension with his wider emphasis on the need to uphold believers' liberty of conscience, Taylor himself did not see this. Instead, he asserted that if the church was to share the gospel meaningfully with others, then ministers must be "bold in checking every iniquity" among their members.[101] With reference to Christ "who wept over a ruined city," Taylor stated that ministers should always be concerned regarding the negative consequences of the ungodliness of church members on the plight of non-believers.[102] His repeated emphasis on the holiness of the church and effective mission should be viewed as a further aspect of his development of a missional spirituality

96. Ibid., 120.

97. Taylor, "Sermon, Dec. 31, 1797," 24.

98. Taylor, "Principal Parts," 40.

99. Ibid., 49.

100. As an example, see Dan Taylor, diary entry, 2 August 1767, in Taylor, Memoirs, 65.

101. Taylor, "Principal Parts," 33.

102. Ibid., 37.

(as examined in chapter 1). This differed from the more introspective approaches to holiness adopted by many Puritans.[103]

A further characteristic of Taylor's engagement with the subject of holiness was the way he urged the New Connexion's ministers to ensure that the exercise of discipline was "properly managed."[104] He highlighted matters such as the need to consider mitigating circumstances and motives that might have led a person to sin, the importance of guarding against the exercise of bias in reaching judgments, and the need for ministers, when dealing with those who had sinned, to ensure they were "filled with the most ardent desires to do them good."[105] This was also something Taylor sought to demonstrate when, similar to the role assumed by Wesley within Methodism, he provided advice regarding issues of discipline within the Connexion's churches. A typical instance was his response in 1800 to concerns expressed by his brother John that some in the fellowship in Queenshead, West Riding were teaching heresy.[106] Taylor proceeded cautiously, firstly advocating the need to ensure they were not simply employing a "different language" to express the same theological convictions found in the Connexion's *Articles*.[107] If this was not the case, he suggested that John excluded them from the church, but only after he had taken "all the pains" to convince them otherwise.[108] Such a carefully considered approach was characteristic of the advice Taylor offered to the Connexion's churches on issues of holiness.

In summary, Taylor's regard for the experiential was central to the importance he placed on the holiness of the church. He argued that the practical outworking of holiness must be underpinned by people first experiencing God's transforming power. The recounting of experiences of faith was essential to membership of the New Connexion with the practice also held by Taylor as important in helping to facilitate a further growth in holiness. His reiteration of the inseparability of the proclamation of the gospel from true holiness, and his determination to model a more reasoned and objective approach to church discipline were significant. As will be demonstrated next, Taylor also emphasized the need for unity.

103. See chapter 1.

104. Taylor, "Principal Parts," 37.

105. Ibid.

106. See Dan Taylor, "Letter to his Brother, Mr. J. T.," 1800 (date not specified), in Taylor, *Memoirs*, 278. Queenshead is today known as Queensbury.

107. Ibid.

108. Ibid.

Importance of Unity

"the Christian's treasure"

A further dimension of Taylor's ecclesiology was the importance he placed on unity. In the first instance, his focus was not how this was to be pursued but how its foundation lay in the church's shared spiritual heritage. All believers were "partakers of the divine nature" with their experience of God's Trinitarian blessings providing a common platform for unity.[109] In *A Good Minister of Jesus Christ* he considered that which constituted believers as "brethren," and drew attention to how "real Christians are properly stiled brethren, because they all partake of the same Spirit."[110] Those led by the Spirit were given a fountain of "living water" which enabled them to walk together in love, prayer, power, and holiness.[111] On other occasions, Taylor turned his attention to God the Father. Speaking in 1793 at the funeral of his wife Elizabeth, he addressed the subject of unity by making particular reference to the shared blessings emanating from knowing God as the "Father of mercies."[112] Regarding the collective life of the church, he was convinced that an authentic experience and understanding of God as "Father, and everlasting Friend" would "produce the best effects in the tempers and lives of real saints."[113] In the *Fundamentals of Religion in Faith and Practice*, he dwelt on believers sharing unity in the Son, and particularly the shared experiences that stemmed from being the object of Christ's varied "offices."[114] Christ as a king, "rules and defends you, and subdues your enemies for you," as a prophet he "enlightens, teaches and instructs," and as a physician he "heals your various returning disorders of soul."[115] The need for believers to experience the power of God's Trinitarian workings in their lives was foundational to Taylor's understanding of the unity of the church.

Taylor described the unity believers shared in God as "the Christian's treasure" and contrasted this with "the dreary wilderness of this world."[116] Similarly, he described the workings of God's power, wisdom, love, and compassion as "treasures of grace and glory" that were "bestowed" on all be-

---

109. Taylor, *Sermon occasioned by Death of Elizabeth Taylor*, 22.

110. Taylor, *Good Minister*, 4, 6.

111. Ibid., 6.

112. Taylor, *Sermon Occasioned by Death of Elizabeth Taylor*, 21. Elizabeth Taylor joined the church at Birchcliff soon after Taylor's arrival. They were married in 1764.

113. Ibid., 21.

114. Dan Taylor, *Fundamentals*, 292.

115. Ibid., 290.

116. Ibid., 288.

lievers.[117] All Christians were heirs of this inheritance and therefore equally entitled to "the same privileges and advantages in the church."[118] Aware of the varied ages, capacities, and temperaments of church members, Taylor frequently employed the metaphor of the church as a household. For example, in *The Faithful and Wise Steward* he described the church as uniting under one father, with all believers sitting at one table—"the Lord's table," eating the same food—"the sacred elements," feeding the same way—by a "living faith," and possessing one rule—"the word of God."[119]

Taylor's advocacy for the active role of women in the life of the church was a further significant aspect of his commitment to unity. For example, Taylor encouraged Birchcliff's female members to voice their opinions at church meetings and in all other settings.[120] In his address at his wife Elizabeth's funeral, he described how at Birchcliff "women were encouraged to speak freely, on every subject," and that they had participated in meetings involving members "conversing on experimental and practical subjects."[121] He also welcomed women to serve as elders and deacons. Elizabeth Mitchel, who was otherwise unknown, was among the first to assume the office of elder at Birchcliff.[122] Such an affirmation of the involvement of women in the church was in contrast to the common General Baptist practice of Taylor's day. From the closing decades of the seventeenth century, the scope of women's involvement in Baptist congregational life had diminished considerably. For instance, while earlier Baptists such as John Smyth and Thomas Helwys endorsed women as eligible to serve as deacons and wider evidence confirms their contribution to early seventeenth-century Baptist life,[123] there is no specific mention of the role of women in any of the later confessions of faith. The greater restrictions placed on them were apparent in the development of rules regulating their speaking at church meetings and participation in worship, as John Briggs highlights.[124] Given this con-

---

117. Ibid., 33.

118. Taylor, *Good Minister*, 5.

119. Taylor, *Faithful and Wise*, 6.

120. See, e.g., Taylor, *Sermon Occasioned by Death of Elizabeth Taylor*, 68.

121. Ibid., 69.

122. Taylor, *Memoirs*, 133.

123. See *Short Confession*, Article sixteen, in Lumpkin, *Baptist Confessions*, 101; *Declaration of Faith*, Article twenty, in ibid., 121. Thomas Helwys was the writer of *A Declaration of Faith*. Adam Taylor drew attention to how women were thought to have been active in openly contributing to discussions at the Bell Alley Church, Whitechapel in the 1640s, see Adam Taylor, *English General Baptists*, 101. See also Briggs, "she-Preachers, Widows and Other Women," 337–40.

124. Ibid., 342. The issues and beliefs that surrounded the participation of women

text, it is not surprising that Taylor, when endorsing the role of women in the church, found it necessary to make it clear twice that women were active—" as well as the men."[125] Taylor also commended the "striking" nature of his wife Elizabeth's spiritual observations on his sermons and "subjects in divinity."[126] Unlike earlier General Baptists such as Grantham and certain of Taylor's contemporaries, such as General Baptist minister Samuel Deacon Sr. (1714–1812), there is also no record of Taylor having ever explicitly endorsed a hierarchical understanding of male headship.[127] The absence of any such emphasis in his writings is again indicative of the depth of Taylor's ecclesiological egalitarianism.

While Taylor's support for the active involvement of women in the church was in keeping with certain Enlightenment influences (see chapter 6), it was also very likely influenced by his years in Methodism. As David Hempton notes, "Methodism was not only a religious movement in which women had an important role, but that Methodism was shaped by women in ways that we still do not fully understand."[128] Phyllis Mack draws attention to how John Wesley supported "women's religious activity and authority," encouraging them, for example, to participate fully as members and leaders in class and band meetings; "to act as informal missionaries" to their neighborhoods; and those who had an "extraordinary call" were authorized to preach.[129] Although Taylor's written works do not contain any acknowledgment of the influence of Methodism on this aspect of his ecclesiology, it is highly probable that his nine-year involvement within its structures and continued awareness of its development influenced his stance regarding the role of women in the church. It is also notable, as Gareth Lloyd notes, that Yorkshire in the eighteenth century was home to several prominent Methodist women, some of whom exercised "very public and extremely popular" ministries.[130]

---

in worship will be considered in chapter 6.

125. Taylor, *Sermon occasioned by Death of Elizabeth Taylor*, 68.

126. Ibid.

127. For consideration of Thomas Grantham's hierarchical understanding, see White, *English Baptists*, 143. Samuel Deacon's emphasis on male authority is apparent in Deacon, *Memoirs*, 102.

128. Hempton, *Methodism*, 149.

129. Mack, *Heart Religion*, 147, 140. For further consideration of the role of women in Methodism, see Cruickshank, "'If God see fit to call you out,'" 55–76. See also, Oh, *John Wesley's Ecclesiology*, 207–12.

130. Lloyd, "Repression and Resistance," 108. Examples include Ann Cutler, and Elizabeth Dickinson. Lloyd also considers the greater restrictions that women faced in Methodism subsequent to John Wesley's death.

Taylor's commitment to the full involvement of women in the church was apparent in his oversight of the New Connexion. It is significant that just two years after the movement's formation, he chaired the process which led to it being "universally agreed" that it was "the duty of all women to attend church meetings when they can conveniently."[131] It was also decided that women should be granted a vote on matters relating to church order and discipline.[132] In addition, Taylor's appreciation for the place of women in the Connexion was apparent within the extensive letter writing he undertook to help foster unity across the Connexion. An example of this was a letter he sent in 1815 to an otherwise unknown Mrs. M. and Mrs. N.[133] Taylor wrote to them due to his concern that their rural location might leave them feeling alienated from others in the Connnexion. He assured them that "Though far distant; we still belong to the same family, and are even members of the same Body. God forbid that we should ever forget our near relation."[134] These sentiments were typical of Taylor's approach.

Given the ecclesiological significance Taylor attached to the function of women in the church and throughout the New Connexion, and the extent to which this differed from the practice of many of his Baptist and certain other evangelical contemporaries, it is unfortunate that it has been widely overlooked by commentators. It is, for instance, absent from Briggs's consideration of women in Baptist life and Rinaldi's examination of the Connexion during the years of Taylor's leadership.[135] Neither does Ruth Gouldbourne draw attention to it in her 1998 Whitley Lecture *Reinventing the Wheel*.[136] Gouldbourne provides an expansive examination of the historical function of women in Baptist life. She includes helpful reflection on the limitations which led to women assuming a "more restricted role" in the eighteenth century and which, she argues, were linked to new patterns of thinking that accompanied the growing institutionalization of the Baptist denomination.[137] However, she makes no mention of Taylor's contrary position. This omission is particularly noticeable given that she does make brief reference to Taylor, noting his support for the Evangelical Revival.[138] Gouldbourne's

131. *Association 1772*. Page not numbered.

132. Ibid.

133. Dan Taylor, "Letter to Mrs. M. and Mrs. N.," 4 April 1815, in Taylor, *Memoirs*, 287–88.

134. Ibid., 287.

135. See, e.g., Briggs, "she-Preachers, Widows and Other Women"; Rinaldi, *Tribe of Dan*.

136. Gouldbourne, *Reinventing the Wheel*.

137. Ibid., 13.

138. Ibid., 14.

oversight is again symptomatic of the limited knowledge that surrounds so much of Taylor's embodiment of a progressive evangelicalism.

A further distinctive dynamic of Taylor's ecclesiological emphasis on unity was the regularity with which he cautioned believers against engaging in contentious disputes. A characteristic example was how, in *The Consistent Christian*, he urged that controversial subjects be avoided as the inevitable outcome would be "diversity in judgement on sacred subjects."[139] This formed a routine part of the instruction he presented at ordinations, such as that of his nephew James in 1800, who he encouraged to steer away from "frequent discussion of controversial subjects" because "few of your hearers can follow you in them to advantage."[140] He also referred to "many other reasons" that led him to issue this caution.[141] Given the central tenets of his evangelicalism, these unspecified reasons likely included a prioritizing of the practical outworking of faith above a cerebral understanding, a preference for brevity above detailed delineation of doctrine, and pragmatic concern that focusing on controversial subjects was detrimental to the task of mission. This approach differed from the way many Reformers and Puritans viewed as imperative the need to teach believers specific principles of faith—irrespective of the contentiousness of the subject matter. An example was how Puritans such as Richard Greenham and William Perkins advocated a strict observance of the Sabbath,[142] despite prescriptive approaches to the Sabbath being contested by most within the Church of England. While, for example, continental Reformed churches generally adopted a freer position regarding the Sabbath, certain English Puritans such as William Ames insisted they made a rigid observance of the Sabbath a hallmark of their piety.[143] A strict Sabbath observance was also advocated by General Baptists such as Thomas Grantham.[144] In contrast, Taylor's works contain only one mention of the subject—a brief note of disappointment that those not resting on the Sabbath were deprived a "treasure" through which God would bless them.[145] As Taylor preached at his nephew's ordination, he instead ad-

139. Taylor, *Consistent Christian*, 125.

140. Taylor, "Outline of a Charge," 263.

141. Ibid.

142. Greenham, *Treatise of the Sabboth*; Perkins, *Whole Treatise*, 453–64.

143. See, e.g., Ames, *Marrow of Theology*, 294–98. For brief reflection on Ames's approach to the Sabbath, see Anthony Milton, "Puritanism," 122. For examples of the seriousness with which Puritans approached Sabbath enforcement, see Hambrick-Stowe, "Practical divinity," 199.

144. See, e.g., Grantham, *Seventh-Day-Sabbath*. See also, *Orthodox Creed*, Article forty, 327–28.

145. Dan Taylor, *Interposition of Providence*, 19.

vocated a sole focus on what he judged as "the essential truths of the gospel" and "Experimental Preaching."[146] Such an emphasis was characteristic of the pragmatic and experiential thrust of his evangelicalism.

Taylor's determination to preserve unity within the church was something he actively sought to model. A prominent example was the way he proceeded regarding the issue of the eating of blood which was a long-standing aspect of General Baptist prohibition.[147] The demand that all members of New Connexion churches "abstained from the eating of blood" was a non-negotiable element of that stipulated by the representatives of the wider body of General Baptists during the 1777 and 1784 attempts at reunion between the two bodies.[148] Although Taylor's understanding of the Scriptures meant he did not believe that the eating of blood was forbidden, it is notable that he "scrupulously abstained from it."[149] He did so to protect unity, not wanting anybody to be "grieved" by his actions regarding this matter.[150] However, because he did not view this as an essential gospel truth, he refused to issue an unequivocal ruling that the Connexion would be expected to follow. Instead, he taught that believers should be granted the "liberty of thinking and acting according to their own views."[151] This demonstrated Taylor's ecclesiological conviction that the Connexion's members "Be positive where Scripture is positive and clear; but modest in every thing doubtful and obscure."[152] The commitment to this principle reflected how the Connexion's churches enjoyed a freer way of functioning when compared to the more restrictive ecclesiological practices commonly found among General Baptists outside the movement.

The importance Taylor attached to believers establishing a "bond of peace" that extended across different denominational affiliations set him apart from the insularity that was sometimes evident among wider General Baptists.[153] He likely had such General Baptists at least partly in mind when he lamented how the fragmented relationships between the

146. Taylor, "Outline of a Charge," 210.

147. See Taylor, *English General Baptists*, 455; Brown, *English Baptists*, 18. This issue had its roots in the correct interpretation of the dietary laws as pronounced by the Council of Jerusalem (Acts 15).

148. Wood, *Condensed History*, 188. These attempts at reunion are examined in the next section.

149. Taylor, *Memoirs*, 292.

150. Dan Taylor. Qtd in Taylor, *Memoirs*, 292. Primary source unknown.

151. Taylor, *New Connection*, 214.

152. Taylor, "Principal Parts," 19–20.

153. Taylor, *Consistent Christian*, 144. The insularity of the General Baptists was noted in chapter 2.

churches of his day had created an "unhappy and divided age," where there were frequent "party broils and contentions."[154] Keen to model a different way of proceeding, he urged all believers to "walk together in harmony, peace and friendship, even though they judge and act differently in matters of religion."[155] He similarly delineated how it was a "particular beauty of Christianity, that it teaches universal love and especially, that all the *saints*, however otherwise distinguished, should maintain a cordial affection one for another."[156] Taylor's strength of conviction on this matter was evident in his 1798 letter to the Connexion's churches where he specified that "a sincere, active, operative affection for all the children of God, is a substantial proof of genuine Christianity."[157] He also stated that those who did not exhibit "a peculiar love to all true believers in Jesus Christ, must be excluded from the number if real Christians."[158] Similarly, he was forceful in *The Consistent Christian* where he argued that to disrespect other believers because they held different theological viewpoints was "to resent their obedience to the Lord Jesus Christ."[159] Such a regard for the wider church confirms Rodney Ambler's claim that Taylor was not "an individualist driven by the imperatives of revival."[160] The same was true for John Wesley who, though strong in his personal convictions, was rarely exclusive in his approach. Taylor himself experienced how believers of all persuasions were warmly welcomed into the Methodist movement.[161] The many close friendships Taylor developed with those of other denominations, and his eclectic spirituality and understanding of unity as a prerequisite to effective mission, were pivotal in shaping his commitment to the wider church.[162] Further typical of Taylor's evangelicalism was the strong experiential motivation that underpinned his resolve on this matter. He was convinced that

---

154. Taylor, *Faithful and Wise*, 26; Taylor, *Consistent Christian*, 82. It was highlighted in chapter 3 how Taylor experienced significant tensions in relationships between General and Particular Baptists during his time at Birchcliff.

155. Taylor, "A Charge and Sermon at Ordination of George Birley," 27. It will be seen in chapter 7 that this was something Taylor also practically demonstrated in the context of mission.

156. Ibid., 28; Taylor's emphasis.

157. Taylor, "Letter to the Churches," in *Minutes of an Association 1798*, 14.

158. Taylor, "Letter to the Churches," 26–28 June 1798, 17.

159. Taylor, *Consistent Christian*, 81.

160. Ambler, "Church, Place and Organization," 240.

161. See chapter 1.

162. Taylor's friendships with those of other denominations and understanding of the importance of unity in mission will be examined in chapter 7.

Jesus pronounced a "*special blessing*" on believers who sought to promote peace with those of other denominations.[163]

To summarize, the significance Taylor placed on unity was a crucial aspect of his ecclesiological understanding. The distinctive aspects of his evangelicalism led him to express his commitment to unity in ways that set him apart from the practice of many General Baptists and Puritans. These include the importance he placed on its experiential origins, his active encouragement of the full participation of women in the life of the church and New Connexion, freer approach to issues such as the eating of blood, pragmatic avoidance of contentious subjects, and the priority he placed on the development of loving relationships with those of other denominations. It will next be seen that Taylor also emphasized the need for churches to be working together and that this involved an inventive outlook.

Importance of Churches Associating Together

"to assist one another . . . in the conversion of
poor sinners to our Lord Jesus Christ"

While Taylor placed significance on the need for the churches of the New Connexion to be associating with each other, it is first necessary to consider how he reconciled the establishment of the movement with the priority he placed on unity. This is particularly pertinent given that it was viewed as divisive by many General Baptists outside the Connexion. For instance, Gilbert Boyce was adamant that the formation of a separate movement would "hurt and divide the churches," "dishonour" Christ, and be understood by non-believers only in terms of "reproach and scandal."[164] Although Taylor was unconvinced by Boyce's reasoning, his initial response to that which he had viewed in the 1760s among his fellow General Baptists as some of the "vilest errors" ever held "by any party of men in former ages" was not to begin a new body of believers, but to challenge these assumptions.[165] In addition, he sought to bring about an evangelical shift in emphasis within the Lincolnshire General Baptist Association by asking the Independent

---

163. Taylor, *Consistent Christian*, 60; Taylor's emphasis.

164. Boyce, "Letter to Taylor," 1770 (date not specified), in Taylor, *Memoirs*, 75, 75; Boyce. "Letter to Taylor," 10 February 1770, in Taylor, *New Connection*, 136. Adam Taylor records that Boyce wrote several letters to Taylor on this subject.

165. Taylor, *Memoirs*, 76. The nature of the views that Taylor encountered and his response to them were considered in chapter 2.

church at Barton-in-the-Beans,[166] Leicestershire, and its associated group of churches, to join the Association.[167] The Barton church was formed into a society of believers in 1744 and entered the Church of England, but seceded in 1745. It then came under Methodist influence (through the ministry of David Taylor), embraced Arminianism, and adopted believers' baptism in 1755.[168] Taylor was struck by their fervor for the gospel and evangelism when he first visited them in 1764.[169] However, his invitation to join the Association was declined by the Barton pastor Samuel Deacon Sr. who declared it "the duty of all who maintained the truth, to have no fellowship with such as had so grossly fallen from it," and had become so "highly erroneous in their creed."[170] His rejection was firm.

It was immediately after the Barton grouping of churches declined Taylor's plan that he resolved to establish the New Connexion. Although his heart was "full and pained" at the thought of separation from the wider General Baptists, he was convinced of its need.[171] Significantly, Taylor's prime reason for beginning the Connexion was not his discontent with what he viewed as the theological errors of many of his General Baptist colleagues, but a mindfulness of how the gospel could be effectively propagated by partnering with such "strenuous advocates" for gospel truth as the Barton churches.[172] They, in turn, formed five of the Connexion's initial sixteen churches.[173] Nevertheless, Taylor prioritized the sustaining

166. This spelling of Barton-in the-Beans is consistent with how it was known in Taylor's day.

167. See Taylor, *Memoirs*, 76. The daughter churches of the Independent church at Barton-in-the-Beans were established in 1760 and consisted of Melbourne, Kegworth, Loughborough, and Kirby Woodhouse. Hinckley church also emerged from Barton Church in 1798. An account of the origins of the church at Barton-in-the-Beans and influence of David Taylor (who was at this time a servant of the Countess of Huntingdon) was written by John Deacon as part of his history of the emergence of the New Connexion that he continued across several issues of the first volume of the *General Baptist Magazine*, see John Deacon, "History of New Connection," 181–90, 225–30. See also Wood, *Condensed History*, 157–68; Godfrey, *Historic Memorials*; Betteridge, "Barton-In-The-Beans," 70–79.

168. See Welch, "Origins," 65–66.

169. Taylor, *Memoirs*, 30.

170. Ibid. Adam Taylor lists Deacon's doctrinal concerns as including General Baptist approaches to Christ's divinity, the atonement by Christ's death, justification by faith alone, and regeneration by the Holy Spirit, see Taylor, *New Connection*, 133.

171. Dan Taylor. Qtd in Taylor, *Memoirs*, 76. Primary source unknown.

172. Ibid., 29. Primary source unknown.

173. The formal decision to begin the New Connexion was taken in a meeting at the close of 1769 by Taylor, William Thompson and other representatives of the Leicestershire churches including John Grimley (Loughborough), and Nathaniel Pickering

of "cordial relationships" between the New Connexion and other General Baptists.[174] He freely appeared before the General Assembly of the older General Baptist body in 1770,[175] maintained good friendships with leading General Baptists such as Boyce, and periodically served General Baptist churches that were outside the Connexion.[176] These efforts underline the importance Taylor placed on unity.

The primacy Taylor attached to unity was also apparent in his willingness to engage in the earlier noted reunion discussions that were instigated by the General Assembly of the wider General Baptists.[177] While Taylor, writing on behalf of the Connexion, concluded that it was not appropriate to unite with believers who "deny the proper atonement of Christ for the sins of men," he engaged seriously in the discussions that took place.[178] It is also significant that there is no record of the Barton churches opposing Taylor's willingness to discuss the proposals for reunion. This apparent softening of stance towards the long established body of General Baptists, compared to their earlier strong rejection of the possibility of joining the Lincolnshire General Baptists, was likely a consequence of their trust in Taylor's oversight of the Connexion, and particularly how he demonstrated that a commitment to unity and peace did not in itself compromise evangelical convictions. As noted in chapter 3, it was not until 1803 that Taylor finally felt compelled to end relations with the General Assembly, when he judged its continued departure from key gospel tenets to have reached a point where he considered there was no longer sufficient theological accord between the two bodies.[179]

Taylor's regard for the merits of ecclesiological unity saw him place great importance on the development of a coherent collective identity throughout the Connexion. It was for this reason he urged churches to ensure their representation at the annual Association.[180] It was "The Nature and Importance of the Annual Associations" which formed the subject of

(Castle Donnington), see Taylor, *Memoirs*, 30.

174. Brown, *English Baptists*, 69.

175. See Taylor, *Memoirs*, 76.

176. Examples of how Taylor served General Baptist churches outside the Connexion will be considered in chapter 7.

177. See Taylor, *New Connection*, 213–16.

178. Dan Taylor, "Letter to the General Assembly," 1784 (date not specified), in Whitley, *Minutes of General Baptist Assembly, 1731–1811*, 183.

179. See Taylor, *Memoirs*, 224–25. See also Whitley, *Minutes of General Baptist Assembly, 1654–1728*, xxv.

180. Churches were represented at the annual Association by ministers, elders or chosen representatives. Further consideration is given to this in the next section.

his 1793 letter to the churches.[181] With much scriptural reference, Taylor advocated the need to replicate the practice of the early church apostles who met regularly to discuss "the affairs of the churches."[182] The establishment of quarterly regional conferences also enabled ministers, deacons and chosen church representatives to associate at "appointed seasons" and "to confer on the difficult concerns of their churches," both practical and theological.[183] An indication of the significance of these meetings is provided by John Taylor who commended the Yorkshire Conference as having provided him with "very special benefit."[184] In direct reference to the nature of his brother Dan's involvement at these regional conferences, he also mentioned that "I needed correction and instruction. I generally got both at these meetings."[185] The central influence Taylor exerted over the churches through his successful fostering of a commitment to participation in the movement's limited structures and personal oversight should not be overlooked. The scope of his influential and strategic coordinating of initiatives was distinct from the way Particular Baptists began to associate more meaningfully from the late eighteenth-century, and exceeded the advisory powers that General Baptists outside the Connexion gave to its Assembly.[186] Within Baptist life, Taylor was the architect of an innovative framework within which churches associated together.

As Taylor urged the Connexion's members to associate with each other, it was in keeping with the nature of his evangelicalism that he appealed for this by highlighting its benefits for the cause of mission. Indicative of the influence of the years he had spent in Methodism, he asked "Can we believe that *Methodism* would have ever spread so universally, had Mr. WESLEY and his preachers never associated?"[187] He therefore emphasized that it was "by mutual intercourse, we may be able to contribute a considerable share toward the effectual propagation of the gospel."[188] It was in this respect, that he noted the importance of the annual Association, referring to it as able "to assist one another in endeavours so very important, as

---

181. See Dan Taylor, "Nature and Importance," 12–19.

182. Ibid., 13.

183. [Deacon], *Comprehensive Account*, 124. The five district conferences consisted of the original Leicester Conference and Yorkshire established in 1772, London—1779, Nottingham—1803, and Warwickshire—1816, see Taylor, *New Connection*, 329.

184. John Taylor. Qtd in Taylor, *John Taylor*, 36.

185. Ibid.

186. Nicholson, "Office of Messenger," 214.

187. Taylor, "Nature and Importance," 15; Taylor's emphasis.

188. Ibid., 16.

well as in the conversion of poor sinners to our Lord Jesus Christ."[189] His emphasis on the representatives of churches meeting together to consider how to share the gospel more effectively was very much in accord with the rationale on which he founded the Connexion.[190] It also reflected Taylor's determination to avoid, what he held as, the "glaring fact" of how, for General Baptists who were not part of the Connexion, "their cause in many places was nearly extinct" due to what he judged as their failure to prioritize meaningful associations with other churches.[191] This further strengthened the resolve with which he urged that the annual Association and regional conferences be attended "with all possible diligence."[192] His firmness also stemmed from his conviction that the discipline of attending had benefited the movement. He was unequivocal that "much of the success of the New Connexion of General Baptists, is owing to the love and zeal of their ministers and members, and *their frequent conferences* with each other."[193] The advantages of the Connexion's strong relational bonds were also noted by New Connexion minister Samuel Deacon Jr. (1746–1816) as of "great use" in uniting "the remotest ministers and congregations" and "cementing in one common Christianity and friendship the supporters of the General Baptist interest, in the whole kingdom."[194] The sense of togetherness Taylor fostered in the Connexion was an important catalyst to its unity and aided the movement's missional focus.

A reason why Taylor viewed the practice of churches associating together as helpful to the spread of the gospel was the way in which it enabled "a mutual communication of our difficulties."[195] Chief among these were financial considerations, with Taylor's attendance at regional conferences and the annual Association making him aware that many churches were "hampered, distressed, and almost destroyed" by their financial need.[196] As he noted in a 1795 letter to George Birley, this was something that "grieved" him.[197] He responded innovatively by implementing a coordi-

189. Ibid., 13.

190. It was also in keeping with the outward facing direction of Taylor's evangelicalism.

191. Taylor, "Nature and Importance," 15.

192. Ibid.

193. Ibid.; italics added.

194. [Deacon], *Comprehensive Account*, 124.

195. Taylor, "Nature and Importance," 16.

196. Dan Taylor, *Important Advice*, 10. This pamphlet comprises an address that Taylor gave on an unspecified occasion. Subsequent to Taylor's death it was then published at the request of the London Conference of the New Connexion.

197. Dan Taylor, "Letter to George Birley," 5 March 1795. Page not numbered.

nated approach to monetary giving. From 1789 onwards, churches were encouraged to share their financial requests with the annual Association, which selected a limited number of needs to which all the churches were expected to contribute.[198] This was the closest expression of New Connexion inter-dependency, with all those desiring financial assistance encouraged to recognize that the movement's "general interest should be regarded in preference to any individual" request.[199] While some churches were able to pursue financial endeavors independently such as the Barton church which was the first within the Connexion to self-finance the building of a meeting house,[200] such an occurrence was rare. Instead, a shared approach to such ventures was normal. The nurturing of this colsignilective perspective proved effective, enabling the building of numerous churches.[201] It also provided financial aid for ministers with Taylor establishing both an Aged Ministers Fund and Itinerant Fund.[202] The introduction of such a thorough approach to financial need illustrates how Taylor's influence over the Connexion's churches exceeded the coordinating efforts of the Association of the wider General Baptists, which was largely restricted to resolving differences between individuals and churches. It was indicative of how Taylor, like Wesley in Methodism, used the structures and relational bonds that existed between the churches of the New Connexion in both a practical and progressive way.

Taylor's approach to monetary giving included other aspects of his core ecclesiological framework. In his commitment to Christ as the church's master, he encouraged believers not to look to their own interests in their personal giving, but to fix their eyes on Christ their "glorious leader and pattern."[203] In line with the importance he placed on holiness, he asked believers to give "according to their ability," as this produced a practical demonstration of Christ's "great rule" concerning the need to do to others what you would have them do to you.[204] He also highlighted the experiential benefits of giving. This included reference to an expectation of future heavenly rewards, and that God would materially honor the everyday lives

198. See Taylor, *Important Advice*, 10.

199. *Minutes of an Association 1789*, 8.

200. See Deacon, *Memoirs*, 68

201. See, e.g., Taylor, "Nature and Importance," 18.

202. See Rinaldi, *Tribe of Dan*, 53–55.

203. Taylor, *Humble Essay on Earthly Treasure*, 12.

204. Taylor, *Important Advice*, 7. Taylor urged those who were poor to consider how "nothing can excuse them from giving a little," even if this was a small as one half penny, once or twice a week, 7. He encouraged those in "better circumstances" to give at least two pence a week, 7.

of those who financially gave to the church. Taylor was explicit regarding the heavenly rewards due to God's "faithful servants" and how "this doctrine runs through the New Testament."[205] He stipulated in his 1780 *An Humble Essay on the Right Use of Earthly Treasure* that believers "need not fear making any capital mistake" for "Blessings on our labours and possessions are frequently promised by the blessed God to those who are thus liberal to the poor."[206] The frankness of Taylor's stance caused an anonymous reviewer of this publication to question if this was "a proper subject for positive assertion and practical urgency."[207] However, Taylor adopted the same tone on another unspecified occasion with the content of his address published after his death in a pamphlet entitled *Important Advice to Churches Involved in Pecuniary Difficulties*. In return for people's generous giving, he declared with confidence that "God will abundantly supply and reward it, so that none will be poorer by it."[208] This conviction stemmed from his frequently cited literal interpretations of Scripture that God would financially bless the giver.[209] Even during his financial hardship of 1785 when, to raise funds for his move to London, he was forced to sell his collection of books, he expressed his hope that "I am able to trust in him who has hitherto helped me."[210] It was this vibrancy of faith that Taylor desired all people across the churches to exhibit in their giving and commitment to church fellowship.

In summary, Taylor stressed the need for churches to associate meaningfully together. He successfully developed a strong collective identity throughout the Connexion. He advocated an active participation in the movement's shared structures and commitment to its joint ventures. His approach again illustrates the distinctiveness of his ecclesiology and further confirms his importance within the history of the English Baptists. As will be demonstrated next, his overall style of leadership was similarly significant.

205. Taylor, *Good Minister*, 26.

206. Taylor, *Humble Essay on Earthly Treasure*, 21.

207. [Anon.], "A Review of Taylor's *A Good Minister of Jesus Christ*," in *The Evangelical Magazine*, vol. 4, 84.

208. Taylor, *Important Advice*, 7.

209. These Scriptures included Deut 15:10, Prov 3:9–10, 11:25, Mal 3:10–11, Luke 6:38, and 2 Cor 9:6, see Taylor, *Humble Essay on Earthly Treasure*, 21–22.

210. Dan Taylor, *Letter to William Thompson*, 4 July 1785, 131.

Taylor's Style of Leadership

"common friend and guardian"

Consideration of Taylor's ecclesiology necessitates an examination of the influence and authority he commanded over the Connexion's churches, for this was largely without precedent in English Baptist history. Adam Taylor recorded that by the 1780s, "his opinion was considered almost as an oracle."[211] Similarly, Independent minister John Kello (1750–1827), a close friend of Taylor's, drew attention at Taylor's funeral to the way he was viewed across the Connexion with "deference, esteem and expectation."[212] An indication of the almost prestigious regard with which Taylor was sometimes held is found in the diary entries of New Connexion minister Joseph Goadby (1774–1857). He emphasized his deference for Taylor, making particular reference to how he was always impacted by "the frightful appearance of his white wig before my eyes" during his training at the Connexion's Academy in 1798.[213] Within the Connexion, Taylor commanded unrivaled respect.

It is pertinent to consider how Taylor acquired this status, particularly as he generally never sought it because it militated against his emphasis on the church having no master but Christ. Similar to the source of some of John Wesley's influence over Methodism, the respect given to Taylor emanated chiefly from his centrality to all aspects of the movement. He chaired all but one of its annual Associations, oversaw all aspects of training, represented the Connexion to wider evangelical bodies and defended the movement from its theological detractors. From the perspective of the members of the Connexion, Taylor's commitment to them was clear. It is estimated that his oversight of the Connexion involved him traveling approximately 25,000 miles, preaching 20,000 sermons, and assisting at thirty-eight ordinations.[214] His visible prominence within the movement was evident to all. The churches he visited were normally well attended. His description of

211. Taylor, *Memoirs*, 109.

212. Kello, "Tribute to Taylor," in Taylor, *Memoirs*, 307. John Kello was pastor of the Congregational church at Bethnal Green, London. Taylor and Kello's friendship will be examined in chapter 7. Kello provided Adam Taylor with a copy of his text which was never published. Adam Taylor also intersperses his own reflection in his provision of key extracts of Kello's tribute.

213. Joseph Goadby, diary entry, in Goadby and Goadby, *Not Saints but Men*, 39.

214. See [Anon.], "The Brief Memoirs of Taylor's life," in Dan Taylor, *Christian Religion*, 22. Taylor's demanding pattern of ministry continued even into his seventies, with him embarking in 1814 on a typical seventeen day preaching itinerary which took him from London to Yorkshire, Birmingham, Burton Upon Trent, Nottingham, and Leicestershire, see Taylor, *Memoirs*, 243.

how "all the places were wonderfully crowded" following his return from an extensive preaching trip in 1801 was a common experience.[215] In addition to his preaching, and ordaining of ministers, he opened new meeting houses, offered advice to churches, and settled disputes. In fulfilling these varied roles, Taylor assumed many of the tasks associated with the General Baptist office of Messenger which was a position he did not adopt within the structures of the Connexion. An essential aspect of the ministry of Messenger was, for example, how they were sent to settle disputes or discuss matters of concern.[216] While Frank Rinaldi's description of the New Connexion as *The Tribe of Dan* is slightly unfortunate as it could imply a sense of control, the Connexion's members however certainly saw themselves as belonging to Taylor. As Henry Vedder stated, he was "the life and soul of the movement."[217] Taylor's relational energy and commitment to the movement's churches formed a vital consolidating function and, although never his intention, is important in accounting for the scope of his authority.

The Connexion's deference to Taylor gave him the opportunity for directive oversight, yet it is significant that he was rarely forceful or overbearing. Instead, he exercised leadership as the Connexion's "common friend and guardian."[218] It was from this basis that he sought to advance core aspects of his ecclesiological perspective. A characteristic example is how his earlier mentioned pamphlet *Important Advice to Churches Involved in Pecuniary Difficulties* contains a plan that he formulated to help churches with accumulated debt.[219] Mindful of the importance to the unity of the Connexion that all its churches were financially contributing to commonly shared objectives (as noted in the previous section), he approached this subject very seriously, advocating proposals such as the holding of six monthly meetings where finances were outlined and all members expected to attend and respond accordingly.[220] Even more specifically, he proposed a detailed three month debt removal plan and creation of a three tier class-based system with members encouraged to group together on the basis of whether they were able to give two, five or ten shillings.[221] While Taylor was firm in his advice, he insisted, in typical manner, that "I pretend to

---

215. Dan Taylor, "Letter to George Birley," 4 September 1801. Page not numbered.

216. The different aspects of the office of Messenger were considered in chapter 2.

217. Vedder, *Short History*, 247.

218. Taylor, *Memoirs*, 170.

219. See Taylor, *Important Advice*, 7–9.

220. Ibid., 9.

221. Ibid.

dictate nothing."[222] Despite his refusal to compel debt-ridden churches to adopt the plan, it was warmly received. The unnamed writer of the preface to the pamphlet declared that it was useful not only to those "of the Baptist persuasion, but of the great Christian family at large."[223] Taylor's plan illustrates his progressive and practical response to ecclesiological problem solving. It was also symptomatic of how his refusal to act in a domineering way was not an obstacle to successfully initiating change, such was the relational influence he commanded.

Taylor's determination to serve the Connexion in the manner of friend, rather than master, led him to ensure that decision making in the Connexion did not rest with himself but with the annual Association.[224] It is similarly notable that this body, which for the Connexion's first twenty-five years functioned as a "synod of officers" comprising mainly ministers and elders, did not possess the authority to make decisions on behalf of the churches.[225] Instead, its role was restricted to guidance and recommendation. A typical example was its response to a 1787 request for guidance from the New Connexion church in Gosberton, Lincolnshire, concerning a situation where some of its members had asked someone to preach, who had left the church in dubious circumstances.[226] While the Association, chaired by Taylor, judged that those involved should be called to account, it did not compel this course of action.[227] A further example was how the same annual Association extended liberty to the churches regarding worship. The question had been raised whether it was a necessity for churches to meet on Christmas day. The Association answered with the flexible judgment that, because it was not a command of Scripture, "every church ought to consult circumstances, and act accordingly."[228] This decision was in keeping with the less restrictive nature of Taylor's evangelical framework of approach to ecclesiological matters when compared, for example, to the theological precision and primacy on correct patterns of order that were generally common among movements such as the Puritans. Consequently, as Samuel Deacon Jr. noted, the common perception among the Connexion's churches towards the Association was that they "do not esteem it a tribunal" but instead "only

---

222. Ibid.
223. [Anon.], in Taylor, *Important Advice*, Preface. Page not numbered.
224. See, e.g., *Assembly of Free Grace General Baptists 1770*. Page not numbered.
225. Taylor, *New Connection*, 211.
226. *Minutes of an Association 1787*, 14.
227. Ibid.
228. Ibid., 13.

ask advice."[229] A similar sense of freedom emanated from the letters Taylor wrote on behalf of the Association. For instance, when offering guidance on the prevalence of "ungoverned passions" among youth and seeking to encourage holiness, he emphasized that "We are very far, Brethren, from wishing to lord it over your consciences, in this or any other instance of your conduct."[230] This declaration was indicative of how Taylor fused a desire to protect and nurture the Connexion's churches, alongside a commitment to preserving their liberty.

The priority Taylor placed on the protection of liberty within the Connexion's churches was evident in his lack of prescriptive direction concerning ecclesiastical order. He was convinced this should remain at the discretion of the churches and impressed this on the annual Association. This was expressed in his 1778 letter to the churches where he insisted,

> In every part of church-business, in maintaining and improving order and discipline in it . . . the power is entirely lodged in the church, (the officers being included) nor can her members justly give away this power to any other person or persons whatsoever.[231]

Even after the Association's composition was altered in 1795 so that it included only those appointed by their churches and therefore functioned as "an assembly of delegates," there remained a strong commitment to protecting the liberty of churches on matters of ecclesiastical order.[232]

Neither was Taylor dogmatic about the precise offices that the churches should adopt. He viewed the New Testament as endorsing the three offices of "*Bishop*, or Overseer, who is also called an *Elder*" whose function was to have oversight of a particular community of believers and to administer the Lord's Supper; a "*ruling* elder," whose duty was to assist the overseer and provide "private instruction, exhortation, reproof, &c. but who does not labour publicly in the word and doctrine"; and deacons, who were concerned with the "secular interests of the church" such as distribution of aid to the poor.[233] However, he rarely sought to convince others of his viewpoint. Instead, he was adamant that each church possessed the "full power to choose or refuse such officers, as may be judged most conducive to the edification

229. [Deacon], *Comprehensive Account*, 124.

230. Dan Taylor, "Letter to the Churches," in *Minutes of an Association 1788*, 4, 3.

231. Dan Taylor, *Circular Letter 1778*, 5.

232. Payne, *The Baptist Union*, 30. Previously, ministers could attend the annual Association as members—irrespective of whether their churches were in favor of the New Connexion.

233. Taylor, *Charge and Sermon at Ordination of John Deacon*, 53; Taylor's emphasis.

of their own souls."[234] While the granting of freedom to the local church was a long established principle of General Baptist ecclesiastical polity, both the Standard Confession, and *Orthodox Creed*, contain Articles regarding the function of church offices and workings of church governance.[235] Although Taylor occasionally addressed these subjects, their absence both from the Connexion's *Articles* and *Confession of Faith* is significant. For Taylor, these matters were not priorities. The nature of his evangelicalism was such that he had no appreciation for unity and truth in terms of correct ecclesiastical order, but instead was far more concerned with their pragmatic capacity for engendering relational bonds of common purpose, focus, and passion for the spread of the gospel. This conviction, when placed alongside his earlier noted Enlightenment-influenced respect for individual freedom and expression of opinion, was a further important contributor to the liberty he extended to the churches in the Connexion.

Taylor's refusal to monopolize control over the Connexion was apparent in his deferential regard for the Association. The letters he wrote to the churches were circulated only after they had been read to the annual Association and approved by the delegates. This was not a formality, for example, it was only "after some corrections" that his 1777 letter on *The Nature and Obligations of Church Fellowship* was approved.[236] Taylor also willingly consented to the Association's requests that he write on specific subjects, such as his earlier noted *Catechism* for children and youth.[237] In keeping with his devolved style of leadership, he shared the responsibility for writing the Association's circular letters with others such as William Thompson and Benjamin Pollard.[238] The chief instance of Taylor's submission to the view of the Association was the process by which he became minister in 1783 of the General Baptist church in Halifax.[239] On receiving the invitation, he im-

234. Ibid., 5.

235. See, e.g., *Brief Confession*, Article twenty-five, 229–30; *Orthodox Creed*, Article thirty-one, 319–20; ibid., Article thirty-four, 322–23.

236. Taylor, *Memoirs*, 101. It has not proved possible to locate this letter.

237. For the Association's request that Taylor write a catechism for youth, see *Association 1779*, Page not numbered. The following question was asked, "Would it not be useful and expedient for us to have a catechism in order to instruct our children in the Christian Religion?" The delegates responded with a commitment that "[i]t is agreed that Bro Taylor compose one and that the same be published as soon as possible." Page not numbered.

238. For an overview of Pollard's ministry, see Wood, *Condensed History*, 221–22.

239. It was through Taylor's pioneering efforts that the work of the General Baptists began in Halifax with Taylor overseeing the building of a meeting house in the town in 1777. For five years this work remained under the oversight of the General Baptist church at Queenshead. In 1782 those involved officially withdrew their membership from Queenshead, leading to the establishment of a distinct General Baptist church in Halifax, see Taylor, *Memoirs*, 99.

mediately referred the matter to the judgment of the annual Association.[240] He also laid the request before the quarterly conference of the Yorkshire New Connexion churches.[241] In a letter to Birley, Taylor noted that this process had left him "much in suspense."[242] Adam Taylor accounted for Taylor's hesitancy on this matter in terms of his unwillingness to create a precedent regarding the moving of ministers between the Connexion's churches, with the practice of ministers changing churches also very unusual among the wider General Baptists.[243] However, even more pertinent was Taylor's conviction that God, through people's corporate decision making and prayer, would provide a "wisdom which is profitable to direct."[244] On this basis, Taylor accepted the judgment of the annual Association which, following his initial six months at Halifax, referred to the "success of this experiment" and voted by sixteen to seven that he continue.[245] The same pattern was followed in 1785 when Taylor moved to London. He noted that the unanimously favorable judgment of the Association enabled his wife Elizabeth to consent to the move "without demur or hesitation," despite opposition from her friends.[246] Again, Taylor demonstrated an ecclesiological confidence in God granting his wisdom through the collective voice of his people. The placing of such importance on this core Baptist value further illustrates the way in which Taylor was the *Baptist* Wesley.

Conclusion

While Taylor subscribed to the core tenets of traditional Baptist ecclesiology, he did so in a way that reflected the dominant facets of eighteenth-century evangelicalism, his earlier Methodist involvement and certain Enlightenment emphases. He frequently articulated and outworked his ecclesiological convictions in ways that were distinct from customary General Baptist and Puritan practices. For example, his application of the principle of Christ's Lordship over the church as a catalyst to his innovative creation of the New Connexion was novel. The distinctiveness of Taylor's evangelicalism was evident in the importance he placed on the experiential and practical, as he endeavored to uphold the church as a "pillar of truth." This accounts for

240. See Taylor, *Consistent Christian*, v.

241. Ibid., vi.

242. Dan Taylor, "Letter to George Birley," 9 December 1782. Page not numbered.

243. Taylor, *Consistent Christian*, vi.

244. Ibid.

245. Taylor, *Memoirs*, 116.

246. Taylor, *Sermon Occasioned by Death of Elizabeth Taylor*, 79. Some of the opposition likely stemmed from the fact that Elizabeth was at his time pregnant. She gave birth to twins just days before the move.

the theological brevity of the Connexion's *Articles* which was in contrast to the far greater detail found in certain earlier General Baptist confessions of faith. Similar to John Wesley, Taylor sought to consolidate truth through relational means, such as his development of experience meetings, monthly gatherings for pastors and extensive mentoring. The primacy Taylor attached to the holiness of the church also included a strong experiential component. In contrast to the moralistic preaching of many of his General Baptist contemporaries, he insisted on the necessity of a prior experience of God's transforming power. He made the recounting of authentic experiences of faith a vital prerequisite to membership of the Connexion. His understanding of the church's holiness included its inseparability from the spread of the gospel. This was typical of the outward looking nature of his evangelicalism and differed from the often more introspective thrust of Puritan approaches to holiness. Taylor also advocated a reasoned and objective way of proceeding regarding church discipline. His accompanying reasoning reflected the influence of certain values that were central to the Enlightenment.

The dominant characteristics of Taylor's evangelicalism led him to advocate, and practically demonstrate, the ecclesiological primacy he placed on unity in ways that differed in certain respects from the common practice of many General Baptists outside the New Connexion and earlier believers such as the Puritans. Examples include his emphasis on its experiential foundations, affirmation of the active participation of women in the church, the pragmatic forcefulness with which he cautioned against engaging in theologically contentious matters, freer approach to certain long-standing aspects of General Baptist prohibition, and advocacy of the merits of engaging fully with believers of other denominations. The importance Taylor attached to unity and liberty was strengthened further by the urges of Enlightenment egalitarianism. A distinctive feature of Taylor's ecclesiological approach was also his use of the Connexion's relational structures and strategic coordination of centralized joint ventures to foster a strong collective identity throughout the movement. He was explicit that his inspiration came from his conviction of the missional benefits of John Wesley's development of the practice of believers associating together within Methodism. Taylor's creation of an innovative framework, where the Connexion's churches prioritized the interests of the movement above their own, and readily expressed a near uniform voluntary submission to his judgments as friend and guardian, was largely without precedent in English Baptist history. Next, it will be seen that the creative tendencies that Taylor's evangelicalism gave rise to were evident in his approach to the sacraments and worship.

6

Creative Proponent

As Taylor exercised his ministerial duties and oversight of the New Connexion, he gave considerable attention to the subject of worship. His practice and underpinning rationale of worship contained certain creative elements. It will be argued that these were evident within his understanding of what he referred to as the "two special ordinances" to be observed in the church, namely believers' baptism and the Lord's Supper.[1] Particular consideration will be given to how his non-sacramental interpretation of baptism differed from that of many earlier General Baptists. It will be argued that his understanding of the Lord's Supper included an emphasis on its efficacy that surpassed that which was commonly found among seventeenth-century General Baptists. Attention will also be given to how some aspects of his approach to the Supper differed notably from those generally adopted by Puritans. Consideration will also be given to Taylor's development of hymn singing throughout the Connexion and the creativity of reasoning and purpose that underpinned his belief that all should be encouraged to participate. As with other aspects of Taylor's evangelicalism, it will be contended that the more creative features of his approach to worship contain evidence of Enlightenment influences.

---

1. Dan Taylor, *Confession of Faith*, 7.

Taylor's Upholding of Believers' Baptism

"the indispensable duty of all who repent and believe"

In 1763 Taylor pronounced that he would "stand up as an advocate" for believers' baptism.[2] His doubts regarding the appropriateness of infant baptism increased during his years within Methodism,[3] and when he became leader of the Wadsworth fellowship, he resolved "to satisfy his own mind" on the matter.[4] Soon afterwards, he reached the judgment that "none are to be baptized before conversion."[5] He argued that an "inseparable" consequence of the prerequisites of faith and repentance was that the baptism of infants was invalid.[6] This placed him in a doctrinally marginalized position. Believers' baptism was practiced only by the General and Particular Baptists and certain Independent fellowships.[7] Those who were most influential on the early development of his evangelical thinking such as William Grimshaw, George Whitefield, and John Wesley all upheld the baptism of infants. After Taylor's baptism by immersion in 1763,[8] he introduced believers' baptism at Birchcliff and opposition soon followed. A 1769 entry in Taylor's diary is typical, "Today, I have preached and baptized nine persons amidst much scorn and persecution from the world."[9] Taylor included believers' baptism in the New Connexion's *Articles of Religion*. He specified in Article six that it was "the indispensable duty of all who repent and believe the gospel, to be baptized, by immersion in water," and that "no person ought to be received into the church without submission to that ordinance."[10] A correct understanding of the "proper subjects of

2. Adam Taylor, *Memoirs*, Preface, (iv).

3. Taylor, *Memoirs*, 10–11.

4. Ibid., 10.

5. Anon. [Dan Taylor], *Humble Essay Christian Baptism*, 32. Adam Taylor identifies Taylor as the author of this publication, see Taylor, *Memoirs*, 27. Dan Taylor attached his name to its second edition which was almost identical in content (other than the occasional minor adjustment of word choice), see Dan Taylor, *Humble Essay Christian Baptism*, 2nd edition.

6. [Taylor], *Humble Essay Christian Baptism*, 32.

7. Examples of such Independent fellowships include those believers associated with the Barton-in-the-Beans grouping of churches in Leicestershire—as examined in chapter 5.

8. The events that surrounded Taylor's baptism were noted in the introductory chapter.

9. Dan Taylor, diary entry, 23 February 1769, in Taylor, *Memoirs*, 54.

10. *Articles*, in Lumpkin, *Baptist Confessions*, 344. As noted in chapter 5, it was Taylor who drafted the *Articles* for the Connexion's approval.

baptism" was among the written elements required from churches wanting to join the Connexion.[11] This is again indicative of the importance Taylor placed on believers' baptism.

Taylor's 1768 *An Humble Essay on Christian Baptism* was his largest work on the subject. He was persuaded to write through "the solicitations of his friends" who asked him to defend the doctrine from its detractors.[12] Taylor wrote anonymously, first focusing on the appropriate recipients of baptism, and then how it should be administered. Although routinely overlooked by commentators, *Humble Essay* was a significant publication.[13] While eighteenth-century Particular Baptists such as John Gale and Joseph Stennett Sr. wrote detailed defenses of believers' baptism,[14] no equivalent works were produced by General Baptists. The last substantial work on baptism written by a General Baptist was Thomas Grantham's 1687 *Presumption no Proof*.[15] Given this context, Taylor's *Humble Essay* was an important initiative.

Taylor began *Humble Essay* by insisting that baptism be restricted to believers. He viewed this as "so very clear" in the Scriptures, both "by precept and precedent."[16] Although appeals to the scriptural veracity of baptismal practice were a long-standing feature of dialog between proponents of believers' baptism and paedobaptists, Taylor specifically urged that this be done impartially. His "chief request" was that the reader would "*impartially* examine the Scriptures with regard to the ordinance of baptism and regard this pamphlet, as far as will be found consistent with them."[17] This emphasis was indicative of how, as Rhodri Lewis notes, the importance of impartiality was drawn on during the Enlightenment as a "framing device with which to neuter those who may not agree with the arguments one is advancing."[18]

11. Adam Taylor, *New Connection*, 212.

12. Taylor, *Memoirs*, 28.

13. An example is how Anthony Cross reflects on the thinking towards baptism of eighteenth-century Baptists but makes no mention of Taylor, see Cross, "The Myth of English Baptist Anti-Sacramentalism," 128–62.

14. See Gale, *Reflections*; Stennett Sr., *Answer to David Russen's Book, Entitul'd, Fundamentals Without a Foundation*.

15. Grantham, *Presumption no Proof*. This work formed part of Grantham's response to the works of Samuel Petto and Giles Firmin who were Independent Puritan ministers and strong proponents of infant baptism. For more on the context of Grantham's publication, see Essick Jr., "Messenger, Apologist, and Nonconformist," 79–81.

16. [Taylor], *Humble Essay Christian Baptism*, 5.

17. Ibid., iii; italics added. Similarly typical was Taylor's assertion that because baptism is "an ordinance of so great importance . . . it must be the indispensable duty of both ministers and people, impartially to examine what is meant by it," see ibid., 5–6.

18. Lewis, "Impartiality and Disingenuousness in English Rational Religion," 227.

Despite Taylor's creative integration of the merits of impartiality alongside his support for believers' baptism, certain presuppositions are evident. These are apparent within his provision of New Testament "proofs of the baptism of believers" rather than infants.[19] While carefully delineating his thinking on matters such as Christ's baptism; the Pentecost baptisms (Acts 2) which comprised those who received the gospel—"not them and their children"; the practice of the apostles who "first taught and then baptized" and the presence of an active faith in all household baptisms, some subjective interpretations are apparent.[20] For example, his accusation that infant baptism stemmed from "The plain Scripture method being forsook" ignores the fact that it is not actually prohibited in the Scriptures.[21] He was also sweeping in his judgment that Christ's commission to make disciples and to baptize must be obeyed in its literal order of "faith before baptism."[22] Neither did he acknowledge that the New Testament pattern of baptism concerns the first generation of believers who were baptized in this way. His neglect of any recognition of the implications of this is apparent in his failure to consider why the Scriptures would instruct someone to be baptized as an infant if they had already passed that stage of their life. His judgment that it was "natural" for the "sacred *historians . . .* to have added—*and children*" if any had been baptized in the New Testament household baptisms, was also an overly simplistic basis from which to claim that these examples applied only to believers.[23] The nature of Taylor's approach was, at least in part, indicative of the influence of his presuppositions.

Taylor's defense of believers' baptism lacked the meticulous attention to Scripture that was modeled by many earlier proponents of both believers' and infant baptism. Richard Baxter's extensive *Plain Scripture Proof of Infants* was a typical example.[24] Taylor responded tersely to arguments in favor of infant baptism that he had become familiar with through his study of works such as *A History of Infant Baptism* by Church of England minister William Wall,[25] and David Russen's anti-Baptist tract *Fundamentals Without Foundation*.[26] He provided only minimal reflection on Scriptures regularly cited by paedobaptists as evidence of baptism succeeding

19. [Taylor], *Humble Essay Christian Baptism*, 46.
20. Ibid., 29, 45.
21. Ibid., 46.
22. Ibid., 34.
23. Ibid., 46; Taylor's emphasis.
24. Baxter, *Plain Scripture Proof.*
25. Wall, *History.*
26. Russen, *Fundamentals Without Foundation.*

circumcision as the sacrament that signified and sealed the admission of God's people into his covenant of grace. For instance, he briefly dismissed Col 2:11–12 as "express against" any link between the covenantal sign of circumcision and baptism.[27] Taylor considered it sufficient to argue that neither John the Baptist, Christ, nor the apostles even "hinted" at any connection between circumcision and baptism.[28] This contrasted with how Thomas Grantham, a century earlier, provided close scriptural exegesis in *The Paedo-Baptists Apology* as he attacked circumcision as a type of baptism.[29] Taylor also offered no qualification of his declaration that "Neither circumcision nor baptism are ever called *seals* of any covenant, in all the Bible, and much less seals of the *covenant of grace*."[30] This again differed from earlier General Baptist approaches. Article twenty-eight of the 1678 *Orthodox Creed* describes baptism as "a sign of our entrance into the covenant of grace."[31] The way that Taylor distanced himself from such an outlook, typified his dislike of arguments that he deemed too nebulous. Similar to his engagement with subjects such as election and the Trinity, he sought to uphold believers' baptism by referring to what he held as the plain and practical teaching of Scripture.

Taylor's approach to baptism demonstrates a non-sacramental interpretation. His writings contain no mention of its efficacy. This was different from the sacramental leanings evident among many seventeenth-century General Baptists. Although the way baptism is described in Article twenty-seven of the *Orthodox Creed* as a "sacrament" and as an "ordinance" is a reminder, as Stanley Fowler notes, "not to read modern distinctions back into the expressions of our predecessors," there is wider evidence of General

27. Col 2:11–12: "In him you were also circumcised with a circumcision not performed by human hands. Your whole self ruled by the flesh was put off when you were circumcised by Christ, having been buried with him in baptism, in which you were also raised with him through your faith in the working of God, who raised him from the dead."; [Taylor], *Humble Essay Christian Baptism*, 36. Taylor argued that Paul was referring to circumcision of the heart and that it was therefore of no relevance to water baptism.

28. Ibid., 35.

29. Grantham, *Paedo-Baptists Apology*. For consideration of this publication, see Essick Jr., "Messenger, Apologist, and Nonconformist," 66.

30. [Taylor], *Humble Essay Christian Baptism*, 38; Taylor's emphasis. Taylor's very general approach saw him fail to offer any explanation or even recognition of the apostle Paul's designation in Rom 4:11 of Abraham's circumcision as a sign and seal of his faith.

31. *Orthodox Creed*, Article twenty-eight, in Lumpkin, *Baptist Confessions*, 317. This is similar to that stated in the 1646 *Westminster Confession of Faith*, see *Westminster Confession of Faith*, chapter 28, in Jones, Long, and Moore, eds., *Protestant Nonconformist Texts*, 186. The extent to which the *Orthodox Creed* was modeled on the *Westminster Confession* was considered in chapter 3.

Baptist sacramentalism from the seventeenth century.[32] Examples include Thomas Helwys who viewed baptism as inseparable from the work of the Spirit in a believer's life. Helwys stated in *A Short Declaration of the Mystery of Iniquity* that "you cannot divide the water and the spirit" but that "the baptism of Christ is the washing with water and the Holy Ghost."[33] Thomas Grantham noted that "it is Christ who is held forth in baptism, which saveth,"[34] referred to it as the "sacrament or washing of Regeneration" in *The Loyal Baptist*,[35] and again described it as a sacrament in *Christianismus Primitivus*.[36] While Clint Bass in his consideration of Grantham's approach to baptism emphasizes the need for interpretative caution due to the way in which Grantham sometimes used figurative language, his description of Grantham viewing baptism "as a means of sanctification" and as having "kindled his [Christ's] presence in an extraordinary way," extended far beyond that posited by Taylor.[37] Examples of sacramental interpretations can also be found among the seventeenth-century Particular Baptists. *The Baptist Catechism* which emerged following a meeting of the General Assembly of Particular Baptists in 1693 and which became identified with the prominent Particular Baptist minister Benjamin Keach (1640–1704), although this is contested by some, describes baptism as a means through which "Christ communicates to us the benefits of redemption" and which becomes "effectual to the elect."[38] Fowler observes that the "theology of baptism" that was held by seventeenth-century Baptists "may not have been uniform, but they consistently asserted that God, by his Spirit, bestowed spiritual benefit

---

32. *Orthodox Creed*, Article twenty-seven, 317. These same terms were also applied in this Article to the Lord's Supper; Stanley K. Fowler, *More Than a Symbol*, 19.

33. Helwys, *Short Declaration* [1612], in Early Jr., *Life and Writings of Thomas Helwys*, 257.

34. Grantham, *St. Paul's Catechism*, 35–36.

35. Grantham, *The Loyal Baptist*, Part 2, 15. That which Grantham stipulates regarding baptism in *The Loyal Baptist* is considered by Anthony Cross, see Anthony R. Cross, "Baptismal Regeneration," 154.

36. Grantham, *Christianismus Primitivus*, Book 2, Part 2, 4. For consideration of Grantham's understanding of baptism as a sacrament, see Philip E. Thompson, "sacraments and Religious Liberty, 48.

37. Bass, *Thomas Grantham*, 85, 84.

38. Anon. *The Baptist Catechism*, 26. For an examination of the evolution of *The Baptist Catechism* and questions that surround its authorship, see Arnold, *Reformed Theology of Benjamin Keach*, 57–59. Arnold does not hold to the view that it was the "sole work" of Keach although states that its contents are in accord with that found in his wider catechetical works, see 59. It should also be noted that Keach was formerly a General Baptist.

through baptism."[39] Philip Thompson similarly draws attention to how Baptists of this period believed Christ to be "active in the rite."[40] This was in contrast to Taylor who viewed baptism only as a symbol of Christ's death, burial and resurrection, and command to be obeyed. Taylor made no mention of the more sacramental orientation of the seventeenth-century Baptists towards baptism. It is conceivable that he was not aware of this.

Taylor's non-sacramental interpretation differed, by degree, from the understanding of baptism held by many eighteenth-century Baptists. While Fowler highlights the works of Particular Baptists such as John Gill (1697–1771), Abraham Booth, Anne Dutton (1695–1765), Andrew Fuller, and John Ryland Jr. as evidence of a "retreat from a more clearly sacramental view of baptism," they all contain sacramental elements not held by Taylor.[41] Examples include Gill's emphasis on how baptism facilitates a cleansing from sin,[42] "discharges a good conscience,"[43] and provides "a means of leading faith to Christ's resurrection for justification."[44] Even Booth, who as Fowler argues "moved strongly in an anti-sacramental direction,"[45] did not hesitate to cite that "theological writers have often called baptism, the sacrament of regeneration."[46] Dutton's description of baptism as God's "seal" of salvation and means of providing "solemn Assurance in the very ordinance of all the great Things represented therein" were also absent from Taylor's understanding.[47] Unlike Taylor, Fuller viewed baptism as a "sign" which "when rightly used, leads to the thing signified."[48] Fuller understood it as "promoting piety in individuals," serving to "sanctify the soul," and a means by which "sin is washed away."[49] Ryland's assertions that "baptism

39. Fowler, *More Than a Symbol*, 32.

40. Thompson, "Sacraments and Religious Liberty," 48. See also P. E. Thompson, "A New Question in Baptist History," 51–72.

41. Fowler, *More Than a Symbol*, 56.

42. Gill, *Complete Body of Doctrinal and Practical Divinity*, 565–66.

43. Ibid., 566.

44. Gill, *Exposition of the New Testament*, 505.

45. Fowler, *More Than a Symbol*, 56.

46. Booth, *Works*, 2:376. Booth made this point when arguing that baptism must precede participation in the Lord's Supper. For an overview of Booth's defense of believers' baptism, see James, "Booth's Defence of Believers' Baptism".

47. Dutton, *Brief Hints*, 21. Anne Dutton's second husband, Benjamin, became the minister of the Particular Baptist church in Great Gransden, Huntingdonshire, in 1732. For the next thirty years she wrote many pamphlets, see Ford Watson, "Anne Dutton," 51–56. See also Ford Watson, *Selected Spiritual Writings of Anne Dutton*.

48. Fuller, *Practical Uses of Christian Baptism* [1802], in Fuller, *Works*, 728.

49. Ibid.

doth now save us, by the resurrection of Jesus Christ, to which our faith is therein directed," and that it enables a "communion with him, of which infants are absolutely incapable," were also absent from Taylor's thinking.[50] The continuing sacramental tendencies of these Particular Baptists all extended beyond Taylor's understanding of baptism.

It is unfortunate that Fowler does not consider Taylor's approach to baptism. Instead, he states that "Given the drift of the General Baptists away from orthodoxy and their numerical decline, there was virtually nothing in their literature of this period which addressed baptismal theology."[51] Whether Fowler is even aware of Taylor's relevant publications is unknown. If Taylor's failure to give any credence to the efficacious nature of baptism had been acknowledged by Fowler, this would have drawn attention to Taylor as an innovator. Taylor's outlook anticipated the approach to baptism that became ascendant in the nineteenth century. As Fowler notes, "By the end of the 19th century, it was widely assumed by Baptists that baptism is an "ordinance" as *opposed* to a "sacrament," an act of human obedience as opposed to a means of grace."[52] This perspective was the same as that taught by Taylor.

Although neither Fowler nor Thompson mention Enlightenment values as a factor in the gradual transition of Baptists away from sacramental understandings of baptism, their influence on Taylor is apparent.[53] An example was the way in which his defense of believers' baptism emphasized that which was logical or provable. This is evident in his dismissal of paedobaptist claims that infants were qualified for baptism due to Paul's pronouncement in 1 Cor 7:14 that the children of one believing parent were not unclean, but holy.[54] Taylor emphasized the "fundamental maxim" that "like causes will have like effects" and therefore viewed the holiness of the children, to which Paul referred, as the same "in kind" as that of the unbelieving parent (also noted in the passage)—namely a lawful holiness, rather than an inner holiness, which "set apart" the child as "intirely the believers'

50. John Ryland Jr., *Candid Statement*, 28. Ryland was here writing a summary of what he regularly preached at baptismal services.

51. Fowler, *More Than a Symbol*, 33.

52. Ibid., 87; Fowler's emphasis.

53. Fowler argues that Baptists at this time were instead often occupied by other foundational matters, see ibid., 32. Thompson accounts for the changed outlook regarding baptism with reference to the "individualist, conversionist soteriology bequeathed to Baptists by revivalism," see P. E. Thompson, "An address to the National Association of Baptist Professors of Religion in Wisconsin," June 1999. Qtd in Cross, "Myth of English Baptist Anti-Sacramentalism," 132.

54. See [Taylor], *Humble Essay Christian Baptism*, 49–58.

property."⁵⁵ It was typical that Taylor made no reference here to the possibility that baptism might convey grace which superseded the power of sin.
This stance was again apparent in his response to the arguments in favor of
infant baptism propounded by Independent minister Stephen Addington
(1729–96).⁵⁶ Whereas Addington claimed that the baptism of infants signified their "spiritual purity,"⁵⁷ Taylor considered this unprovable, dismissing
it as a "vague and indeterminate" judgment.⁵⁸ He also viewed it as illogical,
asking "How can this be done to an infant?"⁵⁹ His emphasis on that which
was logical or provable was akin to an Enlightenment scientific outlook.
This influenced Taylor's disregard of any viewpoint that was rooted in an
efficacious understanding of baptism.

Taylor sought to prove that infant baptism was not practiced in the
earliest centuries by referring to the writings of the Early Church Fathers.⁶⁰
His approach reflected the emphasis found within the Enlightenment on
establishing facts on which claims to truth could be judged. He cited Justin
Martyr's *First Apology* as "clear and full evidence" that infant baptism was
not administered in the second century.⁶¹ He was aware that Wall cited Justin Martyr's description of people being "discipled to Christ . . . from their
childhood" as evidence of infant baptism.⁶² Taylor argued that baptism was
not explicitly mentioned, and that the Greek word *matheteusate* (to disciple)
was primarily about teaching.⁶³ As further evidence that Justin Martyr was
not referring to infants, he highlighted his description that those seeking
baptism needed to be "persuaded that the things spoke and taught by us are
true" and then to fast for "the pardon of their past sins."⁶⁴ Taylor adopted the
same approach to the writings of Irenaeus and Tertullian. For example, he
highlighted Tertullian's statement that those desiring baptism should come

55. Ibid., 56, 56, 57.

56. Taylor's response to Addington is examined later in this section.

57. Addington, *Summary*, 5.

58. Dan Taylor, *Strictures*, 5.

59. Ibid.

60. See [Taylor], *Humble Essay Christian Baptism*, 59–70.

61. [Taylor], *Humble Essay Christian Baptism*, 59. See *First Apology of Justin Martyr*,
in *ANF*, 1:159–87, esp. 155–57. Taylor incorrectly refers here to *The Second Apology*.
His mistake is particularly evident considering that he then proceeds to quote from *The
First Apology*.

62. *First Apology of Justin Martyr*, in *ANF*, 1:167. Qtd in Wall, *History*, Part 2, 351.

63. [Taylor], *Humble Essay Christian Baptism*, 60.

64. *First Apology of Justin Martyr*, in *ANF*, 1:187. Qtd in [Taylor], *Humble Essay
Christian Baptism*, 59.

"when they are *grown up*; let them come when they understand."[65] Pointing his readers to the writings of John Gill (thereby again demonstrating his willingness to learn from Particular Baptists) he refuted the view that Origen's *Commentary on the Epistle to the Romans* confirmed infant baptism as an apostolic tradition by the beginning of the third century.[66] He also contested Wall's claim that the apostles understood children to be included in Christ's command to baptize, due to their familiarity with the baptism of infants of Gentile proselytes to Judaism.[67] Taylor argued that there is no evidence in the Scriptures, Apocrypha, first-century works of Josephus and Philo, and stipulations concerning worship in the Jewish Mishnah that this practice preceded Christian baptism.[68] Taylor's thoroughness reflected the importance he placed on that which he held as provable.

Enlightenment influences were again apparent as Taylor adopted the terminology of experience and observation.[69] For instance, he stated,

> We find, by unhappy experience, and constant observation, that persons who are told they were baptized in their infancy, do naturally place some hope of their salvation on this; and imagine they are in a better state than others, because of it.[70]

His belief that infant baptism led to a false assurance of personal salvation was evident on other occasions. It led him, at the 1786 ordination of the General Baptist minister John Deacon, to criticize those who "mutilated" the practice of baptism by causing "pernicious consequence to the souls of men."[71] For this reason, he repeatedly stated that the prerequisites for baptism of faith and repentance were essential in preventing people acquiring

---

65. Septimi Florentis Tertulliani, *De Baptismo*, 51. Qtd in [Taylor], *Humble Essay Christian Baptism*, 63; italics added. Taylor did not cite the translation of Tertullian's publication that he was using.

66. Taylor particularly focused on how Gill, through the insights of Erasmus and particularly Heutius (who provided the Greek edition of Origen's commentaries on Romans), carefully exposed the deficiencies in the Latin translation of Origen's works provided by Rufinus. See Gill, *Antipaedo-baptism*, 25. For Taylor's thinking on this matter, see [Taylor], *Humble Essay Christian Baptism*, 64–65. See also Origen, *Commentary on Epistle to the Romans*, 367.

67. See Wall, *History*, Part 1, Preface, v. This argument was propounded by the twelfth-century Rabbi, Moses Maimonides, see Bannerman and Grew, *Practices of the Early Christians*, 18. This viewpoint was then revived in the seventeenth century by the rabbinical scholar John Lightfoot and Anglican theologian Henry Hammond, see [Taylor], *Humble Essay Christian Baptism*, 40–41.

68. [Taylor], *Humble Essay Christian Baptism*, 40–41.

69. The significance of Taylor's use of these terms was examined in chapter 2.

70. [Taylor], *Humble Essay Christian Baptism*, 30.

71. Dan Taylor, *A Charge and Sermon at Ordination of John Deacon*, 51.

only "the form of religion."[72] It is likely that this warning reflected Taylor's mindfulness of his own experience of religion prior to his entrance into evangelicalism (see chapter 1).Given this parallel and his readiness to incorporate the merits of observation and personal experience into his argument, it again appears that his upholding of believers' baptism was influenced by certain subjective presuppositions. This perhaps accounts for his failure to attempt to reconcile or even to acknowledge that, within Methodism, there was a commitment to infant baptism and yet also an accompanying vibrancy of faith and worship. Such an omission further exposes the way that Taylor's advocacy of believers' baptism was at times founded on inaccurate generalizations.

In 1777 Taylor wrote the second of his works on baptism—*Strictures on the Rev. Mr. Addington's Summary.* As noted earlier, this was a response to Addington's defense of infant baptism. Addington first wrote on the subject in 1771 with his publication of *The Christian Minister's Reasons for Baptizing Infants.*[73] Taylor did not reply at that time which was almost certainly a consequence of how, shortly after its publication, he was writing responses to the teachings of Socinianism and Unitarianism (see chapter 2). The Particular Baptist minister Samuel Stennett wrote a reply to Addington's publication in 1772 which Taylor viewed as "nobly executed."[74] However, Taylor was concerned that Stennett's response was "too large for the lower class of readers."[75] It was after Addington produced a compact question and answer style *Summary of The Christian Minister's Reasons for Baptizing Infants* in 1776,[76] that Taylor acquiesced to the New Connexion's request that he make a response. The urgency of the request may have been strengthened by Addington being a minister in Leicestershire where the Connexion had a strong presence. It was as Taylor responded to Addington's *Summary* that he wrote *Strictures*, a modest sized tract containing no etymology and only limited reference to the historical practice of baptism. From the outset, the need for the tract to be affordable for the less wealthy was at the forefront of Taylor's thinking. He stated in a letter to Birley that "I wish the pamphlets to be stitched in blue paper as frugally as possible so that they may be sold cheap."[77] Taylor's approach was in keeping with how the production of similarly small and affordable pamphlets and tracts were a notable feature of

72. Dan Taylor, *Our Saviour's Commission*, 38.

73. Addington, *Christian Minister's Reasons for Baptizing Infants.*

74. Taylor, *Memoirs*, 97. See Samuel Stennett, *Remarks.*

75. Ibid., 97.

76. See Addington, *Summary.*

77. Dan Taylor, "Letter to George Birley," 18 September 1777. Page not numbered.

eighteenth-century evangelicalism.[78] It was typical of Taylor's willingness to embrace new forms of innovation that he adopted this form of communication as he acted as a proponent for believers' baptism.

Within *Strictures* Taylor reiterated his central arguments in favor of believers as the correct subjects of baptism. He was clear that "Baptism is the immersion of that person in water, who gives credible evidence that he believes in Jesus Christ."[79] Whereas Addington viewed faith and repentance as imperatives to baptism only for those who were the first to be baptized in the early church,[80] Taylor insisted it was "very natural" that they remain essential unless contrary scriptural evidence could be found.[81] He was again very rational in his dismissal of 1 Cor 7:14 as a justification for baptizing infants.[82] He was bewildered at how "a Minister of the gospel is not ashamed of a cause which stands in need of supports so far-fetched, and so feeble."[83] In line with the traditional Baptist position, Taylor added his concern that Scriptures such as 1 Cor 7:14 had been used by "some ancient Christians" to justify baptismal regeneration.[84] This knowledge likely strengthened his resistance to efficacious interpretations of baptism. Taylor once more rejected the sufficiency of God's covenant as a foundation for baptizing children. He likened such reasoning to "throwing dust in the air to prevent persons discerning the plain path in which they ought to walk."[85] In addition, he accused Addington of having "taken for granted what you ought to prove."[86] As evident in this section, this same criticism can occasionally also be applied to Taylor.

To summarize, Taylor's defense of believers as the only appropriate recipients of baptism contained notable distinctions. Examples include his succinctness, concentration on that which he viewed as the plain meaning of the Scriptures (albeit influenced by certain presuppositions), non-sacramental interpretation, attempts to prove the historic facts of baptismal practice, the merits of "observation and experience," and innovative design

78. This will be examined in chapter 7.

79. Taylor, *Strictures*, 5.

80. Addington, *Summary*, 29.

81. Taylor, *Strictures*, 27.

82. Ibid., 20.

83. Ibid. Addington emphasized the capacity for one part to sanctify the whole and the relevance of the underlying principle of Rom 11:16 ("If the part of the dough offered as firstfruits is holy, then the whole batch is holy; if the root is holy, so are the branches") to a proper understanding of 1 Cor 7:14, see Addington, *Summary*, 17.

84. Taylor, *Strictures*, 20.

85. Ibid., 19.

86. Ibid., 24.

of *Strictures*. Aspects of this approach set him apart from the nature of the defense of believers' baptism provided by seventeenth-century Baptists. His non-sacramental interpretation was similar to that which became common among Baptists later in the nineteenth century. Consideration will next be given to certain creative elements that were evident within his understanding of how baptism should be administered.

Taylor's Upholding of Baptism by Immersion

"the validity of immersion"

In *Humble Essay*, Taylor sought to demonstrate that immersion was "the plain Scripture method" of baptism.[87] He began by examining the meaning of the Greek word *baptizo*, understanding it as signifying to dip, overwhelm, sink or plunge.[88] He was convinced that "every place where the word is found, if duly examined would tend to prove the validity of immersion."[89] For example, he cited the baptismal practice of John the Baptist and the apostles of "going *into* and coming *out of*" the water as proof that "the ordinance of baptism never was, nor can be properly administered any other way than by immersion."[90] He was adamant that "There is no passage in the sacred oracles, in which it can fairly be interpreted, as signifying to *sprinkle* nor to wash any other way than by dipping."[91] To contend otherwise was to argue from the "silence of the Scriptures."[92] It is likely that his categorical stance contributed to his failure to engage with Addington's highlighting of Scriptures and arguments that were regularly used by paedobaptists to justify baptism by sprinkling or pouring. These included the attention Addington gave to Scriptures such as Ezek 36:25.[93] Addington also sought to demonstrate that the term *baptizo* does not always refer to immersion in the New Testament. He noted how the plural form of *baptizo* is used in Heb 9:10 to refer to priestly ceremonial washings and how the priests sprinkled unclean

87. [Taylor], *Humble Essay Christian Baptism*, 25.

88. Ibid., 8–9.

89. Ibid., 8.

90. Ibid., 14, 18; Taylor's emphasis. Taylor also responded to common objections such as that the Philippian jailer in Acts 16 could not have been immersed as it was claimed he was baptized at home, see ibid., 18.

91. Ibid., 7; Taylor's emphasis.

92. Ibid., 40.

93. Ezek 36:25: "I will sprinkle clean water on you, and you will be clean."

people with water and the blood of animals, and poured oil on sacrifices.[94] Addington pointed to how the word *baptizo* is found in 1 Cor 10:2 which describes the Israelites as being baptized as they crossed the Red Sea.[95] Taylor dismissed all of Addington's evidence as "extraordinary intelligence."[96] He did not even acknowledge the possibility that Addington's scriptural references demonstrated a link in the New Testament between baptism and sprinkling or pouring. Taylor's belief that "the sprinkling of infants is not proper Christian baptism" seemed to stifle his desire to engage meaningfully with the points raised by Addington.[97]

Taylor's advocacy of baptism by immersion not only stemmed from his interpretation of the Scriptures but from a set of presuppositions. This is evident from his judgments regarding the practice of baptism in church history. An example was his insistence that sprinkling was not practiced until the second half of the third century. Referring to Tertullian and Eusebius of Caesarea, he delineated in *Humble Essay* how baptism was first administered only by immersion.[98] He specified that there was "not a hint concerning *pouring or sprinkling* till pretty far in the third century."[99] Taylor argued that even at this time, baptism by pouring was only in "extraordinary cases" where the recipient was excessively sick or weak.[100] While Taylor's handling of this extra-biblical evidence was credible for his time, he overlooked important evidence that modern scholars would be quick to point out. A significant example is how the instructions on baptism within the *Didache* state that, if there was insufficient water for immersion, then it could be poured three times on the head.[101] Given that the *Didache* has been dated by most scholars to the late first or early second century, it is very likely that this provision concerning pouring was applied at that time.

As Taylor acted as a proponent of immersion, he made creative use of knowledge from other disciplines. For example, he responded to concerns that immersion was damaging to health by highlighting the medical

94. Addington, *Summary*, 8. Heb 9:10: "They are only a matter of food and drink and various ceremonial washings—external regulations applying until the time of the new order."

95. Ibid. 1 Cor 10:2: "They were all baptised into Moses in the cloud and in the sea."

96. Taylor, *Strictures*, 10.

97. Ibid., 7. Taylor's insistence that the sprinkling of infants was not Christian baptism was a response to Addington's use of the term "Anabaptists" to describe Baptists. For Addington's use of this term, see Addington, *Summary*, 7.

98. [Taylor], *Humble Essay Christian Baptism*, 16.

99. Ibid., 20; Taylor's emphasis.

100. Ibid., 22.

101. James Stevenson, and Frend, *New Eusebius*, 9–10.

writings of Sir John Floyer, a doctor in the late seventeenth and early eighteenth century. He cited Floyer's endorsement of the "usefulness of *cold bath*" as a remedy against many disorders.[102] In addition, he drew attention to Floyer's highlighting of how the "TRUE OLD USEFUL MODE" of baptism by immersion had taken place in countries far colder than England.[103] When interpreting the Scriptures, Taylor also drew on information from other disciplines. This is evident as he justified his claim that the description of King Nebuchadnezzar as baptized in the Septuagint was because he was "immersed in the dew" rather than sprinkled, as Addington argued.[104] Taylor pointed to the "propriety" of his judgment by claiming that those with a knowledge of geography had the "sense and learning" to know that "dews are very abundant" in "the countries where Nebuchadnezzar's dominions lay, and in all countries in the same latitude."[105] He therefore reasoned that Nebuchadnezzar would have been "very wet as if he had been immersed in water."[106] Taylor's conviction that extra-biblical evidence supported his arguments, led him to pronounce all doubts concerning the validity of immersion as "contrary to the truths derived from daily observation, and constant experience."[107] Again, this was indicative of Enlightenment influences on his thinking.

Taylor considered the correct method of baptism in *A Compendious View of the Nature and Importance of Christian Baptism*.[108] He wrote this in 1789 and it was his final publication on the subject. Its nine editions confirm Adam Taylor's assertion that it was "one of the most successful of his compositions."[109] As specified in the title, it was intended *For the Use of Plain Christians*. This again reflected Taylor's desire to act as a proponent of believers' baptism in a way that engaged the broadest number of people. He crafted his core arguments from within *Humble Essay* and *Strictures* into "a narrow compass" of questions and answers regarding the correct

---

102. Floyer, "Letter I. To the Learned Physician, Dr. William Gibbons," 21 October 1701, in Floyer, and Baynard, 25. Qtd in [Taylor], *Humble Essay Christian Baptism*, 18; Taylor's emphasis.

103. Ibid.

104. Taylor, *Strictures*, 9; See Addington, *Christian Minister's Reasons for Baptizing Infants*, 17–18.

105. Taylor, *Strictures*, 9.

106. Ibid., 9.

107. [Taylor], *Humble Essay Christian Baptism*, 18.

108. Dan Taylor, *Compendious View*. There is no date attached to this first edition, but Adam Taylor recorded that it was published in 1789, see Taylor, *Memoirs*, 187.

109. Taylor, *Memoirs*, 187.

recipients and method of baptism.[110] In addition to that noted in these two publications on the subject, he emphasized the inappropriateness of sprinkling due to the greater significance of that which he believed immersion symbolized. He stated that immersion was "designed to be a standing representation of the burial and resurrection of Christ, and a profession of our death to sin, and recovery to holiness."[111] Taylor's language of "representation" and "profession" was typical of his non-sacramental interpretation. This is also pronounced in the *Confession of Faith* that Taylor wrote four years later and which includes the description of baptism as "an emblematical representation of the burial and resurrection of Jesus Christ."[112] His unwillingness to move beyond a symbolic understanding of baptism was an unchanging facet of his approach.

A further distinctive aspect of Taylor's thinking regarding the administration of baptism was his insistence that it did not need to be accompanied by the laying on of hands for the gift of the Holy Spirit.[113] Within Baptist worship, the laying on of hands had seventeenth-century origins, when it often followed baptism.[114] Keach's description of the laying on of hands as an ordinance through which believers can "meet with more of Christ and his Spirit," was typical of the importance that was placed on it.[115] While its popularity began to wane among Particular Baptists with its frequency of practice declining at baptismal services and at the reception of new members,[116] General Baptists demonstrated a far greater resistance to change. James Wood recorded that it retained an "extensive prevalence."[117] Leading General Baptists such as Thomas Grantham and William Jeffrey insisted that it remained a "necessity."[118] While a very small number of General Baptists disagreed with this judgment,[119] a strong commitment to its practice was certainly the norm. The 1656 General Baptist Assembly ruled that it was illegal to share the Lord's Supper with any who denied the necessity of

110. Taylor, *Compendious View*, 4.

111. Ibid., 16.

112. Taylor, *Confession of Faith*, Article twenty-one, 7.

113. See *Minutes of an Association 1798*, 8.

114. See Adam Taylor, *English General Baptists*, 136, 410–11; Payne, "Baptists and the Laying on of Hands," 203–5; White, *English Baptists*, 36–40; Bass, *Thomas Grantham*, 103–34.

115. Keach, *Laying on of Hands*, 58.

116. See Brown, *English Baptists*, 45.

117. Wood, *Condensed History*, 134.

118. Taylor, *English General Baptists*, 411.

119. Occasional exceptions are highlighted by White, see White, *English Baptists*, 37.

the laying on of hands.[120] This ruling is indicative of how John Briggs argues that the laying on of hands formed an aspect of the denomination's "internal sectarianism."[121] Pedantic tendencies also developed regarding issues such as the number of people required for it to be administered.[122] The 1660 General Baptist Standard Confession also specified that it was the duty of all those baptized to "draw nigh unto God in submission" by receiving prayer through the laying on of hands for the Holy Spirit.[123] Article thirty-two of the *Orthodox Creed* is similarly clear that the "imposition of hands . . . is a principle of Christ's doctrine, and ought to be practised and submitted to by every baptized believer in order to receive the promised Spirit of the Father and Son."[124] Grantham was typical of many regarding how, as Bass notes, he required baptismal candidates to agree to the laying on of hands before he would baptize them.[125] Given this background, Taylor's insistence that the laying on of hands "be treated as a matter of indifference" is an important indicator of his progressive outlook.[126]

Taylor's determination to initiate a change in attitude among General Baptists regarding the laying on of hands was apparent in his disagreement on this matter with the General Baptist Messenger Gilbert Boyce. He opposed the way Boyce had made the regular practice of the laying of hands a non-negotiable element within the 1777 and 1784 proposals for reunion between the wider General Baptists and the New Connexion.[127] Although Taylor's written response cannot be located, Adam Taylor noted that he viewed Boyce's stipulation as an inappropriate condition due to his belief that the laying on of hands was "not of divine institution."[128] Dan Taylor instead urged that people be allowed "the liberty of thinking and acting

120. The judgment was reached that "mixt communion in breaking of bread with persons denying laying on of hands is not lawful," see Whitley, *Minutes of General Baptist Assembly, 1654–1728,* 6. Adam Taylor provides examples of how this ruling was applied as an important principle, see Taylor, *English General Baptists,* 330–31. For further reflection and examples of the seriousness with which General Baptists approached this issue, see Winter, "Lord's Supper," 267–71.

121. Briggs, "Changing Pattern of Baptist Life," 4.

122. See Wood, *Condensed History,* 134.

123. *Brief Confession,* in Lumpkin, *Baptist Confessions,* 229

124. *Orthodox Creed,* Article thirty-two, 320–21.

125. Bass, *Thomas Grantham,* 120. See also Grantham, *Fourth Principle.*

126. Dan Taylor, "Letter to George Birley," [1789], 261. It has not proved possible to establish if Taylor himself laid hands on people after baptism.

127. The attempts at reunion that were instigated by the wider body of General Baptists were mentioned in chapter 5.

128. Taylor, *New Connection,* 214.

according to their own views."[129] This reflected the ecclesiological primacy that he placed on the exercise of liberty.[130]

In a 1789 letter to George Birley, Taylor emphasized that a correct way of proceeding regarding the laying on of hands was of "essential importance for the welfare and peace of the church."[131] He noted how his ministry at Church Lane had taught him that a prescriptive approach could cause contention. Difficulty had arisen due to his co-pastor, John Brittain, viewing the rite as "an ordinance of Christ and essential to church fellowship," whereas Taylor insisted it should not always accompany baptism as a prerequisite to membership.[132] Brittain's stance was shared by others in the Connexion, even by Birley—Taylor's closest confidant.[133] Taylor charged them with failing to provide any scriptural evidence that it was an ordinance. He stated, "It astonishes me that both of you . . . render persuasion unnecessary."[134] The fact that Taylor wrestled on this matter with some members of the Connexion casts doubt on the reliability of Raymond Brown's claim that the laying on of hands was of "little significance" in the churches of the New Connexion.[135] The pertinence of the issue was such that the Connexion's 1798 annual Association gave specific consideration to the question "Why is the laying on of hands considered as a principle of the doctrine of Christ, and yet nowhere commanded in the New Testament?"[136] The answer, written by Taylor, was that "If laying of hands be not enjoined in the New Testament, we think that Christians may be easy about it, whether it were or were not always in the primitive church attended to."[137] The way in which this judgment was unanimously accepted is testimony to Taylor's ability as a proponent of change.

In summary, Taylor's upholding of baptism by immersion was outworked with a commitment to what he understood as the plain meaning of the Scriptures. The influence of his presuppositions was also apparent, particularly in his delineation of how baptism was administered during the first three centuries. Taylor also drew creatively on the findings of wider disciplines as he attempted to strengthen his arguments in favor of immersion.

129. Ibid.
130. This was examined in chapter 5.
131. Taylor, "Letter to George Birley," [1789], 261.
132. Ibid.
133. Ibid.
134. Ibid.
135. Brown, *English Baptists*, 98.
136. *Minutes of an Association 1798*, 8.
137. Ibid.

Taylor's affinity with the Enlightenment emphasis on truth being in accordance with observation and experience was apparent. His non-sacramental interpretation of baptism was dominant. Taylor's progressive tendencies and willingness to embrace change were evident as he advocated a freer approach to the laying on of hands than customarily practiced by the General Baptists. It will next be argued that his high regard for the Lord's Supper also contained certain creative distinctions.

The Lord's Supper

"reviving ordinance"

Taylor frequently mentioned the importance of sharing in the Lord's Supper. He particularly emphasized the "precious advantages" that could be experienced.[138] While he referred to the Supper as an "emblematical representation" of Christ's death for all, it was the "spiritual nourishment" that it brings to the "souls of true believers" that occupied his greatest attention.[139] Whenever Taylor referred to the Supper in his works he acted as a proponent of how believers could be blessed by God in different ways through their participation at the Table. For example, within his published works he first referred to the Supper in *The Faithful and Wise Steward* where he encouraged believers in their approach to the Table to "Wait on the Lord with desire and expectation of a blessing from him."[140] Other examples include his drawing of attention in *Scripture Directions and Encouragements to Feeble Christians* to the way it was a crucial means through which "the weak Christian" could be upheld by God.[141] He again sought to foster an expectation of experiencing God at the Table in *Fundamentals*. He declared,

> In a believing attendance on the sacred ordinance of the Lord's Supper, we may almost say we make a near approach even to heaven itself, and do, by faith, in a most sensible manner, behold the King in his beauty; and the sight raises, and sometimes almost ravishes the soul.[142]

---

138. Taylor, *Circular Letter 1778*, 9.

139. Taylor, *Confession of Faith*, Article twenty-two, 7; ibid., 8.

140. Dan Taylor, *Faithful and Wise*, 6.

141. Dan Taylor, *Scripture Directions*, 18. The first edition was published in 1766, although it has not proved possible to locate this.

142. Dan Taylor, *Fundamentals*, 295.

This assertion was typical of the experiential significance he placed on the Supper.

Taylor promoted an appreciation of the benefits of sharing in the Supper throughout the New Connexion. He emphasized its importance as a source of "refreshment"[143] and means of "comfort of all members."[144] While in line with mainstream Baptist and Protestant thinking he viewed the elements of the Supper as remaining unchanged when received,[145] his regard for its spiritual advantages was to the extent that he encouraged the Connexion's churches to view it as the "chief means of your edification."[146] He often upheld this aspect of his understanding of the Supper at notable public occasions, such as John Deacon's ordination. He was explicit regarding the connection between "eating bread, and drinking wine" and "the blessings we enjoy through him [Christ]."[147] As he warned those present to "beware of *formality* in religion," he urged that the Supper be "accompanied with such improving instructions, as will tend, by the blessing of God, to promote the great ends for which they were appointed."[148] He impressed upon his listeners that the Supper was "designed to bring us nearer to God."[149] It was, he urged, a "reviving ordinance."[150] Although referring to the Supper as an ordinance, Taylor's appreciation of its sacramental function is apparent.

The importance Taylor placed on the efficacy of the Lord's Supper surpassed that commonly found in earlier General Baptist understandings of the Table. For example, John Smyth's 1609 *Short Confession of Faith* refers to the Supper as an "external sign"[151] and it is described in Thomas Helwys's 1611 *A Declaration of Faith of English People Remaining at Amsterdam in Holland* as an "outward manifestacion" of Christ's communion with his people.[152] The fifty-third Article of the General Baptist confession that appeared in 1651, following a meeting of representatives from thirty congregations, refers to the Table only in terms of "a memorial of his [Christ's] suffering."[153]

143. Taylor, *Confession of Faith*, Article twenty-two, 7. As previously noted, this same Article also refers to the Supper as nourishing believers spiritually.

144. Taylor, *Circular Letter 1778*, 4.

145. He did not, for example, hold to the view that the bread changed into the body of Christ or the substance of the wine into Christ's blood.

146. Taylor, *Circular Letter 1778*, 9.

147. Taylor, *Charge and Sermon at Ordination of John Deacon*, 52.

148. Ibid., 70; Taylor's emphasis.

149. Ibid.

150. Ibid., 52.

151. *Short Confession*, in Lumpkin, *Baptist Confessions*, 101.

152. *Declaration of Faith*, Article fifteen, in Lumpkin, *Baptist Confessions*, 120–21.

153. *Faith and Practice*, Article fifty-three, in Lumpkin, *Baptist Confessions*, 183.

Neither does the Standard Confession mention God meeting with people in a particular way when they shared the Supper. It contains only brief reference in its thirteenth Article to believers "assembling together in fellowship, in breaking of bread."[154] Seventeenth-century General Baptists did sometimes offer interpretations of the Table that extended beyond the memorialist view. For instance, Article thirty-three of the *Orthodox Creed* refers to the Supper as a "holy sacrament" that confirms believers "in all the benefits of his [Christ's] death and resurrection, and spiritual nourishment and growth in him."[155] As Bass states, the content of this Article provides an example of its composers having "borrowed the language" of *The Westminster Confession of Faith* (1646).[156] Chapter twenty-nine of the *Westminster Confession* contains various points of similarity and even precise wording such as that already cited regarding a believer's spiritual nourishment and growth in Christ.[157] The way that Article nineteen of the *Orthodox Creed* briefly compares the "spiritual nourishment" provided by the sacraments with how God nourished his people in the wilderness through his provision of manna, is however, distinct from that stipulated in the *Westminster Confession*.[158] Overall, the sacramental interpretation of the Supper in the *Orthodox Creed* does not assume quite the same prominence as in Taylor's works. Its chief focus remained on other elements of the Supper such as it being a "perpetual remembrance," and on what the "outward elements" of the bread and wine "signify."[159]

The dominance of Taylor's regard for the experiential advantages of participation at the Table is pronounced when compared to Thomas Grantham's approach to the Supper. While that which Curtis Freeman refers to as Grantham's "spiritual sacramentarianism" led Grantham to view the Supper as "a real offer of the flesh and blood of Christ" that believers were "to feed upon by faith," this was not the central thrust of his understanding of the Table.[160] Grantham's greater emphasis was on how the Supper provides a remembrance of the cross; a visible representation that there was no other

---

154. *Brief Confession*, 229.

155. *Orthodox Creed*, Article thirty-three, 321. In earlier General Baptist creeds and confessions the Lord's Supper was referred to as an ordinance or by a different title other than a sacrament. The way that sacraments provide spiritual nourishment is also noted in Article nineteen of the *Orthodox Creed*, 312.

156. See Bass, *Thomas Grantham*, 99.

157. *Westminster Confession of Faith*, chapter 29, 187.

158. *Orthodox Creed*, Article nineteen, 312.

159. Ibid., Article thirty-three, 321.

160. Freeman, "To Feed Upon by Faith," 196; Grantham, *Christianismus Primitivus*, Book 2, Part 7, 88.

means by which people can obtain forgiveness of sin; a promoter of Christian unity; a stabilizing influence; and an external motivation to spur believers on in their spiritual lives.[161] Although not noted by Freeman, such emphases help substantiate his claim that Grantham exhibited "little sacramental latitude."[162] Similarly, Bass states that Grantham's approach to the Supper was typical of his General Baptist contemporaries in the way that

> the administration of the elements was for the edification of Christians by way of commemoration . . . commemorative meditation dominated Grantham's view of the Lord's supper. While Christ's presence was an important feature of sacramental schemes, it received only minimal attention from Grantham.[163]

Grantham's core understanding of the Supper differed from how Taylor, as highlighted earlier, placed foundational importance on the way in which participation at the Table could lead to the reviving of spiritual life.

The way Taylor promoted the efficacy of the Lord's Supper shared some similarities with the understanding of many Particular Baptists in the seventeenth and eighteenth centuries. Michael Haykin describes how Particular Baptists frequently "come to the Table believing that there Christ would meet them and give them something deeply satisfying and precious."[164] Keach's depiction of the Supper as a "soul-reviving Cordial"[165] and Anne Dutton's reference to how participation at the Table enables "the nearest Approach to his glorious self" and to "the presence of his Glory in Heaven" are examples.[166] The similarity of these descriptions to that which Taylor wrote, as previously noted, concerning the Supper as a "reviving ordinance" and means by which "we make a near approach even to heaven," is apparent. Similar to Taylor, Keach and Dutton referred to the Supper as an ordinance, while interpreting it in sacramental terms.[167] Although there is no evidence that Taylor was familiar with these specific works by Keach and Dutton, it is possible that he became aware of their reasoning through his many Particular Baptist acquaintances. However, not all of Taylor's Particular Baptist friends maintained a sacramental interpretation of the Supper. For example, Haykin highlights the works of John Fawcett Sr., Abraham

---

161. Ibid., Book 2, Part 2, 85–90.
162. Freeman, "To Feed upon by Faith," 205.
163. Bass, *Thomas Grantham*, 96.
164. Haykin, "His soul-refreshing presence," 193.
165. Keach, *TROPOLOGIA*, 621.
166. Dutton, *Thoughts on the Lord's Supper*, 25, 28.
167. Keach, *TROPOLOGIA*, 638; Dutton, *Thoughts on the Lord's Supper*, 3–4.

Booth, and John Sutcliff as examples of how the final decades of the eighteenth century saw Particular Baptists increasingly using memorialist terms to describe the significance of the Supper.[168] Haykin chiefly accounts for this shift in interpretation by drawing attention to the transition that many Particular Baptists underwent during this period from an "inward-looking" to "outward-looking" body of believers.[169] In particular, Haykin cites Reginald Ward's reflection that the primacy evangelicals placed on conversion meant that "ordinances which did not convert . . . were a matter of diminishing interest."[170] While this was perhaps true of the Particular Baptists, the importance Taylor placed on both mission and the Lord's Supper provides a contrary example to that which Ward puts forward.

It is necessary to consider why Taylor was so emphatic regarding the spiritual benefits of the Supper. This is particularly pertinent given his non-sacramental understanding of baptism. In seeking to revolve this apparent tension, it should be noted that his stance towards this aspect of the Table does not appear to have been influenced by his General Baptist colleagues. For instance, when advocating the experiential advantages of the Supper to the Lincolnshire General Baptists in 1766, he complained that "Too many alas!" had "no such view as this."[171] It is also significant that Samuel Deacon Jr.'s mention of the Table, within his 1795 description of attitudes to worship in the New Connexion, did not include any reference to its spiritual benefits but only to "the duty of receiving the Lord's Supper."[172] This view is typical of that which Michael Walker identifies as the increasing trend among nineteenth-century Baptists to "distance themselves from sacramentalism."[173]

Although not recorded by Taylor, it is likely that his sacramental interpretation of the Supper developed during his regular participation, from the mid-1750s to early 1760s, in worship led by William Grimshaw at Haworth Parish Church.[174] As Frank Baker notes, "the Haworth revival, like the Methodist Revival in general, was associated with a sacramental revival."[175]

168. Haykin, "His soul-refreshing presence," 188–92. Taylor's friendship with Booth will be examined in chapter 7.

169. Ibid., 192. The transition in approach towards mission that the Particular Baptists underwent was considered in chapters 3 and 4.

170. Ward "Evangelical Revival," in Gilley and Sheils, *History of Religion in Britain*, 271. Qtd in Haykin, "His soul-refreshing presence," 193.

171. Taylor, *Faithful and Wise*, 69.

172. See Anon. [Samuel Deacon Jr.], *Comprehensive Account*, 93.

173. J. M. Walker, *Baptists at the Table*, 4.

174. The significance of Taylor's visits to Haworth on his spiritual formation was examined in chapter 1.

175. Baker, *William Grimshaw*, 181.

George Cragg similarly points to Grimshaw as an example of how "early evangelicals stressed the importance of the sacramental life."[176] Baker demonstrates Grimshaw to have administered a minimum of a monthly communion which differed from the way it was commonly administered by Church of England clergy three or four times a year.[177] The nature of Grimshaw's sacramentalism was typified within *The Believer's Golden Chain*, where he attributed importance to the Supper as a "Means of Grace," and emphasized how "receiving the Sacrament without CHRIST" was "like an Empty Glass without a Cordial."[178] Taylor was likely influenced by Grimshaw's sacramental outlook during his trips to Haworth to hear the preaching of notable evangelicals such as John Wesley and George Whitefield, whose visits were often accompanied by "huge communion services."[179] It is, for example, possible that Taylor participated in the Lord's Supper at Haworth when George Whitefield visited in 1753 and when Grimshaw notes that as many as thirty-five bottles of wine were drunk with the occasion being "a High day indeed. A Sabbath of Sabbaths."[180] Similar to Taylor, Grimshaw valued the Supper as a "sacrament" through which all participants could receive a "blessing," provided they "receive in faith."[181] Henry Venn, when speaking at Grimshaw's funeral, asked "Which of you ever received with him the holy communion, without perceiving it was an exquisite feast of joy to his [Grimshaw's] soul?"[182] This question was indicative of the impact of Grimshaw's sacramental approach. Taylor's appreciation of the Supper's spiritual benefits may also have increased as a consequence of his involvement in Methodism. While Taylor is very unlikely to have received communion at the Halifax Society, with John Bowmer highlighting that the Supper was generally not administered in Methodist chapels until towards the end of the century,[183] John Wesley taught that the Supper was a means of "conveying his [Christ's] grace to the souls of men."[184] The spiritually formative years that surrounded

176. George G. Cragg, *Grimshaw*, 6.

177. See Baker, *William Grimshaw*, 180–81.

178. Grimshaw, *Believer's Golden Chain*, Section 15. Page not numbered. Qtd in Baker, *William Grimshaw*, 179; Grimshaw's emphasis.

179. Baker, *William Grimshaw*, 183.

180. Grimshaw, "Letter to Mrs. Gallatin," 19 September 1753. Page not numbered.

181. Grimshaw, "Letter to Mrs. Gallatin," 2 May 1755. Page not numbered.

182. Venn, *Christ the Joy*, 12.

183. Bowmer, *Sacrament*, 72. With only a few exceptions, Bowmer states that there is little evidence that communion services were held among Methodists before 1780.

184. John Wesley, *Means of Grace*, 381. For examination of how Wesley viewed the Supper as a means of grace, see Maddox, *Responsible Grace*, 202–5.

Taylor's introduction to evangelicalism should be considered the most likely catalyst to his experiential regard for the Supper.

Taylor's approach to the Supper was different from certain outlooks that were common among Puritans. The brevity with which he taught on the subject differed from the exegetical tendencies of many prominent Puritans, such as the addresses given by John Owen prior to presiding at the Table.[185] Taylor did not share Owen's priority of providing detail on the precise "nature" and "obligations" of the Supper so as to secure "an intelligent and scriptural observance."[186] The "model meditations and prayers for disciplines" that Charles Hambrick-Stowe identifies as a common aspect of Puritan preparation for receiving the Lord's Supper were also absent from that which Taylor taught.[187] While Owen outlined different *Meditations and Ejaculations* as specified in the title and content of *The Lord's Supper Fully Considered*, nothing of this nature is found within Taylor's writings.[188] Taylor demonstrated less regard for that which Paul Lim describes as the "Puritan preoccupation with Eucharistic piety and purity."[189] The specifics of correct self-preparation were not a priority for Taylor. This was in keeping with how the nature of his evangelicalism led him to advocate that the practices of spiritual self-examination be focused primarily in an outward direction, particularly regarding a believer's commitment to the spread of the gospel.[190]

The regularity with which Taylor invited believers to share in the Supper differed from the frequency of participation that was generally practiced by Puritans. While most Puritans in England shared the Supper only occasionally and those in New England monthly,[191] Taylor administered the elements every Sunday.[192] He also urged the churches of the New Connexion to share the Supper regularly. As noted in his *Confession of Faith*, which was in turn adopted by the Connexion, the Supper was to be "performed as often as can be made convenient."[193] This reflected John Wesley's view that

185. See Owen, *Twenty-five Discourses*.

186. Alexander, in Owen, *Twenty-five Discourses*, Preface, iv.

187. Hambrick-Stowe, "Practical divinity," 197.

188. Owen, *Lord's Supper*.

189. Lim, "Puritans and the Church of England," 234.

190. The outward looking nature of Taylor's approach to spiritual disciplines was considered in chapter 1.

191. For consideration and evidence of its less regular practice in England, see Hambrick-Stowe, "Practical divinity," 197. See also Bremer, "Puritan experiment in New England," 132.

192. Taylor, *Memoirs*, 234.

193. Taylor, *Confession of Faith*, Article twenty, 7.

"it is the duty of every Christian to receive the Lord's Supper as often as he can."[194] Taylor's commitment to administering the Supper is also evident from his diary entries. For example, despite returning "very weary" from a nineteen day preaching trip in 1796, he made particular reference to how "blessed be God . . . I was enabled on the day following, to administer the Lord's Supper."[195] He also administered the Supper on special occasions, such as at ordinations and services marking the opening of new church buildings.[196] Taylor was mindful that only ordained pastors were allowed to officiate at the Table within the Connexion, but that not all congregations had such leaders. He therefore proposed that pastors be granted jurisdiction to serve the elements beyond their own fellowships. This was agreed by a "great majority" at the 1773 annual Association.[197] Taylor's resolve to bring about this structural change stemmed from his desire that all might benefit as regularly as possible from sharing in the Supper.

It is appropriate to consider why Taylor opposed participation at the Table being open to all believers. In his *Catechism* for children and youth, he stated that the Supper be restricted to baptized believers, designating the "proper subjects" of the ordinance as "those who gladly receive the word, and are baptized, and added to the church."[198] The issue particularly commanded his attention after he was sent two pamphlets written by authors using the pseudonyms Candidus and Pacifus in 1772.[199] Although Taylor was not aware at the time, it soon emerged as "an open secret" that the writers were Particular Baptist ministers.[200] Candidus was Daniel Turner (1710–98) of Abingdon, and Pacifus was John Collett Ryland of Northampton.[201] While a closed approach to the Table dominated among Baptists, the

194. John Wesley, *Duty of Constant Communion*, 427. It was also Wesley's personal practice to receive bread and wine very regularly, see Bowmer, *Sacrament*, 55–56. Randy Maddox highlights that some have sought to qualify Bowmer's figures, although Maddox is in broad agreement with Bowmer's central finding that Wesley participated in the Supper approximately once every five days during his adult life, see Maddox, *Responsible Grace*, 202.

195. Dan Taylor, diary entry, 9 July 1796, in Taylor, *Memoirs*, 212.

196. An example is how Taylor led the believers in sharing the Supper together at the opening of the General Baptist meeting house in Great Suffolk Street, London in 1809, see ibid., 234.

197. *Association 1773*.

198. Dan Taylor, *Catechism*, 32.

199. Candidus [Daniel Turner], *Modest Plea*; Pacifus [John Collett Ryland], *Modest Plea for Free Communion*. These pamphlets were sent to Taylor by George Birley, see Taylor, *Memoirs*, 86.

200. Oliver, *History*, 60.

201. See Oliver, "John Collett Ryland." It was the Particular Baptist minister

question of whether believers who had not undergone baptism by immersion be admitted to the Lord's Table was a long-standing point of debate among the Particular Baptists.[202] A consequence of Turner and Ryland collaborating to produce near identical works in favor of an open position was that it "reopened the whole debate among a new generation of Baptists."[203] Taylor viewed the subject to be of "considerable importance" and, using the pseudonym Philalethes, wrote *Candidus Examined with Candour*.[204] This was a reply to Turner's *A Modest Plea* and contains a delineation of the basis on which Taylor's closed approach to the Table was predicated. It is unfortunate that this publication has been frequently overlooked by commentators. For example, Peter Naylor in his examination of the reactions to Turner and Ryland's pamphlets makes no mention of it,[205] while Robert Oliver includes only the very briefest of references.[206] Although George Birley sent Taylor's reply to the printers prematurely, with Taylor complaining it was only "a rough draught,"[207] Oliver is incorrect to imply that as a "hurried production" it does not therefore merit close consideration.[208] For instance, although Oliver and Naylor highlight the significance of Abraham Booth's defense of

<hr/>

Abraham Booth who first identified the authors as Turner and Ryland, see Booth, *Apology for the Baptists*, in Booth, *Works*, 2:491. Daniel Turner was pastor of the Particular Baptist church in Abingdon from 1748 to 1798. For more on Turner's understanding of the sacraments and church, see Fiddes, "Daniel Turner," 112–27. John Collett Ryland was originally a member of the Baptist church at Bourton-on-the-Water. He then attended Bristol Baptist Academy and subsequently became pastor at Warwick and then at College Lane, Northampton. He was also father of John Ryland Jr.—friend of Andrew Fuller and subsequent President of Bristol Baptist Academy.

202. See Oliver, *History*, 58. This was typified in the theological dialog that took place in the late seventeenth century between the Particular Baptist minister William Kiffin who upheld a closed position and John Bunyan whose church in Bedford practiced an open approach. For further reflection on Kiffin's engagement with Bunyan on the subject of the Lord's Supper, see Michael Haykin's chapter on Kiffin in Haykin, *Kiffin, Knollys and Keach*, 49–51.

203. Oliver, *History*, 58.

204. Philalethes [Dan Taylor], *Candidus*, 3. For evidence that Taylor was the author of this work, see, e.g., Taylor, *Memoirs*, 86.

205. Naylor, *Calvinism*, 119–20.

206. Oliver, *History*, 65–66. While both Naylor's neglect of attention to Taylor's publication and Oliver's lack of detailed examination is unfortunate, it should be noted that it was the Particular Baptists who were the chief subject matter of their respective works.

207. Dan Taylor, "Letter to George Birley," 17 November 1772, 86. Taylor here expressed rare annoyance towards Birley. It is conceivable that Taylor might have intended to temper some of his earlier noted language before sending that which he was writing for publication. The hasty actions of Birley in sending Taylor's draft to the publishers meant that he was denied this opportunity.

208. Oliver, *History*, 66.

the practice of closed communion in his *Apology for the Baptists* which was written six years after Taylor's *Candidus Examined with Candour*,[209] Taylor's response to Turner included many similar points, albeit in briefer form.

Taylor responded to Turner's insistence that all believers be granted "*equal right*" of access to the Supper by stating that the New Testament provides a "directory" of the correct order of initiation into the church.[210] This involved repentance of sin, faith in Jesus, and lastly baptism by immersion.[211] Taylor viewed this as the only basis from which people were to be admitted into church fellowship. He was firm that baptism was "clearly appointed in Scripture to be administered at, or before, the admission of persons to the Lord's Table."[212] His puzzlement at Turner's stance was evident as he declared "I cannot think it possible that a real Baptist, as such, can think the Scripture authorises the admission of unbaptized persons into the church."[213] Whereas Turner argued that "liberty of conscience" should govern approaches to the Table,[214] Taylor claimed this would leave believers "wholly at uncertainties, in a matter of very great importance."[215] He refused to accept Turner's view that "divine benevolence" necessitated an inclusive approach.[216] Instead, Taylor urged that believers must firstly "act by rule" as revealed in the Scriptures.[217]

While Taylor's upholding of the baptism of believers by immersion as a prerequisite to the Lord's Supper was the ascendant viewpoint among General Baptists until the mid-nineteenth century,[218] his rejection of Turner's arguments is significant. On other occasions, Taylor's theological reasoning included emphases that Turner here advanced, such as Turner's citing of the merits of liberty and benevolence.[219] The fact that these were also impor-

209. Ibid., 70–77; Naylor, *Calvinism*, 120–24.

210. Candidus [Turner], *Modest Plea*, 5; Turner's emphasis; Philalethes [Taylor], *Candidus*, 5.

211. Philalethes [Taylor], *Candidus*, 5–6.

212. Ibid., 14.

213. Ibid., 9.

214. Candidus [Turner], *Modest Plea*, 6. Qtd in Philalethes [Taylor], *Candidus*, 14.

215. Philalethes [Taylor], *Candidus*, 4.

216. Candidus [Turner], *Modest Plea*, 5. Qtd in ibid., 10.

217. Philalethes [Taylor], *Candidus*, 11.

218. The dominance of a closed approach to the Supper among the General Baptists until the mid-nineteenth century is a point emphasized by Rinaldi, *Tribe of Dan*, 65. It should also be noted that Rinaldi failed to offer any examination of Taylor's approach to the ordinance.

219. Notable examples include the emphasis Taylor placed on liberty in his ecclesiology (see chapter 5) and in his discourse with Andrew Fuller (see chapter 4).

tant Enlightenment values further demonstrates how Taylor occasionally sought to step aside from Enlightenment influences, when he felt they were contrary to the biblical witness. In addition, it is likely that the firmness of Taylor's response to Turner was influenced by the nature of Taylor's recent engagement with proponents of Socinianism and Unitarianism such as William Graham (see chapter 2).[220] This may have left him particularly sensitive to ideas that he thought might indicate a downgrading of commitment to matters that he believed were clearly outlined in the Scriptures. More typical of Taylor was that his approach included no acknowledgment that earlier General Baptist confessions of faith prohibited participation at the Supper of those who were not baptized as believers. Examples include the 1610 *A Short Confession of Faith*,[221] John Smyth's 1612 *Confession of Faith*,[222] Standard Confession,[223] and *Orthodox Creed*.[224] Such an absence of mention was indicative of the lack of creedal emphasis found within Taylor's evangelical expression of faith.

To summarize, Taylor's approach to the Lord's Table demonstrates certain creative distinctions. His repeated emphasis on its efficacy was of greatest significance. This was found across a range of his works and surpassed the sacramental leanings of earlier General Baptists and certain of his contemporaries. His conviction of the Supper's spiritual benefits was likely fostered during his entrance into evangelicalism as he attended the ministry of William Grimshaw at Haworth. It is also possible that it was strengthened during his years in Methodism. His lack of emphasis on self-preparation prior to participating at the Table, and encouragement that the Supper be shared weekly, differed from approaches that were generally practiced by

220. It was examined in chapter 2 how Taylor had previously responded to the Unitarian teachings of those such as William Graham and Joseph Priestley.

221. Article thirty-one of the 1610 *A Short Confession* stipulates that "The Holy Supper, according to the institution of Christ, is to be administered to the baptized," see *Short Confession of Faith, 1610*, Article thirty-one, in Lumpkin, *Baptist Confessions*, 110.

222. Article seventy-two of the 1612 *Confession of Faith* refers to the "outward Supper which only baptised persons must partake," see *Propositions and Conclusions*, Article seventy-two, in Lumpkin, *Baptist Confessions*, 137. The spelling of "baptised" in this quotation is as found in the text of the 1612 Confession in Lumpkin's *Baptist Confessions*.

223. Article thirteen of the Standard Confession refers to the need for believers to be breaking bread with one another. It specifically states that this was "the duty of such who are constituted as aforesaid," which was a direct reference to the previous two Articles which cite the imperative that all believers be baptized and provide a critique of infant baptism. See *Brief Confession*, Article thirteen, 229.

224. Article thirty-three of the *Orthodox Creed* stipulates that "no un-baptized, unbelieving, or open profane, or wicked heretical persons, ought to be admitted to this ordinance," see *Orthodox Creed*, Article thirty-three, 321.

Puritans. His refusal to embrace an open practice of participation stemmed from his belief that this was not in line with the teachings of Scripture. As will be examined next, Taylor's position regarding hymn singing was also marked by his propensity for creativity.

Taylor's Endorsement of Hymn Singing

"The most common is to sing a Hymn"

An important dimension of Taylor's approach to worship was his commitment to hymn singing. He was introduced to it during his initial exposure to the Evangelical Revival and regularly engaged in singing during his nine years in Methodism.[225] The importance he attributed to hymn singing was apparent as he made its inclusion in worship a priority from early in his ministry at Birchcliff. It was first mentioned in a 1767 entry in his diary.[226] However, his regard for singing was such that he likely introduced it as soon as he commenced his ministry in 1763. After John Taylor visited Birchcliff in the early 1770s, he noted that a typical service comprised "reading the Scripture, singing, and prayer."[227] Dan Taylor's emphasis on congregational hymn singing differed from customary General Baptist practice. While the Particular Baptists through the influence of hymn writers such as Keach— "the seminal figure in congregation singing among Baptists"[228]—had progressively embraced congregational hymn singing, the General Baptists maintained a strong resistance. The minutes of the 1733 General Baptist Assembly record that "there is very few who belong to this Assembly, that either practice or approve, the Way of singing Mens Composures."[229] This was also a point emphasized by Adam Taylor in his description of the practice of worship among the seventeenth-century General Baptists.[230] The

225. See chapter 1.

226. Dan Taylor, diary entry, 14 July 1767, in Taylor, *Memoirs*, 62.

227. John Taylor. Qtd in Adam Taylor, *John Taylor*, 26. The date of John Taylor's visit is not specified.

228. Anon. [John Fawcett Jr.], *Account*, 256–57. Keach was the Particular Baptist minister of a church in Horsly-down (today Horsleydown) Southwark from 1668 to 1704. It was during this period of Keach's ministry that he wrote many hymns and published a hymn book in 1691, see Keach, *Spiritual Melody*. For more on Keach's significance as a hymn writer and of his wider ministry, see Hugh Martin, *Benjamin Keach*; Vaughn, "Public Worship"; Austin Walker, *Benjamin Keach*; Arnold, *Reformed Theology of Benjamin Keach*.

229. "1733 Assembly at White's Alley," in Whitley, *Minutes of General Baptist Assembly, 1731–1811*, 18.

230. Taylor, *English General Baptists*, 424–25.

prescriptive restrictions that prominent General Baptists such as Thomas Grantham applied even to the singing of psalms were influential in consolidating a lasting culture of opposition to the collective singing of composed hymns, as will be shown in the next section.[231] Taylor advocated and modeled a very different stance.

Taylor sought to foster a commitment to hymn singing throughout the New Connexion. It is significant that his early efforts to encourage its adoption did not involve him doing so in written form, but by providing opportunities for the movement's members to become convinced of its merits through personal participation in the practice. This approach was in keeping with the very practical nature of his evangelicalism. He made hymn singing a routine aspect of worship at New Connexion gatherings, such as ordination services and meetings of the regional and national associations. A characteristic example was the record provided in the minutes of the 1772 annual Association which note that "brother Taylor opened the meeting with singing" and similarly "concluded with singing."[232] When Samuel Deacon Jr. described patterns of worship across the Connexion he noted that,

> The most common is to sing a Hymn—to deliver a kind of general prayer—to sing another Hymn—to take a text of Scripture, and to preach from it about an hour—taking another Hymn, and conclude in prayer.[233]

The way Taylor created opportunities for people to participate in singing was essential to its uptake across the Connexion.

Taylor's efforts to promote full participation in hymn singing led him to undertake certain pioneering initiatives. In 1772 he became the first General Baptist to produce a hymn book, entitled *Hymns and Spiritual Songs*.[234] Whereas the Particular Baptists had a strong hymn writing tradition, the rejection of hymn singing by most General Baptists meant that a hymn book had not been previously compiled.[235] Although Adam Taylor drew attention to Taylor's hymn book, and cited its use throughout the

---

231. It will be seen in the next section that Grantham's arguments were perpetuated in the second half of the eighteenth century by people such as Gilbert Boyce.

232. *Association 1772*. Page not numbered.

233. [Deacon], *Comprehensive Account*, 6.

234. [Dan Taylor], *Hymns*. The evidence that Taylor was editor of this work is considered subsequently.

235. Particular Baptist hymn writers included those such as Benjamin Keach (noted earlier), Joseph Stennett Sr., Anne Steele, Benjamin Beddome, Samuel Stennett, and Taylor's close friend John Fawcett.

New Connexion, he did not specify its title.[236] Neither is it identified in Dan Taylor's writings, the contributions that comprise the *General Baptist Magazine*,[237] nor Wood's history of the Connexion. Frank Rinaldi also fails to note it as he does not consider hymn singing in the New Connexion.[238] Taylor is however identified as the editor of *Hymns and Spiritual Songs* by Henry Burrage in *Baptist Hymn Writers and Their Hymns*.[239] Despite the hymn book not mentioning Taylor, but instead attributed to certain anonymous "compilers," several factors point to this as Taylor's publication.[240] Similar to many of Taylor's pre-1785 works, it was published in Halifax by Edward Jacob. Moreover, its preface is characteristic of Taylor's style of writing and theology. For example, Christ is described as having "died for all men without exception" and salvation promised as "full, complete, and free, to every sinner desirous to enjoy it."[241] The claim by David Music and Paul Richardson that the preface exclusively "sets out the theology of the general atonement" is, however, an exaggeration.[242] It also includes reference to humanity's depravity, Christ's divinity and humanity, salvation only by faith in Christ's atoning work and the pursuit of holiness.[243] In keeping with Taylor's theological generosity of spirit, its 293 hymns and six doxologies include contributions not only from Arminians such as Charles Wesley, but also Calvinists such as Isaac Watts, Philip Doddridge, and Robert Seagrave. Taylor chose hymns on the basis of their suitability "to promote the advantage and edification of the common people" who he recognized "compose the chief part of our assemblies," this was typical of his constant regard for the interests of the less educated.[244] When the language of the hymns was viewed as too "lofty" for the poor to understand, individual words, lines, and verses were altered, and replaced with "more easy and familiar" phrases.[245] Such an approach was symptomatic of Taylor's creativity and likely aided the popularity of the work. By 1789, as many as 3,500 copies of *Hymns and Spiritual Songs* had been sold.[246] Considering

236. Taylor, *Memoirs*, 79.

237. Dan Taylor, *General Baptist Magazine*.

238. See Rinaldi, *Tribe of Dan*.

239. Burrage, *Baptist Hymn Writers*, 629.

240. [Taylor], *Hymns*, iii.

241. Ibid., iv, v.

242. Music, and Richardson, *"I Will Sing the Wondrous Story,"* 48.

243. See [Taylor], *Hymns*, iii–ix.

244. Ibid., viii.

245. Ibid.

246. *Minutes of an Association 1789*, 8. The name of the hymn book is not cited in

the Connexion's membership was at this time 2,792,[247] it is conceivable that the popularity of this book extended beyond the movement.

Taylor's persuasive influence on the uptake of hymn singing across the Connexion led to a demand for a new hymn book that would include a greater number of hymns. The idea was first mooted at the 1789 annual Association, where all ministers were encouraged to "embrace any opportunity" to collect new hymns.[248] A committee was then established in 1791 "to examine and decide upon" their scriptural merit.[249] While Taylor chaired the committee, his participation alongside others such as William Thompson, George Birley, Benjamin Pollard, and Robert Smith was in keeping with that noted in chapter 5 regarding his reluctance to exercise an overbearing style of leadership. The project was completed in 1793, with the number of hymns expanded to 632 and composers' names inserted alongside each hymn.[250] Although Taylor's inspiration was again central to the formation of this new hymn book, the collective process by which these hymns were gathered and their suitability judged, suggests the need for caution against viewing its emergence only in terms of his influence. It is, for example, something of a misrepresentation for Music and Richardson to refer to this hymn book simply as comprising "Dan Taylor's hymns."[251] The claim by the nineteenth-century hymnologist William Stevenson that John Deacon's publication of his own collection of hymns in 1800 stemmed from him having "disapproved of the treatment" received from Taylor after he had compiled material for the 1793 hymn book is similarly dubious.[252] The 1791 Association minutes state that Deacon's responsibility was not to produce the hymn book, but "to form a collection" of possible contributions for submission to the committee.[253] Stevenson also failed to acknowledge that it was now increasingly common for people to produce their own hymn books. This not only included Particular Baptists such as John Ash, Caleb Evans, and John Rippon,[254] but also others in the New Connexion

---

the minutes but Taylor's collection of hymns is mentioned.

247. See Rinaldi, *Tribe of Dan*, 213.

248. *Minutes of an Association 1789*, 14.

249. *Minutes of an Association 1791*, 9. Wisbeach is today known as Wisbech.

250. Dan Taylor and John Deacon, *Hymns and Spiritual Songs*. Unlike the 1772 hymn book, this new collection of hymns does not have a preface.

251. Music and Richardson, "*I Will Sing the Wondrous Story*," 50.

252. William R. Stevenson, "Dan Taylor," 1117. See John Deacon, *New and Large Collection*.

253. *Minutes of an Association 1791*, 9.

254. See, e.g., Ash, and Evans, *Collection of Hymns*. Though no date of publication is provided in the first edition, the preface is dated 27 September 1769. This work was

such as Samuel Deacon Jr. who produced a hymn book in 1784.[255] The way Taylor was a key motivational catalyst to the further expansion of hymn singing across the Connexion, but acted in a non-overbearing way, was again indicative of how his ecclesiological understanding was underpinned by a creative fusion of the merits of coordinated visionary leadership and protection of liberty.[256]

To summarize, the commitment and creative means by which Taylor promoted the singing of hymns was a core aspect of his approach to worship. These characteristics were evident from the outset of his ministry at Birchcliff and throughout his oversight of the New Connexion. In particular, the way he increased the uptake of singing by giving people opportunities to participate, the priority he placed on seeking to ensure that it was accessible to the less educated, and being the first General Baptist to produce a hymn book, were all typical of the pioneering nature of his evangelicalism. Such an approach set him apart from the thinking of many other General Baptists. Next it will be seen that the innovative nature of Taylor's underlying convictions on this subject became particularly apparent through his discourse with Gilbert Boyce.

Taylor's Response to Gilbert Boyce's Opposition to Hymn Singing

"truly alive to God"

The dedication to hymn singing found throughout the New Connexion, and which was embodied most fully by Taylor, differed from the common resistance to this form of worship among the older body of General Baptists. Their different approaches were apparent within the earlier cited 1777 and 1784 reunion discussions. While Gilbert Boyce insisted that the Connexion's churches ceased singing hymns, Taylor remained resolute that they be granted liberty to exercise their own judgment.[257] Boyce's determination to persuade Taylor to change his stance led him in 1785 to publish *Serious Thoughts on the Present Mode and Practice of Singing in the Public*

---

popularly referred to as the "Bristol Collection." See also Rippon, *Selection of Hymns.*

255. Samuel Deacon Jr., *New Composition of Hymns.* This was enlarged in 1797 and became known as Barton Hymns, see Samuel Deacon Jr., *Barton Hymns.*

256. This significant aspect of Taylor's exercise of leadership was examined in chapter 5.

257. See Taylor, *New Connection*, 214–15.

Worship of God.[258] This was a strong repudiation of the "matter and manner" of all forms of joint singing.[259] It was the first time that Taylor had been presented with the collective arguments against congregational singing in such a coherent way. Although Taylor stated that he was "very averse to taking up my pen" with his "much esteemed friend," the passion for singing that he had developed across the Connexion led many in the movement to urge him to issue a reply.[260] He consented, and in 1786 wrote *A Dissertation on Singing in the Worship of God.* After briefly defining what it means to sing, he firstly sought to establish its legitimacy from the Scriptures. He provided Old and New Testament references that aimed to illustrate his belief that "SINGING the praises of God, is plainly and frequently recommended in the sacred Scriptures."[261] As he summarized his evidence, he pointed to how singing was "so manifest" in the Old Testament that "none will pretend to deny it."[262] Given that Christ had not declared anything to the contrary, he argued that sung praises of God should not cease.[263] His approach was again typical of the importance he attached to that which he viewed as the plain message of the Scriptures.

Taylor was mindful that Boyce's opposition to the joint singing of both psalms and hymns was underpinned by a belief that Scriptures such as Eph 5:19, Col 3:16, and 1 Cor 14:15 were not endorsements for all to sing.[264] Boyce instead applied these verses only to those specifically enabled by the Spirit in the congregational setting to "sing one by one, as well as the prophets might prophesy one by one."[265] Boyce was perpetuating a view that had been dominant among the General Baptists since the previous century. An example was Thomas Grantham's insistence at the 1689 General Baptist Assembly,

258. Boyce, *Serious Thoughts.*

259. Ibid., 7.

260. Dan Taylor, "Letter to Gilbert Boyce," 7 January 1786, in Dan Taylor, *Dissertation*, iii; Taylor, "Memoir Rev. Gilbert Boyce," 348.

261. Taylor, *Dissertation*, 8; Taylor's emphasis.

262. Ibid., 26.

263. Ibid.

264. Eph 5:19: "[A]s you sing psalms and hymns and spiritual songs among yourselves, singing and making melody to the Lord in your hearts"; Col 3:16: "Let the word of Christ dwell in you richly; teach and admonish one another in all wisdom; and with gratitude in your hearts sing psalms, hymns, and spiritual songs to God."; 1 Cor 14:15: "What should I do then? I will pray with the spirit, but I will pray with the mind also; I will sing praise with the spirit, but I will sing praise with the mind also."

265. Boyce, *Serious Thoughts*, 19. For Boyce's examination of these Scriptures, see 14–17.

That as prayer of one in the Church is the prayer of whole
Church so the singing of one in the church is the singing of the
whole church, and as he that prayeth in the church is to pforme
the service as of the ability wch. God giveth even so he that sin-
geth praises in the church ought to pforme that service as of the
Ability reced. of God.[266]

Although Taylor acknowledged that spontaneous Spirit empowered
singing might have taken place among the first believers, he contended that
the Scriptures provided by Boyce "cannot be a rule for other churches, or for
after ages to be *confined* to."[267] He drew attention to Jesus and his disciples
having sung following their sharing of the Passover meal (Matt 26:30) and
pointed to the Greek text as "plainly denoting" that this was joint singing.
He gave similar attention to Paul and Silas singing together in jail (Acts
16:25). Taylor was adamant that the directives on singing in Eph 5:19 and
Col 3:16 were not relevant to whether hymns should be sung jointly. He
viewed them as only concerning *"personal* instruction and admonition," not
public worship.[268] He argued that the pronoun that was translated as "yourselves" and "one another" in these two verses was found another 250 times
in the New Testament and that on only four occasions did it contain "even
the appearance of *mutuality*."[269] Taylor, in a footnote, also referred his readers to the thoughts of John Gill on this issue. In particular, he referenced
Gill's *A Discourse on Singing of Psalms as a Part of Divine Worship From I.
Corinthians xiv.15* which provided a defense of joint singing.[270] Taylor's use
of Gill's works again demonstrates how Taylor's evangelicalism sometimes
gave rise to a generosity of spirit concerning insights gained from others,
even if some of their beliefs differed from his own, such as the scope of
Christ's atoning work in the case of Gill.

Taylor and Boyce held contrary viewpoints regarding the benefits of
composed hymns. Boyce accused those who used "words devised by others"

266. Grantham, "1689 City of London Assembly," in Whitley, *Minutes of General
Baptist Assembly, 1654–1728,* 1:27–28.

267. Taylor, *Dissertation,* 56; Taylor's emphasis.

268. Ibid., 55; Taylor's emphasis.

269. Ibid.; Taylor's emphasis. Taylor pointed to Eph 4:10, Col 3:13, Heb 3:13, and
1 Pet 4:10 as the four exceptions. He argued that these four verses would need to be
submitted to those who were more "capable judges," see ibid., 55.

270. See ibid., 14. It is likely that Taylor appreciated aspects of this work such as
Gill's claim that singing was not confined to the Old Testament dispensation and his
reflection concerning how singing with the Spirit was not necessarily a reference to
the extraordinary gift of the Spirit, but to how the Spirit "is absolutely necessary to the
spiritual performance of this duty," see Gill, *Discourse on Singing,* 43.

of bringing their *"praises* with them in their *pockets"* rather than in their hearts and stipulated that this led to "dry, empty" worship.[271] This was rejected by Taylor who, instead, argued that the singing of composed songs indicated a vibrancy of faith. He stated that the singing of hymns was "a practice peculiarly suitable to the disposition of one who is truly alive to God."[272] He, therefore, quickly dismissed certain of Boyce's other claims such as that the singing of "human compositions" was unnecessary when the Scriptures could be read.[273] Taylor instead urged that any

> Hymn, or Spiritual Song, that is founded on Scripture, and consistent with it, though not in its very words, may be as properly, and as profitably used in divine worship, as any prayer or sermon, though ever so scriptural, which is not in the very words of Scripture.[274]

Taylor's liberated stance was typical of that often found among eighteenth-century evangelicals. It differed from the concern for precise scriptural warrant that generally accompanied Puritan approaches to singing.[275] With the exception of certain innovators such as Isaac Watts, Puritans restricted God's praise to the singing of metrical psalms.[276] As Taylor upheld the advantages of composed hymns, he also emphasized the experiential benefits of singing. This is apparent as he conveyed his delight at how "the melody raises the spirits, and excites pleasure."[277] Taylor noted that "the contents of the song, more easily engage the attention and affect the heart; and

271. Boyce, *Serious Thoughts*, 7, 8, 7; Boyce's emphasis.

272. Taylor, *Dissertation*, 17.

273. Boyce, *Serious Thoughts*, 10. Taylor also rejected Boyce's charge of inconsistency concerning the Connexion's use of the words of others in singing, but not in prayers or sermons. While Taylor believed there was scriptural precedent for singing, he argued that there was no "Divine Authority" for sermons and prayers written by others, see Taylor, *Dissertation*, 44. For Boyce's thoughts on this matter, see Boyce, *Serious Thoughts*, 35.

274. Taylor, *Dissertation*, 52.

275. For an examination of Puritan approaches to singing, see J. R. Watson, *English Hymn*, 103–32. See also Scholes, *Puritans and Music*. Similar to the approach popularized by John Calvin, most Puritans insisted that the only songs authorized to be sung in worship were those that God had provided in the book of Psalms. Puritans such as Thomas Sternhold, John Hopkins, William Kethe, and John Marckant assumed a significant role in the production of the influential 1562 *The Whole Booke of Psalmes*, which was the first complete English metrical version of the Psalms, see Sternhold and Hopkins, *Whole Booke of Psalmes*.

276. Isaac Watts assumed a more pioneering approach, which involved paraphrasing biblical texts for the purpose of hymn singing.

277. Taylor, *Dissertation*, 53.

the instructions more agreeably insinuate themselves into the mind."[278] His comments suggest he had personally experienced that which John Watson notes regarding how Charles Wesley's hymns "have a kind of urgency which comes from a direct application to the self."[279] Taylor's regard for singing as a spiritual experience, and the capacity for composed hymns to stimulate spiritual renewal were influential on the resolute way that he upheld this form of worship.

Taylor's endorsement of congregational singing was intertwined with his conviction regarding its experiential advantages for non-believers. He emphasized that as non-believers participated in sung worship they had "often been instructed, admonished, and otherwise benefitted."[280] It is likely that he reached this judgment as a consequence of his experience of hymn singing during his earlier involvement in Methodism and from his wider observations of the benefits of singing from his oversight of the Connexion. He was therefore unequivocal that they "be not only permitted but encouraged to join in the exercise" of corporate hymn singing.[281] Compared to the common practice of the wider General Baptists, Taylor's position was again pioneering. Outside of the New Connexion there was widespread General Baptist agreement that collective singing was inappropriate, as congregations might include some who were non-believers. Grantham's warning that this would lead to God being offered an unedifying composition of "mixed voices" and "promiscuous singing" was influential.[282] Boyce's opposition to people "promiscuously" singing together was typical.[283] Boyce was incredulous that anybody could think there was scriptural authority for the active participation in worship of "openly profane and scandalous sinners . . . who know nothing of the solemnity of praising God."[284] Given Boyce's position, it is pertinent to note the inaccuracy of Leon McBeth's assertion that "*along with Boyce*, Taylor admitted that the unsaved might join in singing."[285] While McBeth should be commended for how he alone, among contemporary commentators, offers limited reflection on Taylor's discourse with Boyce, his assertion that Boyce also advocated that non-believers participate in singing is a notable error. Taylor responded to Boyce by insisting that the singing

---

278. Ibid.

279. Watson, *English Hymn*, 222.

280. Taylor, *Dissertation*, 28.

281. Ibid., 71.

282. Grantham, *Christianismus Primitivus*, Book 2, Part 2, 101.

283. Boyce, *Serious Thoughts*, 11.

284. Ibid.

285. McBeth, *Baptist Heritage*, 167; italics added.

of praises was a moral duty for all and, therefore, that "carnal people ought to attend to it."[286] With reference to the many "facts" and "moral precepts" found in the Psalms, Taylor further specified that singing did not have to be conducted from a basis of relationship with God, for it was designed "to strike and engage the mind."[287] In turn, he accused Boyce and all opponents of the inclusion of non-believers of having a "mistaken idea of the nature and design of singing in divine worship."[288] Taylor was convinced that it was an important means by which God met with non-believers. The way he brought his concern for the spread of the gospel, even into the center of his understanding of public worship, was indicative of how his evangelicalism fostered within him a concern for mission that was intrinsic to all aspects of his theological thinking.

Another pioneering aspect of Taylor's position, that became apparent through his engagement with Boyce, was his wholehearted support for the participation of women in singing.[289] This was another important issue where he and Boyce thought differently. Boyce argued that women should not sing, as this was "contrary to the nature of things and the tenor of Scripture."[290] This viewpoint was previously advocated by Grantham and was common among General Baptists outside of the New Connexion. In response, Taylor highlighted scriptural examples of women who sang with men. These included Miriam, Deborah, and the daughters of Heman.[291] He also urged Boyce to recognize that the apostle Paul's commands that women be silent (1 Cor 14:34) and not teach (1 Tim 2:12) had no relevance to the subject of singing.[292] Taylor believed that Paul's appeal for silence applied only to the specific situation of disorder at Corinth, and was unconvinced that his instruction in his letter to Timothy referred to public worship. Taylor was therefore firm that Paul's apparent prohibitions against women were applicable only in their "most strict and limited sense."[293]

It is significant that a belief in women's equality with men was central to Taylor's justification of women's full participation in singing. This led him

286. Taylor, *Dissertation*, 28.

287. Ibid., 29.

288. Ibid., 28.

289. Ibid., 28–40. Taylor's position was consistent with the ecclesiological importance he attached to the role of women—see chapter 5.

290. Boyce, *Serious Thoughts*, 38.

291. Taylor, *Dissertation*, 34.

292. Ibid.

293. Ibid.

to argue that they were "under an obligation" to sing.[294] He underlined this by stating,

> Women, as well as men have rational capacities;—they as well as men, have immortal souls;—they, as well as men, are made for an eternal duration; they, as well as men, are the creatures of God;—they, as well as men, have received many blessings from God, which they ought to praise him for.[295]

Taylor's reasoning reflects that which Karen O'Brien outlines regarding the way that the Enlightenment values of toleration and equality enabled the development of a framework for appreciating the moral capacity and shifting social roles of women.[296] Similarly, the Enlightenment influences and innovative tendencies that were central to evangelicalism were probably a factor in accounting for the readiness with which Taylor embraced this new outlook. Symptomatic of the increasing credence shown to women at this time was how the English social philosopher Mary Wollstonecraft wrote her influential *A Vindication of the Rights of Women*, only six years after Taylor wrote his *Dissertation*.[297] Taylor's high regard for the place of women led him to assert "I am persuaded there are many things which some of the women understand better than some of the men."[298] He was, in turn, unequivocal that women should be free to "enjoy the advantages of singing, and experience the *goodness* of it, and the *pleasantness* of it."[299] Such a plea not only epitomized his conviction that women engage fully in sung worship, but again reflected his regard for its experiential benefits.

In 1787, Boyce responded to Taylor's dissertation with *A Candid and Friendly Reply*.[300] He reiterated each aspect of his earlier critique and particularly accused Taylor of failing to validate the singing of God's praises as a universal and obligatory moral duty.[301] Although Taylor believed he had adequately demonstrated this principle, he replied with *A Second Dissertation on Singing in the Worship of God*.[302] He outlined eight propositions

294. Ibid.
295. Ibid.
296. O' Brien, *Women and Enlightenment*, 1–34.
297. Wollstonecraft, *Vindication*.
298. Taylor, *Dissertation*, 33.
299. Ibid.; Taylor's emphasis.
300. Boyce, *Candid and Friendly Reply*.
301. Ibid., 21–28.
302. Dan Taylor, *Second Dissertation*.

that aimed to prove the scriptural basis of singing in public worship.[303] This largely involved a recasting of his previously cited material. However, the way he emphasized his conviction that churches be granted freedom of judgment regarding the specifics of worship was particularly noteworthy. This was something he had earlier sought to impress on Boyce when he outlined his belief that the New Testament did not vindicate any one particular method of worship, but established only "general rules" concerning its edifying nature.[304] Boyce stated his disapproval of this position, and accused Taylor of advocating a way of proceeding that appealed only to "lovers of their own contrived forms."[305] To safeguard unity, Boyce was convinced that it was to "the benefit and advantage of the churches of Christ, to be joined together in one scriptural way of public worship."[306] In contrast, Taylor was firm within his *Second Dissertation* regarding the merits of a non-uniform approach. He rejected any need for "precise rules, with regard to the punctilios of mode and form," insisting on "a law of liberty, as far as it relates to modes and forms of worship."[307] His emphasis on the importance of liberty accorded with that often found in other aspects of his evangelical understanding of the practice of faith.[308]

A further prominent feature of Taylor's *Second Dissertation* was his continued rejection of Boyce's entrenched opposition to the participation of women and non-believers in singing. It is again evident that Taylor viewed himself as a guardian of the full involvement of women in worship. This is apparent in his stated goal that he "endeavoured to vindicate them" from the prohibitive stance assumed by Boyce.[309] The sense of injustice he felt towards Boyce's position was evident as he asked "What right have we, without Scripture warrant, to forbid them, or dissuade them from it?"[310] He also failed to conceal any longer his frustration at Boyce's judgment that those who did not love God should not sing his praises. Taylor sarcastically retorted that non-believers might as well "lie down and die."[311] Boyce's

303. Ibid., 38–77.

304. Taylor, *Dissertation*, 50. Taylor stipulated that these rules included: "let all things be done edifying" (1 Cor 14:26), "let all things be done decently and in order" (1 Cor 14:40), "whatever ye do, do all to the glory of God" (1 Cor 10:31), and "let all your things be done with charity" (1 Cor 16:14), see ibid., 57.

305. Boyce, *Candid and Friendly Reply*, 52.

306. Ibid.

307. Taylor, *Second Dissertation*, 54.

308. This was particularly examined in chapter 5.

309. Taylor, *Second Dissertation*, 52.

310. Ibid., 63–64.

311. Ibid., 65.

declaration that "never until now, did I hear from the mouth of a *Baptist preacher*" that non-believers should praise God, again typified the extent to which Taylor's approach to worship was challenging and innovative when compared with much wider General Baptist practice.[312]

A final important aspect of Taylor's reply was his rejection of the view that singing be accompanied by instruments.[313] The appropriateness of instruments became a particular point of debate in the later decades of the eighteenth century when the singing of psalms in parish churches was increasingly accompanied by instruments.[314] They also began to be used in Methodist societies. Taylor briefly referred to his position in his earlier dissertation, arguing that there is no mention of instruments in the New Testament.[315] Although Boyce did not agree with the playing of instruments in worship, his knowledge of the use of instruments in the Old Testament meant he was surprised by Taylor's resistance. Boyce was unclear why Taylor had not followed the same principle that he applied to joint singing, namely that "nothing less than a divine prohibition can vindicate our refusing to use them in public worship."[316] Taylor's failure to do this led Boyce to accuse him of an inconsistency that undermined his entire defense of singing. He challenged Taylor to "set up instruments of music as well as singing in the worship of God, or neither."[317] However, Taylor refused to accept their inseparability. In addition to his belief that there was no New Testament warrant for accompanied singing, he cited its lack of teaching purpose and absence from the practice of worship that was embraced by the early church.[318] While his stance was contrary to the support given to the use of instruments by some early Baptist pioneers of congregational singing such as Keach, it reflected the outlook that was common during his earlier years in Methodism. Even when, towards the end of the century, an increasing number of Methodist societies began to use orchestral instruments to accompany their worship, their use was not officially approved by the Methodist Conference.[319]

---

312. Boyce, *Candid and Friendly Reply*, 46; Boyce's emphasis.

313. See Taylor, *Second Dissertation*, 72–76.

314. For an examination of this changing aspect of worship, see Drage, "John Fawcett of Bolton," 59–69.

315. Taylor, *Dissertation*, 63.

316. Boyce, *Candid and Friendly Reply*, 64.

317. Ibid.

318. Taylor, *Second Dissertation*, 73–76.

319. The minutes of the 1808 Methodist Conference record its refusal to "sanction or consent to the erection of any organs in our chapels" and warned that where they already existed, they were no longer "to overpower or supersede the congregational singing." Qtd in Curwen, *Studies in Worship-music*, 29.

Although the New Connexion's annual Association throughout Taylor's lifetime was also unsupportive of instruments accompanying singing, it is significant that there is no evidence of Taylor seeking to dissuade the "very few" New Connexion churches that utilized instruments.[320] Moreover, Taylor softened his stance. For example, in his sermon on a national day of thanksgiving in 1789 for the recovery from ill health of King George III, he made particular reference to how such occasions of great praise of God merited the playing of instruments. He was specific that

> Nor will I by any means deny the propriety of musical instruments on these occasions. I cheerfully grant that an instrument of music, or a concert of music, may be well adapted to seasons of peculiar joy and festivity.[321]

He even went so far as to say that it could serve "some moral purposes, when employed in the fear, and to the honour of God."[322] His comments reflect a change of position from that voiced two years earlier in his dialog with Boyce. It is conceivable that Boyce's critique caused him to adopt a more progressive stance. The way Taylor was now acting as a proponent of instrumental accompaniment, albeit in particular circumstances, was more in keeping with the creative thrust of his approach to worship.

Conclusion

The subject and practice of worship was a central element of Taylor's theological thinking. It was also a priority within the exercise of his ministry and oversight of the New Connexion. Elements of his reasoning displayed creative thinking and inventive argument. These were apparent as he acted as a proponent of believers' baptism. His publication of *Humble Essay* was the first substantial defense of believers' baptism by a General Baptist since Thomas Grantham's *Presumption no Proof.* Taylor's concentration on baptism as a duty and command to be obeyed was underpinned by a non-sacramental interpretation. This set him apart from the greater sacramental tendencies of many earlier General Baptists. Taylor's non-sacramental understanding of baptism was similar to that which became common among Baptists later in the nineteenth century. Other creative aspects of Taylor's outlook towards baptism include his advocacy of the merits of observation and experience, use of material from wider disciplines that he felt strengthened his reasoning, and innovative design of *Strictures*. Enlightenment influences were also apparent. Taylor's judgments demonstrate the strength

320. [Deacon], *Comprehensive Account*, 6.
321. Dan Taylor, *Interposition of Providence*, 9.
322. Ibid.

of certain presuppositions. These were particularly evident in both his handling of the Scriptures and extra-biblical material. His refusal to accept that the laying on of hands was a compulsory aspect of baptism was also distinct from customary General Baptist practice. Taylor's understanding of the Lord's Supper was also notable. In particular, his regard for its efficacy extended beyond that outlined by many earlier General Baptists. It is likely that his early exposure to the ministry of William Grimshaw, who held a sacramental understanding of the Supper, influenced the way Taylor repeatedly drew attention to its spiritual benefits. This conviction may have been strengthened during his years within Methodism. His lack of attention to the need for self-preparation prior to participating at the Table, and frequency that he celebrated the Supper, set him apart from approaches commonly adopted by the Puritans. Given Taylor's progressive tendencies and propensity for innovation, it is surprising that he upheld a restricted approach to participation. This reflected his reluctance to innovate when he believed that this was contrary to his understanding of the Scriptures.

Taylor's commitment to hymn singing was an important aspect of his approach to worship. Within the context of General Baptist life, his advocacy of hymn singing was significant. He successfully encouraged its adoption throughout the New Connexion and did so by seeking to ensure that its members had opportunities to engage in the practice for themselves. Taylor became the first General Baptist to produce a hymn book. The conviction and creativity that underpinned his actions as a proponent of this aspect of worship were apparent during his discourse on the subject with Gilbert Boyce. As Taylor challenged many of Boyce's assumptions, he placed particular emphasis on singing as an indicator of a vibrancy of faith and its experiential benefits. In contrast to Boyce and earlier General Baptists such as Grantham, Taylor argued that non-believers be encouraged to participate. Contrary to established General Baptist thinking, and in accordance with the Enlightenment emphasis on the principle of equality, he was also unequivocal that women be allowed to join in. Taylor's change of mind from his initial resistance to singing being accompanied by instruments was also significant. It will be seen in the next chapter that the same creativity that was evident in Taylor's approach to worship, was central to his understanding of mission.

7

Religious Entrepreneur

A DISTINCTIVE FEATURE OF Taylor's ministry was the way in which he introduced new endeavors, embraced new practices, and developed new outlooks. As David Bebbington notes, he was a "religious entrepreneur."[1] It will be argued that Taylor's proclivity for innovation was in keeping with the ethos of the eighteenth-century evangelical movement. Firstly, consideration will be given to Taylor's entrepreneurship as he adopted certain methods of evangelism and established the New Connexion for the purpose of mission. This will be followed by an examination of his innovative approach to church planting. It will be seen that his missiology was underpinned by a deep regard for the need to mobilize every member of the Connexion in evangelism and the importance of cooperating with those of other denominations. Attention will also be given to how the primacy he attached to mission was central to his creation of the General Baptist Academy and establishment of the General Baptist Missionary Society. It will become apparent that his entrepreneurship was fueled by his missiological convictions and certain cultural influences of his day, and that it was intrinsic to the evangelicalism he espoused. It will be contended that this set Taylor apart from certain ways of proceeding and outlooks found within Puritanism and among the wider General Baptists.

---

1. Bebbington, *Baptists*, 85. The term religious entrepreneur was defined in the introductory chapter.

Practical Innovation for the Cause of Mission

"exert ourselves by every means"

Taylor's approach to ministry attests to Reginald Ward's observation that a combination of "theological conservatism with practical innovation" was a characteristic of the eighteenth-century Evangelical Revival.[2] For example, when Taylor assumed oversight in 1763 of the believers in Heptonstall who subsequently formed the fellowship in Wadsworth, he immediately embraced some of the new practices he had been exposed to within the revival. He sought to increase their numbers through the adoption of open air preaching he had witnessed in the ministries of those such as William Grimshaw, George Whitefield, and the Wesley brothers.[3] Taylor delivered all his early sermons from the fields surrounding Wadsworth.[4] Adam Taylor emphasized that the results of this were "encouraging" considering the inhabitants of the area were "few, scattered and in general depraved."[5] It was through open air preaching that Taylor sought to introduce the gospel to neighboring communities. According to an unnamed colleague, Taylor regularly traveled "a considerable distance" to preach "in a wild country, the inhabitants of which were hardly civilized and generally great strangers to religion."[6] Similarly Adam Taylor, when referring to Dan Taylor's field preaching, stated,

> He did not confine his attention to Wadsworth, nor his labours to the meeting house, but went out on all sides to a considerable distance to preach on the evenings of the Lord's day and frequently on the week days.[7]

These accounts bear witness to how Taylor, from the earliest stage of his ministry, demonstrated a dynamic centrifugal approach to mission as he took the gospel to others.

While open air preaching, prior to its re-emergence as a standard feature of the Evangelical Revival, was practiced in different forms throughout church history, it is important not to underestimate the extent to which Taylor was a pioneer of this approach within the context of the eighteenth-century

2. Ward, *Protestant Evangelical Awakening*, 355.
3. The open air preaching of these evangelical preachers was referred to in chapter 1.
4. Adam Taylor, *Memoirs*, 9.
5. Taylor, *Memoirs*, 10.
6. [Anon.]. Qtd in ibid., 30.
7. Taylor, *Memoirs*, 30.

General Baptists.[8] He appears to have been the first General Baptist of his generation to engage in open air preaching. This was not surprising given the resistance exhibited by many General Baptists to both the conversionist impulse of the Evangelical Revival and wider innovation and change.[9] The way in which Taylor modeled and endorsed field preaching soon led other General Baptists to embrace this method of evangelism. A notable convert was William Thompson—Taylor's close friend and colleague in the ministry. Through Taylor's influence, Thompson began open air preaching in 1771.[10] When Taylor received this news, he let Thompson know that his reaction was to "rejoice to hear that you are so hearty a friend to field preaching."[11] He then tried to persuade Thompson to visit him, emphasizing that "We have plenty of field room in the West Riding of Yorkshire."[12] Such a response was typical of Taylor's passion for the practice. Within the Baptist context, the significance of Taylor's adoption of open air preaching was also noteworthy due to the caution shown to field preaching by most Particular Baptists. When Taylor began his open air preaching in the early 1760s, there still existed opposition among many Particular Baptists to issuing indiscriminate gospel invitations.[13]

Similar to how Taylor's participation in the Evangelical Revival encouraged him to adopt field preaching, his years in Methodism led him to become active in the publication of tracts. While the distribution of tracts preceded the invention of the printing press,[14] evangelicals such as John Wesley printed and circulated religious tracts on a larger scale and to greater widespread effect.[15] As evident throughout this book, Taylor wrote tracts on subjects such as the importance of the Scriptures, baptism, the atonement, and process of conversion.[16] Distinct from the common practice of both the

---

8. For an examination of the history of open air preaching, see Byington, *Open-Air Preaching*.

9. This has been demonstrated throughout this book.

10. Taylor, *Memoirs*, 143.

11. Dan Taylor, "Letter to William Thompson," 4 September 1771, 143.

12. Ibid.

13. As examined in chapter 4, it was not until the later decades of the eighteenth century that an increasing number of Particular Baptist began to change their outlook on this matter.

14. For an examination of the history of tract distribution, see M'Clintock, and Strong, "Tracts and Tract Societies," 511–16.

15. The large scope of Wesley's tract distribution was emphasized by Richard Watson, his biographer. See R. Watson, *Life of John Wesley*, 513.

16. Examples that have previously been examined include Dan Taylor, *Absolute Necessity*; Dan Taylor, *Strictures*; Dan Taylor, *Friendly Conclusion*.

General Baptists and seventeenth-century Puritans, he often wrote specifically with non-believers in mind. Examples include his 1764 *The Absolute Necessity of Searching the Scriptures* where he emphasized how justification before God was only possible by faith, and then demonstrated that "This is a doctrine fully maintained in the Scriptures."[17] His 1777 publication of a tract entitled *Entertainment and Profit United* was also typical.[18] As the title states it was written *For the Use of Poor Children and Youth* and contained many Scriptures that he encouraged all children to commit to memory. This tract was "well received by the public," partly due to the "plain, honest, searching style which he adopted" whenever he wrote this form of literature.[19] Through his distribution of tracts, Taylor demonstrated a further notable means by which the gospel could be shared in a style and language that meaningfully connected with non-believers.

Taylor's belief in the evangelistic importance of tracts was such that, in addition to devising his own tracts, he actively encouraged the New Connexion to adopt the practice. He was explicit on this matter in a letter he wrote to the churches in 1801. As he urged them to take up this approach, he stated,

> You can take part with us in disseminating sacred knowledge by the distribution of small and useful Tracts for the instruction of the poor. Much, in the present age, is done in this way; and, so far as we can judge from report, to no small advantage.[20]

Taylor also commended the work of the Cheap Repository which, with a sizable contribution from the literary writer and evangelical moralist Hannah More, published a series of religious and political tracts between 1795–97.[21] He also drew attention to the Religious Tract Society which was established in 1799 to develop and distribute More's writings.[22] Taylor rejoiced at how tracts had been "widely circulated" by these bodies.[23] His

17. Taylor, *Absolute Necessity*, 4. The contents of this tract were examined in chapter 2.

18. Dan Taylor, *Entertainment and Profit*. Mention was made of this tract in chapter 3.

19. Taylor, *Memoirs*, 96.

20. Dan Taylor, "Concurrence of People," 19.

21. See ibid. For consideration of the significance of Hannah More, see Stott, *Hannah More*.

22. Taylor, "Concurrence of People," 19. For more detail on the Religious Tract Society, see W. Jones, *Jubilee Memorial*.

23. Taylor, "Concurrence of People," 19. For the commonplace nature of tract distribution within eighteenth-century evangelicalism, see Bebbington, *Evangelicalism*, 69.

appreciation of this was probably influential in the Connexion's own establishment of the Derby General Baptist Religious Tract Society in 1810.[24] Although little is known of its precise manner of functioning, its formation was in keeping with how tract distribution had become an increasingly commonplace feature of the evangelicalism of Taylor's day.

As Taylor impressed the merits of tracts on the members of the Connexion, he insisted that they "see the propriety of distributing these" and stressed the accessibility of this form of communication to the poor.[25] He noted,

> Many know not what to read; and will be glad to read any thing entertaining and useful; but know neither what to enquire for, nor how to pay for what they would wish to read. To many of these, your little presents will be acceptable; and many others, of a worse disposition, may, by proper means be induced to read them.[26]

This assertion indicates that one of the influencing factors to produce and distribute tracts was that they were an affordable means by which the poor could grow in their understanding of the faith.

It is significant that Taylor's endorsement of tracts in his 1801 letter to the churches was preceded by a strongly expressed lament concerning the poor condition of education. His strength of feeling on this matter was plainly apparent as he referred to it as "most abominably neglected."[27] He therefore urged the New Connexion to "exert ourselves by every means" so that they might "inform the minds" of others on all subjects.[28] Such sentiments exemplify Bebbington's observations that eighteenth-century evangelicals were "a force dedicated to the advance of education" and that the "fulfilment of religious duty was in harmony with the goal of eighteenth-century progressive thinkers: the enlightenment of the masses."[29] These convictions underpinned Taylor's active endorsement of both charity schools, and Sunday schools which during the last two decades of the century had become increasingly popular through the influence of Robert Raikes.[30] Also it should not be forgotten that Taylor, alongside his ministry at Birchcliff, both

24. See Adam Taylor, *New Connection*, 465.
25. Taylor, "Concurrence of People," 19.
26. Ibid.
27. Ibid.
28. Ibid.
29. Bebbington, *Evangelicalism*, 69.
30. For Taylor's support for Charity Schools and Sunday Schools, see Taylor, "Concurrence of People," 19.

founded and taught at a school that grew to a size of nearly fifty children.[31] Pupils who boarded came from different parts of the country.[32] It is therefore evident that Taylor's evangelistic passion for tract distribution should be placed within the context of the broader eighteenth-century educational framework and associated evangelical perceptions.

While Taylor's participation in field preaching and tract distribution provide examples of his willingness to engage in practical innovation for the advancement of the gospel, his establishment of the New Connexion was in itself an important expression of his entrepreneurship. This was not only apparent in the attention given throughout this book to its many innovative features, but also in how it comprised the pinnacle of his response to the missional inertia and theological drift from orthodoxy that he encountered among many General Baptists.[33] Even though his entrance into General Baptist life had seen him take every opportunity to challenge and stimulate his fellow ministers to develop a greater evangelistic passion, and to hold to that which he understood as the key tenets of the gospel, ultimately he held this approach as insufficient.[34] Instead, he viewed the development of a coordinated movement of churches as imperative, hence his establishment of the Connexion. This initiative was without precedent among the Baptists,[35] and was typical of how a propensity for evangelicals to pioneer had led to the emergence of wider bodies of believers, such as the different streams within Methodism. As John Coffey notes, these were similarly "devoted to propagating vital evangelical religion," and "coalesced around dynamic itinerant evangelists" like John Wesley, George Whitefield, and Howell Harris.[36] The Connexion was certainly in this mold.

A further point of commonality between Taylor's establishment of the New Connexion and wider evangelical emphases was the prominence of his hope that God would bring about a revival of repentance and faith.[37] This was central to the overarching goal that he set for the Connexion, that it might serve "To revive experimental religion or primitive Christian-

31. Taylor, *Memoirs*, 91. Taylor's establishment of a school was mentioned in the introductory chapter.

32. Typical was how Taylor received fourteen boarders to the school from Leicestershire in 1775, see ibid., 91.

33. These characteristics of wider General Baptist life have been highlighted throughout this book, particularly in chapter 2.

34. See chapter 2.

35. This was noted in chapter 5.

36. Coffey, "Puritanism," 276.

37. It was outlined in chapter 1 that the importance Taylor placed on the subject of revival was part of his missional spirituality.

ity in faith and practice."[38] He reinforced the importance of this regularly. A typical example was how shortly after Birley had assumed leadership responsibility for the General Baptist church in St Ives, Huntingdonshire in 1778, Taylor began a letter to him by writing "I am in hope you'll see the redeemer's interests revive at St Ives."[39] In this regard, Frank Rinaldi's description of the emergence of the Connexion exclusively in terms of a "theology of protest" against the "lack of conversion zeal on the part of the General Baptists" is somewhat insufficient.[40] Although Rinaldi refers to the Connexion as a *Revival Movement* in the title and contents of his publication and thesis he does not consider how the hope of further revival was so important to its *raison d'être*. Taylor's overriding motivation was for the Connexion to be a catalyst to effective mission and not, in the first instance, a tool of corrective theology.

The importance of revival within Taylor's thinking concerning the New Connexion was again apparent in his 1793 written response to General Baptist Messenger Gilbert Boyce's questions about the church growth experienced in the movement.[41] In addition to Taylor's emphasis on the need for a powerful preaching of Christ's death for all, he mentioned his underlying and constant hope that God would bring about "genuine reformation."[42] As he highlighted the Connexion's commitment to declaring the need for repentance and faith in Christ as the crucified Son of God, he was explicit that "in every age and in every part of the world where remarkable revivals have been known, they have been effected by a system which included this doctrine as a fundamental."[43] For Taylor, the "system" consisted of his evangelical convictions and particularly their espousal and articulation through the means of the Connexion as he sought to promote revival.

In summary, Taylor's willingness to engage in practical innovation for the cause of mission is evident in the way he embraced field preaching and tract distribution, and, most significantly, in his creation of the New Connexion. As will be demonstrated in the next section, it is also apparent in his dynamic approach to church planting.

---

38. *Assembly of Free Grace General Baptists*. Page not numbered.

39. Dan Taylor, "Letter to George Birley," 6 February 1778. Page not numbered.

40. Rinaldi, *Tribe of Dan*, 11.

41. As was noted in chapter 3, Taylor's response took the form of two letters. See Dan Taylor, "Letter I to Gilbert Boyce," 25 May 1793, in Taylor, *Memoirs*, 267–71; and Dan Taylor, "Letter II to Gilbert Boyce," 25 May 1793, in Taylor, *Memoirs*, 271–74.

42. Taylor, "Letter II to Gilbert Boyce," 25 May 1793, 273.

43. Ibid.

Taylor's Church Planting Initiatives

"the great Apostle of the Gentiles"

An aspect of Taylor's ministry where his strategic thinking and organizational development were vividly demonstrated was his role in the initial development and continued oversight of church planting across the New Connexion. The forming of new churches was an important part of the movement's work. Of the seventy churches that comprised the Connexion in 1817 (one year after Taylor's death), twenty were church plants from existing Connexion churches.[44] Taylor's involvement was pivotal from the beginning. He assumed a lead role in the emergence of the movement's first church plant in Queenshead, West Riding in 1773.[45] The venture began with Taylor engaging in open air preaching which led to the establishment of a preaching station in the home of an early convert.[46] This was followed by the enterprising adaptation of part of the Queenshead Inn as a place of worship, the transfer of seventeen members from Birchcliff, the construction of a meeting house in 1773 and appointment of a pastor—Taylor's brother John.[47] Given the "rapid growth" of the Queenshead fellowship, it is not surprising that the model of planting Taylor adopted became something of a prototype throughout the Connexion.[48] As described by Rinaldi, there was common acceptance that "The strategy was simple; there would be open air preaching during the summer months, followed by the renting of a room in winter."[49] This was a further reason why Taylor so enthusiastically encouraged the churches to adopt open air preaching. This is evident in his 1778 letter to the churches where he "strongly advised the churches to encourage their ministers to preach as often as they could, in the villages around their respective stations."[50] Taylor's "unabated zeal" for church planting "laid the foundation for the raising of churches in various places."[51] In addition to Queenshead, Taylor was personally involved in church planting in Burnley, Lancashire (1780), Shore, Lancashire (1795), Quorndon, Leices-

---

44. See Rinaldi, *Tribe of Dan*, 101.

45. This fellowship is today known as Queensbury Baptist.

46. Blomfield, "Yorkshire Baptist Churches," 106. The convert and owner of the home was John Bairstow.

47. See ibid.

48. Ibid. The growth of this fellowship to its 160 members by 1818 is noted by John Hargreaves. See Hargreaves, "Religion and Society," 111.

49. Rinaldi, *Tribe of Dan*, 98.

50. Dan Taylor, *Circular Letter 1778*, 10.

51. Taylor, *Memoirs*, 88, 31.

tershire (1804), and Duffield, Derbyshire (1810).[52] An unnamed colleague mentioned that, through Taylor's labors, "several meetings for prayer and Christian conference were established around the country" and "many were brought to repentance."[53] Such endeavors led General Baptist minister Robert Smith, in his tribute to Taylor at his funeral, to refer to him as "the great Apostle of the Gentiles."[54] This reflection was representative of the regard for Taylor as a skilled and dedicated apostle and entrepreneur.

Within Taylor's approach to church planting, he sought to ensure that the New Connexion made effective inroads into the fast developing working class communities found in the industrial towns and cities. Examples included the Connexion plants in Nottingham (1775), Halifax (1782), Birmingham (1786), and Derby (1789).[55] While Alfred Underwood pointed to how churches were planted in these places as evidence that the Connexion was "much more alive to the needs of the time" than other General Baptists, his failure to appreciate Taylor's extensive personal involvement and strategic coordination is illustrative of other commentators who have reflected on the Connexion's church planting.[56] The way Rinaldi describes the movement's church planting only in terms of G. Jackson's reference to it as involving "spontaneous extension of preaching to new centres," is similarly inadequate.[57] An example of the careful consideration that Taylor gave to the development of church plants is evident in the process by which, as mentioned earlier, a church was planted in Burnley. Taylor was the sole instigator of the 1779 decision to relocate one of the Connexion's preaching stations from Worsthorne, a village on the outskirts of Burnley, into the center of the town.[58] Indicative of his strategic approach was his assertion, in a letter to Thompson, that his motivations for this decision stemmed from his recognition that Burnley was now "a town of some note."[59] He proceeded to outline to Thompson that, for preaching purposes, he had therefore "ventured to hire a house in the market place" and was delighted to report that "The room is filled, and the prospect encouraging."[60] Taylor's optimism was

---

52. In 1889 Quorndom was shortened to Quorn.

53. [Anon.]. Qtd in Taylor, *Memoirs*, 88.

54. Taylor, *Memoirs*, 251.

55. As previously noted and is considered later in this paragraph, the development of a New Connexion church in Burnley was another significant example.

56. Alfred Underwood, *History of English Baptists*, 157.

57. G. Jackson "Evangelical Work," 276. Qtd in Rinaldi, *Tribe of Dan*, 108.

58. See Dan Taylor, "Letter to William Thompson," 29 October 1779, 102.

59. Ibid.

60. Ibid., 103.

well grounded with a church founded the following year and a steady ministry subsequently maintained. This achievement was notable, particularly given Taylor's initial candid observation that "The town is a wretched place; no religion in, or near it, that we know of. The Methodists have made several attempts there, I am told, but have always been beaten out."[61] John Wesley noted in a 1784 journal entry that the town had proved resistant to Methodist advances, stating "I went to Burnley, a place which had been tried for many years, but without effect."[62] The nature of church planting ventures, such as in Burnley, suggests the inappropriateness of assessments of the New Connexion's founding of new churches that fail to recognize Taylor's role as an enterprising and strategic thinker—particularly concerning the larger urban settings.

A further instructive example of Taylor's pioneering approach to church planting and his effective coordination of the New Connexion's churches in this endeavor, was his critical involvement in the establishment of the church in Derby. He first visited the town on 31 May 1789 and, typical of his normal practice when beginning evangelistic work in a new place, engaged in open air preaching.[63] He took as his text Luke 2:10 "I bring you good news that will cause great joy," and strategically positioned himself at Willow Row—a piece of open land which served as a busy thoroughfare due its close proximity to the central market place and prison.[64] This occasion was significant, for neither the General nor Particular Baptists had engaged in any evangelistic activity in the town.[65] Taylor was keen for his evangelistic efforts to be developed, and was thankful that Nathaniel and Thomas Pickering from the Connexion's Castle Donnington church followed his example by preaching regularly at Willow Row.[66] After this, services were held in the open air, and a room rented where the believers could meet and regular preaching begun.[67] However, tensions surrounded both the long-term ownership of the venture and its resourcing.[68] Again,

61. Ibid., 102.

62. John Wesley, Journal entry, 13 July 1784, 322. While records indicate the presence of a Methodist society in Burnley from 1763, this appears to have been very small, see B. Moore, *History of Wesleyan Methodism*, 53–56.

63. Taylor, *Memoirs*, 187.

64. Ibid.

65. Adam Taylor recorded that Dan Taylor's preaching visit was "the first time that a General Baptist minister had been heard at Derby," see Taylor, *Memoirs*, 187. It was not until 1794 that the first Particular Baptist chapel was opened in Derby (Agard Street).

66. See Wood, *Condensed History*, 193.

67. Ibid.

68. Ibid.

Taylor's intervention was crucial. He made the creative suggestion that the Connexion's churches in Castle Donnington, Melbourne, and Ilkeston together take responsibility for the successful birthing and consolidation of a church plant.[69] A rota of involvement was established across the three churches. By August 1791 nine people had been baptized and a church formed.[70] The determination, which underpinned the founding of this church, exposes doubts concerning the strength of Fred Harrison's claim that in the East Midlands the Connexion demonstrated "little indication" of the strategic significance of the industrial towns.[71] Instead, it should be confidently assumed that, as with the Burnley church plant, Taylor resolved to see the venture in Derby succeed as he was mindful of the need to establish a church in a town of such increasing significance, and that this reasoning was pivotal to his successful raising of support for the plant. In addition, two of the most significant decisions Taylor made in the course of his ministry, namely his moves to Halifax and then to London, were both underpinned by his understanding of the need to have growing New Connexion churches in places of influence.[72]

Taylor's development within the New Connexion of a vibrant evangelistic ethos, as reflected in its commitment to church planting, contrasted with the missional lethargy of many General Baptists outside of the movement. It also stood apart from the way in which Puritans typically engaged in mission. For example, the establishment of exclusively missional evangelical movements such as the New Connexion were distinct from the evangelistic efforts of Puritans, such as John Bunyan and Cotton Mather, or David Brainerd's evangelistic work with the Native Americans. These examples of Puritan activism are highlighted by commentators such as Michael Haykin, Douglas Sweeney, and Brandon Withrow in response to Bebbington's assertion that eighteenth-century evangelicals placed "new emphasis on mission."[73] While Bebbington, in turn, acknowledges that examples of evangelistic activism can be found prior to the 1730s, his basic standpoint remains unchanged.[74] This concerns his conviction that nothing emerged from within Puritan-

69. Ibid.

70. Ibid., 194.

71. Harrison, "Approach of the New Connexion," 16. Harrison states that they instead simply went to the towns "in due course," 16.

72. See Taylor, *Memoirs*, 113, 125–26.

73. Bebbington, *Evangelicalism*, 40. For Haykin's response to Bebbington and specific reference to Bunyan, and Mather, see Haykin, "Evangelicalism," 52. For the response of Douglas Sweeney and Brandon Withrow and their reference to Brainerd and Edwards, see Sweeney and Brandon, "Jonathan Edwards," 298–99.

74. Bebbington, "Response," 420.

ism akin to the "sustained character" of evangelistic endeavor as found in the missionary societies that developed towards the end of the eighteenth century.[75] The Connexion during the years of Taylor's oversight, and despite its initial focus solely on England, is a further example of the purposeful and continued commitment to evangelism to which Bebbington refers. The movement's embodiment of a dedicated and continuous primacy on the task of mission provides a glimpse of the same characteristics that assumed prominence in the later missionary societies.[76]

To summarize, Taylor's progressive and strategic approach to church planting exemplified his skills as a religious entrepreneur. It has been argued that his successful cultivation throughout the Connexion of a vigorous commitment to mission, while illustrative of that emanating from the eighteenth-century evangelical movement, differed from typical Puritan approaches to mission. The pioneering ways Taylor sought to nurture this all-pervading evangelistic ethos are considered in the next section.

Participation of the Laity in Evangelism

"helpers in Christ Jesus"

The way that the New Connexion embraced Taylor's innovative practices such as field preaching, tract distribution, and church planting is testimony to the extensive lay activity he successfully fostered throughout the movement. For this reason it is unfortunate that neither Taylor nor the Connexion are mentioned in Deryck Lovegrove's influential *The Rise of the Laity in Evangelical Protestantism*.[77] Taylor's missiology exemplified the "new orientation towards the laity" that Lovegrove describes as commonplace within eighteenth-century evangelicalism.[78] Taylor was convinced that the Connexion's goal of promoting a revival in experimental religion required an embracing of the task of evangelism by all its members. This was encapsulated his 1778 letter to the churches where he stated,

> It is therefore incumbent upon you, brethren, to walk humbly with God, and to act conscientiously before him, and zealously for him, in every situation, and in every relation, in which the Lord in the course of his wise providence, may place you. By

75. Ibid.

76. Consideration is given to the emergence of missionary societies in the final section of this chapter.

77. Lovegrove, *Rise of the Laity*.

78. Lovegrove, "Lay leadership," 120.

this means, your light will so shine before men, that they will see your good works, and glorify your Father, who is in heaven.[79]

Similarly, in 1795 he laid great importance on the involvement of every member concerning "the necessity of reminding our children, servants, and friends of their fallen condition and of the change they must experience in order to be truly happy."[80] Rinaldi commends Taylor's strategy in this area, stating "In addressing the personal responsibility of each member for the work of evangelism amongst friends and family, Taylor drew attention to a sphere of activity that was potentially most fruitful."[81] It is also notable that, unlike the seventeenth-century establishment of the role of General Baptist Messengers for the task of evangelism, no such office was created in the New Connexion.[82] Taylor's approach therefore differed from how, as Clint Bass notes, the influential seventeenth-century General Baptist minister Thomas Grantham believed that "evangelism be largely restricted to the service of messengers" with this and the Messenger's wider responsibilities "suggestive of a slightly hierarchical polity."[83] Neither did the offices of pastor, elder or deacon within the New Connexion's member churches include any extra responsibility for mission. Instead, this was viewed as a mandate for all believers.

Taylor expounded his understanding of the importance of the role of the laity in mission in his 1801 letter to the churches, entitled "The Concurrence of People with Their Pastors."[84] His starting place and whole thrust of the letter was the imperative that pastors and church members work together and fully involve themselves in evangelism.[85] He considered this "the most momentous object that can be placed before us."[86] In accordance with his conviction that it was collectively embraced, he insisted that "all engage, and that you will animate one another, in giving us all the assistance in the accomplishment of it of which you are capable; that you may be our 'helpers in Christ Jesus.'"[87] His belief in the essential role of laity in mis-

79. Taylor, *Circular Letter 1778*, 10–11.

80. Taylor, "Letter to the Churches," in *Minutes of an Association 1795*, 20.

81. Rinaldi, *Tribe of Dan*, 103.

82. The evangelistic focus of the seventeenth-century General Baptist Messengers was noted in chapter 2. The absence of the office of Messenger from within the structures of the New Connexion was considered in chapter 5.

83. Bass, *Thomas Grantham*, 52, 57.

84. See Taylor, "Concurrence of People," 15–22.

85. Ibid., 15.

86. Ibid.

87. Ibid.

sion was evident as he encouraged church members to share the gospel with non-believers on the basis that "for various reasons, what you say to such persons, is more likely to be acceptable and effectual, than the same things said by your ministers will probably be."[88] This view was important in his desire to see lay people released into evangelism.

Taylor was firm that all the Connexion's members should be active in sharing the gospel because "otherwise few will go out to seek it."[89] While this view reflected his non-determinate understanding of election, and belief that humankind's sinful condition was such that if the good news was not offered few would choose to embrace the truth, Enlightenment influences should not be overlooked. For instance, his emphasis on the assumption of individual responsibility for mission was in accord with the Enlightenment belief in the great transforming capacity of individual ability and initiative. Bruce Hindmarsh argues that "the rise of the laity within evangelicalism in the eighteenth century owed much to the appearance of a new individualism in modern society."[90] Although making no reference to Taylor or the Connexion, Hindmarsh's outlining of the emergence of "an articulate and involved laity" describes that found in the Connexion.[91] This provides a further example of how the defining facets of the evangelicalism of this period were replicated in Taylor's approach.

A prominent feature of Taylor's conviction that all believers engage in evangelism was the way he sought to facilitate this throughout the Connexion by developing a readiness to share the gospel in every situation. Taylor insisted that believers "contrive means of conveying the word of truth into every town and village; and if possible, into every neighbourhood, and every family."[92] As Rinaldi notes, it was "personal conversation about the gospel, by the members of the Connexion churches, that was key to the effectiveness of outreach."[93] Regarding non-believers, Taylor emphasized that "Opportunities for speaking to such persons, may often be found."[94] In the daily interactions of life, he accordingly encouraged believers to learn "the happy and beneficial art of directing the conversation, in as prudent and inoffensive manner as possible to spiritual subjects."[95] When church

88. Ibid., 20.

89. Ibid., 18.

90. Hindmarsh, "Reshaping Individualism," 81.

91. Ibid., 68.

92. Taylor, "Concurrence of People," 18.

93. Rinaldi, *Tribe of Dan*, 103.

94. Taylor, "Concurrence of People," 20.

95. Ibid., 18.

members visited the sick, he placed importance on "making your visits as spiritual as possible," emphasizing that "Affliction often disposes the mind to hear those things, with which the same person, who is under it, would, at another time be disgusted."[96] Travels to or from church were to be spent "conversing with those who do hear the gospel, but do not much understand it."[97] Similarly, "secular concerns" should not distract from the objective that "our glorious Redeemer's name may be made known in every corner of our land."[98] Taylor's aim was to mobilize a movement of believers into an intentional, evangelistic, and vigorous lay activism which included nearly every sphere of life.

The ways that Taylor shaped the New Connexion into a body of believers dedicated to evangelism are relevant to consideration of what was distinct about eighteenth-century evangelicalism. Taylor's approach suggests the inadequacy of reasoning that views the lay involvement of evangelicals as only a continuation of what was articulated in the Reformation by those such as Martin Luther. For example Carl Trueman argues that evangelical lay participation "must be understood as a development of the Reformation, not as an innovation of the Wesleys, Whitefield or whoever else."[99] However, the scope, strategic thinking, and all-embracing nature of the lay activity that Taylor successfully nurtured across the New Connexion differed from models of activism that were commonly applied only at an individual level by Puritans such as Richard Baxter.[100] The examples of activism in the post-reformation period that are closest to the ethos of the New Connexion are generally found in the eighteenth century, and include what Hindmarsh refers to as the "motivated laity" associated with John Wesley, George Whitefield, Henry Venn, John Newton, and the Moravians.[101] The weakness of Trueman's continuity argument is also suggested by how the seventeenth-century General Baptists, and those of Taylor's day who remained resistant to the Evangelical Revival, also held firmly to the doctrine of the priesthood of all believers, yet Taylor tended to outwork this doctrine in a more dynamic and progressive manner. For example, no similar movement to the New Connexion emerged among the seventeenth-century General Baptists.

96. Ibid., 21.

97. Ibid., 20.

98. Ibid., 18.

99. Trueman, "Reformers, Puritans and Evangelicals," 33.

100. For an overview of the nature of Richard Baxter's activism, see Baxter, *Practical Works.*

101. Hindmarsh, "Reshaping Individualism," 68.

The difference in approach can, at least in part, be accounted for by the nature of Taylor's platform of evangelicalism.

Further underlining the importance Taylor attached to laity was the priority he put on the regular accumulation of precise facts and figures concerning the activism of the New Connexion's membership and the growth of the whole movement. Taylor insisted that the churches annually record their main evangelistic enterprises, and provide statistics on the numbers of people newly baptized, admitted into membership, removed from membership, and the total current size of their churches.[102] This reflected the Enlightenment emphasis on the acquisition of empirical observation and evidence so that clear and seemingly objective judgments could be formed. In a rational and almost mechanistic manner, the statistics were discussed in detail at the annual Association and the "Total Increase" and "Total Decrease" of the Connexion's overall membership was calculated.[103] In addition, churches were expected to write reports that accounted for the figures they had submitted. The minutes of the 1787 annual Association in London provide a typical example. Although churches such as those in Castle Donnington and Long Sutton rejoiced at how they were "Well attended with hearers" and how "true religion is making gradual advances," others such as the church in Maltby referred to more difficult contexts with "Religion low" and "members decrease in number."[104] This empirical approach fostered a sense of collective accountability regarding the task of mission and should be viewed as an important contributor to the way in which the Connexion maintained its missional focus and its initial phase of continuous growth.[105]

Examination of the reports submitted by the New Connexion's churches to the Association demonstrates that the primacy on mission, which Taylor sought to engender, was widely emulated. It also reveals that where situations were difficult, there was often a resolve to see spiritual breakthrough. An example concerns the church in Kirkby Woodhouse, Nottinghamshire whose leaders lamented in 1787 that "the gospel has had so little success in this place for so many years past," but expressed their hope that "it is on the advance in some respects, as several young people seem to embrace the gospel."[106] It should be noted that once Taylor was provided with sufficient facts and observations from the churches, he was not afraid to challenge.

102. See, e.g., *Minutes of an Association 1787*, 6.

103. Ibid., 8.

104. Ibid., 8, 8, 10.

105. The movement's membership increased from 1,635 in 1770 to 3,715 in 1802, and then to 6,624 (as noted in the introductory chapter) by the time of Taylor's death in 1816, see Rinaldi, *Tribe of Dan*, 103.

106. *Minutes of an Association 1787*, 9.

For instance, in his 1802 letter concerning "Observations On The State of The Churches," he declared that when "conversion work goes on slowly" sometimes the reason for this is "in part in yourselves."[107] Taylor's empirically based approach fostered a culture of attention to mission, accountability, and challenge that was without comparison within the context of eighteenth-century General Baptist life.

The greater intensity towards mission developed by Taylor throughout the New Connexion, compared to that found among the older body of General Baptists of his day, led to several of the long established General Baptist churches that had joined the Connexion at its inception to withdraw. James Wood, for example, noted how the General Baptist churches in Essex and Kent "in a short time, relinquished their connexion."[108] This was carefully considered by Rinaldi who noted that these churches "were not comfortable with the evangelistic demands that membership of the Connexion entailed."[109] There was possibly a dislike towards Taylor's previously highlighted wish for the production of statistics, which carried with it a pressure to be experiencing numerical growth, or at least to have the expectancy that this would soon occur. While those General Baptists who withdrew were sufficiently orthodox in their belief to have been accepted into the Connexion, it appears that the priority Taylor placed on the need for all members to be seeking the personal conversion of their family, friends, and colleagues was uncomfortable for some churches. Taylor's evangelistic stance was indicative of the approach to personal conversion that was prevalent among eighteenth-century evangelicals. Although commentators such as Hindmarsh identify the emergence of a personal "conversion narrative" among the mid-seventeenth-century Puritans that was akin to that found in eighteenth-century evangelicalism, distinct features of the evangelicalism of Taylor's day were the intensely vigorous and enterprising ways that the conversion of others was sought, and its dependence on lay activism.[110]

In summary, the importance Taylor attributed to lay activism was an essential element of his approach to mission. Outside of the eighteenth century, such an extensive mobilization of a whole movement of believers, who intentionally shared their faith in a variety of different contexts, was unusual in the post reformation period. Taylor's approach did, however, share some common emphases with other movements of his era. A further

107. Taylor, "Letter to the Churches," in *Minutes of an Association 1802*, Angus Library and Archives. Page not numbered.

108. Wood, *Condensed History*, 180.

109. Rinaldi, *Tribe of Dan*, 43.

110. Hindmarsh, *Evangelical Conversion Narrative*, vi.

central aspect of his missiology was his commitment to working together with believers outside of the New Connexion. This will be examined next.

Cooperation for the Sake of Mission

"there are some . . . of every denomination, who
'worship him in spirit and truth'"

A further distinctive facet of Taylor's approach to mission was his determination to develop close relations with believers outside of the New Connexion. These included General Baptists, with Taylor regularly ministering in General Baptist churches in places such as Poplar, London.[111] The extent to which Taylor sought to strengthen the ministry and mission of the General Baptists outside of the Connexion should not be underestimated. The minutes of the 1789 General Baptist Assembly of the older body of General Baptists contain reference to the acceptance of "A plan proposed by Brother Taylor to supply vacant places" in their churches that lacked ministers.[112] This plan likely acted as a catalyst in Taylor's later decision to deploy the Connexion's Academy students to this end (see next section). Taylor remained active among wider General Baptist churches even beyond his 1803 withdrawal from its Assembly. This is significant, for the commonly accepted assumption of those such as Underwood is that Taylor ceased all further involvement at this time.[113] However, Taylor ministered at the General Baptist church in Salisbury in 1806, demonstrating such a commitment that the New Connexion's Association charged him with the task of "forming a plan for future operations."[114] He was active in 1816 among the General Baptists of Kent where, as Adam Taylor detailed, "a considerable attention to the distinguishing truths of the gospel had been excited . . . Mr. T. was earnestly invited to pay them a visit in order to strengthen their hands."[115] Taylor's willingness to partner in these wider General Baptist interests reflected his generous disposition to associate with General Baptists outside of the Connexion, despite what he considered to be striking denominational failings such as the 1802 acceptance

---

111. See Taylor, *Memoirs*, 221.

112. *Proceedings of General Assembly, June 3d, 1789*, 4. It has not proved possible to locate this plan.

113. See Underwood, *History of English Baptists*, 156.

114. Taylor, *Memoirs*, 229.

115. Ibid., 244–45.

into its Assembly of William Vidler.[116] In keeping with what commentators such as Roger Martin identify as an increasingly common characteristic of the evangelicals of this period, Taylor sought to cut across denominational affiliations and unite with others who shared a commitment to the spread of the gospel.[117] This was in contrast to the tendency for insularity found among the wider General Baptists of his day.[118]

Taylor also cultivated rich friendships with Particular Baptists. In addition to his previously examined relationships with John Fawcett Sr. and John Sutcliff,[119] he became particularly close to Abraham Booth, minister of Prescot Street Church, London.[120] After Taylor moved to London he initiated contact with Booth.[121] This is notable as Booth was previously a General Baptist and had rejected Taylor's 1768 efforts to persuade him to remain in the denomination.[122] Taylor's actions were typical of the generosity he extended to mission-minded believers of other denominations. Subsequently, they developed a "very cordial friendship" with their "common bond of union" emphasized by Taylor.[123] Booth died in 1806 and his family asked Taylor to collate a catalog of his works.[124] Despite their differences regarding the scope of the atonement, Taylor claimed that they never shared an "unpleasant word" but instead recognized that "there were other subjects on which we were agreed, we could converse with more pleasure and to greater advantage."[125] Given Booth's support for the formation of the Particular Baptist Missionary Society and his involvement in the London Baptist Educational Society,[126] it is likely that an exchange of ideas on mission and

116. Taylor's disapproval of Vidler's acceptance into the Assembly was noted in chapter 3.

117. See H. R. Martin, *Evangelicals United*.

118. The common place insularity of the wider General Baptists has been noted throughout this book.

119. Taylor's relationship with Fawcett and Sutcliff was examined in chapter 3.

120. For an overview of Abraham Booth's life and ministry, see Payne, "Abraham Booth," 28–42. Helpful reflections are also found in Haykin and Haykin, *"First Counsellor of Our Denomination"*.

121. Taylor, *Memoirs*, 207.

122. Adam Taylor recorded how Booth stayed at Taylor's Yorkshire home prior to joining the Particular Baptists, see ibid., 301.

123. Dan Taylor, "Tribute to Booth," in Taylor, *Memoirs*, 301.

124. Taylor, *Memoirs*, 229.

125. Taylor, "Tribute to Booth," 301.

126. For Booth's involvement in these areas, see Payne, "Abraham Booth," 37, 40.

ministerial training, subjects so precious to Taylor, would have been central to the "many agreeable and profitable hours" they spent together.[127]

A further significant point of agreement shared by Taylor and Booth was their disapproval of the slave trade. Booth followed the examples of Particular Baptists, such as Robert Robinson and James Dore, in being active within the Christian abolitionist movement that emerged at the end of the eighteenth century.[128] Taylor wrote forcibly in favor of abolition in 1795 and his arguments reflected those outlined by Booth in his influential 1792 sermon entitled *Commerce in the Human Species*.[129] Taylor referred to the "abominable" trade as a contravention of humankind's shared equality and liberty before God.[130] He argued that England would "become the object of divine vengeance" unless its people opposed the practice.[131] In addition, he was strong in his condemnation of its "glaring and horrid enormities" as family members were "torn from one another," "stowed up in ships" and treated "with the utmost barbarity."[132] Taylor's respect for Booth led him to send his Academy students to hear him preach. One such example was the New Connexion minister Joseph Goadby, who trained at the Academy for six months in 1798, and recorded how he was sent to listen to Booth who he described as teaching a "rigid Calvinism."[133] It is conceivable that these visits were suggested by Taylor due to how, as Goadby's biographers suggested, "Much talk must have taken place around Dan Taylor's table about the possible abolition of the Slave Trade," and Booth's status as "one of the first in England to declare the trade a sin and advocate the freedom of the slaves."[134] Although Christian social concern has been found in every age of the church, there is much credence to Bebbington's assertion that the Enlightenment's regard for "Benevolence, happiness and liberty, three leading principles of the time, all created a presumption in favour

127. Taylor, "Tribute to Booth," 301.

128. For reflection on Booth's role within the abolitionist movement, see Coffey, "Abolition of the slave trade," 1–6. Robert Robinson was a leading Baptist in Cambridge and James Dore was pastor of Maze Pond Baptist Church, London.

129. Booth, *Commerce in the Human Species*, in Booth, *Works*, 3:185–219. As noted by Ernest Payne, the slavery abolitionist Thomas Clarkson viewed this sermon as one of the most important documents in the early stage of the anti-slavery movement, see Payne, "Abraham Booth," 37.

130. Dan Taylor, *Cause of National Calamities*, 20.

131. Ibid.

132. Ibid., 20, 21, 20.

133. Joseph Goadby, diary entry, in Bertha Goadby, and Lilian Goadby, *Not Saints but Men*, 37. It should be noted that Goadby's diary entries are not dated in this publication.

134. Ibid.

of abolition."[135] These principles underpinned Taylor's abolitionist stance. They were also apparent in Taylor's advocacy for the need to safeguard "the comfort of the industrious poor," which provides another example of his concern for social welfare.[136]

Another Particular Baptist minister with whom Taylor enjoyed a "long and intimate friendship" was Samuel Stennett, pastor of the church at Little Wild Street, London.[137] Taylor's diary and personal correspondence contain many references to them meeting together. Examples include his diary entry on 6 August 1784 where he noted "I dined with Dr. Stennett," and a reference in a 1788 letter to George Birley that "I spent yesterday with Dr. Stennett."[138] Considering Stennett was among the more progressive Particular Baptists who endorsed Andrew Fuller's belief that the gospel be preached to all, it can be confidently assumed that Taylor and Stennett were united by this shared imperative. The importance they put on mission almost certainly accounts for how according to Taylor, Stennett believed there was "very little different in judgement between him and me," despite their different positions regarding the extent of Christ's atoning work.[139] It also likely explains Stennett's keenness that Taylor might "spend a day with him, and preach for him."[140] Given Taylor's contention that the "grand end" of a minister's calling was the conversion of poor perishing sinners,"[141] he therefore had no hesitation in entitling the sermon he published in honor of Stennett's life—*A Good Minister of Jesus Christ*.[142] As in his relationship with Booth, it is significant that despite Taylor's key motivation for mission stemming from his general view of the atonement, he refused to let this form a barrier between Stennett and himself.[143] This pragmatic, respectful, and mission-orientated way of proceeding was in contrast to the combative attitudes that had tended to characterize General and Particular Baptist relations.[144]

---

135. Bebbington, *Evangelicalism*, 71.

136. Taylor, *Cause of National Calamities*, 38.

137. Taylor, *Memoirs*, 210.

138. Dan Taylor, "Letter to William Thompson," 6 August 1784, 159; Dan Taylor, "Letter to George Birley," 30 August 1788, 257.

139. Dan Taylor, "Letter to William Thompson," 4 July 1778, 153.

140. Ibid.

141. Dan Taylor, "Letter to George Birley," 3 November 1777. Page not numbered.

142. Dan Taylor, *Good Minister*. Mention was made to this publication in chapter 5.

143. The centrality of Taylor's understanding of a general view of the atonement to the spread of the gospel was examined in chapter 3.

144. This was also noted in chapter 3, particularly regarding Taylor's harmonious relationship with John Fawcett Sr.

Taylor sought to foster an approach to mission based on a realization of the common perspectives that existed across the evangelical tradition. This was typified in a 1789 sermon where he stated,

> Blessed be God, there are some, I trust, of every denomination, who 'worship him in spirit and truth' . . . whose hearts are right with God; whose families, whose closets, and whose consciences, have repeatedly witnessed their concern for our national welfare.[145]

Such generous and inclusive sentiments reflect Bebbington's assertion that an "interdenominational temper" emerged within evangelicalism that sometimes enabled the "abandonment of exclusive denominationalism."[146] Even commentators such as John Coffey, who points to a "rejection of party spirit" also having been apparent among Puritans such as Oliver Cromwell and Richard Baxter, acknowledge that "the difference is one of degree."[147] Coffey notes that ecumenical hopes were "more fully realized in the eighteenth century than in the seventeenth."[148] Taylor embodied the greater degree of resolve for ecumenical relations that emanated from the eighteenth-century evangelical movement.

Taylor gladly united in the cause of mission with several Independent ministers. The most noteworthy example is how the New Connexion was formed through Taylor's partnering with the group of Independent churches of Arminian conviction that were associated with the fellowship in Barton-in-the-Beans.[149] The readiness of these churches to innovate would have been known to Taylor and very likely formed a further reason for his willingness to enter into partnership. Both their church planting, and evangelistic practices, perpetuated the entrepreneurship that had been modeled by their founder, David Taylor, who engaged in practices such as open air preaching.[150] Samuel Deacon Sr., minister of the Barton fellowship and with whom Taylor developed a good friendship, was converted through David Taylor's field preaching.[151]

Taylor worked closely with Independent ministers who were of Calvinist persuasion. An example was his "intimate and uninterrupted" friendship

---

145. Dan Taylor, *Interposition of Providence*, 16. Taylor noted that his reference to worshiping God in spirit and truth was from John 4:24.

146. Bebbington, *Evangelicalism*, 66.

147. Coffey, "Puritanism," 269.

148. Ibid.

149. The nature of this partnership was examined in chapter 5.

150. See Godfrey, *Historic Memorials*, 12.

151. Ibid., 4.

with John Kello, minister of the Congregational church in Bethnal Green, London.[152] Kello confessed to having initially felt "great prejudice" towards Taylor.[153] His familiarity with the theological drift of many General Baptists had led him to presume that Taylor's "views and preaching were deficient in point of evangelical savour."[154] It is conceivable that Kello had never met a General Baptist of firm evangelical conviction. Kello was therefore relieved when he discovered that Taylor shared an "adherence to the grand truths, which are the foundation of a Christian's faith."[155] He held a deep regard for how Taylor's "charity" and generous disposition enabled their friendship to be "promoted, strengthened and confirmed."[156] The sincerity of Kello's comments was further underlined by his important role at Taylor's funeral where he led the procession of mourners and delivered a tribute at his graveside to the "piety, humility and activity of his departed friend."[157] The fact that Taylor and Kello met weekly to pray for "the state of our nation" should also not be overlooked.[158] Again, this points to the pre-eminence Taylor placed on mission in his ecumenical friendships.

A further indicator of the importance Taylor attached to the development of strong relationships with those outside of the Connexion was his active involvement in some cross-denominational groups. In 1787, he joined the General Body of Protestant Dissenting Ministers which met at Dr. Williams's Library and comprised Congregationalists, Presbyterians, and Baptists both from London and its vicinity.[159] An important component of its work was consideration of issues relevant to the spread of the gospel in the capital. In addition, it took seriously that which was central to the reason for its formation in 1727—namely the need to provide representation of the interests and viewpoints of Dissenters before Parliament and the King.[160] Taylor was a member of two of its committees.[161] The respect he commanded was evident in 1800 when he was chosen, among a small group of ministers, to offer "congratulatory addresses" before King

152. John Kello, "Tribute to Taylor," in Taylor, *Memoirs*, 307.

153. Ibid., 302.

154. Ibid.

155. Ibid.

156. Ibid.

157. Taylor, *Memoirs*, 251.

158. Kello, "Tribute to Taylor," 302.

159. Taylor, *Memoirs*, 185.

160. For more on the function and resolutions of the General Body of Protestant Dissenting Ministers, see Protestant Dissenting Ministers of the Three Denominations, *At a Numerous and Respectable Meeting.*

161. Taylor, *Memoirs*, 220.

George III who had survived an assassination attempt in the May of that same year.[162] As a supporter of the King, Taylor humbly noted that this episode brought him a "measure of pleasure."[163] It is conceivable that Taylor also welcomed this opportunity to demonstrate that Dissenters were not necessarily interested in furthering the cause of revolution. Taylor's involvement in wider ecumenical groups was further apparent in his weekly attendance, from 1803 onwards, at a prayer meeting that comprised dissenting ministers.[164] His willingness to serve in these ways again demonstrated his desire to model an understanding of mission that was outworked beyond fixed denominational boundaries.

In summary, Taylor's entrepreneurship was apparent in the importance he placed on working in the cause of mission with believers outside of the New Connexion. This was practically embodied in the priority he placed on ministering in wider General Baptist churches, the time he invested in friendships with different Particular Baptists, and his fostering of relationships with Independent believers. Taylor was also very active within certain cross-denominational groups which he viewed as important in the task of mission. Taylor placed importance on how working with believers of other denominations would lead to more effective mission. This emphasis was a feature of eighteenth-century evangelicalism which, by degree, surpassed that found within earlier Christian movements such as Puritanism. It will be seen next that the task of mission also influenced Taylor's establishment of the General Baptist Academy.

Formation of the General Baptist Academy

"Enlarged scenes now open on our view"

Taylor's establishment of the General Baptist Academy in 1797 was one of the most significant achievements of his ministry. It was a landmark in the New Connexion's approach to training. Its process of formation and way of functioning exemplified Taylor's enterprising spirit. He originally proposed the establishment of an academy for the training of ministers at the 1779 annual Association.[165] While his precise recommendations are unclear, as there appears to be no surviving copy of the proposal, the As-

162. Ibid. This significant moment in Taylor's life was noted in the introductory chapter.

163. Dan Taylor, "Letter," (addressee and date not specified), in Taylor, *Memoirs*, 220.

164. Taylor, *Memoirs*, 225.

165. See *Association 1779*. Page not numbered.

sociation was at that time unwilling to embrace the initiative. It preferred to maintain the status quo of the churches being generally led by those with little education and lack of theological training.[166] In contrast, Taylor was resolute about the need for change. He recognized that, as a consequence of the movement's growth and planting of new churches, there was a large shortfall in the provision of training to meet the demand for new ministers. Taylor referred to this as "a common and affecting complaint" and drew attention to how "as we increase in number of meeting places, we need not wonder that it is so."[167] He was therefore convinced of the need to develop a more rigorous approach to training that went beyond his mentoring of prospective ministers.[168]

Alongside Taylor's appreciation of the need for a different approach to training was his growing unease at what he perceived as a deficit of biblical knowledge throughout the New Connexion. He referred to "the ignorance on religious subjects, which prevails in too many professors" and viewed this as "lamentable."[169] His anxiety regarding the implications this might have for mission was apparent. This was evident in his declaration that "You cannot talk, with propriety, on a subject which you do not understand."[170] The link between a grasp of the essentials of the faith and effective sharing of the gospel was at the core of his hopes for an academy. This was reflected in his 1800 address to the annual Association when he expressed his desire that the academy would enable students to acquire "literary and theological knowledge," and lead to "the conversion of sinners, and the greater extension of the kingdom of our Lord Jesus Christ."[171] This suggests the need for caution regarding Rinaldi's claim that the Academy's establishment was a product of the Connexion's "developing denominationalism" and priorities being diverted away from mission "As the power of the Evangelical Revival began to wane."[172] Instead, Taylor viewed the formation of an academy as essential in helping to maintain and extend a powerful proclamation of the gospel.

Despite the Association's initial failure to support the formation of an academy, Taylor still took the first steps in pursuit of the venture. He

166. See Rinaldi, *Tribe of Dan*, 158.

167. Taylor, "Letter to the Churches," in *Minutes of an Association 1802*. Page not numbered.

168. The importance Taylor placed on mentoring was noted in chapter 5.

169. Taylor, "Concurrence of People," 17.

170. Ibid.

171. Taylor, "Address in Behalf of the Academy," in *Minutes of an Association 1800*, 14.

172. Rinaldi, *Tribe of Dan*, 158.

established a fund for the assistance of young ministers who wished to undergo training.[173] This was the sole instance that he ever proceeded on a significant initiative without the Association's specific support. It is apt that Adam Taylor described his nephew as sometimes acting "with a pertinacity which bordered on obstinacy."[174] As well as Taylor's determination stemming from his conviction of the necessity of an academy for the continued spread of the gospel, it perhaps also reflected his unwillingness to allow the Association to thwart the outworking of his organizational energies and desire to innovate. In addition, Taylor was probably spurred on by developments in training that were undertaken among the Particular Baptists. It is likely that the regular letters he received from his good friend John Sutcliff, during Sutcliff's studies at Bristol Baptist Academy in the early 1770s,[175] kept him informed that Hugh Evans's establishment of the Bristol Education Society in 1770 had led to an expansion of the college's training capacity and wider work.[176] A further example of the emphasis on training among Particular Baptists was Sutcliff's own establishment of an academy dedicated to the training of missionaries within the Particular Baptist Missionary Society.[177] Given that Sutcliff's friendship with Taylor continued to develop since their time together in the West Riding, he probably drew on Taylor's valuable experience as he began to provide personal tutelage. The way Sutcliff also interlinked mission so closely with the establishment of a training academy indicates that this was not a phenomenon personal to Taylor, but a further emerging characteristic of late eighteenth-century evangelicalism.

In 1796, the annual Association finally recommended that a means be developed by which prospective ministers could be trained.[178] The next year saw explicit endorsement given to the establishment of a training academy "to instruct young men in biblical knowledge, in order to fit them for

173. See Dan Taylor, "Letter to Birley," 6 August 1779, in Taylor, Memoirs, 103.

174. Taylor, Memoirs, 321.

175. Adam Taylor referred to Sutcliff when he stated that "Mr. T. corresponded with his young friend while at the academy," see Taylor, Memoirs, 33. Taylor's friendship with Sutcliff was considered in chapter 3.

176. For an overview of the origins of the Bristol Education Society, see Bristol Education Society, Account of the Bristol Education Society. See also Moon, Education for Ministry; Foreman, "Baptist Provision for Ministerial Education in the 18th Century," 363.

177. The academy was established in 1798 after Sutcliff was approached to begin the venture by the executive committee of the Baptist Missionary Society, see Haykin, One Heart and One Soul, 251–54. Sutcliff trained at least thirty-three people, most notably—William Carey and William Robinson, see Foreman, "Baptist Provision for Ministerial Education in the 18th Century," 366.

178. See Taylor, New Connection, 330.

the work of the ministry."[179] A commitment was also made to establish a permanent fund for the purposes of training and into which churches and individuals were encouraged to make financial contributions. Unsurprisingly, Taylor deemed this a momentous decision. He spoke, in visionary language, of the "Enlarged scenes now open on our view," and the "abundant blessings" that would be experienced for "many generations to come."[180] Rinaldi accounts for the Association's eventual decision in favor of an academy as it realized its necessity due to the Connexion's growth in members and respectability, and the challenge from the wider General Baptists who had revived their original 1702 plan for a training college.[181] Unfortunately, Rinaldi makes no mention of Taylor's influence. He fails even to acknowledge Taylor's proposal for an academy made to the Association in 1779 (as previously noted). Adam Taylor stated that the proposal gained increasing "credit and reputation" due to the way Taylor "laboured much to promote it at almost every association."[182] This relentlessness means that Taylor should be viewed as a key catalyst in the Association's decision to pursue a more rigorous approach to training.

The Academy began functioning in 1797 with Taylor accepting the position of tutor, opening his home in Mile End, London for this purpose.[183] His determination that the Academy would promote a new depth of learning was reflected in the earnestness with which he approached his preparation. This is apparent in Adam Taylor's description of how "He read authors, made extracts, consulted and corresponded with persons who had been employed in the same work, and took every method, which his opportunities afforded him, to render himself, in some measure, equal to the task."[184] This illustrates the activism that characterized so much of his evangelicalism. Significantly, the chief focus of his teaching was the instilling of practical skills for ministry. This is evident within the recollections of Joseph Goadby who, as highlighted earlier, underwent training at the Academy. Goadby recorded that morning lectures typically included "The Work of the Ministry" and the "Art of Sermon Making."[185] A similar practical orientation is evident in Adam Taylor's description of what was taught. He had access to

179. Ibid.

180. Taylor, "Address in Behalf of the Academy," 14.

181. Rinaldi, *Tribe of Dan*, 158. For more details of the developments surrounding the General Baptist training college, see Foreman, "Baptist Provision for Ministerial Education in the 18th Century," 362–63.

182. Taylor, *New Connection*, 215.

183. See Taylor, *Memoirs*, 216.

184. Ibid., 314.

185. Joseph Goadby, diary entry, in Goadby, and Goadby, *Not Saints but Men*, 32.

the outline of 135 of Taylor's lectures and noted that these included subjects such as the most effective forms of preaching delivery, styles of exhortation, choice of appropriate texts, and the development of wider disciplines such as scriptural remembrance.[186]

While Taylor's lectures included themes such as how the Scriptures should best be studied, the chronology of the Bible, prophecy, and prayer, it is notable that Goadby and Adam Taylor made no mention of Taylor lecturing on biblical doctrine. Although the absence of an exhaustive list of all that was taught means that this possibility cannot be entirely precluded, a neglect of any mention of doctrinal themes was in keeping with Taylor's aversion to becoming embroiled within the intricacies of doctrine—particularly once he was assured that his listeners had a good grasp of the fundamentals. This was something that he repeatedly reinforced, such as in a 1788 letter to George Birley when, in response to an unspecified doctrinal question from Birley, Taylor stated "I have neither time nor taste for controversy."[187] Taylor's greater priority was the provision of practical forms of training and nurture that he deemed most relevant to the spread of the gospel. For this reason, a further emphasis in his program of teaching was his series of lectures on "The Evidences of Christianity."[188] Given that which was outlined earlier in this book, this subject likely included Taylor's Enlightenment-inspired regard for the *reasoned* basis on which he believed the Bible should be viewed as the word of God, and how people's *observation and experience* of sin pointed to the need of a savior.[189] Equipping prospective ministers to explain the evidence for their faith complemented Taylor's hope that the Academy would help churches in their evangelistic endeavors.

A further distinctive dynamic of Taylor's training was the importance he placed on wider academic disciplines. Adam Taylor and Goadby noted the inclusion of English, History, Geography, and Moral Philosophy.[190] While Taylor's willingness to teach on these subjects reflected his awareness that most of the students had "few advantages of education previous to their admission," it is a further indicator that he was influenced by one of the prime motors of the Enlightenment—namely that human beings could be improved through education and the development of their rational

186. Taylor, *Memoirs*, 315. It has not proved possible to locate any surviving manuscripts of these lectures.

187. Dan Taylor, "Letter to George Birley," 10 May 1788. Page not numbered.

188. Taylor, *Memoirs*, 315.

189. These emphases were highlighted in chapter 2.

190. Taylor, *Memoirs*, 315; Joseph Goadby, diary entry, in Goadby, and Goadby, *Not Saints but Men*, 32.

faculties.[191] Taylor impressed on his students the need to gain knowledge of many different forms. For this reason, he sent Goadby and James Taylor (Dan Taylor's nephew) to visit Adam Taylor in Shadwell who, as Goadby noted, "gave us a lecture on the 'latitudes and longitudes' and the 'diurnal and periodical revolutions of the earth.'"[192] It is also notable that Taylor included logic on the syllabus.[193] Goadby stated that part of his training included writing as a "school exercise" an abridgement of Isaac Watts's *Logic; Or the Right Use of Reason*.[194] The way Taylor sought to develop this skill among his students resonated with wider cultural emphases. Although the discipline of logic dated back to the ancient Greeks, and was commonplace in subsequent periods such as medieval scholasticism, it was again brought to the fore during the Enlightenment. John Locke, for instance, included an exposition of the "new way of ideas" in *An Essay Concerning Human Understanding* and the same epistemological principles were found in the works of René Descartes, Nicolas Malebranche, and the logicians of the Port-Royal school.[195] The way the Academy's syllabus included the increasing prominence given to logic and the general pursuit of knowledge that was often evident in the eighteenth century, underlines the extent to which Taylor's approach to the process of ministerial formation was alive to the spirit of the age.

Taylor's belief that the need to train ministers in ways that were in keeping with the cultural ethos of his day was a vital prerequisite for effective mission provides an important response to those who have expressed puzzlement as to why he devoted his time to the development of the Academy. For example, this aspect of Taylor's thinking appears to have been unknown to Peter Shepherd who stated his surprise at Taylor's willingness to stand "behind the lectern of a classroom" given that so much of his wider time was spent "trampling the moors of the North to a preaching station, or engaging in a lively debate with an opponent."[196] Taylor's desire for his students to engage meaningfully with their surroundings was further apparent in Goadby's reflections that Taylor expected them to take a "walk of two hours each day around London."[197] Visits were made to places such as St.

---

191. Taylor, *Memoirs*, 315.

192. Joseph Goadby, diary entry, in Goadby and Goadby, *Not Saints but Men*, 37. It was noted in the introductory chapter that Adam Taylor was a schoolmaster.

193. Ibid., 33.

194. Ibid. See Isaac Watts, *Logic*.

195. Locke, *Essay Concerning Human Understanding*, 6. See also Yolton, "John Locke," 431; Lennon, "Locke," 155–77.

196. Shepherd, *Making of a Northern Baptist College*, 25.

197. Joseph Goadby, diary entry, in Goadby, and Goadby, *Not Saints but Men*, 33.

James's Palace where the students stood among many thousands watching an appearance of King George III, the House of Commons to listen to the Prime Minister William Pitt "the younger," the British Museum, a Jewish funeral, and a public hanging.[198] The significance of this enterprising aspect of the training Taylor provided should not be underestimated. Goadby implied that it was of great importance in the students' development. The returning students likely spoke with Taylor about all they had witnessed and how the gospel could be shared relevantly in such contexts.

In 1799, Taylor chose to hire a property close to Mile End for worship so that his students could have "an opportunity of exercising their ministerial abilities."[199] This was in keeping with his propensity for starting new ventures. The seriousness with which this endeavor was undertaken is evident in how it soon became a growing New Connexion church.[200] Taylor also secured preaching opportunities for his students at struggling General Baptist churches such as in Hoddesdon, Hertfordshire,[201] and the Park meeting house in Southwark.[202] Neither of these churches were, at that time, members of the Connexion, which again reflects the expansive experience that Taylor was keen to give to his students. It also demonstrates his desire to foster within them a willingness to develop good ecumenical relations. The church in Southwark was transformed into a "reviving society," helped to erect its own building, and subsequently joined the Connexion.[203] This provides further evidence of the vibrancy of faith and commitment to the gospel that emanated from the Academy.

To summarize, Taylor's establishment of the General Baptist Academy demonstrated his entrepreneurial skills and ways in which his evangelicalism was influenced by certain Enlightenment values. This is apparent in how the Academy functioned, the nature of the syllabus, the emphasis on the development of practical skills, and engagement with different aspects of life that Taylor sought to ensure that the students were exposed to through their travels around London and preaching visits to other churches. This was all undergirded by a belief that the Academy was essential to mission. As will be examined next, a similar commitment to the spread of the gospel was foundational to Taylor's belief that the New Connexion should establish a missionary society.

198. See ibid., 32–40.

199. Taylor, *Memoirs*, 218.

200. Ibid., 221.

201. Ibid., 217.

202. Ibid., 218.

203. Ibid.

Development of the General Baptist Missionary Society

"What is to be done that the interest of our Redeemer
may be advanced in the world?"

Another area of Taylor's ministry, where his evangelicalism was outworked in a ground-breaking way, was his involvement in establishing the General Baptist Missionary Society in 1816. Its creation is testimony to the truth of Brian Stanley's assertion that "The eighteenth-century Protestant missionary awakening was intimately associated with the birth of evangelicalism."[204] While commentators such as Glyn Prosser have focused on the Society's emergence with reference to its first secretary, the New Connexion minister John Pike (1784-1854),[205] Taylor's contribution has regularly been overlooked. Rinaldi's brief examination of the Society does not even include any mention of Taylor.[206] This is a significant omission, for Taylor was an important catalyst to its formation. He chaired the crucial June 1816 annual Association in Boston where the forty-five representatives of the movement unanimously passed the resolution that paved the way for its creation. The resolution unequivocally confirmed that the Association "heartily approves of a foreign General Baptist Mission and recommends it to the friends of the measure to form themselves immediately into a society for the prosecution of this important object."[207] This was very significant as it led to General Baptists being sent into world mission for the first time, particularly to countries such as India, China, and the West Indies.

Taylor's efforts to raise awareness of God's concern for the nations contributed to the Association's unanimous support for establishing the Society. A typical example is found within *Cause of National Calamities* where he drew attention to how "The eyes of God are continually upon all the nations of the earth, and upon every individual among men in every station, and of every rank and character."[208] Even more importantly, it was something he specifically addressed in his letters to the Connexion's churches. For instance, in 1801 he urged the churches to consider the question, "What is to be done that the interest of our Redeemer may be advanced in the world?"[209]

204. Stanley, "Christian Missions," 2.

205. Prosser, "Formation of the General Baptist Missionary Society," 23–29.

206. See Rinaldi, *Tribe of Dan*, 56–57.

207. *Minutes of an Association 1816*, 10.

208. Taylor, *Cause of National Calamities*, 6.

209. Taylor, "Concurrence of People," 15.

He declared that the only appropriate response was to propagate "the gospel of Christ" and, pointing to the first apostles, insisted that they needed "to walk in their steps" and go into the world and preach the gospel.[210] Given the importance that the Connexion's members placed on Taylor's letters, his declarations in favor of overseas mission were likely influential in paving the way for the Connexion's favorable response to establishing its own missionary society. These references, in Taylor's letters and general writings, to God's care for the world and the need for an accompanying advancement of the gospel are notable for a further reason. They demonstrate that the later formation of the General Baptist Missionary Society, when compared to the Particular Baptist Missionary Society established in 1792 and Church Missionary Society in 1799, should not be interpreted in terms of Taylor lacking sufficient conviction to take the gospel to the nations.

The comparatively late establishment of the General Baptist Missionary Society should best be understood on the basis that the Connexion lacked the necessary material means to start such an enterprise. This is evident in how the annual Association granted its consent for the commencement of some smaller scale missionary initiatives, but that when the possibility of beginning a missionary society was discussed in 1802 and 1809, it was judged that "the resources of the Connexion were unequal to such an effort."[211] This should not be understood as evidence of Taylor's disinterest in the spread of the gospel overseas. While some commentators such as Martin attribute the absence of a missionary organization within Methodism during Wesley's lifetime to how "Wesley preferred to concentrate the resources of his connexion on the harvest at home,"[212] and Henry Rack suggests "overseas missions were not among Wesley's priorities,"[213] there is no evidence that this was true for Taylor. Furthermore, Taylor's already noted support for the establishment of the General Baptist Missionary Society suggests otherwise. This is important as Haykin argues that the time taken to establish missionary societies was indicative of there being a far greater measure of continuity between Puritanism and the evangelical movement than Bebbington allows. Haykin asserts that a missional activism could not have been integral to evangelicalism to the extent that Bebbington stipulates, as there was "little manifestation of what was its distinctive feature" (namely in the form of

210. Ibid.

211. Wood, *Condensed History*, 316. For reference to the smaller scale missionary initiatives that were undertaken, see Prosser, "Formation of The General Baptist Missionary Society," 25.

212. Roger H. Martin, "Missionary Competition," 81.

213. Rack, "John Wesley and Overseas Missions," 45. For further consideration of this subject, see Bennett, "John Wesley," 159–70.

mission organizations) "until the second or even third generation of the movement."[214] Certainly, in the case of the New Connexion, the issue was not a lack of inclination but of material constraint.

Taylor exercised a beneficial influence on those who, in time, occupied positions of central importance within the Missionary Society. Its first missionaries James Pegg and William Brampton, who were sent to Orissa, India,[215] both underwent training at the General Baptist Academy established by Taylor.[216] Although widely overlooked, Pike, whose secretarial responsibilities gave him much influence, also experienced substantial input from Taylor during the two years that he spent with him during Taylor's ministry at Church Lane.[217] The training that Taylor gave Pike enabled him to become minister at Brook Street church, Derby in 1810.[218] Though Prosser and Rinaldi failed to highlight this link between Pike and Taylor, the influence of Taylor's activism on Pike is almost certainly evident in Rinaldi's reference to Pike's "vigorous effort and extent of his missionary journeys promoting the cause of the work."[219] Others who became important supporters of the Missionary Society, such as Benjamin Pollard, also worked closely with Taylor in the Connexion for many years.[220] Pollard's enthusiastic declaration that he "could almost have sold his coat from his back for the missionary cause" was indicative of Taylor's commitment to the spread of the gospel.[221]

Taylor's support for overseas mission was demonstrated in other public ways. A typical example was how he prioritized speaking at a "missionary prayer meeting" in Birmingham in 1814, as noted by Adam Taylor.[222] In 1816, he accepted a request from the General Body of Protestant Dissenting Ministers to chair a large gathering of London ministers concerned about the persecution of Protestants in Southern France.[223] His readiness to serve in this way illustrates that, even at the age of seventy-eight and with declining health, his passion for the spread of the gospel across the nations was such that he refused to confine his labors only to the needs of the New Con-

---

214. Haykin, "Evangelicalism," 54.

215. Orissa is today known as Odisha, a state in Eastern India.

216. See Rinaldi, *Tribe of Dan*, 159.

217. See [Anon.], "Pike, Rev. John G.," 921.

218. Ibid.

219. Rinaldi, *Tribe of Dan*, 56.

220. See Wood, *Condensed History*, 316.

221. Pollard. Qtd in ibid., 316. Primary source unknown.

222. Taylor, *Memoirs*, 243.

223. Ibid., 245.

nexion or issues of national concern. This was his last public engagement as Taylor died just five days later.

Conclusion

Taylor's entrepreneurship became apparent soon after he began his ministry at Birchcliff. Notable examples include his embracing of field preaching and tract distribution, which were practices he had become familiar with during his period in Methodism. Taylor's initiative was also demonstrated in his response to the missional inertia of the wider General Baptists by establishing the New Connexion. Its mission focused objective had much in common with other movements that emerged from within eighteenth-century evangelicalism. Taylor's emphasis on "revival" was significant and, in contrast to seventeenth-century Puritanism, was a commonplace feature of the evangelicalism of his day. His entrepreneurship was also displayed by his commitment to church planting, particularly in how he led the Connexion to develop churches in towns that were growing quickly as a consequence of the industrial revolution. Taylor's personal involvement in these initiatives, and wider strategic coordination of the Connexion's approach to church planting exemplified his skills as a pioneer. Such an intentional, carefully planned, and sustained way of proceeding regarding the task of mission differed from the missional lethargy that was commonplace among General Baptists outside of the Connexion. It also stood apart from the evangelistic efforts of the Puritans which tended to be more individualistic than the Connexion's often coordinated strategy.

Another noteworthy aspect of Taylor's approach to mission was how he successfully fostered a culture of personal responsibility for evangelism throughout the Connexion. Taylor was convinced that the goal of promoting a revival in experimental religion required a comprehensive lay activism. Such an emphasis reflected the new individualism that was evident in eighteenth-century society, with the development of a more engaged laity a key characteristic of the evangelical movement of this period. In keeping with the greater sense of tolerance and flexibility that began to permeate the society of Taylor's day, he also demonstrated a regard for the importance of establishing good relationships with those in other denominations. Where there was a shared imperative on mission, he gladly worked with those outside of the Connexion and assumed an important function on several dissenting committees. Taylor's primacy on mission was evident in the resolve he displayed in the process which led to establishing the General Baptist training Academy. The thrust of the syllabus on subjects such as the work of the ministry and sermon preparation was also indicative of the distinctive way in which Taylor, in keeping with the ethos of eighteenth-century evangelicalism, attributed greater importance to the provision of practical skills that would aid the spread of the gospel than on the intricacy of doctrine. The way in which Taylor taught subjects that were prominent within the context of the Enlightenment and ensured that the students fully engaged with London's multifaceted cultural life further demonstrated his innovativeness. Taylor's scope as a pioneer also extended internationally, as evident in his role in establishing the General Baptist Missionary Society. In keeping with many of his evangelical contemporaries, Taylor had long drawn attention to God's concern for the nations and the need for churches to respond accordingly. Overall, the way that Taylor's evangelicalism contributed to how he functioned as a religious entrepreneur should be considered as one of his most defining characteristics.

Conclusion

THIS BOOK HAS EXAMINED the evangelicalism of Dan Taylor, the pre-eminent General Baptist minister of his era. Despite the breadth of his ministry, his large number of written works, theological engagement with significant figures such as Particular Baptist minister Andrew Fuller, formation of the New Connexion of General Baptists and general widespread respect he commanded, the nature of his evangelicalism has been a very neglected area of study. Through my close consideration of the underpinning facets and central tenets of Taylor's theological understanding and ways in which these were practically outworked, I have sought to provide new insight into the precise characteristics and particular nuances of the evangelicalism on which the entire framework of Taylor's thinking and ministry was based. In turn, this has proved crucial to my consideration of the origin and defining features of evangelicalism as a movement.

Taylor was first exposed to evangelical teaching when as a youth he traveled to listen to the preaching of William Grimshaw at Haworth and visiting preachers, such as the Wesley brothers and George Whitefield. While at Haworth, Taylor was introduced to the conversionism, activism, Biblicism, and crucicentrism that David Bebbington identifies as the core distinguishing marks of evangelicalism.[1] Despite being raised in a household which maintained a respect for the Bible and moral living, and having regularly attended Halifax Parish Church with his parents, Taylor was moved by the clarity of gospel understanding he gained as he heard the Christian message expounded by evangelical preachers. During his participation in the Evangelical Revival, he entered progressively into a stronger personal commitment to the gospel, particularly his new understanding of

1. Bebbington, *Evangelicalism*, 2–17.

Christ's atoning work. This was firstly expressed at an emotional level as he sometimes wept at the profundity of Christ's sacrifice, and then in other ways, such as his quickly developing fervor for prayer and intense desire to share the faith with others.

A further significant influence on the initial shaping of Taylor's evangelicalism was his subsequent nine-year involvement in the structures of Methodism. Joining the Methodist society in Halifax gave him the opportunity to consider more fully those aspects of evangelical teaching that had produced within him a new sense of liberty and understanding of the gospel. This proved crucial to the further development of his theological thinking, spirituality, and ecclesiological understanding. His active participation in Methodist class and band meetings instilled in him a lasting regard for the importance of an experiential and practical outworking of all the teaching that he received. Importantly, these years also provided Taylor with continued exposure to aspects of evangelical innovation such as field preaching, the use of "market language" when communicating the gospel to the poor, tract distribution, hymn singing, and extensive opportunities for lay participation within the society and in the task of sharing the gospel with others.

Overall, both the preaching of the gospel by evangelical preachers and Taylor's participation within the structures of Methodism were vital in his acquisition of a vibrant platform of evangelicalism. He then found himself needing to uphold his evangelical convictions as he entered into fellowship with the General Baptists, most of whom were untouched by the Evangelical Revival and resistant to its overarching ethos. When Taylor stepped out as a proponent and practitioner of an evangelical understanding of the gospel, the pioneering distinctions of his evangelicalism became particularly evident.

Creative Emphases

I have argued throughout the book that Taylor's evangelicalism was marked by a notable creativity. This was first evident in how, soon after he embraced evangelicalism, he placed mission as the focal point of his regular participation in spiritual disciplines such as self-examination, fasting, and scriptural meditation. He sought to establish a missional spirituality throughout the New Connexion by encouraging all believers to use these same disciplines in an outward orientated direction. This approach stood apart from the more introspective use of these disciplines by earlier movements, such as the Puritans. As has been argued, the confident platform of assurance of salvation that Taylor shared in common with many wider evangelicals was a crucial factor in his ready employment of these disciplines as an aid to the spread of the gospel.

Taylor's creativity was evident when, as an evangelical apologist, he engaged with those of Socinian and Unitarian persuasion such as the Unitarian minister William Graham. For example, in the *Scriptural Account of the Way of Salvation*[2] Taylor not only defended doctrines such as human depravity, the humanity and deity of Christ, and acquisition of salvation only as a free gift through faith in Christ's atoning work, but also emphasized aspects of his thinking such as the compatibility between reason and revelation. Taylor was influenced by the empiricism that was central to the Enlightenment writings of John Locke. Regularly, this led Taylor to attempt to convince others of the truth with reference to the merits of observation and experience. As frequently noted, a wariness of the corrupting effects of sin meant that even Arminian Puritans, such as John Milton, refused to uphold the benefits of rational thinking in the process of salvation.

Taylor's dominant soteriological metaphor, that of God as moral governor, was also marked by an inventive approach. Influenced by the writings of Hugo Grotius, he viewed God's divine justice and moral government as upheld by Christ's death. Beyond that posited by Grotius, he also advocated a propitiatory understanding of Christ's atonement as a sacrificial ransom that paid humankind's debt before God, and a penal substitutionary view of the atonement. It seems likely that Taylor was the first eighteenth-century Baptist to have fused these elements of thought together.

As Taylor acted as a proponent for his evangelical understanding of the gospel, a further novel feature of his approach was his theological succinctness. A typical example was the brevity of the New Connexion's six *Articles of Religion*.[3] Their conciseness is particularly evident when compared to the expansive scope of General Baptist creeds and confessions of faith such as the Standard Confession and *Orthodox Creed*.[4] Irrespective of subject matter, the nature of Taylor's evangelical Arminianism was such that he preferred to isolate only core principles and offer minimal reflection. This put him at variance with the way many earlier General Baptists articulated central aspects of the faith and the tendency for detailed exegesis and precision among Calvinist Puritans, such as John Owen and those of Arminian persuasion like John Goodwin. As argued, Taylor's focus on

---

2. Dan Taylor, *Scriptural Account.*
3. *Articles*, in Lumpkin, *Baptist Confessions*, 342–44.
4. See Lumpkin, *Baptist Confessions*, 224–35, 297–334.

the plain meaning of the text and avoidance of abstractionism and mystery was again distinctly Lockean.

Taylor's approach to his favorite theme of Christ's death for all was typical of his creativity. Whereas the works of many earlier General Baptists, such as Thomas Monk and Thomas Grantham, reveal a lack of specific attention to the upholding of general redemption, it was central to all that Taylor taught. Examples include his material on the duties of ministers,[5] *The Chief Subjects of Christianity* for the use of children and youth,[6] and *Mourning Parent Comforted.*[7] Taylor's foremost emphasis was that all should know the depth of God's love as exemplified in the general scope of Christ's death. He was adamant that this should motivate believers to share the gospel with others. The missional thrust of his drawing attention to general redemption extended beyond how certain Puritan proponents of the doctrine, such as Laurence Saunders and Thomas Moore Sr., emphasized the scope of God's love only with the hope of undermining belief in a limited view of the atonement.

Taylor's belief that Christ's death for all was the prime motivation for mission was pivotal to his opposition to the basis on which Particular Baptists, such as Robert Hall Sr. and Andrew Fuller, advocated that the gospel be offered to all. This is apparent in Taylor's response to Fuller's *The Gospel of Christ Worthy of All Acceptation.*[8] His reasoned critique of Fuller's framework, such as his differentiation between natural and moral inability, was significant. It caused Fuller to change his position and accept that Christ's death was sufficient for all humanity, so that whoever came to God could be saved. Their dialog revealed wider aspects of Taylor's creative thinking, such as his apparent acknowledgment that he held to the doctrine of perseverance of believers. This was typical of the pioneering nature of Taylor's evangelical Arminianism. Certain concessions that Taylor made to Fuller were also indicative of his pragmatism. Aware that Fuller's regard for the efficacy of Christ's death was an obstacle to his acceptance of Christ's death for all, Taylor argued that the Spirit's operations could not always be resisted and even allowed for the possibility of special design within Christ's atoning work. These sentiments were not intimated in any of Taylor's wider works. Whereas such a theological pragmatism was rare among Puritans, it was an important aspect of Taylor's evangelicalism.

5. Dan Taylor, "Principal Parts," in Dan Taylor and William Thompson, *Respective Duties.*

6. Dan Taylor, *Entertainment and Profit.*

7. Dan Taylor, *Mourning Parent Comforted.*

8. Fuller, *Gospel Worthy.*

As evident, Taylor was a creative proponent of his evangelical understanding of the faith. A dynamic creativity was interwoven throughout his evangelicalism. This is apparent within the private sphere of his exercise of different spiritual disciplines, and the very public ways in which he sought to foster a missional spirituality throughout the Connexion. His upholding of core tenets of the gospel, and understanding and articulation of key aspects of his theological schema such as God's moral governance and Christ's death for all, were marked by similarly creative facets.

Innovative Distinctives

I have endeavored to demonstrate that Taylor's evangelicalism was marked by a tendency for innovation. This was exemplified in his 1770 formation of the New Connexion of General Baptists which was established principally as a catalyst to spread the gospel more effectively. The strategic coordination and sense of inter-dependency that Taylor brought to the movement's churches was without precedent in Baptist life. Taylor used the Connexion's relational structures, joint ventures, and collective approach to financial giving, to establish a powerful corporate identity and sustained focus on evangelism. As has been argued, Taylor's structural skills, organizational ability, and pivotal influence were such that he should be viewed as the Baptist Wesley.

A significant example of Taylor's inclination for innovation during his oversight of the Connexion was his establishment of weekly experience meetings, which were an adaptation of the Methodist class meetings. The importance Taylor attributed to this practice, as well as how the recounting of faith experiences came to form the chief basis on which people were admitted into membership, were typical of the reduced importance he attached to creedal assent in the process of spiritual formation. Taylor's regard for the experiential was also central to his endorsement of hymn singing. Given the almost uniform opposition of General Baptists outside the New Connexion to collective singing, Taylor's stance was particularly notable. As demonstrated, Taylor was emphatic concerning its experiential benefits, and this set him apart from the concentration on precise scriptural warrant that often accompanied Puritan approaches to singing. I have contended that it was Taylor's belief in its spiritual benefits which accounted for him initially seeking to convince the movement's members of its merits simply by providing opportunities for them to participate in this form of worship. Through this means, hymn singing became one of the Connexion's most renowned characteristics. Taylor was also the first General Baptist to produce a hymn book. In addition Taylor, in his discourse with General Baptist Messenger Gilbert Boyce, argued that the way God impacted the minds of non-believers through hymn singing necessitated they be encouraged to join in. Compared to the outlook of the wider General Baptists this was again a novel viewpoint. It was indicative of the primacy on mission that his evangelicalism fostered within him.

Taylor's defense of believers' baptism by immersion also demonstrated certain distinctive elements. The extent to which he maintained a non-sacramental interpretation was different from the understanding of baptism commonly held by earlier General Baptists and it anticipated the interpretation of baptism that became dominant among Baptists later in the nineteenth century. His succinctness of argument and attempts to convince others of the strength of his position by drawing on the claims of observation and experience were important. In addition, Taylor displayed a different approach to the Lord's Supper. In particular, his regard for its efficacy extended beyond that of most earlier General Baptists. His lack of attention to the precise nature of the Supper, absence of interest in the specifics of self-preparation, and belief it should be celebrated weekly differed from the approach often assumed by Puritans.

A further point of differentiation between Taylor and customary General Baptist practice was his outlook towards certain longstanding contentious matters. Examples include the way in which he granted liberty of judgment regarding issues such as the eating of blood and laying on of hands after baptism and for the reception of new members. This was another indication of his more progressive outlook. Taylor applied the same principle of liberty in his refusal to be overly prescriptive regarding the precise offices that churches should adopt. Matters of precise ecclesiastical order were not a priority for him.

Taylor's emphasis on liberty was also influential in the way he advocated the active role of women in the church as office holders, their full participation in all issues discussed at church meetings and engagement in all aspects of church life such as hymn singing. This is evident from the earliest years of Taylor's ministry at Birchcliff and was something he purposefully encouraged throughout the Connexion. It contrasted with the restrictions that limited the involvement of women in wider General Baptist life. As noted, Taylor's stance was indicative of his ecclesiological egalitarianism and his sensitivity to the increasing appreciation found within the Enlightenment concerning the role of women.

Taylor's entrepreneurship was epitomized in wider aspects of his approach to ministry, such as, being the first eighteenth-century General Baptist to engage in open air preaching, in his commitment to church planting—many of which were strategically located in the emerging industrial cities and towns, and in his extensive use of tracts frequently produced for non-believers. Following Taylor's modeling of each of these practices, they were subsequently adopted throughout the Connexion. Further creative dimensions of Taylor's ministry included his 1797 establishment of the General Baptist Academy with its innovative features, notably how Taylor, as tutor, taught the students to engage meaningfully with their cultural situation and compiled a syllabus that was alive to the spirit of the age. In addition, he was an advocate for the movement establishing the General Baptist Missionary Society in 1816, which proved crucial in enabling General Baptists to participate in world mission.

Overall, Taylor's orientation to innovation was a central hallmark of his evangelicalism. It was found throughout his oversight of the Connexion, was apparent in his approach to worship and the Lord's Table, as well as a dominant feature of his ecclesiology and approach to mission. Taylor was certainly a religious entrepreneur.

Wider Implications of Taylor's Evangelicalism

It has been argued that the defining characteristics of Taylor's theological thinking are of relevance to the debate surrounding the distinguishing features and origins of evangelicalism. In particular, this book contends that the creative emphases and progressive distinctions of Taylor's evangelicalism affirm much of what Bebbington argues was new and distinct about eighteenth-century evangelicalism. In response to fresh scrutiny of his position in the 2008 publication of *The Emergence of Evangelicalism*, Bebbington accepts he under-appreciated certain individual evangelical emphases which pre-dated the eighteenth century, yet remains firm in his refusal to assume an unbroken tradition of gospel based evangelical Christianity.[9] He instead continues to view evangelicalism's inception as primarily rooted in the eighteenth century. I have contended throughout this book that the nature of Taylor's pioneering evangelicalism supports Bebbington's central argument.

Although Taylor's theological framework contains elements of continuity such as an upholding of the core Reformation doctrines of the authority of the Scriptures, justification by faith alone, and priesthood of all believers, I have sought to demonstrate that its distinguishing facets gave rise to an expression of faith that differed markedly. This was not only a consequence of the collective effect of the dynamic combination of the four

9. Bebbington, "Response," 427.

principal marks of evangelicalism as highlighted by Bebbington, but also stemmed from other underpinning tenets of Taylor's understanding and articulation of the faith. These include the importance he attached to certain core values of the Enlightenment, such as his regard for reason, the merits of observation and experience, liberty, and equality. This, in turn, affirms Bebbington's assertion that evangelicalism was not principally a reaction against the values of the Enlightenment but was itself an expression of certain emphases that were central to this phenomenon.[10]

It has been seen that Taylor's framework of thought was predicated on a creative synthesis of differing influences that were congruent with that which was distinct about eighteenth-century evangelicalism. These include several elements. Taylor emphasized the experiential over the cerebral, pragmatism over the metaphysical, reason and observation over abstraction, succinctness over verbosity, innovation over inertia, tolerance over dogmatism, and liberty over rigid doctrine. He also wove the task of mission into all aspects of his understanding of faith. Together these characteristics challenge any understanding of eighteenth-century evangelicalism that views it as only a continuum of earlier patterns of theological thinking, particularly those associated with the Reformation and Puritanism.

I have argued that an appreciation of the distinctions of Taylor's outworking of faith challenges the strength of particular criticisms that have been leveled against Bebbington's emphasis on the newness of evangelicalism. Examples include how proponents of the continuity of evangelicalism such as Garry Williams, Carl Trueman, and Michael Haykin have respectively referred to the use of spiritual disciplines by evangelicals, the parallels in evangelical approaches to lay participation, and also questioned the distinctness of evangelical methods regarding the spread of the gospel.[11] In addition to Taylor's creative approach to the spiritual disciplines, it has been contended that the collective vigorous lay activism which he mobilized throughout the Connexion, and accompanying evangelistic ethos he created and sustained, was innovative compared to both the general practices of the seventeenth-century General Baptists and those of his day who remained resistant to the Evangelical Revival. It was also contrary to the approaches frequently assumed by Puritans. As has been noted, an unwillingness to acknowledge the newness of evangelicalism, and particularly its eighteenth-century roots, has sometimes stemmed from a reluctance to recognize that Arminianism, as articulated within Methodism, was a formative influence

---

10. Bebbington, *Evangelicalism*, 53.

11. See Williams, "Enlightenment Epistemology," 351; Trueman, "Reformers, puritans and evangelicals," 33; Haykin, "Evangelicalism," 54.

on its emergence. This, in turn, has very likely contributed to the lack of scholarly attention given to certain Arminians such as Taylor.

Conclusion

The overarching aim of Taylor's ministry, as evident in his objective for the New Connexion, was "To revive experimental religion or primitive Christianity in faith and practice."[12] This encapsulates the thrust of the twenty-one years that he spent as minister at Birchcliff. In addition, it reflects the sole motivation in his acceptance of the invitation to become minister in 1783 of the newly planted General Baptist church in Halifax and rationale behind his subsequent move, two years later, to Church Lane, London where he remained for the duration of his ministry. As he endeavored to fulfill this aim, he did so from a platform of evangelicalism that was pioneering. This was not only apparent within its underpinning facets, many of which were influenced by the Enlightenment, but also in the practical expression of faith that emerged. Neither was this unique to Taylor, but was instead consistent with both the overriding attributes and more subtle nuances of eighteenth-century evangelicalism. As I have sought to demonstrate throughout this book, it was the pioneering nature of Taylor's evangelicalism which led him to function as an innovative apologist, novel advocate, enlightened critic, the Baptist Wesley, a creative proponent, and religious entrepreneur of an evangelical understanding of the gospel that he hoped would revive Christianity in faith and practice.

12. *Assembly of Free Grace General Baptists.* Page not numbered.

Bibliography

Primary Sources—Manuscripts

Angus Library and Archives, Regent's Park College, Oxford

Taylor, Dan. Letters from the Revd Dan Taylor to the Revd George Birley, 1771–1808, Hughes Collection, D/HUS 1/6.

Methodist Archives and Research Centre,
The John Rylands Library, Manchester

Grimshaw, William. "Letter" (no addressee specified), The Early Preachers Collection, DDPR 2/65.

———. "Letter to Charles Wesley," 31 March 1760, The Early Preachers Collection, DDPR 2/63.

———. "Letter to Mrs. Gallatin," 19 September 1753, PLP 47–15–8.

———. "Letter to Mrs. Gallatin," 10 May 1754, PLP 47–15–9.

———. "Letter to Mrs. Gallatin," 13 September 1755, PLP 47–15–11.

———. "Letter to Mrs Gallatin," 31 July 1757, PLP 47–15–21.

West Yorkshire Archives Office, Wakefield

Halifax St John the Baptist, Register of Baptisms, Marriages, and Burials 1726–1756, WDP53/1/1/10.

Primary Sources—Minutes

General Baptists of the New Connexion, Minutes of Association, 1770–1796. Manuscripts. Angus Library and Archives, Regent's Park College, Oxford, GB NC Association Minutes 1770–96.

305

General Baptists of the New Connexion, Minutes of Association, 1797–1827. Manuscripts. Angus Library and Archives, Regent's Park College, Oxford, GB NC Association Minutes 1797–1827.

Minutes of an Association of General Baptists, and Representatives of Churches, holden at Spalding, Lincolnshire, June 24th, 25th, 26th, 1800. London: Printed by J.G. Barnard, 1800.

Minutes of an Association of General Baptists, held at Nottingham, June 24th, 25th & 26th, 1795. London: Printed by R. Hawes, 1795.

Minutes of an Association of General Baptists, held at Retford, Nottinghamshire, the 27th and 28th Days of May, 1789. London: Printed by Henry Fry, 1789.

Minutes of an Association of General Baptists, held at Wisbeach, Cambridgeshire, the 27th and 28th of April, 1791. St. Ives: Printed by P. Croft, 1791.

Minutes of an Association of General Baptists, held in Birmingham, Warwickshire, the 26th and 27th Days of March, 1788. n.l.: n.p., 1788.

Minutes of an Association of General Baptists held, in Church-Lane, White Chapel, London, the 11th and 12th Days of April, 1787. London: n.p., 1787.

Minutes of an Association of General Baptists, holden at Hinckley, Leicestershire, on Wednesday and Thursday, April 3d and 4th, 1793. London: Printed by R. Hawes, 1793.

Minutes of an Association of General Baptist Ministers, and Representatives of Churches, held at Loughborough, Leicestershire, July 1st, 2d, and 3d, 1801. Derby: Printed by G. Wilkins, 1801.

Minutes of an Association of General Baptist Ministers, and Representatives of Churches, holden at Halifax, June 26th, 27th, 28th, 1798. London: Printed by J. Sammells, 1798.

Minutes of an Association of General Baptist Ministers, held in Church-Lane, London, June the 26th and 27th, 1794. London: Printed by R. Hawes, 1794.

Minutes of an Association of The New Connection of General Baptists, held at Boston, June 25th and 28th, 1816. Derby: Printed by G. Wilkins, 1816.

The Proceedings of the General Assembly held on Wednesday, June 3d, 1789, at the Baptist Meeting-House, in Worship Street, Near Bishops-Gate Street, London. London: Brown, 1789.

Primary Sources—Periodicals and Newspapers

The Arminian Magazine.

The Evangelical Magazine

General Baptist Magazine.

The Gentleman's Magazine and Historical Chronicle.

Leeds Intelligencer.

The Monthly Review; or Literary Journal.

Primary Sources—Books, Pamphlets and Letters

Anon. *The Baptist Catechism: Commonly Called Keach's Catechism: Or, A Brief Instruction in the Principles of the Christian Religion: Agreeably to the Confession of Faith Put Forth by Upwards of an Hundred Congregations in Great Britain, July 3, 1689, and Adopted by the Philadelphia Baptist Association, September 22, 1742.* Philadelphia: American Baptist, 1851.

Addington, Stephen. *The Christian Minister's Reasons for Baptizing Infants and for Administering the Ordinance by Sprinkling or Pouring of Water.* London: Buckland, 1771.

———. *A Summary of the Christian Minister's Reasons for Baptizing Infants, and for Administering the Ordinance by Sprinkling or Pouring of Water with some Remarks on the Rev. Dr. Stennett's Answers, in a Letter to the Doctor.* London: Buckland, 1776.

Aequus [Author unknown]. *Scrutator's Query Respecting the Extent of Our Blessed Saviour's Death, Re-proposed; With Responsor's Answer to it; Scrutator's Reply to Responsor; Observator's Remarks on Both; and Scrutator's Answer to Observator.* Leeds: Wright & Son, n.d., [1780].

Ames, William. *The Marrow of Theology.* London: n.p., 1642.

Arminius, James. *The Works of James Arminius.* Vol. 2. Translated by James Nichols and William R. Bagnall. Auburn, NY: Derby & Miller, 1853.

Ash, John, and Caleb Evans. *A Collection of Hymns Adapted to Public Worship.* Bristol: Pine, n.d., [1769].

Bannerman, Henry, and Henry Grew. *The Practices of the Early Christians Considered: Comprising, I. An Exhibition of the First Churches by H. Grew, Hartford, U. S. II. Notes Containing Objections to some of Mr. Grew's Statements. III. Letters on Baptism, Containing Strictures on the Notes.* London: Whitaker et al., 1838.

Baxter, Richard. *Plain Scripture Proof of Infants Church-Membership and Baptism: Being the Arguments Prepared for (and Partly Managed in) the Publick Dispute with Mr. Tombes at Bewdley on the First Day of Jan. 1649: With a Full Reply to What He Then Answered, and What is Contained in His Sermon Since Preached, in His Printed Books, His M.S. on 1 Cor 7.14. Which I Saw, Against Mr. Marshall, Against These Arguments. With a Reply to His Valedictory Oration at Bewdley and a Corrective for His Antidote.* London: Printed for Robert White, 1653.

———. *Practical Works of the Rev. Richard Baxter; With a Life of the Author and a Critical Examination of His Writings.* Vol. 1. Edited by William Orme. London: Duncan, 1830.

Beattie, James. *An Essay on the Nature and Immutability of Truth in Opposition to Sophistry and Scepticism.* 10th ed. London: Lackington & Allen, 1810.

Blackwall, Anthony. *The Sacred Classics Defended and Illustrated, or, An Essay Humbly Offered towards Proving the Purity, Propriety, and True Eloquence of the Writers of the New Testament. In Two Parts.* London: Printed by Bettenham, for Rivington & Cantrell, 1725.

Booth, Abraham. *The Reign of Grace: From Its Rise to Its Consummation.* Philadelphia: Whetham, 1838.

———. *The Works of Abraham Booth, Late Pastor of the Baptist church, Little Prescot Street, Goodman's Fields, London. With Some Account of His Life and Writings.* 3 vols. London: Button & Sons, 1813.

Boyce, Gilbert. *A Candid and Friendly Reply to Mr. Dan Taylor's Dissertation on Singing in the Worship of God.* Wisbech: Nicholson, 1787.

———. *Serious Thoughts on the Present Mode and Practice of Singing in the Public Worship of God.* Wisbech: Nicholson, 1785.

Bristol Education Society. *An Account of the Bristol Education Society, begun anno 1770.* Bristol: Ward, 1776.

Brooks, Thomas. *The Complete Works of Thomas Brooks.* Vol. 2. Edited by Alexander B. Grosart. Edinburgh: Nichol, 1866.

Bunyan, John. *The Works of John Bunyan.* Vol. 1. Edited by George Offor. London: Blackie & Son, 1856.

Butler, Charles. *The Life of Hugo Grotius: With Brief Minutes of the Civil, Ecclesiastical, and Literary History of the Netherlands.* London: Murray, 1826.

Butler, Joseph. *Analogy of Religion, Natural and Revealed, to the Constitution and Course of Nature, to Which are Added Two Brief Dissertations: I. Of Personal Identity. II. Of the Nature of Virtue.* London: J. & P. Knapton, 1736.

Calamy, Edmund. *The Nonconformist's Memorial: Being an Account of the Ministers, Who were Ejected or Silenced after the Restoration, Particularly by the Act of Uniformity, Which Took Place on Bartholomew-day, Aug. 24, 1662. Containing a Concise View of Their Lives and Characters, Their Principles, Sufferings, and Printed Works. Originally Written by the Reverend and Learned Edmund Calamy, D.D. Now Abridged and Corrected, and the Author's Additions Inserted, with Many Further Particulars, and New Anecdotes, by Samuel Palmer.* Vol. 1. London: Printed for W. Harris, 1775.

Calvinisticus [Author unknown]. *Calvinism Defended and Arminianism Refuted; or Remarks on a Pamphlet (Lately Published) by Philalethes, Entitled A Solemn Caution against the Ten Horns of Calvinism.* Leeds: Printed by Binns, 1780.

Chetham, John. *A Book of Psalmody, Containing Variety of Tunes for all the Common Metres of the Psalms in the Old and New Versions and Others for Particular Measures, with Chanting Tunes and Fifteen Anthems, All Set in Four Parts.* London: Pearson, 1718.

Clarke, Samuel. *A Discourse concerning the Being and Attributes of God, the Obligations of Natural Religion, and the Truth and Certainty of the Christian Revelation. In Answer to Mr. Hobbs, Spinoza, the Author of the Oracles of Reason and other Deniers of Natural and Revealed Religion. Being Sixteen Sermons, Preach'd in the Cathedral-church of St. Paul, in the Year 1704, and 1705, at the Lecture Founded by the Honourable Robert Boyle, esq.* London: Printed by W. Botham, for James & John Knapton, 1728.

Cottle, Joseph. *Essays in Reference to Socinianism.* London: Longman, 1812.

Crabtree, John. *Concise History of the Parish and Vicarage of Halifax, in the Country of York.* Halifax: Hartley & Walker, 1836.

Crosby, Thomas. *The History of the English Baptists, from the Reformation to the Beginning of the Reign of King George I.* 4 vols. London: Printed for the author, and sold by Aaron Ward et al., 1738–1740.

Deacon, John. *A New and Large Collection of Hymns and Psalms, Selected from More Than Forty Different Authors: The Whole Being Classed and Arranged According to Their Respective Subjects.* London: Printed by C. Whittingham, sold by H.D. Symonds, 1800.

Deacon, Samuel, Jr. *Barton Hymns: A New Composition of Hymns and Poems; Chiefly upon Divine Subjects. Designed for the Amusement and Edification of Christians of all Denominations: More Particularly Those of the General Baptist Persuasion.* Coventry: Printed by Luckman and Firm, and sold by Taylor, Pollard, & Deacon, 1797.

———— Anon. [Samuel Deacon Jr.]. *A Comprehensive Account of the General Baptists with Respect to Principle and Practice in Which Are Displayed Their Manner of Worship, Church Order and Discipline. By a Mechanic Who Was Long Conversant with Them.* Coventry: Luckman, 1795.

————. *Memoirs of the Late Mr. Samuel Deacon Who Was Nearly Forty Years Pastor and Fifty Years a Member of the General Baptist Church, Barton, Leicestershire; With Extracts from His Various Writings, Letters, &c.* Edited by Joel Green. Loughbrough: Winks, n.d., [1827].

————. *A New Composition of Hymns and Poems, Chiefly on Divine Subjects; Designed for the Amusement, and Edification of Christians of all Denominations. More Particularly Them of the Baptist Persuasion.* Leicester: Printed for the author by George Ireland, 1784.

Dutton, Anne. *Brief Hints concerning Baptism: Of the Subject, Mode, and End of This Solemn Ordinance.* London: Hart, 1746.

————. *Thoughts on the Lord's Supper, Relating to the Nature, Subjects, and Right Partaking of This Solemn Ordinance.* London: Hart, 1748.

Early, Joe, Jr., ed. *The Life and Writings of Thomas Helwys.* Macon, GA: Mercer University Press, 2009.

Edwards, Jonathan. *The Works of Jonathan Edwards.* 26 vols. Edited by Perry Miller, John E. Smith, and Harry S. Stout. New Haven, CT: Yale University Press, 1957–2008.

Evershed, William. *The Messenger's Mission, or the Foundation and Authority for such an Order of Officers in the Christian Church, Called Messengers, Being (as Far as Concerned the Authority for that Office) the Substance of a Sermon Preached at Canterbury, at an Ordination of Messengers, July, 29th 1783. To Which is Added an Appendix Showing the Work and Business of Those Messengers.* London: Printed for the author by J. Brown, 1783.

Anon. [Fawcett, John, Jr.]. *An Account of the Life, Ministry, and Writings of the Late Rev. John Fawcett.* London: Baldwin et al., 1818.

Fawcett, John, Sr. *Christ Precious to Those that Believe: The Preciousness of Jesus Christ, to Those Who Believe—Practically Considered and Improved.* Halifax: n.p., 1799.

Fletcher, John. *A Rational Vindication of the Catholic Faith: Being the First Part of a Vindication of Christ's Divinity; Inscribed to the Reverend Dr. Priestley, Left Imperfect by the Author, and Now Revised, and Finished at Mrs. Fletcher's Request, by Joseph Benson.* Hull: Prince, 1790.

Fowler, Edward. *The Design of Christianity; Or a Plain Demonstration and Improvement of This Proposition, that the Enduing Men with Inward Real Righteousness or True Holiness, Was the Ultimate End of Our Saviour's Coming Into This World, and is the Great Intendment of His Blessed Gospel.* London: Printed for R. Royston, 1676.

Fuller, Andrew. *A Defence of a Treatise Entitled the Gospel of Christ Worthy of All Acceptation; Containing a Reply to Mr. Button's Remarks and the Observations of Philanthropos.* Northampton: Dicey, 1787.

————. *The Gospel of Christ Worthy of All Acceptation: Or the Obligations of Men Fully to Credit, and Cordially to Approve, Whatever God Makes Known. Wherein is Considered the Nature of Faith in Christ, and the Duty of Those Where the Gospel Comes in that Matter.* Northampton: Dicey, 1785.

———— [Agnostos]. *The Reality and Efficacy of Divine Grace; With the Certain Success of Christ's Sufferings, in Behalf of All Who are Finally Saved. Considered in a Series of Letters to the Rev. A. Fuller: Containing Remarks upon the Observations of the Rev. Dan Taylor, on Mr. Fuller's Reply to Philanthropos.* London: Sold by Lepard, n.d., [1790].

————. *The Works of Andrew Fuller.* Edited by Andrew G. Fuller. 1841. Edinburgh: Banner of Truth, 2007.

Gale, John. *Reflections on Mr. Wall's History of Infant Baptism.* London: Printed & sold by Darby, 1711.

Gill, John. *Antipaedo-baptism; or, Infant-Baptism an Innovation: Being a Reply to a Late Pamphlet, Entitled, Paedo-baptism; Or, A Defence of Infant-baptism, in Point of Antiquity, &c.* London: Keith & Robinson, 1753.

————. *A Complete Body of Doctrinal and Practical Divinity: Being a System of Evangelical Truths Deduced from the Sacred Scriptures* [1769–70]. Abridged by William Staughton. Philadelphia: Printed for Delaplaine et al., 1810.

————. *A Discourse on Singing of Psalms as a Part of Divine Worship, from I. Corinthians xiv.15. Preached the 25th December, 1733. To a Society of Young Men Who Carry on an Exercise of Prayer on Lord's-Day Mornings, at a Meeting-House on Horsly-down.* Southwark. London: n.p., 1734.

————. *An Exposition of the New Testament.* Vol. 1. Philadelphia: Woodward, 1811.

Gillies, John. *Historical Collections Relating to Remarkable Periods of the Success of the Gospel.* Kelso: Rutherford, 1845.

Godfrey, R. John. *Historic Memorials of Barton and Melbourne General Baptist Churches; Including Their Numerous Offshoots since 1760; Biographical Sketches of the Leading Ministers and Laymen; Together with Portraits and Other Illustrations.* Leicester: Buck et al., 1891.

Goodwin, John. *An Exposition of the Nineth Chapter of the Epistle to the Romans: Wherein is Proved that the Apostles Scope Therein is to Maintain His Great Doctrine of Justification by Faith.* n.l.: Printed by John Macock, for Lodowick Lloyd & Henry Cripps, 1653.

————. *Redemption Redeemed Wherein the Most Glorious Work of the Redemption of the World by Jesus Christ, is by Expressness of Scripture, Clearness of Argument, Countenance of the Best Authority, as Well Ancient as Modern, Vindicated and Asserted in the Just Latitude and Extent of it, According to the Counsel and Most Gracious Intensions of God, Against the Encroachments of Later Times Made Upon it, Whereby the Unsearchable Riches and Glory of the Grace of God Therein, Have Been, and yet are, Much Obscured, and Hid from the Eyes of Many.* n.l.: Printed by John Macock, for Lodowick Lloyd & Henry Cripps, 1651.

————. *The Remedie of Unreasonableness; Or the Substance of a Speech Intended at a Conference or Dispute, in Al-hallows the Great London. Feb 11. 1649. Exhibiting the Heads of John Goodwin's Judgement Concerning the Grace of God.* n.l.: Printed by John Macock, for Lodowick Lloyd & Henry Cripps, 1650.

Goodwin, Thomas. *The Works of Thomas Goodwin.* 12 vols. Edinburgh: Nichol, 1861.

Graham, William. *Repentance the Only Condition of Final Acceptance: A Sermon Delivered Before the Dissenting Clergy at Mill-Hill-Chapel in Leeds. September 18, 1771.* London: Johnson, 1772.

Grantham, Thomas. *Christianismus Primitivus, or, The Ancient Christian Religion, in its Nature, Certainty, Excellency, and Beauty, (Internal and External) Particularly Considered, Asserted, and Vindicated from the Many Abuses Which Have Invaded that Sacred Profession, by Humane Innovation, or Pretended Revelation: Comprehending Likewise the General Duties of Mankind, in Their Respective Relations: and Particularly the Obedience of All Christians to Magistrates, and the Necessity of Christian-Moderation About Things Dispensible in Matters of Religion: With Divers Cases of Conscience Discussed and Resolved.* London: Smith, 1678.

————. *The Fourth Principle of Christ's Doctrine Vindicated Being a Brief Answer to Mr. H. Danvers Book, Intituled, A Treatise of Laying on of Hands, Plainly Evincing the True Antiquity and Perpetuity of that Despised Ministration of Prayer with Imposition of Hands for the Promise of the Spirit. To Which is Added, a Discourse of the Successors of the Apostles, Wherein the Office of the Messengers of Christ and the Church is Asserted to be Perpetual, and of Divine Authority, In the Same Nature as Bishops, Elders, &C.* London: n.p., 1674.

————. *The Loyal Baptist, or, an Apology for the Baptized Believers: Occasioned by the Great and Long Continued Sufferings of the Baptized Believers in This Nation.* London: Printed for the author, sold by Thomas Fabian, 1678.

————. *The Paedo-Baptists Apology for the Baptized Churches Shewing the Invalidity of the Strongest Grounds for Infant Baptism Out of the Works of the Learned Assertors of that Tenent, and that the Baptism of Repentance for the Remission of Sins is a Duty Incumbent Upon All Sinners Who Come Orderly to the Profession of Christianity: Also the Promise of the Spirit [B]Eing the Substance of a Sermon on I Cor. 12, I, to Which is Added a Post-script out of the Works of Dr. Jer. Taylor in Defence of Imposition of Hands as a Never Failing Ministry.* London: n.p., 1671.

————. *Presumption No Proof, or, Mr. Petto's Arguments for Infant-Baptism Considered and Answered and Infants Interest in the Convenant* [sic.] *of Grace Without Baptism Asserted and Maintained: Whereunto is Prefixed an Answer to Two questions Propounded by Mr. Firmin About Infants Church-membership and Baptism.* London: n.p., 1687.

————. *The Seventh-Day-Sabbath Ceased as Ceremonial and yet the Morality of the Fourth Command Remaineth, or, Seven Reasons Tending to Prove that the Fourth Command in the Decalogue is of a Different Nature from the Other Nine: Also Certain Answers to some of the Said Reasons Proved Insufficient: Whereunto is Added a Postscript, Shewing the Judgement of the Jews and Antient Christians, Touching the Sabbath-day.* London: n.p., 1667.

————. *St. Paul's Catechism, or, a Brief and Plain Explication of the Six Principles of the Christian Religion, as Recorded Heb. 6.1, 2 with some Considerations of the Principles of Natural and Universal Religion, as Previous, and yet Subservient to the Rules of Revealed and Positive Religion: Containing also, the Duties of Children to Their Superiors, Written Chiefly for the Instruction of Young Christians, Children and Servants in All Christian Families.* London: n.p., 1687.

Greenham, Richard. *A Treatise of the Sabboth.* London: n.p., 1599.

Grimshaw, William. *An Answer to a Sermon Lately Published against the Methodists by the Rev. George White, A.M. Minister of Colne in Lancashire.* Preston: Stanley & Moon, 1749.

Grotius, Hugo. *A Defence of the Catholick Faith concerning the Satisfaction of Christ.* Translated by W. H. London: Printed for Thomas Parkhurst & Johnathan Robinson, 1692.

Hall, Robert, Sr. *Help to Zion's Travellers: Being an Attempt to Remove Various Stumbling Blocks Out of the Way Relating to Doctrinal, Experimental and Practical Religion.* Bristol: Printed by William Pine, sold by Evans & Mills, 1781.

Hanbury, Benjamin. *An Enlarged Series of Extracts from the Diary, Meditations and Letters of Mr. Joseph Williams of Kidderminster: With Notes Biographical and Explanatory, to Which are Annexed some Original Letters from Ministers, &c., Occasioned by His Death, and an Index.* London: Printed for Westley & Davis, 1826.

Hoadly, Benjamin. *The Works of Benjamin Hoadly.* Vol. 3. London: Hoadly, 1773.

Hoard, Samuel. *God's Love to Mankind; Manifested by Disproving His Absolute Decree for Their Damnation.* London: Clark, 1673.

Hopkins, John, and Thomas Sternhold, eds. *The Whole Booke of Psalmes Collected into English Metre.* London: Day, 1562.

Ivimey, Joseph. *A History of the English Baptists.* Vol. 3. London: Holdsworth & Ball, 1830.

Jeffrey, William. *The Whole Faith of Man.* London: Printed by G. Dawson, 1659.

Jones, William. *The Jubilee Memorial of the Religious Tract Society: Containing a Record of its Origin, Proceedings, and Results A.D. 1799—A.D. 1849.* London: The Religious Tract Society, 1850.

Keach, Benjamin. *Laying on of Hands Upon Baptized Believers, as such, Proved an Ordinance of Christ: In Answer to Mr. Danvers's Former Book Intituled, A Treatise of Laying on of Hands: With a Brief Answer to a Late Book Called, A Treatise Concerning Laying on of Hands; Written by a Nameless Author.* 2nd ed. London: Printed and sold by B. Harris, 1698.

———. *Spiritual Melody, Containing Near Three Hundred Sacred Hymns.* London: Printed for J. Hancock, 1691.

———. *TROPOLOGIA: A Key to Open Scripture Metaphors, in Four Books to Which are Prefixed, Arguments to Prove the Divine Authority of the Holy Bible. Together with Types of the Old Testament.* London: Otridge, 1778 [1681–82].

Klein-Nicolai, George [Paul Siegvolk]. *The Everlasting Gospel, Commanded and Preached by Jesus Christ Judge of the Living and the Dead, unto All Creatures, Mark xvi.15, Concerning the Eternal Redemption Found Out by Him whereby Devil, Sin, Hell, and Death, Shall at Last be Abolished and the Whole Creation Restored to its Primitive Purity: Being a Testimony Against the Present Anti-Christian World.* Translated by John S. 1753. Stonington-Port, CT: Trumbull, 1801.

Lambe, Thomas. *A Treatise of Particular Predestination.* London: n.p., 1642.

Legh, George [A Christian]. *An Answer to the Reverend Mr. Stebbing's Remark on the B. of Bangor's Doctrine of Religious Sincerity.* 2nd ed. London: Printed by W.W., for J. Roberts, 1719.

——— [A Christian]. *A Case of an Erroneous Conscience.* London: Printed by W.W., for J. Roberts, 1719.

———— [Gilbert Dalrymple]. *A Letter from Edinburgh to Dr. Sherlock, Rectifying the Committee's Notions of Sincerity. Defending the Whole of the B. of Bangor's Doctrine.* 3rd ed. London: Printed for Roberts et al., 1718.

———— [A Christian]. *A Letter to the Reverend Mr. Stebbing; Being Remarks upon His Late Book Relating to Sincerity.* London: Printed by W.W., for J. Roberts, 1718.

Lévesque de Burigny, Jean. *The Life of the Truly Eminent and Learned Hugo Grotius Containing a Copius and Circumstantial History of the Several Important and Honourable Negotiations in Which He Was Employed, Together with a Critical Account of His Works.* Originally written in French. London: Whiston & White, 1754.

Locke, John. *An Essay Concerning Human Understanding.* 27th ed. Cheapside: Tegg, 1836 [1689].

————. *The Works of John Locke.* Vol. 7. 11th ed. London: Otridge, 1812.

Miall, G. James. *Congregationalism in Yorkshire: A Chapter of Modern Church History.* London: Snow, 1868.

Milton, John. *A Treatise on Christian Doctrine: Compiled from the Holy Scriptures Alone.* Translated by Charles R. Sumner. Vol. 1. Boston: Cummings & Billiard, 1825.

Monk, Thomas. *A Cure for the Cankering Error of the New Eutychians: Who (Concerning the Truth) Have Erred, Saying, that Our Blessed Mediator Did Not Take His Flesh of the Virgin Mary, Neither Was He Made of the Seed of David According to the Flesh, and Thereby Have Overthrown the Faith of some Further Information.* London: n.p., 1673.

Monk, Thomas, et al. *Sions Groans for Her Distressed, or Sober Endeavours to Prevent Innocent Blood, and to Stablish the Nation in the Best of Settlements: Grounded Upon Scripture, Reason, and Authority. Proving it the Undoubted Right of Christian liberty Under Different Perswasions, in Matters Spiritual, to Have Equal Protection as to Their Civil Peace. Unto Which is Added the Testimony of Fifteen Antients. Humbly Offered to the Kings Majesty, Parliament and People, and Left unto Their Serious View.* London: n.p., 1661.

Moore Sr., Thomas. *The Universality of Gods Free Grace in Christ to Mankind.* n.l.: n.p., 1646.

Morris, W. John. *Memoirs of the Life and Writings of the Rev. Andrew Fuller, Late Pastor of the Baptist Church at Kettering, and First Secretary to the Baptist Missionary Society.* Boston: Lincoln & Edmands, 1830.

Murton, John. *Truth's Champion.* n.l.: n.p., 1617.

Nelson, John. *An Extract of John Nelson's Journal; Being an Account of God's Dealing with Him, from His Youth, to the Forty-Second Year of His Age and His Working by Him: Likewise the Oppressions He Met with from People of Different Denominations.* London: Waugh & Mason, 1835.

Newton, John. *Memoirs of the Life of the Late Rev. William Grimshaw, with Occasional Reflections by John Newton, in Six Letters to the Rev. Henry Foster.* London: Bensley, 1799.

Nye, Stephen. *A Brief History of the Unitarians, Called also Socinians, in Four Letters, Written to a Friend.* London: n.p., 1687.

Origen. *Commentary on the Epistle to the Romans.* Translated by Thomas P. Scheck. Washington, WA: Catholic University of America Press, 2001 [246].

Osborn, George. *Outlines of Wesleyan Bibliography; or, A Record of Methodist Literature from the Beginning. In Two Parts: The First Containing the Publications of John and Charles Wesley, Arranged in Order of Time; The Second Those of Methodist Preachers, Alphabetically Arranged.* London: Wesleyan Conference Office, 1869.

Owen, John. *Christologia: Or A Declaration of the Glorious Mystery of the Person of Christ—God and Man with the Infinite Wisdom, Love, and Power of God in the Contrivance and Constitution Thereof; As also, of the Grounds and Reasons of His Incarnation; The Nature of His Ministry in Heaven; The Present State of the Church Above Thereon; and the Use of His Person in Religion, with an Account and Vindication of the Honour, Worship, Faith, Love, and Obedience Due Unto Him, in and from the* Church. London: Printed by John Darby, for Nathaniel Ponder, 1679.

———. *The Lord's Supper Fully Considered, in a Review of the History of its Institution with Meditations and Ejaculations Suited to the Several Parts of the Ordinance. To Which are Prefixed Three Discourses Delivered at the Lord's Table.* 2 vols. Edinburgh: Ogle, 1798.

———. *Twenty-five Discourses Suitable to the Lord's Supper, Delivered Before the Observance of that Ordinance.* Edinburgh: Ogle et al., 1844 [1760].

———. *The Works of John Owen,* edited by William Goold. 24 vols. Edinburgh: Johnston & Hunter, 1850–53.

Perkins, William. *The Whole Treatise of the Cases of Conscience.* Cambridge: n.p., 1606.

Priestley, Joseph. *Institutes of Natural and Revealed Religion.* Vol. 1. London: Johnson, 1772.

Protestant Dissenting Ministers of the Three Denominations in and about the Cities of London and Westminster. *At a Numerous and Respectable Meeting of the General Body of the Protestant Dissenting Ministers in and About the Cities of London and Westminster, Convened for the Purpose of Expressing our Concurrence with Our Brethren in the Country, in Their Resolutions on the Subjects of the Corporation and Test Acts.* London: n.p., n.d., [1789].

Rees, Thomas, ed. *The Racovian Catechism with Notes and Illustrations, Translated from the Latin: To Which is Prefixed a Sketch of the History of Unitarianism in Poland and the Adjacent Countries.* London: Longman et al., 1818.

Rippon, John. *A Selection of Hymns from the Best Authors, Intended as an Appendix to Dr. Watts's Psalms and Hymns.* London: Wilkins, 1787.

Roberts, Alexander, and James Donaldson, eds. *Ante-Nicene Fathers: The Apostolic Fathers, Justin Martyr, Ireneaus.* Vol. 1. 1885. Peabody, MA: Hendrickson, 2004.

Russen, David. *Fundamentals Without Foundation or, A True Picture of the Anabaptists in Their Rise, Progress and* Practice. London: Bassett, 1703.

Ryland Jr., John. *A Candid Statement of the Reasons Which Induce the Baptists to Differ in Opinion and Practice from so Many of Their Christian* Brethren. London: Button & Son, 1814.

Ryland, C. John [Pacifus]. *A Modest Plea for Free Communion at the Lord's Table; Between True Believers of All Denominations: In a Letter to a* Friend. n.l.: n.p., n.d., [1772].

———. *The Work of Faith, the Labour of Love, and the Patience of Hope, Illustrated; In the Life and Death of the Rev. Andrew Fuller, Late Pastor of the Baptist Church at Kettering and Secretary to the Baptist Missionary Society, from its Commencement in 1792,* 2nd ed. London: Button & Son, 1818.

Saunders, Laurence. *The Fullnesse of Gods Love Manifested.* n.l.: n.p., 1643.

Seymour, Aaron, C., ed. *Memoirs of the Life and Character of George Whitefield. Faithfully Selected from His Original Papers, Journals and Letters. Illustrated by a*

Variety of Interesting Anecdotes, from the best Authorities. Originally Compiled by the Late Rev. John Gillies, D.D. Minister of the College Church of Glasgow. 4th ed. Philadelphia: Simon Probasco, 1820.

Smalbroke, Richard. *Reformation Necessary to Prevent Our Ruine. A Sermon Preached to the Societies for Reformation of Manners, at St. Mary-le-Bow, 10 January 1727.* London: Printed by J. Downing, 1728.

Stennett Sr., Joseph. *An Answer to Mr. David Russen's Book, Entitul'd, Fundamentals Without a Foundation, or a True Picture of the Anabaptists, &c: Together with some Brief Remarks on Mr. James Broome's Letter Annex'd to that Treatise.* London: Brown et al., 1704.

Stennett, Samuel. *Remarks on the Christian Minister's Reasons for Administering Baptism by Sprinkling or Pouring of Water: In a Series of Letters to a Friend.* London: Keith et al., 1772.

Stone, M. Edwin. *Biography of Rev. Elhanan Winchester.* Boston: Brewster, 1836.

Stonehouse, James. *Universal Restitution a Scripture Doctrine: This Prov'd in Several Letters Wrote on the Nature and Extent of Christ's Kingdom; Wherein the Scripture Passages, Falsely Alleged in Proof of the Eternity of Hell Torments, are Truly Translated and Explained.* London: Dodsley & Cadell, 1761.

Taylor, Adam. *The History of the English General Baptists in Two Parts. Part First: The History of the English General Baptists. Part Second: The History of The New Connection.* London: Printed for the author by T. Bore, and sold by Button & Son, 1818.

———. *Memoirs of the Rev. Dan Taylor, Late Pastor of the General Baptist Church, Whitechapel, London; With Extracts from His Diary, Correspondence, and Unpublished Manuscripts.* London: Baynes & Son, 1820.

———. *Memoirs of the Rev. John Taylor, Late Pastor of the General Baptist Church at Queenshead, Near Halifax, Yorkshire: Chiefly Compiled from a Manuscript Written by Himself.* Halifax: n.p., 1821.

Taylor, Dan. *The Absolute Necessity of Searching the* Scriptures. Halifax: Darby, 1764.

——— [Philalethes]. *Candidus Examined with Candour, or A Modest Inquiry Into the Propriety and Force of What is Contained in a Late Pamphlet; Intitled, A Modest Plea for Free Communion at the Lord's Table; Particularly Between the Baptists and Poedobaptists* [Sic.]. *By Candidus. in Which it is Attempted to Prove, that This Kind of Free Communion Has Not Sufficient Foundation in the Scriptures.* London: Keith, 1772.

———. *A Catechism; Or Instructions for Children and Youth in the Fundamental Doctrines of Christianity.* 6th ed. London: Button, 1805.

———. *The Cause of National Calamities and the Certain Means of Preventing or Removing Them. A Sermon, on I Sam. xii.14.15.* London: Button, 1795.

———. *A Charge and Sermon Delivered at the Ordination of the Rev. Mr. John Deacon, on Wednesday, April 26, 1786, at Leicester. Together with the Introductory Discourse, the Questions Proposed to the Church, and the Minister, the Answers Returned; And Mr. Deacon's Profession of Faith.* London: Buckland, 1786.

———. *A Charge and Sermon, Together with a Confession of Faith, Delivered at the Ordination of the Rev. George Birley on Wednesday, October 18, 1786, at St. Ives Huntingdonshire. The Charge Delivered by D. Taylor of London, the Sermon by R. Robinson, of Cambridge.* n.l.: Buckland, n.d, [1786].

————. *The Christian Religion: An Exposition of its Leading Principles, Practical Requirements and Experimental Enjoyments.* London: Smith, 1844 [1802].

————. *A Circular Letter from the Ministers of the General Baptist Denomination, Assembled at St. Ives, Huntingdonshire, June 10th, and 11th, 1778. To Their Respective Churches.* London: Printed by J. W. Pasham, 1778.

————. *A Compendious View of the Nature and Importance of Christian Baptism; For the Use of Plain Christians.* London: Wayland, n.d., [1789].

————. *Confession of Faith in Twenty-four Articles.* Leicester: Brooks, n.d., [1785].

————. *The Consistent Christian; Or the Truth and Peace, Holiness, Unanimity, Stedfastness, and Zeal, Recommended to Professors of Christianity. The Substance of Five Sermons. To Which is Prefixed, a Brief Account of the Author's Removal from Wadsworth to Halifax.* Leeds: Wright & Son, 1784.

————. *The Consistent Christian; Or the Truth and Peace, Holiness, Unanimity, Stedfastness, and Zeal, Recommended to Professors of Christianity. The Substance of Five Sermons. With an Appendix on Self-Examination.* 2nd ed. Leeds: Printed for the author and Sold by W. Button, n.d., [1795].

————. *A Dissertation on Singing in the Worship of God: Interspersed with Occasional Strictures on Mr. Boyce's Late Tract, Entitled, "serious Thoughts on the Present Mode and Practice of Singing in the Public Worship of God."* London: Buckland & Mortom, 1786.

————. *Entertainment and Profit United: Easy Verses on some of the Chief Subjects of Christianity for the Use of Poor Children and Youth.* 3rd ed. London: Hawes, n.d., [1777].

————. *An Essay on the Truth and Inspiration of the Holy Scriptures.* London: Knott et al., 1790.

————. *The Eternity of Future Punishment, Asserted and Improved; A Discourse on Matthew, xxv.46.* London: Printed by Henry Fry, for J. Buckland et al., 1789.

————. *The Eternity of Future Punishment, Re-asserted; The Importance of the Doctrine Stated, and the Truth of it Vindicated, in a Reply to the Exceptions of the Rev. Mr. Winchester Against it. In Six Letters to the Rev. G. - - B. - - of C.* London: Printed by Henry Fry, for J. Buckland, B. Ash, J. Marsom, n.d., [1789].

————. *The Faithful and Wise Steward, Being the Substance of a Discourse, Delivered by Way of Address to Young Ministers, at an Association of Ministers and Others, at Conningsby in Lincolnshire, May 13, 1766, from Luk. xii.42.* Leeds: Wright, 1766.

————. *The Friendly Conclusion: Occasioned by the Letters of Agnostos to the Rev. Andrew Fuller, Respecting the Extent of Our Saviour's Death, and Other Subjects Connected with that Doctrine: In Four Letters to a Friend.* London: Ash, Marsom & Button, 1790.

————. *Fundamentals of Religion in Faith and Practice; Or, An Humble Attempt to Place some of the Most Important Subjects of Doctrinal, Experimental, and Practical Divinity in a Clear and Scripture Light.* Leeds: n.p., 1775.

————. *A Good Minister of Jesus Christ. A Sermon Occasioned by the Death of the Rev. Samuel Stennett.* London: Button et al., n.d., [1795].

———— Anon. [Dan Taylor]. *An Humble Essay on Christian Baptism.* Leeds: Wright, 1768.

————. *Humble Essay on Christian Baptism,* 2nd edition. London: Pashan, 1777.

————. *An Humble Essay on the Right Use of Earthly Treasure. In Three Letters to a Fellow-Labourer in the Work of the Ministry.* 2nd ed. Leeds: Wright & Son, 1780.

———— [ed.]. *Hymns and Spiritual Songs, Mostly Collected from Various Authors; With a Few that Have Not Been Published Before.* Halifax: Jacob, 1772.

————. *Important Advice to Churches Involved in Pecuniary Difficulties, with Motives to Enforce it. From an Occasional Address by the Late Rev. D. Taylor.* London: Printed by P.&F. Hack, sold by J. Mann et al., 1819.

————. *The Interposition of Providence in the Late Recovery of His Majesty King George the Third, Illustrated and Improved; The Substance of a Sermon, Preached March 15, 1789.* London: Buckland et al., 1789.

————. *Letter on the Duties of Church Members to Each Other; Addressed Principally to the General Baptist Churches; and Read by Desire, at the Annual Association of General Baptist Ministers and Representatives of Churches; Holden at Boston, in Lincolnshire, June 28th, 29th, 30th, and July 1st, 1796.* London: Printed by R. Hawes, 1796.

————. *Memoirs of the Life, Character, Experiences, and Ministry, of the Late Rev. William Thompson, of Boston in Lincolnshire: who Died February 7th, 1794. To Which is Prefixed a Discourse on 2 Cor. xiii.II Occasioned by His Death; and Recommended to the Church over Which He Presided, as the Advice of a Dying Pastor.* London: Hawes et al., 1796.

————. *Mourning Parent Comforted: Or, an Humble Attempt to Relieve the Minds of Those Christians Who are Lamenting the Loss of Their Children, or Labouring Under Any Other Trial. The Substance of Two Sermons.* Halifax: Jacob, 1768.

———— [Lover of All Mankind]. *Observations on the Rev. Andrew Fuller's Late Pamphlet, Entitled, "The Gospel of Christ Worthy of All Acceptation." In which it is Attempted, Farther to Confirm His Leading Idea, Viz. that "faith in Christ is the Duty of All Men, who Hear the Sound of the Gospel." In Nine Letters, to a Friend.* London: Buckland et al., 1786.

————. *Observations on the Rev. Andrew Fuller's Reply to Philanthropos; Or a Further Attempt to Prove that the Universal Invitations of the Gospel are Founded on the Universality of Divine Love, and the Death of Jesus Christ, as the Propitiation for the Sins of the Whole World. In Thirteen Letters to a Friend.* London: Buckland et al., 1787.

————. *Observations on the Rev. Andrew Fuller's Reply to Philanthropos; Or a Further Attempt to Prove that the Universal Invitations of the Gospel are Founded on the Universality of Divine Love, and the Death of Jesus Christ, as the Propitiation for the Sins of the Whole World. In Thirteen Letters to a Friend.* 2nd ed. St. Ives: Buckland et al., 1788.

————. *Our Saviour's Commission to His Ministers, Explained and Improved. The Substance of a Sermon Delivered at Canterbury, and in Worship-Street, London, at the Administration of the Ordinance of Baptism.* Leeds: Wright, 1785.

———— [Philagathus]. *A Practical Improvement of the Divinity and Atonement of Jesus, Attempted in Verse; Humbly Offered as a Supplement to the Tracts Lately Published by Mr. Cayley, the Rev. Mr. Morgan, Verus and Biblicus.* Halifax: Jacob, 1772.

————. *The Scriptural Account of the Way of Salvation in Two Parts: The Former, an Appeal to the Conscience of Every Reader, Respecting some Important Doctrines of Scripture and His Own Personal Concern in Them. The Latter, a Free Examination of a Sermon Lately Published by the Rev. W. Graham, M.A. Intitled "Repentance the Only Condition of Final Acceptance."* Halifax: Jacob, 1772.

———. *Scripture Directions and Encouragements to Feeble Christians.* 3rd ed. Leeds: Wright, 1777.

——— [Scrutator]. *Scrutator to Responsor; Or an Introduction to a Farther Proof, (If need be,) that Jesus Christ, the Blessed Son of God, Laid Down His Life for the Sins of all Mankind, in Two Letters to Responsor. With a short letter to Considerator,* 2nd ed. Leeds: Printed by J. Bowling for the author, n.d., [1781].

———. *A Second Dissertation on Singing in the Worship of God; Introduced with Two Letters to the Revd. Mr. Gilbert Boyce, in Defence of a Former Dissertation on that Subject.* London: Buckland, 1787.

———. *A Sermon Occasioned by the Death of Mrs. Elizabeth Taylor, Who Departed This Life October 22, 1793, in the 49th Year of Her Age. With a Short Account of Her Life, and a Description of Her Character.* London: Marsom et al., 1794.

———. *Strictures on the Rev. Stephen Addington's Late Summary of the Christian Minister's Reasons for Baptizing Infants and for Administering the Ordinance by Sprinkling or Pouring of Water.* London: Pasham, 1777.

——— Anon. [Dan Taylor]. *A Thought on the Death of the Late Reverend Mr. Wm. Grimshaw, Who Died the 7th April 1763.* Halifax: Darby, 1763.

———., and John Deacon, eds. *Hymns and Spiritual Songs. Selected from Various Sources.* London: Sold by D. Taylor, 1793.

———., and William Thompson. *The Respective Duties of Ministers and People Briefly Explained and Enforced: The Substance of Two Discourses, delivered at Great-Yarmouth, in Norfolk, Jan. 9th, 1775, at the Ordination of the Rev. Mr. Benjamin Worship, to the Pastoral Office. The Former by Dan Taylor, of Wadsworth, Yorkshire. The Latter by Wm. Thompson, of Boston, Lincolnshire.* Leeds: Wright, 1775.

Taylor, Thomas [Philalethes]. *A Solemn Caution Against the Ten Horns of Calvinism. By Philalethes Lately Escaped.* 4th ed. Leeds: Nichols, 1780.

Toland, John. *Christianity not Mysterious: Or, a Treatise Showing that There is Nothing in the Gospel Contrary to Reason, Nor Above it, and that No Christian Doctrine Can Be Properly Call'd a Mystery.* 2nd ed. London: Buckley, 1696.

Turner, Daniel [Candidus]. *A Modest Plea for Free Communion at the Lord's Table; Particularly between the Baptists and Paedobaptists. In a Letter to a Friend.* London: Printed for J. Johnson, 1772.

Underwood, William. *The Life of the Rev. Dan Taylor: A Monograph.* London: Simpkin & Marshall, n.d., [1870].

Venn, Henry. *Christ the Joy of the Christian's Life and Death his Gain: The Substance of a Sermon Preached April 10th, in Haworth Church on the Death of the Reverend Mr. W. Grimshaw, A.B. Minister of that Parish and Published at the Request of His Friends. To which is added, a Sketch of His Life and Ministry.* Leeds: Wright, 1763.

Vidler, William. *A Sketch of the Life of Elhanan Winchester: Preacher of the Universal Restoration, with a Review of His Writings.* London: Gillet, 1797.

Walker, U. James. *A History of Wesleyan Methodism in Halifax and its Vicinity from its Commencement to the Present Period.* London: Hartley & Walker., 1836.

Wall, William. *A History of Infant Baptism in Two Parts. The First Being an Impartial Collection of all such Passages in the Writers of the First Four Centuries as do Make For, or Against it. The Second, Containing several things that do Illustrate the Said History.* London: Printed by J. Downing, 1705.

Watson, Richard. *The Life of the Rev. John. Wesley.* London: Mason, 1831.

Watts, Isaac. *Logic; Or the Right Use of Reason, in the Inquiry After Truth: With a Variety of Rules to Guard against Error in the Affairs of Religion and Human Life, as well as in the Sciences*. New ed. London: Cuthell, 1792 [1724].

Wesley, Charles. *The Letters of Charles Wesley: A Critical Edition, with Introduction and Notes*, edited by Kenneth G.C. Newport, and Gareth Lloyd. Vol. 1. Oxford: Oxford University Press, 2013.

Wesley, John. *The Bicentennial Edition of the Works of John Wesley*. Edited by Frank Baker and Richard P. Heitzenrater. Oxford: Clarendon, 1975–83; and Nashville: Abingdon, 1984–.

———. *Free Grace: A Sermon Preach'd at Bristol*. Bristol: S. & F. Farley, 1739.

———. *The Letters of the Rev. John Wesley*. 8 vols. Edited by John Telford. 1931. Repr., London: Epworth, 1960.

———. *Predestination Calmly Considered*. London: Printed by W. B., 1752.

———. *The Works of the Rev. John Wesley*, edited by Thomas Jackson. Vol. 8. 3rd ed. London: Wesleyan Conference Office, 1872 [1831].

Whiston, William. *Historical Memoirs of the Life of Dr. Samuel Clarke: Being a Supplement to Dr. Sykes's and Bishop Hoadley's Accounts; Including Certain Memoirs of Several of Dr. Clarke's Friends*. London: Sold by Gyles and Roberts, 1730.

Whitefield, George. *George Whitefield's Journals*. New ed. London: Banner of Truth, 1960.

———. *The Works of the Reverend George Whitefield, M.A. Late of Pembroke-college, Oxford, and Chaplain to the Rt. Hon. the Countess of Huntingdon. Containing All His Sermons and Tracts Which Have Been Already Published: With a Select Collection of Letters Written to His Most Intimate Friends and Persons of Distinction in England, Scotland, Ireland and America, from the Year 1734 to 1770, Including the Whole Period of His Ministry also some other Pieces on Important subjects Never Before Printed; Prepared by Himself for the Press. To Which is Prefixed, an Account of His Life, Compiled from his Original Papers and Letters*. Vol. 1. London: Printed for Edward Dilly et al., 1771.

Whitley, William T., ed. *Minutes of the General Baptist Assembly of the General Baptist Churches in England, with Kindred Records 1654–1811*. 2 vols. London: Kingsgate, 1909–10.

Winchester, Elhanan. *A Letter to a Friend, Containing some Remarks upon the Rev. Dan Taylor's Sermon on "The Eternity of Future Punishment Asserted and Improved,"* in Elhanan Winchester, *the Holy Conversation, and High Expectation, of True Christians. A Discourse, Delivered in London April 29 MDCCLXXXIX. To Which are Added a Few Remarks on the Rev. Dan Taylor's Discourse, Entitled "The Eternity of Future Punishment Asserted and Improved."* London: Printed and sold by R. Hawes, n.d., [1789].

———. *The Restitution of All Things (Which God Hath Spoken by the Mouth of All His Holy Prophets Since the World Began) Defended: Being an Attempt to Answer the Reverend Dan Taylor's Assertions and Re-Assertions in Favour of Endless Misery, in Five Letters to Himself*. London: Printed for the author, sold by Parsons, 1790.

———. *The Universal Restoration: Exhibited in Four Dialogues Between a Minister and His Friend: Comprehending the Substance of Several Conversations that the Author Hath Had with Various Persons, Both in America and Europe, on that Interesting Subject. Chiefly Designed and Fully to State and Fairly to Answer the Most Common*

Objections that are Brought Against it, from the Scriptures. Boston: Mussey, 1831 [1788].

Wollstonecraft, Mary. *A Vindication of the Rights of Women: With Strictures on Political and Moral Subjects.* London: Johnson, 1792.

Wood, H. James. *A Condensed History of the General Baptists of The New Connexion. Preceded by Historical Sketches of the Early Baptists.* London: Simpkin & Marshall, 1847.

Woodward, Josiah. *An Account of the Rise and Progress of the Religious Societies in the City of London and of Endeavours for the Reformation of Manners Which Have Been Made Therein.* London: Printed by J.D., for the author, and sold by Ra. Simpson, 1698.

Wyclif, Iohannis. *Opus Evangelicum.* 4 vols. Edited by Iohann Loserth. London: Published for the Wyclif Society by Trubner, 1895–96.

Secondary Sources

Anon. "Pike, Rev. John G." In *The Baptist Encyclopaedia. A Dictionary of the Doctrines, Ordinances, Usages, Confessions of Faith, Sufferings, Labors and Successes, and of the General History of the Baptist Denomination in All Lands. With Numerous Biographical Sketches of Distinguished Americans and Foreign Baptists, and a Supplement*, edited by William Cathcart, 921–22. Philadelphia: Everts, 1881.

Aaron, I. Richard. *John Locke.* Oxford: Clarendon, 1955.

Ambler, Rodney W. "Church, Place and Organization: The Development of the New Connexion General Baptists in Lincolnshire, 1770–1891." *BQ* 37, no. 5 (1998) 238–48.

Anstey, Roger. *The Atlantic Slave Trade and British Abolition, 1760–1810.* London: Macmillan, 1975.

Arnold, W. Jonathan. *The Reformed Theology of Benjamin Keach (1640–1704).* Oxford: Regent's Park College, 2013.

Arrington, Robert L., ed. *A Companion to the Philosophers.* Oxford: Blackwell, 1999.

Baker, Frank, *John Wesley and the Church of England.* 2nd ed. London: Epworth, 2000

———. *William Grimshaw 1708–63.* London: Epworth, 1963.

Bangs, Carl. *Arminius: A Study in the Dutch Reformation.* Nashville: Abingdon, 1971.

Bass, C. Clint. *Thomas Grantham (1633–1692) and General Baptist Theology.* Oxford: Regent's Park College, 2013.

Bebbington, W. David. *Baptists Through the Centuries: A History of a Global People.* Waco, TX: Baylor University Press, 2010.

———. "British Baptist Crucicentrism since the Late Eighteenth Century: Part 1." *BQ* 44, no. 4 (2011) 223–37.

———. *Evangelicalism in Modern Britain: A History from the 1730s to the 1980s.* London: Unwin Hyman, 1989.

———. "Response." In *The Emergence of Evangelicalism: Exploring Historical Continuities*, edited by Michael A.G. Haykin, and Kenneth J. Stewart, 417–32. Nottingham: Apollos, 2008.

Bebbington, W. David, et al., eds. *Protestant Nonconformist Texts: The Nineteenth Century.* Vol. 3. Aldershot: Ashgate, 2006.

Beckwith, Frank. "Dan Taylor (1738–1816) and Yorkshire Baptist Life." *BQ* 9, no. 5 (1939) 297–306.

Bennett, Christi-An C. "John Wesley: Founder of a Missionary Church?" *PWHS* 50, no. 5 (1996) 159–70.

Betteridge, Alan. "Barton-in-the-Beans, Leicestershire: A Source of Church Plants." *BQ* 36, no. 2 (1995) 70–79.

Blom, Hans W. "Grotius and Socinianism." In *Socinianism and Arminianism: Antitrinitarians, Calvinists, and Cultural Exchange in the Seventeenth-Century Europe*, edited by Martin Mulsow and Jan Rohls, 121–47. Leiden: Brill, 2005.

Blomfield, W. E. "Yorkshire Baptist Churches in the 17th and 18th Centuries." In *The Baptists of Yorkshire: Being the Centenary Memorial Volume of the Yorkshire Baptist Association*, edited by C. E. Shipley, 53–112. Bradford: Byles & Sons, 1912.

Bowmer, C. John. *The Sacrament of the Lord's Supper in Early Methodism*. London: Dacre, 1951.

Brackney, H. William. *A Genetic History of Baptist Thought*. Macon, GA: Mercer University Press, 2004.

Bremer, Francis J. "The Puritan Experiment in New England, 1630–1660." In *The Cambridge Companion to Puritanism*, edited by John Coffey and Paul C.H. Lim, 127–42. Cambridge: Cambridge University Press, 2008.

Bremer, Francis J., ed. *Puritanism: Transatlantic Perspectives on a Seventeenth-Century Anglo-American Faith*. Boston: Massachusetts Historical Society, 1993.

Briggs, John H. Y. "The Changing Pattern of Baptist Life in the Eighteenth Century." In *Pulpit and People: Studies in Eighteenth-Century Baptist Life and Thought*, edited by John H.Y. Briggs, 1–24. Eugene, OR: Wipf and Stock, 2009.

———. 'She-Preachers, Widows and Other Women: The Feminine Dimension in Baptist Life since 1600." *BQ* 31, no. 7 (July 1986) 337–52.

Briggs, John H. Y., ed. *Pulpit and People: Studies in Eighteenth-Century Baptist Life and Thought*. Eugene, OR: Wipf and Stock, 2009.

Brown, Raymond. *English Baptists of the Eighteenth Century*. London: Baptist Historical Society, 1986.

Brown, Stewart J., and Timothy Tackett, eds. *The Cambridge History of Christianity: Enlightenment, Reawakening and Revolution 1660–1815*. Vol. 7. Cambridge: Cambridge University Press, 2006.

Burrage, S. Henry. *Baptist Hymn Writers and Their Hymns*. Portland, ME: Thurstow, 1888.

Butt-Thompson, Frederick W. "William Vidler, Baptist and Universalist." *Transactions of the Baptist Historical Society* 1, no. 1 (1908) 42–55.

Byington, H. Edwin. *Open-Air Preaching: A Practical Manual for Pastors, Evangelists, and Other Christian Workers*. Hartford, CT: Hartford Theological Seminary, 1892.

Campbell, A. Ted. *The Religion of the Heart: A Study of European Religious Life in the Seventeenth and Eighteenth Centuries*. Eugene, OR: Wipf and Stock, 2000.

Cassirer, Ernst. *The Philosophy of the Enlightenment*. Princeton, NJ: Princeton University Press, 2009 [1932].

Cathcart, William, ed. *The Baptist Encyclopaedia. A Dictionary of the Doctrines, Ordinances, Usages, Confessions of Faith, Sufferings, Labors and Successes, and of the General History of the Baptist Denomination in All Lands. With Numerous Biographical Sketches of Distinguished Americans and Foreign Baptists, and a Supplement*. Philadelphia: Everts, 1881.

Chun, Chris. *The Legacy of Jonathan Edwards in the Theology of Andrew Fuller*. Leiden: Brill, 2012.

Clipsham, Ernest F. "Andrew Fuller and Fullerism: Fuller as a Theologian." *BQ* 20, no. 6 (1964) 268–76.

———. "Andrew Fuller and Fullerism: The Gospel Worthy of All Acceptation." *BQ* 20, no. 5 (1964) 214–25.

Coffey, John. "The Abolition of the Slave Trade: Christian Conscience and Political Action." *Cambridge Papers* 15, no. 2 (2006) 1–6.

———. *John Goodwin and the Puritan Revolution: Religion and Intellectual Change in Seventeenth-Century England*. Woodbridge: Boydell, 2006.

———. "Puritanism, Evangelicalism and the Evangelical Protestant Tradition." In *The Emergence of Evangelicalism: Exploring Historical Continuities*, edited by Michael A. G. Haykin and Kenneth J. Stewart, 252–77. Nottingham: Apollos, 2008.

———., and Paul C.H. Lim, eds. *The Cambridge Companion to Puritanism*. Cambridge: Cambridge University Press, 2008.

Coffey, John, and Paul C. H. Lim. "Introduction." In *The Cambridge Companion to Puritanism*, edited by John Coffey and Paul C. H. Lim, 1–15. Cambridge: Cambridge University Press, 2008.

Collins, Kenneth J., and John H. Tyson, eds. *Conversion in the Wesleyan Tradition*. Nashville: Abingdon, 2001.

Collinson, Patrick, *English Puritanism*. London: Historical Association, 1983.

Conforti, A. Joseph. *Samuel Hopkins and the New Divinity Movement*. Grand Rapids: Eerdmans, 1981.

Cook, Faith. *William Grimshaw of Haworth*. Edinburgh: Banner of Truth, 1997.

Cragg, G. George. *Grimshaw of Haworth: A Study in Eighteenth Century Evangelicalism*. London: Canterbury, 1947.

Cragg, R. Gerald. *Reason and Authority in the Eighteenth Century*. Cambridge: Cambridge University Press, 1964.

Cross, Anthony R. "Baptismal Regeneration: Rehabilitating a Lost Dimension of New Testament Baptism." In *Baptist Sacramentalism 2*, edited by Anthony R. Cross and Philip E. Thompson, 149–74. Eugene, OR: Wipf and Stock, 2008.

———. "The Myth of English Baptist Anti-Sacramentalism." In *Recycling the Past or Researching History?*, edited by Philip E. Thompson and Anthony R. Cross, 128–62. Milton Keynes: Paternoster, 2005.

Cross, Anthony R., and Philip E. Thompson, eds. *Baptist Sacramentalism*. Carlisle: Paternoster, 2003.

Cross, Anthony R., and Philip E. Thompson, eds.. *Baptist Sacramentalism 2*. Eugene, Or: Wipf and Stock, 2008.

Cross, Richard. "Duns Scotus on Goodness, Justice, and What God Can Do." *Journal of Theological Studies* 48, no. 1 (1997) 48–76.

Cruickshank, Joanna. ""If God . . . See Fit to Call You Out": "Public" and "Private" in the Writings of Methodist Women, 1760–1840." In *Religion in the Age of Enlightenment*, edited by Brett C. McInelly, 2:55–76. Brooklyn: AMS, 2010.

Curwen, S. John. *Studies in Worship-music, Chiefly as Regards Congregational Singing*. London: Curwen & Sons, 1880.

Daniel, Curt. "Andrew Fuller and Antinomianism." In *"At the Pure Fountain of Thy Word": Andrew Fuller as an Apologist*, edited by Michael A. G. Haykin, 74–82. Milton Keynes: Paternoster, 2004.

Dean, William W. "The Methodist Class Meeting: The Significance of its Decline." *PWHS* 43, no. 3 (1981) 41–48.

Dibble, Jeremy, and Bennett Zon, eds. *Nineteenth-Century British Music Studies.* Vol. 2. Aldershot: Ashgate, 2001.

Drage, Sally. "John Fawcett of Bolton: The Changing Face of Psalmody." In *Nineteenth-Century British Music Studies,* edited by Jeremy Dibble and Bennett Zon, 2:59–69. Aldershot: Ashgate, 2001.

Duncan, Kathryn, ed. *Religion in the Age of Reason: A Transatlantic Study of the Long Eighteenth Century.* Brooklyn: AMS, 2009.

Duncan-Jones, Austin. *Butler's Moral Philosophy.* Harmondsworth: Pelican, 1952.

Elwell, Walter A., ed. *Evangelical Dictionary of Theology.* Grand Rapids: Baker, 1984.

Ferguson, Sinclair B. "John Owen and the Doctrine of the Person of Christ." In *John Owen—The Man and His Theology,* edited by Robert W. Oliver, 69–99. Phillipsburg, NJ: P.&R., 2002.

Fiddes, Paul S. "Daniel Turner and a Theology of the Church Universal." In *Pulpit and People: Studies in Eighteenth-Century Baptist Life and Thought,* edited by John H. Y. Briggs, 112–27. Eugene, OR: Wipf and Stock, 2009.

Forbes, Margaret. *Beattie and His Friends.* London: Constable, 1904.

Ford Watson, JoAnn. "Anne Dutton: Eighteenth Century Evangelical British Woman Writer." *Ashland Theological Journal* 30 (1998) 51–56.

———. *Selected Spiritual Writings of Anne Dutton: Eighteenth-Century, British-Baptist, Woman Theologian.* 6 vols. Macon, GA: Mercer University Press, 2003–2009.

Foreman, Henry. "Baptist Provision for Ministerial Education in the 18th Century." *BQ* 27, no. 8 (1978) 358–69.

Foster, H. Frank. *A Genetic History of the New England Theology.* Chicago: University of Chicago Press, 1907.

Fowler, K. Stanley. *More Than a Symbol: The British Baptist Recovery of Baptismal Sacramentalism.* Carlisle: Paternoster, 2002.

Freeman, Curtis W. ""To Feed upon by Faith": Nourishment from the Lord's Table." In *Baptist Sacramentalism,* edited by Anthony R. Cross and Philip E. Thompson, 194–210. Carlisle: Paternoster, 2003.

Garrett, James Leo, Jr. *Baptist Theology: A Four-Century Study.* Macon, GA: Mercer University Press, 2009.

Gay, Peter. *The Enlightenment: An Interpretation. The Rise of Modern Paganism.* Vol. 1. New York: Knopf, 1966.

———. *The Enlightenment: An Interpretation. The Science of Freedom.* Vol.. 2. New York: Knopf, 1969.

Gerstner, John H. "The Theological Boundaries of Evangelical Faith." In *The Evangelicals: What They Believe, Who They are, Where They are Changing,* edited by David F. Wells, and John D. Woodbridge, 21–37. Nashville: Abingdon, 1975.

Gibson, William. *Enlightenment Prelate: Benjamin Hoadly, 1676–1761.* Cambridge: Clarke, 2004.

Gibson, William, and Robert G. Ingram, eds. *Religious Identities in Britain, 1660–1832.* London: Ashgate, 2005.

Gilley, Sheridan, and W. J. Sheils, eds. *A History of Religion in Britain: Practice and Belief from Pre-Roman Times to the Present.* Oxford: Blackwell, 1994.

Goadby, Bertha, and Lilian Goadby. *Not Saints But Men: Or the Story of the Goadby Ministers. With an Introduction by Dr. John Clifford.* London: Kingsgate, n.d., [1906].

Goldhawk, Norman P. "Darney, William." In *The Encyclopedia of World Methodism,* edited by Nolan B. Harmon, 1:629. Nashville: United Methodist, 1974.

Gouldbourne, M. B. Ruth. *Reinventing the Wheel: Women and Ministry in English Baptist Life.* Oxford: Whitley, 1997.

Gregory, Jeremy. ""In the Church I Will Live and Die": John Wesley, the Church of England and Methodism." In *Religious Identities in Britain, 1660–1832,* edited by William Gibson and Robert G. Ingram, 147–78. London: Ashgate, 2005.

———. "Religion in the Age of Enlightenment: Putting John Wesley in Context." In *Religion in the Age of Enlightenment,* edited by Brett C. McInelly, 2:19–54. Brooklyn: AMS, 2010.

Griffin, I. J. Martin, Jr. *Latitudinarianism in the Seventeenth-Century Church of England.* Edited by Lila Freedman. Leiden: Brill, 2005

Halévy, Elie. *A History of the English People in the Nineteenth Century: England in 1815.* Vol. 1. Translated by E. I. Watkin, and D. I. Barker. London: Benn, 1949.

Hambrick-Stowe, Charles E. "Practical divinity and spirituality." In *The Cambridge Companion to Puritanism,* edited by John Coffey and Paul C.H. Lim, 191–205. Cambridge: Cambridge University Press, 2008.

———. *The Practice of Piety: Puritan Devotional Disciplines in Sevententh-Century New England.* Chapel Hill: University of North Carolina Press, 1986.

———. "The Spirit of the Old Writers: The Great Awakening and the Persistence of Puritan Piety." In *Puritanism: Transatlantic Perspectives on a Seventeenth-Century Anglo-American Faith,* edited by Francis J. Bremer, 277–91. Boston: Massachusetts Historical Society, 1993.

Hardy, S. Robert. *William Grimshaw, Incumbent of Haworth, 1742–1763.* London: Mason, 1860.

Hargreaves, John A. "Religion and Society in the Parish of Halifax c. 1740–1914." PhD thesis, Huddersfield Polytechnic, 1991.

Harmon, Nolan B., ed. *The Encyclopedia of World Methodism.* Vol. 1. Nashville: United Methodist, 1974.

Harrison, Fred M. W. "Approach of the New Connexion General Baptists to a Midland Industrial Town." *BQ* 33, no. 1 (1989) 16–19.

———. "Nottinghamshire Baptists. Church Relations: Social Composition: Finance: Theology." *BQ* 26, no. 4 (1975) 169–90.

———. "The Nottinghamshire Baptists: Mission, Worship & Training." *BQ* 25, no. 7 (1974) 309–28.

———. "Nottinghamshire Baptists: Their Rise and Expansion." *BQ* 25, no. 2 (1973) 59–73.

Haslam, John. "The Yorkshire Baptist Association." In *The Baptists of Yorkshire: Being the Centenary Memorial Volume of the Yorkshire Baptist Association,* edited by C. E. Shipley, 267–318. Bradford: Byles & Sons, 1912.

Hayden, Roger. *Continuity and Change: Evangelical Calvinism among Eighteenth-Century Baptist Ministers Trained at Bristol Academy, 1690–1791.* Milton under Wychwood: Baptist Historical Society, 2006.

———. *English Baptist History and Heritage.* 2nd ed. Didcot: Baptist Union of Great Britain, 2005.

———. "Evangelical Calvinism among Eighteenth-Century British Baptists with Particular Reference to Bernard Foskett, Hugh and Caleb Evans and the Bristol Baptist Academy 1690–1791." PhD thesis, Keele University, 1991.

Haykin, Michael A. G. "Andrew Fuller and the Sandemanian Controversy." In *"At the Pure Fountain of Thy Word": Andrew Fuller as an Apologist*, edited by Michael A.G. Haykin, 223–36. Milton Keynes: Paternoster, 2004.

———. ed. *"At the Pure Fountain of Thy Word": Andrew Fuller as an Apologist*. Milton Keynes: Paternoster, 2004.

———. "Evangelicalism and the Enlightenment: A Reassessment." In *The Emergence of Evangelicalism: Exploring Historical Continuities*, edited by Michael A. G. Haykin and Kenneth J. Stewart, 37–60. Nottingham: Apollos, 2008.

———. "'A Habitation of God, through the Spirit': John Sutcliff (1752–1814) and the Revitalization of the Calvinistic Baptists in the Late Eighteenth Century." *BQ* 34, no. 7 (1992) 304–19.

———. ""His soul-refreshing presence": The Lord's Supper in Calvinistic Baptist Thought and Experience in the "Long" Eighteenth Century." In *Baptist Sacramentalism*, edited by Anthony R. Cross and Philip E. Thompson, 177–93. Carlisle: Paternoster, 2003

———. *Kiffin, Knollys and Keach*. Leeds: Reformation Today Trust, 1996.

———. *One Heart and One Soul: John Sutcliff of Olney, His Friends and His Times*. Darlington: Evangelical, 1994.

Haykin, Michael A. G., and Victoria J. Haykin, eds. *"The First Counsellor of Our Denomination": Studies in the Life and Ministry of Abraham Booth (1734–1806)*. Springfield, MO: Particular Baptist, 2006.

Haykin, Michael A. G., and Kenneth J. Stewart, eds. *The Emergence of Evangelicalism: Exploring Historical Continuities*. Nottingham: Apollos, 2008.

Hempton, David. *Methodism: Empire of the Spirit*. New Haven, CT: Yale University Press, 2005.

Heitzenrater, Richard P. "John Wesley's Principles and Practice of Preaching." *Methodist History* 37, no. 2 (1999) 89–106.

Hindmarsh, D. Bruce. *The Evangelical Conversion Narrative: Spiritual Autobiography in Early Modern England*. Oxford: Oxford University Press, 2005.

———. "Reshaping individualism: The Private Christian, Eighteenth-Century Religion and the Enlightenment." In *The Rise of the Laity in Evangelical Protestantism*, edited by Deryck W. Lovegrove, 67–84. London: Routledge, 2002.

Holmes, R. Stephen. *Baptist Theology*. London: T. & T. Clark, 2012.

———. *God of Grace and God of Glory: An Account of the Theology of Jonathan Edwards*. Edinburgh: T. & T. Clark, 2000.

Horton, Michael Scott, ed. *Power Religion: The Selling Out of the Evangelical Church*. Chicago: Moody Bible Institute, 1992.

Hudson, Wayne. *Enlightenment and Modernity: The English Deists and Reform*. London: Pickering & Chatto, 2009.

Hylson-Smith, Kenneth. *Evangelicals in the Church of England 1734–1984*. Edinburgh: T. & T. Clark, 1989.

Inscore Essick, John D., Jr. "Messenger, Apologist, and Nonconformist: An Examination of Thomas Grantham's Leadership among the Seventeenth-Century General Baptists." PhD thesis, Baylor University, 2008.

————. *Thomas Grantham: God's Messenger from* Lincolnshire. Macon, GA: Mercer University Press, 2013.

Israel, I. Jonathan. *Enlightenment Contested: Philosophy, Modernity, and the Emancipation of Man 1670–1752.* Oxford: Oxford University Press, 2006.

————. *Radical Enlightenment: Philosophy and the Making of Modernity 1650–1750.* Oxford: Oxford University Press, 2001.

Jackson, Jack. "Collecting and Preserving Disciples: Verbal Proclamation in Early Methodist Evangelism." *Wesley and Methodist Studies* 2 (2010) 45–66.

Jacob, Margaret C. "The Enlightenment Critique of Christianity." In *The Cambridge History of Christianity: Enlightenment, Reawakening and Revolution 1660–1815,* edited by Stewart J. Brown, and Timothy Tackett, 7:265–82. Cambridge: Cambridge University Press, 2006.

James, Sharon. "Abraham Booth's Defence of Believers' Baptism by Immersion." In *Grounded in Grace: Essays to Honour Ian M. Randall,* edited by Pieter J. Lalleman, Peter J. Morden and Anthony R. Cross, 53–68. London: Spurgeon's College & Baptist Historical Society, 2013.

Jarvis, Clive. "Gilbert Boyce: General Baptist Messenger and Opponent of John Wesley." In *Pulpit and People: Studies in Eighteenth-Century Baptist Life and Thought,* edited by John H. Y. Briggs, 75–92. Eugene, OR: Wipf and Stock, 2009.

Jennings, W. Theodore, Jr. *Good News to the Poor: John Wesley's Evangelical Economics.* Nashville: Abingdon, 1990.

Jones, David Ceri. "Calvinistic Methodism and the Origins of Evangelicalism in England." In *The Emergence of Evangelicalism: Exploring Historical Continuities,* edited by Michael A. G. Haykin and Kenneth J. Stewart, 103–28. Nottingham: Apollos, 2008.

Jones, T. Robert., Arthur Long, and Rosemary Moore, eds. *Protestant Nonconformist Texts: 1550–1700.* Vol. 1. Aldershot: Ashgate, 2007.

Julian, John, ed. *Dictionary of Hymnology: Setting Forth the Origin and History of Christian Hymns of All Ages and Nations.* Vol. 2. London: Murray, 1892.

Klein, Lawrence E., and Anthony J. La Vopa, eds. *Enthusiasm and Enlightenment in Europe, 1650–1850.* San Marino, CA: Huntingdon Library, 1998.

Kramnick, Isaac. "Explanatory note, John Locke." In *An Essay concerning Human Understanding,* in *The Portable Enlightenment Reader,* edited by Isaac Kramnick, 185. New York: Penguin, 1995.

————. "Introduction." In *The Portable Enlightenment Reader,* edited by Isaac Kramnick, ix–xxviii. New York: Penguin, 1995.

Kramnick, Isaac, ed. *The Portable Enlightenment* Reader. New York: Penguin, 1995.

Lahey, E. Stephen. *John Wyclif.* Oxford: Oxford University Press, 2009.

Lalleman, Pieter J., et al., eds. *Grounded in Grace: Essays to Honour Ian M. Randall.* London: Spurgeon's College & Baptist Historical Society, 2013.

Larsen, Timothy, and Daniel J. Treier, eds. *The Cambridge Companion to Evangelical Theology.* Cambridge: Cambridge University Press, 2007.

Laycock, W. John. *Methodist Heroes in the Great Haworth Round, 1734–84.* Keighley: Wadsworth, 1909.

Lecky, E. H. William. *A History of England in the Eighteenth Century.* New Impression 3. London: Longmans & Green, 1913.

Lennon, Thomas M. "Locke and the Logic of Ideas." *History of Philosophy Quarterly* 18, no. 2 (2001) 155–77.

Lewis, Donald M., ed. *Dictionary of Evangelical* Biography. Oxford: Blackwell, 1995.

Lewis, Rhodri. "Impartiality and Disingenuousness in English Rational Religion." In *The Emergence of Impartiality*, edited by Anita Traninger, and Kathryn Murphy, 224–45. Leiden: Brill, 2013.

Lim, Paul C. H. "Puritans and the Church of England: Historiography and Ecclesiology." In *The Cambridge Companion to Puritanism*, edited by John Coffey, and Paul C. H. Lim, 223–40. Cambridge: Cambridge University Press, 2008.

Lindstrom, G. A. Harald. *Wesley and Sanctification: A Study in the Doctrine of Salvation.* London: Epworth, 1946.

Lloyd, Gareth. "Repression and Resistance: Wesleyan Female Public Ministry in the Generation After 1791." *PWHS* 55, no. 3 (2005) 101–14.

Lovegrove, Deryck W. "Lay Leadership, Establishment Crisis and the Disdain of the Clergy." In *The Rise of the Laity in Evangelical Protestantism*, edited by Deryck W. Lovegrove, 117–33. London: Routledge, 2002.

Lovegrove, Deryck W., ed. *The Rise of the Laity in Evangelical* Protestantism. London: Routledge, 2002.

Lowe, E. Jonathan. *Locke.* London: Routledge, 2005.

Lowery, Ralph. "William Grimshaw." *PWHS* 34, no. 1 (1963) 2–4.

Lumpkin, L. William. *Baptist Confessions of Faith.* Rev. ed. Valley Forge, PA: Judson, 1969.

———. "Locke." In *A Companion to the Philosophers*, edited by Robert L. Arrington, 369–75. Oxford: Blackwell, 1999.

Mack, Phyllis. *Heart Religion in the British Enlightenment: Gender and Emotion in Early Methodism.* Cambridge: Cambridge University Press, 2011.

Maddox, Randy L. *Responsible Grace: John Wesley's Practical Theology.* Nashville: Kingswood, 1994.

Maddox, Randy L., ed. *Aldersgate Reconsidered.* Nashville: Kingswood, 1990.

Maddox, Randy L., and Jason E. Vickers, eds. *The Cambridge Companion to John Wesley.* New York: Cambridge University Press, 2010.

Marsden, George M. "The Evangelical Denomination." In *Evangelicalism and Modern America*, edited by George M. Marsden, vii–xix. Grand Rapids: Eerdmans, 1984.

———. *Evangelicalism and Modern America.* Grand Rapids: Eerdmans, 1984.

Martin, Hugh. *Benjamin Keach (1640–1704): Pioneer of Congregational Hymn Singing.* London: Independent, 1961.

Martin, H. Roger. *Evangelicals United: Ecumenical Stirrings in Pre-Victorian Britain, 1795–1830.* London: Scarecrow, 1983.

———. "Missionary Competition between Evangelical Dissenters and Wesleyan Methodists in the Early Nineteenth Century: A Footnote to the Founding of the Methodist Missionary Society." *PWHS* 42, no. 3 (1979) 81–87.

McBeth, H. Leon, *The Baptist Heritage.* Nashville: Broadman, 1987.

McDonald, H.D. *The Atonement of the Death of Christ: In Faith, Revelation and History.* Grand Rapids: Baker, 1985.

McElwain, Randall D. "Biblical Language in the Hymns of Charles Wesley." *Wesley and Methodist Studies* 1 (2009) 55–70.

McInelly, Brett C. "Method or Madness: Methodist Devotion and the Anti-Methodist Response." In *Religion in the Age of Reason: A Transatlantic Study of the Long Eighteenth Century*, edited by Kathryn Duncan, 195–210. Brooklyn: AMS, 2009.

McInelly, Brett C., ed. *Religion in the Age of Enlightenment*, vol. 2. Brooklyn: AMS, 2010.

McGonigle, B. Herbert. *Sufficient Saving Grace: John Wesley's Evangelical Arminianism.* Carlisle: Paternoster, 2001.

McGowan, Andrew T. B. "Evangelicalism in Scotland from Knox to Cunningham." In *The Emergence of Evangelicalism: Exploring Historical Continuities*, edited by Michael A. G. Haykin, and Kenneth J. Stewart, 63–83. Nottingham: Apollos, 2008.

McLachlan, J. Herbert. *Socinianism in Seventeenth-Century England.* London: Oxford University Press, 1951.

M'Clintock, John, and James Strong. *Cyclopædia of Biblical, Theological, and Ecclesiastical Literature.* Vol. 10. New York: Harper & Brothers, 1891.

———. "Tracts and Tract Societies." In John M'Clintock and James Strong *Cyclopædia of Biblical, Theological, and Ecclesiastical Literature*, 10:511–16. New York: Harper & Brothers, 1891.

McLoughlin, G. William. *Isaac Backus and the American Pietistic Tradition.* Boston: Little Brown, 1967.

Milton, Anthony. "Puritanism and the Continental Reformed Churches." In *The Cambridge Companion to Puritanism*, edited by John Coffey and Paul C. H. Lim, 109–26. Cambridge: Cambridge University Press, 2008.

Moon, S. Norman. *Education for Ministry: Bristol Baptist College, 1679–1979.* Bristol: Bristol Baptist College, 1979.

Moore, Benjamin. *History of Wesleyan Methodism in Burnley and East Lancashire.* Burnley: Gazzette Printing Works, 1899.

Morden, Peter J. "Andrew Fuller: A Biographical Sketch." In *"At the Pure Fountain of Thy Word": Andrew Fuller as an Apologist*, edited by Michael A. G. Haykin, 1–42. Milton Keynes: Paternoster, 2004.

———. *Offering Christ to the World: Andrew Fuller (1754–1815) and the Revival of Eighteenth Century Particular Baptist Life.* Carlisle: Paternoster, 2003.

———. "Andrew Fuller and the Baptist Missionary Society." *BQ* 41, no. 3 (2005) 134–57.

———. "John Bunyan: A Seventeenth-Century Evangelical?" In *Grounded in Grace: Essays to Honour Ian M. Randall*, edited by Pieter J. Lalleman, Peter J. Morden, and Anthony R. Cross, 33–52. London: Spurgeon's College & Baptist Historical Society, 2013.

Mortimer, Sarah. *Reason and Religion in the English Revolution: The Challenge of Socinianism.* Cambridge: Cambridge University Press, 2010.

Muller, Patrick. *Latitudinarianism and Didactism in Eighteenth Century Literature: Moral Theology in Fielding, Sterne and Goldsmith.* Frankfurt: Lang, 2009.

Mulsow, Martin, and Jan Rohls, eds. *Socinianism and Arminianism: Antitrinitarians, Calvinists and Cultural Exchange in Seventeenth-Century* Europe. Leiden: Brill, 2005.

Murray, Derek B. "Robert Sandeman." In *Dictionary of Evangelical Biography*, edited by Donald M. Lewis, 970–71. Oxford: Blackwell, 1995.

Music, W. David., and Paul A. Richardson. *"I Will Sing the Wondrous Story": A History of Baptist Hymnody in North* America. Macon, GA: Mercer University Press, 2008.

Myers, Kenneth. "A Better Way: Proclamation Instead of Protest." In *Power Religion: The Selling Out of the Evangelical Church*, edited by Michael Scott Horton, 39–57. Chicago: Moody Bible Institute, 1992.

Naylor, Peter. *Calvinism, Communion and the Baptists: A Study of English Calvinistic Baptists from the Late 1600s to the Early 1800s.* Milton Keynes: Paternoster, 2003.

Nellen, Henk J. M., and Edwin Rabbie, eds. *Hugo Grotius Theologian: Essays in Honour of G.H.M. Posthumus Meyjes.* Leiden: Brill, 1994.

Nettles, Tom. *The Baptists: Key People Involved in Forming a Baptist Identity.* Fearn: Christian Focus, 2005.

New, F. H. John. *Anglican and Puritan: The Basis of Their Opposition, 1558–1640.* Stanford, CA: Stanford University Press, 1964.

Nicholson, John F. V. "The Office of "Messenger" amongst British Baptists in the Seventeenth and Eighteenth Centuries." *BQ* 17, no. 5 (1958) 206–25.

Noll, A. Mark. *The Rise of Evangelicalism: The Age of Edwards, Whitefield and the Wesleys.* Leicester: InterVarsity, 2004.

O'Brien, Karen. *Women and Enlightenment in Eighteenth-Century Britain.* Cambridge: Cambridge University Press, 2009.

Oh, S. Gwang. *John Wesley's Ecclesiology: A Study in its Sources and Development.* Lanham, MD: Scarecrow, 2008.

O'Hara, Kieron. *The Enlightenment: A Beginner's Guide.* Oxford: Oneworld, 2010.

Oliver, Robert W. "Andrew Fuller and Abraham Booth." In *"At the Pure Fountain of Thy Word": Andrew Fuller as an Apologist,* edited by Michael A. G. Haykin, 203–22. Milton Keynes: Paternoster, 2004.

———. *History of the English Calvinistic Baptists 1771–1892: From John Gill to C.H. Spurgeon.* Edinburgh: Banner of Truth, 2006.

———. "John Collett Ryland, Daniel Turner and Robert Robinson and the Communion Controversy, 1772–1781." *BQ* 29, no. 2 (1981) 77–79.

Oliver, Robert W., ed. *John Owen—The Man and His Theology.* Phillipsburg, NJ: P.&R., 2002.

Olson, C. Gordon. *The Truth Shall Make You Free.* Franklin Park, IL: Bible Research Fellowship, 1980.

Olson, E. Roger. *Arminian Theology: Myths and Realities.* Downers Grove, IL: InterVarsity, 2006.

Outram, Dorinda. *The Enlightenment.* 2nd ed. Cambridge: Cambridge University Press, 2005.

Overton, H. John., and Frederic Relton. *The English Church from the Accession of George 1. to the End of the Eighteenth-Century (1714–1800).* London: Macmillan, 1906.

Packer, I. James. *Honouring the People of God: The Collected Shorter Writings of J.I. Packer.* Vol. 4. Carlisle: Paternoster, 1999.

———. *A Quest for Godliness: The Puritan Vision of the Christian Life.* Wheaton, IL: Crossway, 1990.

Parry, Robin [Gregory Macdonald], ed. *"All Shall be Well": Explorations in Universalism and Christian Theology from Origen to Moltmann.* Cambridge: Clarke, 2011.

———. "Between Calvinism and Arminianism: The Evangelical Universalism of Elhanan Winchester (1751–1797)." In *"All Shall be Well": Explorations in Universalism and Christian Theology from Origen to Moltmann,* edited by Gregory Macdonald [Robin Parry], 141–70. Cambridge: Clarke, 2011.

Payne, Ernest A. "Abraham Booth, 1734–1806." *BQ* 26, no. 1 (1975) 28–42.

———. *The Baptist Union: A Short History.* London: Carey Kingsgate, 1959.

———. "Baptists and the Laying on of Hands." *BQ* 15, no. 5 (1954) 203–15.

Pickles, H.M. *Benjamin Ingham: Preacher amongst the Dales of Yorkshire, the Forests of Yorkshire, and the Fells of Cumbria.* Coventry: n.p., 1995.

Bibliography

Pierard, Richard V. "Evangelicalism." In *Evangelical Dictionary of Theology*, edited by Walter A. Elwell, 379–82. Grand Rapids: Baker Book House, 1984.

Pocock, John G. A. "Enthusiasm: The antiself of Enlightenment." In *Enthusiasm and Enlightenment Europe, 1650–1850*, edited by Lawrence E. Klein, and Anthony J. La Vopa, 7–28. San Marino, CA: Huntingdon Library, 1998.

———. "Historiography and Enlightenment: A View of Their History." *Modern Intellectual History* 5, no. 1 (2008) 83–96.

Pollard, Richard T. "Dan Taylor: A Baptist Entrepreneur." BQ 47, no. 4 (2016) 134–51.

———. *The Pioneering Evangelicalism of Dan Taylor (1738–1816)*. Oxford: Whitley, 2017.

Pope, Robert, ed. *T&T Clark Companion to Nonconformity*. London: Bloomsbury T. & T. Clark: 2013.

Porter, Roy. *Enlightenment: Britain and the Creation of the Modern World*. London: Penguin, 2000.

Priest, Gerald L. "Andrew Fuller's Response to the "Modern Question"—A Reappraisal of The Gospel Worthy of All Acceptation." *The Detroit Baptist Seminary Journal* 6 (2001) 45–73.

Prosser, Glyn P. R. "Formation of the General Baptist Missionary Society." *BQ* 22, no. 1 (1967) 23–29.

Rack, Henry D. "John Wesley and Overseas Missions: Principles and Practice." *Wesley and Methodist Studies* 5 (2013) 30–55.

———. "A Man of Reason and Religion? John Wesley and the Enlightenment." *Wesley and Methodist Studies* 1 (2009) 2–17.

———. *Reasonable Enthusiast: John Wesley and the Rise of Methodism*. 3rd ed. London: Epworth, 2002.

Randall, Ian. *What a Friend We Have in Jesus: The Evangelical* Tradition. London: Darton, Longman and Todd, 2005.

Reill, Peter Hans. "Introduction." In *The Encyclopedia of the Enlightenment*, by Peter Hans Reill and Ellen Judy Wilson, ix–xi. Rev. ed. New York: Facts on File, 2004.

Reill, Peter Hans, and Ellen Judy Wilson, *The Encyclopedia of the Enlightenment*. Rev. ed. New York: Facts on File, 2004.

Rinaldi, W. Frank. *The Tribe of Dan: The New Connexion of General Baptists 1770–1891: A Study in the Transition from Revival Movement to Established Denomination*. Milton Keynes: Paternoster, 2008.

———. "The Tribe of Dan: The New Connexion of General Baptists 1770–1891: A Study in the Transition from Revival Movement to Established Denomination." PhD thesis, University of Glasgow, 1996.

Rivers, Isabel, and David L. Wykes, eds. *Joseph Priestley: Scientist, Philosopher, and Theologian*. Oxford: Oxford University Press, 2008.

Rosenblatt, Helena. "The Christian Enlightenment." In *The Cambridge History of Christianity: Enlightenment, Reawakening and Revolution 1660–1815*, edited by Stewart J. Brown and Timothy Tackett, 7:283–301. Cambridge: Cambridge University Press, 2006.

Royle, Edward. "When Did Methodists Stop Attending Their Parish Churches?" *PWHS* 56, no. 6 (2008) 275–96.

Ryle, C. John. *Christian Leaders of the Eighteenth Century*. Edinburgh: Banner of Truth, 1978 [1869].

Schofield, Robert E., *The Enlightenment of Joseph Priestley: A Study of His Life and Work from 1733 to 1773*. University Park, PA: University Press, 1997.

———. *The Enlightenment of Joseph Priestley: A Study of His Life and Work from 1773 to 1804*. University Park, PA: University Press, 2004.

Scholes, A. Percy. *The Puritans and Music in England and New England: A Contribution to the Cultural History of Two Nations*. London: Oxford University Press, 1934.

Sell, Alan P. F., et al., eds. *Protestant Nonconformist Texts: The Eighteenth Century*. Vol. 2. Aldershot: Ashgate, 2006.

Sellars, Ian, ed. *Our Heritage: The Baptists of Yorkshire, Lancashire and Cheshire 1647–1987*. Leeds: Yorkshire Baptist Association, 1987.

Sheehan, Clint. "Great and Sovereign Grace: Fuller's Defence of the Gospel Against Arminianism." In *"At the Pure Fountain of Thy Word": Andrew Fuller as an Apologist*, edited by Michael A. G. Haykin, 83–121. Milton Keynes: Paternoster, 2004.

Shepherd, Peter. *The Making of a Northern Baptist College*. Manchester: Northern Baptist College, 2004.

Shipley, C. E., ed. *The Baptists of Yorkshire: Being the Centenary Memorial Volume of the Yorkshire Baptist Association*. Bradford: Byles and Sons, 1912.

Sorkin, David. *The Religious Enlightenment: Protestants, Jews, and Catholics from London to Vienna*. Princeton, NJ: Princeton University Press, 2008.

Spurr, John. "Later Stuart Puritanism." In *The Cambridge Companion to Puritanism*, edited by John Coffey, and Paul C. H. Lim, 89–105. Cambridge: Cambridge University Press, 2008.

Stanley, Brian, ed. *Christian Missions and the Enlightenment*. Grand Rapids: Eerdmans, 2001.

———. "Christian Missions and the Enlightenment: A Reevaluation." In *Christian Missions and the Enlightenment*, edited by Brian Stanley, 1–21. Grand Rapids: Eerdmans, 2001.

Starkie, Andrew. *The Church of England and the Bangorian Controversy, 1716–1721*. Woodbridge: Boydell, 2007.

Stevenson, James, and W. H. C. Frend, eds. *A New Eusebius: Documents Illustrating the History of the Church to AD 337*. 2nd rev. ed. London: SPCK, 1987.

Stevenson, William R. "Dan Taylor." In *Dictionary of Hymnology: Setting Forth the Origin and History of Christian Hymns of All Ages and Nations*, edited by John Julian, 2:1117. London: Murray, 1892.

Stewart, Kenneth J. "Did Evangelicalism Predate the Eighteenth Century? An Examination of David Bebbington's Thesis." *Evangelical Quarterly* 77, no. 2 (2005) 135–53.

Stott, Anne. *Hannah More: The First Victorian*. Oxford: Oxford University Press, 2003.

Streiff, Patrick. *Reluctant Saint? A Theological Biography of Fletcher of Madeley*. Translated by G. W. S. Knowles. Peterborough: Epworth, 2001.

Sweeney, A. Douglas, and Brandon G. Withrow. "Jonathan Edwards: Continuator or Pioneer of Evangelical History?" In *The Emergence of Evangelicalism: Exploring Historical Continuities*, edited by Michael A. G. Haykin and Kenneth J. Stewart, 278–301. Nottingham: Apollos, 2008.

Temperley, Nicholas. *The Music of the English Parish Church*. Vol. 1. Cambridge: Cambridge University Press, 1979.

Thompson, Andrew C. ""To Stir Them Up to Believe, Love, Obey"—Soteriological Dimensions of the Class Meeting in Early Methodism." *Methodist History* 48, no. 3 (2010) 160–78.

Thompson, P. Edward. *The Making of the English Working Class*. New York: Vintage, 1963.

Thompson, Philip E. "A New Question in Baptist History: Seeking a Catholic Spirit among Early Baptists." *Pro Ecclesia* 8, no. 1 (1999) 51–72.

———. "Sacraments and Religious Liberty: From Critical Practice to Rejected Infringement." In *Baptist Sacramentalism*, edited by Anthony R. Cross, and Philip E. Thompson, 36–54. Carlisle: Paternoster, 2003.

Tidball, J. Derek. *Who Are the Evangelicals? Tracing the Roots of Today's Movement*. London: Pickering, 1994.

Traninger, Anita, and Kathryn Murphy, eds. *The Emergence of* Impartiality. Leiden: Brill, 2013.

Trueman, R. Carl. *The Claims of Truth: John Owen's Trinitarian Theology*. Carlisle: Paternoster, 1998.

———. "Reformers, Puritans and Evangelicals: The Lay Connection." In *The Rise of the Laity in Evangelical Protestantism*, edited by Deryck W. Lovegrove, 17–35. London: Routledge, 2002.

Tyerman, Luke. *The Oxford Methodists: Memoirs of the Rev. Messrs. Clayton, Ingham, Gambold, Hervey, Broughton, with Biographical Notices of Others*. London: Harper & Row, 1873.

Tyson, John H. "John Wesley's Conversion at Aldersgate." In *Conversion in the Wesleyan Tradition*, edited by Kenneth J. Collins, and John H. Tyson, 27–42. Nashville: Abingdon, 2001.

Tyson, R. John. *Assist Me to Proclaim: The Life and Hymns of Charles Wesley*. Grand Rapids: Eerdmans, 2007.

Underwood, C. Alfred. *A History of the English Baptists*. London: Kingsgate, 1947.

Valentine, Simon R. "Significant Inroads Into 'Satan's Seat': Early Methodism in Bradford: 1740–1760." *PWHS* 51, no. 5 (1998) 141–54.

Van Dyk, Leanne. "The Church in Evangelical Theology and Practice." In *The Cambridge Companion to Evangelical Theology*, edited by Timothy Larsen and Daniel J. Treier, 125–42. Cambridge: Cambridge University Press, 2007.

Vaughn, James Barry. "Public Worship and Practical Theology in the Work of Benjamin Keach (1640–1704)." PhD thesis, University of St. Andrews, 1989.

Vedder, C. Henry. *A Short History of the Baptists*. 2nd ed. Philadelphia: American Baptist, 1907.

Walker, Austin. *The Excellent Benjamin Keach*. Dundas, ON: Joshua, 2004.

Walker, J. Michael. *Baptists at the Table: The Theology of the Lord's Supper amongst English Baptists in the Nineteenth Century*. Didcot: Baptist Historical Society, 1992.

Walsh, John D. "The Yorkshire Evangelicals in the Eighteenth Century: With Especial Reference to Methodism." PhD thesis, University of Cambridge, 1956.

Wall, Robert W. "Wesley as Biblical Interpreter." In *The Cambridge Companion to John Wesley*, edited by Randy L. Maddox and Jason E. Vickers, 113–28. New York: Cambridge University Press, 2010.

Ward, W. Reginald. *Early Evangelicalism: A Global Intellectual History, 1670–1789*. Cambridge: Cambridge University Press, 2006.

———. *The Protestant Evangelical* Awakening. Cambridge: Cambridge University Press, 1992.

———. "The Evangelical Revival in Eighteenth-Century Britain." In *A History of Religion in Britain: Practice and Belief from Pre-Roman Times to the Present*, edited by Sheriden Gilley and W. J. Sheils, 252–72. Oxford: Blackwell, 1994.

Watson, D. Lowes. *The Early Methodist Class Meeting: Its Origins and Significance.* Nashville: Discipleship Resources, 1985.

———. "The Origins and Significance of the Early Methodist Class Meeting." PhD thesis, Duke University, 1978.

Watson, R. John. *The English Hymn: A Critical and Historical* Study. Oxford: Oxford University Press, 1999.

Watson, M. Kevin. *Pursuing Social Holiness: The Band Meeting in Wesley's Thought and Popular Methodist Practice.* Oxford: Oxford University Press, 2014.

Watts, R. Michael. *The Dissenters. I: From the Reformation to the French Revolution.* Oxford: Clarendon, 1978.

Welch, Edwin. "The Origins of the New Connexion of General Baptists in Leicestershire." *The Leicestershire Archaeological and Historical Society* 69 (1995) 59–70.

Wells David F., and John D. Woodbridge, eds. *The Evangelicals: What They Believe, Who They Are, Where They Are Changing.* Nashville: Abingdon, 1975.

White, R. Barrington. *The English Baptists of the Seventeenth Century.* Rev. ed. Didcot: Baptist Historical Society, 1996.

Whitley, T. William. *A History of British Baptists.* London: Charles Griffin, 1923.

Williams, Garry J. "Enlightenment Epistemology and Eighteenth-Century Evangelical Doctrines of Assurance." In *The Emergence of Evangelicalism: Exploring Historical Continuities*, edited by Michael A. G. Haykin and Kenneth J. Stewart, 345–74. Nottingham: Apollos, 2008.

Winter, E. P. "Calvinist and Zwinglian Views of the Lord's Supper among the Baptists of the Seventeenth Century." *BQ* 15, no. 7 (1954) 323–29.

———. "The Lord's Supper: Admission and Exclusion among the Baptists of the Seventeenth Century." *BQ* 17, no. 6 (1958) 267–81.

Withers, W. J. Charles. *Placing the Enlightenment: Thinking Geographically about the Age of Reason.* Chicago: University of Chicago Press, 2004.

Wright, Nigel G. "Election and Predestination in Baptist Confessions of the Seventeenth Century." In *Grounded in Grace: Essays to Honour Ian M. Randall*, edited by Pieter J. Lalleman, Peter J. Morden, and Anthony R. Cross, 16–32. London: Spurgeon's College and Baptist Historical Society, 2013.

Wright, Stephen. *The Early English Baptists, 1603–1649.* Woodbridge: Boydell, 2006.

Wykes, David L. "Joseph Priestley, Minister and Teacher." In *Joseph Priestley: Scientist, Philosopher, and Theologian*, edited by Isabel Rivers, and David L. Wykes, 20–48. Oxford: Oxford University Press, 2008.

Yolton, John W. "John Locke and the Seventeenth-Century Logic of Ideas." *Journal of the History of Ideas* 16, no. 4 (1955) 431–52.